Centuries of Female Days

CENTURIES OF FEMALE DAYS

ENGLISHWOMEN'S PRIVATE DIARIES

Harriet Blodgett

ALAN SUTTON

1989

ALAN SUTTON PUBLISHING
BRUNSWICK ROAD · GLOUCESTER

First published in Great Britain 1989

British Library Cataloguing in Publication Data

Blodgett, Harriet
Centuries of female days : Englishwomen's
private diaries.
1. Diaries in English. Women writers,
1599–1941. Critical studies
I. Title
828'.03

ISBN 0-86299-572-8

Printed in Great Britain by
Dotesios Printers Limited

TO BILL,
WHO MADE IT POSSIBLE

CONTENTS

ACKNOWLEDGMENTS

To the many people who gave of their time and talents to help with this book, I am deeply grateful. I appreciate too my appointments as a visiting, and then an affiliated, scholar at the Institute for Research on Women and Gender at Stanford University, where I accomplished much of my research.

Sandra Gilbert encouraged the project at an early stage by confirming its value. The continued interest of the institute scholars in my papers and their perceptive criticism of my findings ensured its progress. So too did Deputy Director Marilyn Yalom's help in securing otherwise inaccessible books and her always good advice. Karen Offen generously checked my translations, and Sue Bell enabled me to present some of my research at a regional conference. Jane Emery lent me useful materials and read the first draft of the manuscript with a discerning eye, as did Diane Schaffer a portion of it.

Betty Chmaj and Jean Gandesbery also read parts of the manuscript and guided me through initial rewriting with cogent criticism. Doris Earnshaw O'Connor skillfully read the whole at a late stage and took scrupulous care to amend its style. Susan Arpad made a valuable suggestion about reorganizing the introduction. Editor Leslie Mitchner of Rutgers University Press, because of whose enthusiasm the book has seen publication, greatly enhanced the readability and cohesiveness of the completed manuscript and provided repeated and cordial support.

My husband, Bill, whose generosity has been unstinting, saw the book through all its stages with unfailing patience and provided me not only comfort, advice, and editorial assistance but also uninterrupted time to work. His belief in me has been an inspiration; his equanimity, a refuge.

Without the expert guidance of microcomputer consultant Loren Bennett of the University of California at Davis, I could not have prepared the final, word-processed draft; without the services of the interlibrary loan departments at Davis, Sacramento, and Stanford, I could not have written the book at all. I am also grateful to Judy Viargues, who typed a most attractive early copy.

Many fine people have formed the background for this book. I count myself fortunate indeed to have had their friendship and help.

I should acknowledge also that the Afterword is a version of a paper presented as "What Price Change? The Great War and English-women's Diaries" at the North American and Pacific Coast Conference on British Studies, Pacific Grove, California, 24 March 1984, and published in longer form in *Turn-of-the-Century Women* 2 (1985): 18–29. Some text material appeared in "Englishwomen's Diaries: Historical Backgrounds," *Women's Diaries: A Quarterly Newsletter* 4 (Spring 1986): 1, 3–5.

DIARISTS IN THE STUDY

Note that marriage (M) and remarriage (R) dates are given only for Principal Diarists who married during the diary period. Diarists whose status did not change are designated Miss or Mrs.

PRINCIPAL DIARISTS

Amberley, Kate (Katharine Louisa) Russell (née Stanley); Viscountess Amberley (1842–1874). M 8 November 1864
Anonymous (d. 1908)
Anonymous (no dates available)
Asquith, Lady Cynthia Mary Evelyn Charteris (Mrs.) (1887–1960)
Astry, Diana (Mrs. Orlebar) (1671–1716). M December 1708
Bagot, Miss Mary (no dates available)
Bain, Mrs. Louisa (1803–1883)
Barrett, Miss Elizabeth Barrett (later Mrs. Browning) (1806–1861)
Belloc Lowndes, Mrs. Marie Adelaide (1868–1947)
Berry, Miss Mary (1763–1852)
Burney, Fanny Anne (Mrs. Wood) (1812–1860). M 30 July 1835
Butler, Lady Eleanor (Miss) (1739?–1829)
Byrom, Miss Elizabeth (1722–1801)
Carlyle, Mrs. Jane Baillie Welsh (1801–1866)
Carrington, Dora de Houghton (Mrs. Partridge) (1893–1932). M 21 May 1921

Cavendish, Lady Lucy Caroline (née Lyttleton) (1841–1925).
  M 7 June 1864
Clairmont, Miss Claire (Clara Mary Jane) (1798–1879)
Clifford, Anne; Countess of Dorset, then also of Pembroke and
  Montgomery, and Baroness Clifford (1590–1676).
  M 25 February 1608. R 1 June 1630
Cowper, Mary Clavering (Mrs.); Countess Cowper (1685–1724)
Duncannon, Harriet Spencer (Mrs.); Countess of Bessborough
  (1761–1821)
Eastlake, Lady Elizabeth Rigby (Mrs.) (1809–1893)
Eliot, George [Mary Ann Evans] (Mrs. Cross) (1819–1880).
  M 6 May 1880
Fitzgerald, Lady Lucy (Miss) (later Lady Foley) (1771–1851)
Fox, Miss Caroline (1819–1871)
Frampton, Miss Mary (1773–1846)
Freke, Mrs. Elizabeth (1641–1714)
George, Miss Elizabeth (no dates available)
Gladstone, Mary (Mrs. Drew) (1847–1927). M 2 February 1886
Gray, Faith (née Hopwood) (1751–1826). M 9 October 1777
Grove, Miss Harriet (later Mrs. Helyer) (1791–1867)
Guest, Lady Charlotte Elizabeth (née Bertie) (then Mrs. Schreiber)
  (1812–1895). M 29 July 1833. R 10 April 1855
Hamilton, Mary (Mrs. Dickenson) (1756–1816). M 13 June 1785
Hardy, Mrs. Mary (1733–1809)
Hoby, Lady Margaret Dakins (Mrs.) (1571–1633)
Holland, Elizabeth (née Vassall) (Mrs. Webster, then Mrs. Fox);
  became Baroness of Holland House (1770–1845). M 1786.
  R 6 July 1797
Howard, Mrs. Katherine (1672–1765)
Jeune, Mrs. Margaret (1818–1891)
Lumb, Mrs. Anne (later Mrs. Milnes) (no dates available)
Lytton, Edith Villiers (Mrs.); Countess Bulwer-Lytton
  (1841–1936)
Mansfield, Katherine [Kathleen Mansfield Beauchamp] (Mrs.
  Bowden, then Mrs. Murry) (1888–1923). M 2 March 1909;
  R 31 May 1918
Monkswell, Mary Josephine (née Hardcastle) Collier; Baroness of
  Monkswell (1849–1930). M 21 August 1873

Northumberland, Elizabeth Seymour Percy (Mrs.); Duchess of
Northumberland (1716–1776)
Opie, Mrs. Amelia (1769–1853)
Potter, Miss Beatrix (later Mrs. Heelis) (1866–1943)
Powys, Caroline (née Girle) (1739–1817). M 15 August 1762
Raper, Miss Elizabeth (later Mrs. Grant) (d. 1778)
Rothschild, Lady Annie de (Miss) (later the Hon. Mrs. Yorke)
(1844–1926)
Rothschild, Lady Constance de (then Lady Battersea)
(1843–1931). M 22 November 1877
Rothschild, Lady Louisa (née Montefiore) (1821–1910). M 1846
Russell, Frances Anna Maria (née Elliott); Countess Russell
(1815–1898). M 20 July 1841
Schlüter, Miss Auguste (1850–1917)
Shelley, Lady Frances (née Winckley) (1787–1873).
M 4 June 1807
Shelley, Mary Wollstonecraft (née Godwin) (1797–1851).
M 29 December 1816
Shore, Miss Emily (1819–1839)
Sitwell, Miss Florence Alice (1858–1930)
Stevenson, Frances Louise (then Countess Lloyd-George)
(1888–1972). M 1943
Thrale, Mrs. Hester Lynch Salusbury (then Mrs. Piozzi)
(1741–1821). R 23 July 1784
Trant, Clarissa Sandford (Mrs. Bramston) (1800–1844).
M 5 January 1831
Twysden, Lady Isabella Saunder (Mrs.) (1605–1657)
Webb, Beatrice (née Potter) (1858–1943). M 23 July 1892
Weeton, Ellen (Mrs. Stock) (1776–1844). M September 1814
Woodforde, Miss Ann (d. 1861)
Woodforde, Miss Julia (1789–1873)
Woodforde, Mrs. Mary Norton (d. 1730)
Woodforde, Miss Nancy (Anna Maria) (1757–1830)
Woolf, Mrs. Virginia Stephen (1882–1941)
Wynne, Elizabeth (Mrs. Fremantle) (1779–1857).
M 12 January 1797
Wynne, Eugenia (Mrs. Campbell) (b. 1780). M 22 July 1806
Wynne, Miss Harriet (b. 1786)

WORLD WAR I DIARISTS

Adam, Mrs. Helen Pearl Humphrey (1882–?)
Anonymous (no dates available)
Bagnold, Miss Enid Algerine (1889–1981)
Boyle, Mrs. Laura (no dates available)
Brittain, Miss Vera (1893–1970)
Courtney, Lady Kate (Catherine) Potter (Mrs.) (1847–1929)
Farmborough, Miss Florence (1887–1978)
Finzi, Miss Kate John (no dates available)
Houghton, Mrs. Mary (no dates available)
Isherwood, Mrs. Kathleen Machell Smith (1868–1960)
Jephson, Lady Harriet Julia (Miss) (d. 1930)
Kennard, Lady Dorothy Katherine Barclay (Mrs.)
    (no dates available)
Lloyd, Miss Gladys (1889–?)
McDougall, Miss Grace (d. 1963)
Macnaughtan, Miss Sarah Broom (d. 1916)
Morrell, Lady Ottoline Violet Anne Cavendish-Bentinck (Mrs.)
    (1873–1938)
Pless, Daisy (Mary Theresa Olivia) Cornwallis-West
    (Mrs.) Fürstin von (1873–1943)
Sinclair, Miss May (1865–1946)
Thurstan, Miss Violetta (d. 1978)

Centuries of Female Days

INTRODUCTION

PRIVATE MOMENTS AND LITERARY OCCASIONS

> For readily discernible historical reasons women have
> characteristically concerned themselves with matters
> more or less peripheral to male concerns. . . . The dif-
> ference between traditional female preoccupations and
> roles and male ones makes a difference in female writing.
> Patricia Meyer Spacks, *The Female Imagination*

> The female world is worthy of study in and of itself, quite
> apart from its impact on the male world. . . . without
> regard to the male world.
> Jessie Bernard, *The Female World*

Editions from the 1960s of Mary Shelley's and her half-sister
Claire Clairmont's diaries carry interesting commentary by their editors, anticipating sociologist Jessie Bernard's observation that "most
of what we know . . . deals with the male world."[1] Frederick L.
Jones, Shelley's editor, complains in his introduction that Mary's entries are cursory and incomplete, but is thankful for her diary nonetheless, because her diary is "the richest mine of information about
[Percy] Shelley's daily life: where he lived, where he went, and whom
he saw from day to day." Jones indexes and even dates, month by
month, all the books Percy read; "Mary's reading, since it is not of

1

comparable interest to scholars, has not been listed in a similar manner." Viewing Clairmont from a similar angle, editor Marion Kingston Stocking believes "the primary interest of her journals is the light they shed on the Shelley family. . . . were it not for her relationship with Byron and Shelley her journals probably would not have been preserved, much less published."[2] This book is the fruit of my reflections on a large number of private diaries, all published, of Englishwomen from the late sixteenth century to just before the Second World War. It identifies thematic and certain formal contours of female traditions of diary keeping by focusing on the women of one country. My premise is that the diaries of Mary Shelley and Claire Clairmont, as of any woman, are worthy of study in their own right.

Women's diaries provide invaluable testimonials to individual female lives and reveal patterns of female existence over many centuries. Moreover, they constitute a literary tradition of female serial writing. The serial form women use may parallel that of men's diaries; the topics, attitudes, and self-concepts expressed within the form and their manner of expression differ from men's because the interests, status, and lives of the diarists have done so. I have taken an epigraph from Patricia Meyer Spacks because what she says of women's novels is equally applicable to their diaries. In those books of self, differing lives yield differing subject matter, problems of representation, and points of view, and in that sense, differing art. I did not read a mass of men's diaries so that I could compare male and female diaries. I have examined Englishwomen's diaries in relation to one another and to the women's lives, and only incidentally do I compare them to men's. Outside feminist criticism, generalizations are customarily made about the diary as if applicable to both genders' writings, even when based only on male diarists. A few of my claims are likewise widely applicable. But most are not. Fascinated and absorbed by the records women have kept, I have read their diaries not only as a longtime admirer of English literature but also as a feminist scholar actively concerned with introducing a female perspective into learning and knowledge. I write about their diaries in the same spirit. A question I pursue throughout is, how might the diarists' gender have played a role in their diary keeping? The more that question

2

is asked the more will the whole world, as opposed to the male world alone, become known.

Contemporary feminism has directed attention to women's diaries so that they have lately become important documents. Editors in the 1980s no longer risk dismissive declarations such as Jones's and Stocking's. Yet my study was necessary because no other full-length critical books on female English diaries exist.[3] Except for famous women, critical attention has so far favored American diarists.[4] Nor are there books on women's diaries as a general type. Outpaced by the increased publication of diaries themselves, critical attention is still piecemeal, directed not at the genre but at particular women or very limited groups of women, with essays rather than full-length studies the primary mode of discussion. Beyond the essays, ordinarily only the commentary in anthologies hazards theoretical generalizations about female diaries.[5]

And yet, feminism has made the diary prominent because, aside from the general desire to restore the lost voices of female history, feminists take a psychological and an aesthetic interest in the diary form. Diary keeping is a widely acknowledged tool of psychotherapy, and many feminists encourage the practice as an invaluable means of consciousness raising (heightened awareness of sexist devaluation and mistreatment, on the one hand, and of female worth and accomplishment, on the other), as well as of psychic integration. In the act of writing, a sequence of transformations may occur as unconscious matter presents itself to consciousness for assimilation. Both how-to manuals and literary works have encouraged this sense of the diary. Doris Lessing's *Golden Notebook,* for example, was an early inspiration: a novel in diary form "thematically concerned with journal-keeping as a means to personal consciousness and the achievement of dynamic wholeness and sanity by transcending fragmentation and division," as Deena Metzger and Barbara Meyerhoff phrase it in *Chrysalis,* a feminist periodical. Anaïs Nin's influential confessional *Diary* likewise generated admiration for diaries as guides "to those seeking female identity."[6]

However, the diary that deeply investigates the self and may function as therapy or emancipation provides neither the normative standard nor necessarily the epitome of style for diaries. Using a diary to explore personal inner space for the sake of growth into female awareness—the sort of exploration that Charlotte Painter discusses in her afterword to *Revelations: Diaries of Women*—is contemporary practice, not the typical historical reality. Although any personal diary enhances one's sense of selfhood, remarkably few English-women of the past used their diaries for active self-creation or trans-formation. Many diaries are either public diaries, focused on others, or just laconic memoranda. Even those that are not are reticent and protective of the diarist's privacy. A related reality is that most of the women are conventional in their assumptions about womanhood and hence in their aspirations. They also write against a background of centuries of female disparagement. Thus, rather than putting their diaries to work for self-construction, they employ them instead for self-condemnation and, however inadvertently, confessions of low self-esteem. Mary Jane Moffatt's foreword to *Revelations*, an inter-national anthology and one of the few books to reach for a compre-hensive understanding of women's diaries, identifies an emergent "pattern" in the diaries anthologized: "an unconscious call by the women for a redefinition of [Love, Work, Power] into a less divisive, more organic pattern for existence, one where their capacities for both love and work blend, allowing them to be fully human and bal-anced, true to the power of their individual natures." Such sub-liminal feminist voices yearning for fuller, freer, more harmonious lives may at times sound among past English diaries, but they do not resound. Moffatt and Painter encouraged their pattern by limiting their anthology to nineteenth- and twentieth-century women who "demonstrated character as the ability to make moral distinctions and choices according to a personal code rather than the social or religious codes of the age in which they wrote."[7] Naturally such women wanted better lives than they had, but they are not the historical norm. Al-though the Englishwomen studied here reserved certain rights to themselves, most of them adjust to what their contemporary life allows them and observe the codes. The subtexts they encode are not subversive.

Feminist aesthetic interest in diaries, which deplores the periph-eral status of women's diaries as literature, hinges on the assumption

that the loosely structured diary is a valuable form in itself, in addition to being a model for the creation of other forms of art: prose,
whether fiction or autobiography, and poetry of like fragmentary
structure and subjective focus. A literary form the diary is, even if it
has rarely been so entirely communicative and inspirational a model
as is nowadays envisioned. The most speculative aesthetic issue
raised by feminist criticism, however, is not whether the diary is art,
but whether the diary is in some sense a characteristically female literary form or one for which women have a temperamental affinity.[8] I
do not make a case for the diary as an inherently female form, but
rather as a characteristic one. I suggest that diary keeping has been
practiced so extensively by women because it has been possible for
them and gratifying to them. The diary, by its nature as a genre of
personal record, by the opportunity it offers the diarist to record what
is important to her, and by the daily time that it claims for itself,
counters the patriarchal attack on female identity and self-worth. A
diary is an act of language that, by speaking of one's self, sustains
one's sense of being a self,[9] with an autonomous and significant
identity.

As for the aesthetic issue, although I do not evaluate individual
diaries for their stylistic qualities, I do perceive the diaries as forms of
aesthetic representation through language rather than as merely factual data. They are literature subjectively interpreting life. Like
other forms of literature, then, they are potentially subject to influence from models and from devices of rhetoric. But I do not confuse
the diurnal private diary either with the novel or with the public
autobiography in which a life has been retrospectively shaped into
a coherent, self-valorizing fiction. An autobiographer, says critic
Spacks, is like a novelist and "necessarily" depends upon "artifice—
shaping, inventing, selecting, omitting—to achieve effects." She
explains, "When we speak of ourselves, trying to tell someone—an
intimate even—what we are like, we often feel with desperation the
impossibility of accuracy and know that we yield complexity for the
sake of comprehensibility. In the more public kind of communication
involved in writing down an account of the self, such processes become exaggerated." The project Spacks describes is not, however,
that of the private diary, in which there is neither an audience to

impress with effects (except the diarist) nor a whole to arrange. The private diarist, immersed in conversation with herself, speaks as accurately (or deludedly) about herself as does anyone engaged in self-presentation, granted some constraint before the written word. Probably diary critic Margo Culley justly generalizes that "all diarists are involved in a process, even if largely unconscious, of selecting details to create a persona. . . . The pages of a diary might be thought of as a kind of mirror before which the diarist stands assuming this posture or that."[10] It could not be otherwise; selective imagining is a life process. One's self-image is never the whole portrait. Whether or not the diarist tells the whole truth about herself, the context of events the diarist presents is historically verifiable, and the situations are historically explicable. More important here, the diary has aesthetic truth, not because of what it tells, but because of how it does so. The diary's substance is inseparable from its form, and its form, as experienced by a reader, is art even if not in the conventional sense of a highly crafted product. "In the diary the original human need to express oneself . . . coincides with literature as a form of art," as East German novelist Christa Wolf well says.[11]

To define the diary, one can use bibliographer William Matthews's workmanlike terms: "a personal record of what interested the diarist, usually kept day by day, each day's record being self-contained and written soon after the events occurred, the style usually being free from organized exposition."[12] But because my sense of the diary is more expansive, I prefer to supplement Matthews's definition with Virginia Woolf's description for what it implies about the diary's literary possibilities:

> What sort of diary should I like mine to be? Something loose knit, & yet not slovenly, so elastic that it will embrace anything, solemn, slight or beautiful that comes into my mind. I should like it to resemble some deep old desk, or capacious hold-all, in which one flings a mass of odds & ends without looking them through. I should like to come back, after a year or two, & find that the collection had sorted itself & redefined itself and coalesced, as such deposits so mysteriously do, into a mould, transparent enough to reflect the light of our life, & yet steady, tranquil, composed with the aloofness of a work of art. (20 April 1919)[13]

So long as a diary consists of more than the briefest, impersonal snatches—though sometimes even those will work—it constitutes a literary occasion, which, whatever the differing talents of individual writers, has an intrinsic appeal for a reader. As Judith Sloman has argued, women's diaries (indeed, any diaries) should not be cast out as unliterary because, like letters, they do not answer to a traditionally normative, but inadequate concept of literature: "the work designed as a completed whole and readily detached from the author's personal life and motives in writing it." [14] The diary obviously cannot fit such criteria, being preeminently personal and necessarily improvisational; however much the diarist brings her whole life to her writing because it has become part of herself, she articulates only what seems true or valuable for the moment. Woolf vividly captures the improvisational mode of creating diaries when she writes,

> I have just reread my year diary & am much struck by the rapid haphazard gallop at which it swings along, sometimes indeed jerking almost intolerably over the cobbles. Still if it were not written rather faster than the fastest typewriting, if I stopped & took thought, it would never be written at all; & the advantage of the method is that it sweeps up accidentally several stray matters which I should exclude if I hesitated, but which are the diamonds of the dustheap. (20 January 1919). [15]

The normative barriers also exclude male diaries from the critically honored canon; however, the consequences of such exclusion are more serious for women. The barriers nicely discriminate against most of what women have written over the centuries. In either case, by guarding as literature only consciously shaped writing, they exclude that which functions like literature, creating distinctive pleasure through verbal means.

A diary offers an individual perception of existence translated into words, concrete images, and sequences that show a personality in process of being in a particular world. The existence of the diarist, presented in numerous if fragmentary entries, becomes the reader's imaginative experience of participating in the diarist's life as, day by day, in the same formless manner as life, the story unfolds. The diarist has become a character in a construct apart from her life. [16] The

7

material in a diary may be the very stuff of life, but the diary functions with the same verbal medium and imaginative impact as literature—modern literature especially, for, like such literature, the diary remains very close to life in duplicating the multifaceted nature of personality, as well as life's uncertainties, obscurities, and unanticipated events. "I'd give a lot to turn over 30 pages or so, & find written down what happens to us," as Woolf also says (15 January 1915). A diarist cannot foresee the future, and a reader never knows which entries will later prove to be diamonds. To illustrate with an entry more portentious than it first appears, Hester Thrale cannot know that she has named the man who will become her second husband four years hence when she writes, "I have picked up Piozzi here, the great Italian Singer; he shall teach [my daughter] Hester" (14 July 1789).[17] Nor would some readers know.

For the reader, suspense is indigenous to the diary form and gives any diary a quality of tension not unlike the suspense in reading a novel or play. Yet, however unplanned, diaries are not chaotic. The reader awaits, and discovers, the completed actions, the patterns, the sequences, the obsessive concerns that may inform a diary. The reader's mind elicits shapes out of what life is shaping on the diarist's pages. The comparative concision of most diaries and the diarists' selectivity—for all diarists are selective—oblige the reader to stay imaginatively alive, to fill in around the mere framework offered. But it may be difficult not to respond to dramatic sequences such as the following, taken from the diary of Harriet Grove. Typical of the progressions found in diaries, it gains poignancy with the awareness that the first entry was written without knowledge of the last:

Sat. February 4, 1809   Mrs. Bennett[']s youngest child is very ill; they returned home.

Sun. February 5   Mrs. Bennett's child is very ill indeed[.]

Mon. February 6   Mrs. Bennett['s] child is dead—

Reading diaries is an experience that awakens an imaginative identification with other lives and emotional and intellectual responses to them. The province of literature is the terrain of diaries too. Or, as Earl Miner, a scholar of diaries, has said, "The boundaries of literature are as wide as we believe but wider than we pretend."[18]

The intrinsic literary possibilities of diaries do not gainsay that some diarists are both more perceptive and articulate and less self-protective than others, so that their diaries are more engaging to read. Diarists may even attain distinctive rhythmical qualities through their characteristic manner of expression. Lady Anne Clifford's seventeenth-century diary of her last days, its entries laced with refrains, reads like a free-verse drama. But even apart from its rhythms, I find it so effective as art that I have included most of it in an appendix. In this understated drama, an indomitable eighty-six-year-old matriarch holds court in her bedchamber, dispensing largesse and settling her accounts, reliving the past while the present declines towards her death. Clifford creates a whole greater than the sum of its parts. Some diarists do write with a highly developed sense of verbal style and tone. The complete entries for two consecutive days in Caroline Fox's diary, for example, read:

A wet day and all its luxuries.
A fine day and all its liabilities. (23 and 24 October 1848)

Likewise, Lady Eleanor Butler has rationed her words with care when she writes of "a rabbit in the Shrubbery. Sent to the village for hounds to hunt it. No Noses. Nor indeed eyes. Could neither smell nor see the Rabbit which sat before them by the Library window" (3 August 1790). Yet diarists may be appealing for apparently unselfconscious style, like Elizabeth Percy, Duchess of Northumberland, giving her end-of-day summation in which "I came home quite Overcome with heat, settled my Accounts, play'd on my Flute, eat some pease and went to bed" (9 June 1771). Or young Florence Sitwell, for whom "the wedding breakfast [for aunt] was a great success. I awoke next morning with a horrid cold" (30 September 1877). Non sequiturs are a charm of diaries from the first. Witness Lady Margaret Hoby, who "was sent for to Trutsdall to the Trauill [labor] of my Cossine Isons Wiffe, who that Morninge was brought to bed of a daughter: the same day, at night, I hard of a fish that was taken vp at Yarmoth, 53 foott Long and 23 broade" (4 February 1602).[19] Even as the diary's intrinsic appeal lies in its ability to evoke the quality of life in process, so also does the diary thrive on a certain amount of artlessness in its effects. The content of diaries is best when the

9

writer is alert, perceptive, and communicative; the prose is best when she commands the diction and imagery she needs to escape vagueness and triteness; she need not necessarily be a stylist. The history of the diary in England, however, has included diarists' increasing self-consciousness of participating stylistically in a literary form.

My principal diarists, the sixty-nine women on whom my main study is based, were born in England or Wales or lived there through marriage, expatriation, or work.[20] I discuss an additional nineteen diarists in the Afterword. Some of the diaries were published in full, but most appeared as excerpts ranging from brief to nearly complete versions of a diarist's records. The earliest diarist, Margaret Hoby, began her diary in 1599 and continued it until 1605. I chose to terminate the span of history covered with 1939 for reasons I will explain shortly, a decision that meant my latest diarists by chance became Marie Belloc Lowndes and Virginia Woolf. The published private diaries that I found during my research did not yield me anything like scientifically balanced data. By far the largest number of diarists wrote in the nineteenth century and, secondarily, in the eighteenth century; only a handful of the diaries in the main study were composed in the seventeenth and twentieth centuries and, in the latter case, all by women who grew up in the nineteenth century.[21] Moreover, the diarists comprise almost entirely middle- and upper-class women (from lower middle class through landed gentry and aristocracy).[22] Two, however, were servants or the like: Elizabeth George, daughter of a tenant of the duke of Buckingham, who tended the duke's guests, and Auguste Schlüter, maid, then housekeeper, to the Gladstone family. Most were economically secure women, but a few—for example, sometime governesses Claire Clairmont and Ellen Weeton—knew extreme poverty and hard work.

Several are well-known literary figures: Elizabeth Barrett (Browning), George Eliot, and Katherine Mansfield, as well as Marie Belloc Lowndes, Mary Shelley, and Virginia Woolf. A few otherwise achieved distinguished reputations, such as social historian Mary Berry, artist Dora Carrington, collector and translator Lady Charlotte Guest (Schreiber);[23] illustrator-writer Beatrix Potter, and Fabian socialist Beatrice Webb. Several are known because of their male connections, such as Jane Welsh Carlyle, Thomas Carlyle's wife; Mary Gladstone, daughter of the prime minister; Harriet Grove, briefly fiancée of Percy Bysshe Shelley; Frances Stevenson, secretary and lover, then wife, of David Lloyd George; Hester Thrale, close friend to Samuel Johnson. A few, such as Lady Anne Clifford and Lady Elizabeth Holland, are familiar to historians, and a few were minor literary figures in their own day—Lady Cynthia Asquith (daughter-in-law of the prime minister) and Amelia Opie, for example. But many are women with no special hold on fame, who would no longer be known at all were it not that their families or friends or antiquarian societies chose to publish their diaries. Although my principal diarists therefore include many obscure women, I do not highlight the famous diarists; I view all the diarists equally as women, valuable apart from their achievements. Accordingly, I do not treat the diaries of the great writers as adjuncts to the work that made them famous; in those terms, their diaries have had their share of attention already.

Most of the diarists began their records in late childhood or adolescence, so far as is ascertainable; others, only in adulthood and even in middle age. Indeed, diarists Louisa Bain and Amelia Opie respectively began theirs only at fifty-four and fifty-eight. Collectively, the diarists compose for a reader an engrossing drama of female life from early to late, with every shade of joy and despair; and with all that has been said about women, it is refreshing to read what they have to say for themselves. Because the diarists offer such a rich source book of information for further women's studies, I note in some detail what contents their diaries embrace, pertinent to my central topics: why and in what manner these women may have kept diaries, what they most often wrote about, and with what sense of themselves and their personal attachments.

My justification for viewing these Englishwomen's diaries collectively as women's diaries is, as I have already indicated, that even as women writers in other genres manifest recurrent themes, images, and patterns from generation to generation, so in their diaries women resemble one another. What I discovered as I read the diaries was, indeed, striking repetition across the centuries despite modifications in historical circumstances. But the continuity is explicable because the preconditions for writing have been stable. The patriarchal cultural climate dictating an inferior, muted, and service-oriented role in which these women (like women in other societies) lived was constant enough until recently to inspire diaries with similar sentiments and recognizable traits, repeated over the centuries. Even though the current emphasis in research on women, to quote critic Hester Eisenstein, is "uncovering the variety of female experience, rather than its uniformity,"[24] the diaries dictate instead the transhistorical approach I have adopted.

I stop before the Second World War because the postwar world has brought changes affecting ever-increasing numbers of Englishwomen's lives. "Traditions of decades and centuries were uprooted and discarded, sometimes with deliberation and sometimes by force of circumstances," as historian David Bouchier says of English life in the fifties. At that time, too, Simone de Beauvoir's inspirational *Second Sex*, first translated in 1953, fueled a growing interest in the 'woman question.'[25] Englishwomen were ready to start a women's liberation movement by the sixties, and thereafter to expand it. Thus, although change comes slowly for women, who are inclined to be traditionalists, outward and inward change has come to middle- and upper-class Englishwomen during the second half of the twentieth century. They know freer lives and have a better sense of female worth than did women earlier, and presumably their diaries—without necessarily being entirely unlike their predecessors'—would reflect as much. But to ascertain the actual presence and observe the process and extent of such change are matters for another book.

There was material enough available for this one, which includes any private published diaries that I found other than specialized ones such as travel, religious (devotional), and exclusively children's diaries (kept to record children's progress). The eclectic private diary, which is my principle of selection, subsumes these three types as possible contents. I chose to study eclectic private diaries because I wanted to see what women might say when free of others' scrutiny or a limited subject, a stipulation that neither necessitated any uniformity of contents nor precluded women's defining themselves in relation to other people, places, or events. What I observed when I read those diaries was the continuity I accordingly chose as focus of my book; I had not anticipated finding so much similarity. The restriction *private*, which is so important to me, does not signify *domestic*, but rather *personal:* diaries not written or revised by the diarist for publication or intended for immediate reading by a second party. That is why I exclude letter journals and discuss the Great War diaries only in the Afterword. They are not in the relevant sense private. Because of timely contents, the wartime diarists themselves usually published their diaries; moreover, they often wrote them up with hindsight. Yet the wartime diaries seemed to me too significant to omit, because they show women doing sustained writing in relation to a major public event. As it chances, they provide a fitting afterword by implying something of what is to come in after years.

Insisting on truly private diaries meant that I could continue the investigations others had begun on public forms like the novel and poetry, in which women authors historically were forced into covert communication and subversive subtexts to keep their surface meanings acceptable to a male-dominated audience. I could see how women responded to the opportunity (at least potentially) for direct representation, whether subtexts emerged under those circumstances. But insisting on truly private diaries also meant giving up some distinguished diarists. Fanny Burney wrote letter journals, which she edited in her old age for possible publication. Fanny Kemble habitually read her theater diary aloud to her father, then published it and her later plantation diary. Dorothy Wordsworth explicitly kept her Grasmere Journals for her brother William, who read and quoted from her Alfoxden Journal as well. I believe, nonetheless, that if one is seeking to recover the tenor and strategies of female lives, one learns more from diarists like Hester Thrale and Beatrice Webb. Thrale resolved, "Nobody sees the Thraliana but my self" (1 March 1779) and begged her heir in 1813, "Only let it *Never* be printed! oh never, never, never!" Webb in 1866 wrote in her second will, inserted in her diary, "I earnestly beg they [my diary books and letters] may be destroyed immediately . . . I should prefer that no one had looked into them" (1 January).[26]

Common sense says that when a diarist has a live recipient for her words in view, she will have to adulterate her self-expression considerably. She will have to present herself and can no longer just express herself in terms of a personally acceptable image—at least to the extent that self-consciousness and the limitations of androcentric language allow her to. Certainly any diarist who does not personally destroy her diary knows that someday she may chance to be read; some diarists even hope for that reading. Nonetheless, although the anticipation of being read by posterity may affect self-presentation, it still allows for some sense of present privacy and therefore potentially for more forthright self-declaration than does the sense of an immediate reader or a public audience. Virginia Woolf articulates the problem—"affectation or . . . restraint"—bluntly in her review of John Evelyn's diary:

> There can be no doubt that the good diarists are those who write either for themselves or for a posterity so distant that it can safely hear every secret and justly weigh every motive. For such an audience there is no need either of affectation or of restraint. But a diary written to be published in the author's lifetime is no better than a private version of the newspaper, and often worse. The good opinion of our contemporaries means so much to us that it is well worth while to tell them lies.[27]

Dorothy Wordsworth's *Grasmere Journals* (1800–1803) suggests what may occur when a diary is not intended as private. Dorothy begins this diary after brothers William and John have gone to Yorkshire to visit the Hutchinsons, leaving her sad to the point of tears but resolved to keep a journal of the time "because I shall give Wm Pleasure by it when he comes home again."[28] Alec Bond has shown how Dorothy actually uses her diary to deal surreptitiously with her anxieties over losing William and her beloved niche to Mary Hutchinson: "The predominance of Dorothy Wordsworth's concerns for the fate of beggar women, for uprooted birds and plants, for the funerals of women, and of her symbolic identification with them can scarcely be doubted. . . . since we know that William read her journals . . . the entries serve not only as a direct means for communication . . . but also an indirect or symbolic means of communicating . . . her underlying emotional state."[29] What she cannot tell him directly she will tell him indirectly. Such unconscious strategies for communication, like inadvertent revelations, may appear in even the most private diaries. However, were Dorothy keeping a diary for herself alone, she might have acknowledged her anxieties more openly, even if she could not be entirely candid. But she writes for William, and characteristic human behavior is to present oneself to an adored other in ways that one believes will be admired by that other or in ways that one can bear to present oneself. Either way, it would not do for Dorothy to cloud William's happiness with her selfish demands.

The diary of Fanny (Frances) Burney (Mme. D'Arblay) provides a variant illustration of a reader-influenced diary. Kept from 1768 to 1839, her "diary" consists of personal entries, letter journals, and additional personal letters. It was first published in 1842, after her death in 1840, but without her juvenile journals (1768–1778), which were published as the *Early Diary* only in 1889. Burney opens her diary with witty addresses to herself as "Nobody . . . since to Nobody can I be wholly unreserved." The sentiment ironically remains true though the addressee of her diary soon becomes someone other than herself. Perhaps because Burney was a public author at heart, in need of an audience, she soon ignored her original intention to keep a diary "*solely* for my own perusal." [30] Already reading her diary regularly to her sisters, she also converted it to a letter journal for sister Susan. As Burney scholar Joyce Hemlow summarizes, "Indeed almost all the Journals up to 1800 she wrote for her sister Susan." [31]

Hemlow's "almost all" signifies primarily that by 1773 Burney had also branched out to include Samuel "Daddy" Crisp (as she called him), an adored family friend. Burney reports: "I have not entered into a very particular correspondence with Mr. Crisp. I write really a Journal to him, and in answer he sends me most delightful long, and incomparably clever letters." [32] But it is his praise that she delights in, not just his clever letters. Therefore, she adheres to his advice to be spontaneous, not polished, in her writing. By 1776, her journals are being addressed to Susan with the understanding that they will be passed on to Crisp. Spontaneous in tone though they are, in fact they were not written daily but rather reconstructed from memoranda, sometimes months after the event. And "the new commitment to Mr. Crisp," as Hemlow says, "changed the nature of Fanny's diaries. . . . The thought of giving pleasure to [Mr. Crisp and Susan] spurred her best efforts in light and lively writing." [33] For them she perfected her skill at writing apparently artless, candid social comedy.

After Susan died in 1800 (Crisp had died in 1783), Burney's diary changed forever. Her 1802 journals from Paris, addressed to her father and a few other persons, are more stilted, more pretentious: "semi-public productions," in their editor Hemlow's phrase. Journals of the events of later years are also "semi-literary productions" and furthermore composed long after events from notes and memory because Burney's husband had secured her promise to leave a record for their son. Finally, for over twenty years (1817–1838), Burney reworked her manuscripts, rigorously suppressing anything possibly discreditable, embarrassing, or (to her) trivial and adding retrospective commentary,[34] probably with a view to posthumous publication. Throughout her diary career, Burney had the sense of an audience. It kept her a talented raconteur, but it also discouraged penetrating self-portrayal.

Granted, few women's private diaries actually contain candid accounts of the diarists' inner lives (or even full records of their outer lives). Yet I believe one approaches knowledge of female perceptions and attitudes better by concentrating on diaries written to be more, rather than less, private, as I have attempted to do. I do not, however, deceive myself that my endeavor to keep to private diaries has been entirely successful, and I know that some diarists were difficult choices. For example, that Mary Shelley's 1814–1816 diary contains some entries by her husband (a circumstance true of occasional other women's diaries too) argues against her diary's complete privacy before his death. However, since his hand in sporadic early entries does not necessarily mean that she designed her diary for him to read, I decided to retain her diary but to concentrate on entries after 1816.

A few diarists changed their intentions over the years. Mary Collier, Lady Monkswell, for example, kept a private diary until 1907. That year, however, she provides exposition indicating that she has begun to contemplate publication. By 1909, she is forthrightly addressing a reader. I decided to retain her for my study but to focus on her abundant earlier entries. Comparably, what begins as a private diary for Ellen Weeton becomes, at a point of anguish in her life, a record she explicitly leaves for her daughter Mary to read someday in the future—she does not "intend anyone to see these volumes whilst I live" (1809). But so did many other diaries probably become diaries intended for the authors' children to read, sooner or later, without so frank an acknowledgment. I therefore did not rule out Ellen Weeton. A diary such as Caroline Fox's poses another sort of problem. Fox's published diary begins in 1835. In 1855, after the death of her brother Barclay (Robert Barclay Fox), she writes, "I could fill volumes with remembrances and personal historiettes of interesting people, but for whom should I record them now?" (26 April),[35] implying that all preceding entries were intended for Barclay's eyes. However, the nature of her prior entries suggests rather that Caroline kept records of certain experiences so that she could tell Barclay accurately about such interesting matters, for she records his own activities and words to an extent superfluous were he to be reading her diary. Nor does it terminate with his death.

Essentially, my book remains a study of published diaries intended as private, even if diarists could not always be certain that their privacy would be respected and even if occasionally some of them chose to share parts of their diaries with others. Whenever my study does draw incidentally on any diarists outside its intended confines because their diaries were not private or were never published or are otherwise unsuitable, I acknowledge my use of such supplementary sources. Those diarists, along with others not used for my study but of potential interest for other studies, including a few whom I found only belatedly, are included in the Select List of Women's Diaries.

Editors' proclivity to reinforce the privacy of diaries by censoring them is a problem I could not circumvent. With some justice does diary scholar Arthur Ponsonby observe, "No editor can be trusted not to spoil a diary."[36] Editors' zeal to protect the diarist or her family, who may have commissioned the edition—sometimes as the editor's own family, too—invites some distortion of the text. A reader is also at the mercy of the editor's choice of extracts in general. In partial compensation, however, editors provide useful background information about obscure diarists. The accessibility of the published materials, moreover, is an inestimable advantage.

Accessibility determined my own choice to work with published diaries; too few English manuscript diaries are in American collections (nor do they circulate). And while accordingly I cannot speak of all diaries, I suspect that manuscript diaries will largely sustain the conclusions I have drawn about published ones. I found no great differences in characteristics between the published diaries that have been reproduced entire and those that have been extracted. Moreover, as I indicate within my book, I found essential similarities between what I personally saw in these published diaries and what others describe as true of manuscript materials.

That the women's names changed upon marriage created additional problems; that some diaries were published under their writers' marital surnames, yet others under family surnames, compounded the problems. I refer to each diarist by the name used for her published diary, occasionally adding her other surname in parentheses when the context makes it necessary and regularly adding marital surname for Elizabeth Barrett (Browning) because the diarist is more familiar by that name. I furnish a diarist's title only upon first reference to her, except if, as is occasionally true, her titled name has been used for her published diary. I also give the life-span dates of each diarist only the first time she is mentioned within the text, thereafter relying on a dated quotation or, if need be, a descriptive phrase to serve as reminder of her historical period. I have identified the year of a principal diarist's marriage or remarriage if the event occurred during the diary period, so that a curious reader can ascertain whether a diarist's statement was made before or after her marriage (see Diarists in the Study). Except when clarity requires my editing a passage, I quote from the diaries without correcting spelling, punctuation, grammar, or phrasing, and I give as full a date as an entry has provided.

As women's primary form of writing over the centuries along with letters, their diaries have enriched the corpus of literature with experiential evidence of the nature and quality of female existence. Diaries may not provide truth in any indisputable sense because they offer subjective versions of reality, besides coming more or less filtered through a diary tradition. But diaries do tell one what women take to be true about themselves, their world, and its representability. The diarists' own ways of articulating their perceptions and activities are so valuable that I very often allow them to speak for themselves. Whatever the concurrence of attitudes among the women, each voice is unique; in each expression the accent falls a little differently.

18

I suspect—indeed, hope—that my numerous quotations will whet an appetite for the diaries themselves in full. They have much to offer a reader, not because they are unusual revelations, but because they are female enactments of life in process, quick to engage the imagination and absorb the mind.

ONE

"THE FACT OF THINGS":
History and Characteristics of the Diaries

VIRGINIA WOOLF (1882–1941) rightly describes the diary as a "capacious hold-all, in which one flings a mass of odds & ends" (20 April 1919),[1] for the contents of a woman's diary may prove quite heterogeneous. The diary's essential property as a form, however, is not its choice of subject matter, but rather its more or less dailiness. Entries about whatever interests the diarist are made periodically, at dated intervals, by a writer living chiefly at the moment and expressing her immediate self rather than, as in autobiography or memoirs, remembering the self that once she was or creating the self she would like to have been. Yet the diarist brings to her writing all her past experiences and obligatory feminine adaptations, and her diary will reflect that reality. Thus, though the diaries Englishwomen have written belong to the historical tradition of English diary keeping, they are also inevitably a contribution of the women's own: an expression of female lives, perceptions, and behaviors. It is an expression, moreover, marked by great continuity of attitudes.

Englishwomen, like Englishmen, have written diaries recognizable as such since at least the sixteenth century, when they gradually moved away from recording public events to private ones and from detached commentary to more personal mirroring of themselves. When record keepers began fleshing out impersonal records with self, the diary was born. Robert Fothergill finds in the tradition of English

21

diary keeping thereafter a gradual "evolution towards literary self-consciousness," which had become widespread by the beginning of the nineteenth century, for diarists in time also grew more alert to style and manner, sensible of themselves as writers, even if only in private.[2] Women, one discovers, early became uneasy about their writing and continued to be so.

In 1714, for example, Mary, Countess Cowper (1685–1724), apologizes for her style: "I intend this [diary] only for my own *Use*, it being a rough Draft only, which, if *God* bless me with Health and Leisure, I intend hereafter to revise and digest into a better method." In 1760, Caroline Powys (1739–1817) also anticipates someday perfecting her style, for, as she writes with a more conventional flourish, "If the rusticity of a dull pen . . . may be polish'd by exercise, then (as I've scribbled o'er much paper), may I in time, perhaps, have the honorary title of an expert journalist." The candor of Elizabeth George (dates unavailable), a tenant's daughter describing the coming-of-age party of the heir to the manor in 1847, shows her to be even less self-assured about her writing ability: "Well this is a very long and circumstantial account. . . . it has been written in a careless piecemeal sort of way at odd times, and I know it is very badly composed and full of mistakes." When her near-contemporary Lady Lucy Cavendish (1841–1925) describes deeply moving music, she worries on 29 June 1859, "I hope I'm not high-flown.[3]

For female diarists thus to betray uneasiness about their performance as writers makes excellent sense, however. It conforms to the women's penchant to be self-conscious, not just as writers but also as human beings of the secondary sex, who have learned to be ever sensitive to the impression they may be creating on others and habitually self-critical and self-effacing. Englishwomen's diaries may be part of a larger historical tradition, but they also constitute a tradition of their own. Mirroring their writers' female lives and learned behaviors, Englishwomen's diaries prove to be not only "capacious hold-alls" but also personal records that neither laud their writers nor entirely reveal them.

In the larger tradition of English diary keeping, the book reflecting the daily life and impress of an individual personality, the diary proper, was a common form by the eighteenth century. Behind it lay sixteenth-century standardized and fragmentary record-keeping habits to which increasingly the recorders brought more of themselves and which were to persist as foci within the more developed diary form. The travel diary existed by the sixteenth century; so too the businesslike regular-entry record kept largely as a duty, such as the military-campaign annual or record of an embassy or a profession. A handful of such diaries, all written by men, are extant; after midcentury they become more personalized. By the seventeenth century, the regular-entry record had evolved into the public diary, a form focused on public events and persons of interest to the writer. Of these early public diaries, again only male versions are extant. The late sixteenth and seventeenth centuries introduced also the formulaic diary of conscience, kept by both male and female Covenanters, as it would later be by Quakers and Methodists. Such standardized recording of religious soul-searching, in forms prescribed by devotional manuals and embodied in celebrated models, would serve as ancestor of the personal diary preoccupied with the inner life. Last, and most important here, is the diary consisting of brief entries of personal memorabilia and family records, germ of the diary proper.

Sparsely existent by the sixteenth century in both male and female versions—two women's diaries are extant, though only one in its original form—the personal record had lengthened and become comparatively well established by the seventeenth century, when both genders kept such books. During the eighteenth century, its potential contents expanded enormously to include collections of anecdotes and accounts of the famous in the matter of the public diary and self-realizations of the sort found originally only in religious diaries. As the century advanced, romantic, self-dramatizing expressions of feeling might be added. Earlier practice spoke dispassionately even of emotion, but after the 1740s, novels of sensibility inspired some readers themselves to undertake passionate explorations of consciousness, though many diaries remained bare factual records conspicuously lacking in subjective penetration. Not only have Englishwomen over the centuries kept diaries with all four sorts of focus—travel, public events and persons, conscience, personal memorabilia—beginning early to blend the latter two types. They have also occasionally (especially recently) practiced a form imported during the early twentieth century: the French *journal intime,* the serious exploration of the psyche with a "characteristic manner" of "mercurial responsiveness" to stimuli.[4]

By the eighteenth century, the eclectic diary was flourishing. Also, the practice of keeping letter-diaries had begun: writing an ongoing, daily dated letter, addressed to a recipient which functioned simultaneously as a diary and as correspondence, the writer retaining a copy as a personal record. Moreover, it was established procedure for women (as for men) to keep bound pocket diaries that allotted a set bit of space per day wherein to note appointments and other memorabilia. Like letter diaries, bound memo books continued on into the nineteenth century and, with much diminished popularity, still exist. While encouraging women to keep such books, the anonymous author of *My Daughter's Manual: Comprising a Summary View of Female Studies, Accomplishments, and Principles of Conduct,* an 1837 conduct manual, describes the practice with a bit of circular reasoning: "Many persons, of both sexes, accustom themselves to keep a journal of their daily engagements. It is for this purpose that so considerable of number of pocket-books are yearly sold; a fact that substantiates the numerous persons preserving such a diary."[5]

The bound memo books designed for women in the eighteenth and early nineteenth centuries are fascinating curios, at once reference books and diaries. For a sample, *The Suffolk Ladies Memorandum Book: or Polite Pocket Museum for the Year 1793* contains, besides its ruled diary and frontispiece, no less than A Poetical Address to the British Ladies; a poem by Burns, with a note about him; Signs of the Planets and Zodiac, together with Eclipses, Moveable Feasts, Ember Days, Common Notices, Holidays, and Remarkable Days; A Tale of the Moon; The most favorite New Songs and Airs Sung at Public Gardens, &c; The Flower Basket of Poetical Blossoms (original poems by diverse ladies); answers to puzzles, charades, and enigmas posed during 1792 and a new set of the same for the diarist to work at during 1793; and, finally, Country Dances for 1793. The two small leather–bound pocket books kept by diarist Harriet Grove (1791–

1867) in 1809 and 1810 demonstrate another, less frivolous version of the type. *The New Ladies' Memorandum Book for 1809*, after its engraved frontispiece with appropriate verses and its New Songs Sung at Vauxhall and other Public Places, plus the rules for Thomson's Dances for 1809, settles down to the ruled diary. This is printed in red, one week to a page, each page faced by a cash ruling for accounts. The second book is even more businesslike. Its title page declares it *Silvester's Housekeeper's Pocket Book; and Ladies' Daily Journal for 1810*, and its preliminary pages are a Table of Expenses, a New Marketing Table, and a description of Hawkstone, Shropshire. The ruled diary, now printed in black, has in its cash ruling a line for each of various household expenses, such as Meat and Fish, Poultry, Bread and Flour, Cheese and Butter, Rent, Servants' Wages, Washing. The diarist in this case—and she was probably not singular in doing so—according to the editor of her manuscript, Roger Ingpen, simply turned the accounts ledger into extra space for words. Grove also suggests how important such pocket diaries may have become to women. Her mother had given her the first two books as New Year's gifts, but Grove, quick herself to prepare for the future, "went to Church being Christmas day. . . . Bought pocket Book for next year" (25 December 1810).[6]

One could keep both a pocket book and an expanded diary of one's own devising. Apparently, when expanding a diary it was not unusual for the diarist to eliminate records of visits. Diarist Faith Gray (1751–1826), who kept both pocket books and a diary, records that she "went to Acomb" and "took Pocket Books etc. with me to peruse and make extracts from them" (January 1814). Her husband almost clarifies what she means when, upon her death, he scrupulously adds to the diary she had kept faithfully from 1764 to 1826 his "Continuation from my late dear Wife's memorandum books, of some of the principle entries. The details of Visitors and visiting not extracted, which indeed had in part begun to be the case in the foregoing pages." Caroline Powys also decides to omit visits, ending her 1793 diary hastily, "for though in my annual pocket-book I always set down the visits for each day, yet here it would take up too much room."[7] Evidently other women also kept both sorts of diaries. Nancy

Woodforde (1757–1830), for example, did so for at least one year and perhaps for more. Fourteen of Nancy's annual pocket diaries are extant and, for 1792, an expanded diary as well. However, Nancy's nieces, sisters Julia (1789–1873) and Ann (d. 1861) Woodforde, kept only memo books. Since Julia Woodforde engaged in a romance with a renegade Trappist, and her pocket book allotted only a half-inch of space per day, permitting only the barest mention of incidents, posterity may have reason to regret the memo book custom. Hester Thrale (1741–1821) kept not only her massive *Thraliana* but also small pocket diaries. Yet not everyone was ambitious enough to keep two diaries, or even to expand on all the entries when she did. Some women merely used their memo books as the basis for an annual summary, after writing which they destroyed the originals. Whenever a diary appears with summaries one may well suspect memo book antecedents or the like.[8] The supposed diary of Lady Grace Mildmay, covering 1570–1617, is not in fact a daily diary but undated meditations and reminiscences written many years belatedly for her daughter. It was probably based on some sort of daily memoranda, which she afterwards—unfortunately for her fame—destroyed.[9]

To go back to beginnings, therefore, in the history of English-women's diary keeping, means bypassing Mildmay for Lady Margaret Hoby (1571–1633), whose diary for 1599 to 1605 is extant. Hoby is doubly interesting in that she is one of the earliest true diarists, male or female. William Matthews's respected bibliography of British diaries lists as earlier than Hoby only two fifteenth-century embassy and diplomatic diaries and a scattering of sixteenth-century travel, religious, and public ones,[10] which become more personalized after mid-century. Bibliographer Arthur Ponsonby marvels at how Hoby, like a somewhat later Anne Clifford (1590–1676), countess of Dorset, manages "to jump into the correct daily diary method, although it seems unlikely that they were copying any model."[11] The most significant "model" may have been the female engagement with daily trivia and concern with private life in the absence of an active public life. However, as a pious Puritan, Hoby apparently found initial impulsion for her diary keeping in instruction to keep a record of moral and spiritual self-examination and correction. Yet faith alone is inadequate to explain her diary, for it escapes doctrinal justification and account keeping, as it progresses through the years, to become more simply a record of what interests her in her days.

When Hoby's extant diary begins, she has been married for three years to her third husband, Thomas Posthumous Hoby, second son of Sir Thomas Hoby.[12] Thomas Hoby was not only the translator of Castiglione's *Courtier*, but also the author of an autobiographical memoir, *A Booke of the Travaile and Lief of me Thomas Hoby* (*Travels and Life*), covering 1547–1564, in which, for the last eight years of his record, he includes brief annual entries concerning his domestic life. Since Margaret kept no diaries during her first two marriages— or at least no evidence shows her to have done so—her father-in-law's manuscript may have served as some inspiration for the personal, rather than devotional, diary she began gradually to keep during her third marriage. His book was accessible in family archives. The manuscript, which had remained with Thomas's widow, Lady Elizabeth (d. 1609), at some time passed into the hands of Thomas's eldest son, Sir Edward Hoby, who annotated it. Margaret was on visiting terms with her brother-in-law and mother-in-law, according to her diary. But more important, Thomas's *Booke* contains matter potentially of great interest to her: verbatim accounts of speeches by the Puritan martyr Lady Jane Duddley, who, even upon sentence of death by Queen Mary Tudor, refused to convert to Catholicism. Most, though not all, of the Duddley material was also printed by Foxe in his 1563 *Acts and Monuments* (more popularly, the "Book of Martyrs"). The pious Margaret would have been drawn to Thomas's *Booke* for the Duddley account, apart from any possible curiosity about her father-in-law's life. Her own diary shows her interest in Foxe's "Martyrs," which she often reads or has read to her.[13] If Margaret knew Thomas's *Booke*, she had proof that one may properly write of one's domestic affairs without relating them to the divine will, as increasingly she does in her diary, making herself one of the earliest true diarists in England.

But whether or not Thomas's book influenced Margaret, the difference between their books is instructive. Margaret's book is uniquely hers. His brief personal annual entries are strikingly different from her daily ones. To illustrate, a complete personal entry by Thomas looks like this one for 1559:

27

This yeer cam to the Court Monsr. Monmorency, the Constable's eldest sonn, to confirm the peac betwene England and France.

The Queene was visited with sundrie messagers from great princs, as th'Emperor, the King of Suevia, and divers other.

The viii day of July I came to Bissham with my wief, there to remaine.

The ix day of August I entred into a siknes that continued upon me the space of iij weeks.

The xij of November my wief went from Bissham to London, and there continued iij weeks in phisicke for her great belly, which was supposed to have bine a timpanie or dropsie.

Or this one for 1564:

Repairing of outhouses and barnes beyond the stable.

The xvjth. day of November was Anne borne about vij of the clock at night.

Christened the xixth. of the same, Mr. Deane of Westminster being godfather, Mr. Thomas Throgmorton's wief and her aunt Katharine Cooke godmothers.[14]

Sample whole entries in Margaret's diary move in much closer—indeed, increasingly closer—to her life:

After order taken for the house, the priuat praers, I writt notes into my testement and then brak my fast: after, I wrought, and kept Mr Hoby compenie tell almost dinner time: then I praied and, after dimer, I walked awhill and went to church Wth. Mr Hoby, and when I Cam home wrought tell 6:, then I examened my selfe and praied, walked tell supper time: then I hard the Lector, and after wrought a whill, and so went to bed: Lord, for Christs sack, pardone my drousenes which, with a neclegent mind, caused me to ommitt that medetation of that I had hard, which I ought to haue had. (14 September 1599)

After I had praised god for my rest and was readie, I went about the house, then I returned to priuatt praier: after, I did eate my breakfast, and againe was busie tell all most dimer time: then I praied, dined, and, after, went into the toune about som busines: then I was in the granerie receiuing Corne, and againe took order for supper and hard one of my wemen read of perkins, and, after that, returned to priuat praier and examenation: then, soune after, I went to supper, after that to the lector, then to priuat praer, and so to bed: (7 January 1599)

This day, in the afternone, I had had a child brought to se that was borne at Silpho, one Talliour sonne, who had no fundement, and had no passage for excrementes but att the Mouth: I was ernestly in- treated to Cutt the place to se if any passhage Could be made, but, although I Cutt deepe and searched, there was none to be found. (26 August 1601)

Mr. Hoby, my Mother, and my selfe, went to the dalls this day: we had in our Gardens a second sommer, for Hartechokes bare twisse, whitt Rosses, Read Rosses: and we, hauing sett a musk Rose the winter be- fore, it bare flowers now. I thinke the Like hath seldom binn seene: it is a great frute yeare all ouer. (5 October 1603)

After praier I buesied my selfe wt. presaruing, and other thinges whc. was to be done in the House: in the morninge my Mother went to Newton. (6 October 1603) [15]

The difference between 1599 and 1603 in the sample entries from Margaret's diary is conspicuous. Her recorded religious fervor abates considerably as her diary continues; increasingly, the entries become simply domestic. The diary, which breaks off abruptly in 1605, may even have been abandoned because Hoby recognized how far she had strayed from her pious intentions. [16] Although through the years she laconically continues to report private prayers among her activities on many (not all) days, her last few entries concern visitors and guests who came to dine on Sundays, and preceding entries are given to recording gossip garnered from friends. Even in 1601, she expends an entry on a precise description of a two-headed calf (5 May) [17]— clearly she was fascinated by the oddities in Creation for themselves, not only as God's handiwork.

Contents aside, from the start, unlike her businesslike father-in-law, who merely keeps records, including a few about his personal life, Margaret transmits some sense of her feelings: penitence, puzzlement, delight. As the first English female diarist, she anticipates much of what is to come in women's diaries—besides stealing a march on Pepys's "and so to bed." The five sample entries give one a good sense of what her life consisted in: praying, attending church, performing chores—and hers were endless, spanning house and estate—doctoring, entertaining visitors, and taking conjugal walks. Without being confessional or introspective, they convey some sense of her thoughts, self-concept, and reactions. One can see why critic Cynthia Pomerleau, in speaking of seventeenth-century autobiography, implies that diary writing proper is the creation of women: "The idea that oneself, one's feelings, one's spouse and domestic relations were properly and innately worth writing about was essentially a female idea, however tentatively conceived at the time. There is little or no precedent for such a notion, at least in England, in male thinking or practice."[18] Male diaries do offer some scraps of precedent, but female ones offer more than scraps. Before Hoby, Mildmay's missing diary also apparently included a record of herself in her domestic relations, and after Hoby, Clifford's early-seventeenth-century diary, though still not introspective, is even more personally informative than Hoby's, both about states of mind and activities. Clifford even records taking a bath in June 1617.[19]

Yet it would be erroneous to assume that all Englishwomen's diaries are highly personal ones centered on the diarist's own life, for public diaries are well represented too, from the eighteenth century on, especially among women who moved in the great world. The diary that Mary Cowper, for example, planned to rewrite someday covers her court experiences after she became a lady of the bedchamber to the Princess of Wales, wife of George I, in 1714 and is more a record of court gossip and intrigue than of Cowper. While indulging an eighteenth-century penchant for reporting on the doings of persons in high life, she anticipates the numerous court diaries that were to be kept by Queen Victoria's ladies-in-waiting during the next century; for example, by Edith Lytton (1841–1936), Countess Bulwer-Lytton, who from 1895 to 1899 faithfully records her own health and her duties, but whose real interest is the queen's excursions and visitors. She keeps her personal opinions rare and brief, and one learns little more than her admiration for Queen Victoria and for guests who converse easily and dress well.

On the other hand, the 1752–1774 diary of Elizabeth Percy (1716–1776), duchess of Northumberland, a lady of the bedchamber to Queen Charlotte, is generous with opinions—but not about the duchess herself. Her principal aim "throughout these Anecdotes" is to "scatter here & there forms, customs, rules &c of the Court to shew their variations at different periods & likewise the manners of the Times" (2 November 1769).[20] Though in the course of the diary she resigns her post, she does not significantly change her methods as diarist. Lady Northumberland's impulse is like that of Hester Thrale, who for about two years compiled a distinctive collection of anecdotes and gossip about sophisticated life in her *Thraliana* (1776–1809) before settling down to an increasingly more self-centered diary. Mary Frampton (1773–1846) kept a diary spanning 1779–1846, which, besides retrospection to her youth for its personal contents, consists largely of gossip and yearly summaries of public events. The sayings of the famous and near-famous consume the larger part of the 1835–1867 diary of Caroline Fox (1819–1871), who knew many intellectuals and envisioned her diary as notetaking on conversations. She reports others' discourse faithfully, but rarely her own reactions, even when the speaker is John Sterling, whom she reveres. An anonymous spinster (d. 1908) left a diary of anecdotes and conversations that is nearly devoid of self.[21] And Frances Stevenson (1888–1972), who became Countess Lloyd-George, kept a diary from 1914 to 1937 that is so much more about her lover (later, her husband) than about herself that it was publishable as *Lloyd George: A Diary by Frances Stevenson*.

For all that diary keeping implies an interest in oneself, then, female English diary need not connote a diary focused on self. Nonetheless, even the more public female diaries do remain personal diaries in an important sense: their interest in persons; in human behaviors, attachments, opinions, fates. Thus, Englishwomen's diaries on the whole reflect what critic Estelle C. Jelinek has found true of female autobiography: "emphasis by women on the personal, especially on other people, rather than on their [own] work life, their professional success, or their connectedness to current political events

31

or intellectual history."[22] Of course, since most women historically have not had careers or extensive educations to write about and have not been at the center of political life, it could scarcely be otherwise. Female lives have customarily hinged on relationships rather than achievements.

A second caveat is necessary. Englishwomen's diaries, even those without public intentions and despite women's peripheral public roles, are not necessarily diaries of domesticity. Jelinek also asserts, "In both English and American . . . personal diaries of the seventeenth and eighteenth centuries, it is domestic details that comprise the larger part of their accounts."[23] Women's diaries across the centuries do rely heavily on domestic details—on daily lives at home, on family matters, on social activities so often a part of family responsibilities. Even the most public diaries carry homey touches. The diary of Jacobite Elizabeth Byrom (1722–1801) for 1745–1746, for example, is devoted to Pretender Prince Charles Edward's invasion of Manchester, but amidst the mounting tension of events she remembers to record when she is "smoothing" (ironing) and washing (12, 16, 24, and 31 December 1745 for the former; 23 and 30 December for the latter).[24] Yet one must beware of stereotypical assumptions like those of Adrian Henstock, editor of the 1751–1810 "diary," actually retrospection, of Abigail Gawthern of Nottingham:

> Another factor colouring the entries in the diary is of course that events were seen through a woman's eyes. As with most women of her station at the period, her interests are in the social round. . . . She is naturally also concerned with bringing up her children, and, latterly, with their liaisons with intending suitors; many of her pages are taken up with social gossip, especially notices of births, marriages and deaths of local people.[25]

Over the centuries, despite variations in historical circumstances, themes and attitudes recur because so much of women's history has been lived under cultural assumptions about separate spheres for female and male life. Nonetheless, women's "eyes" have very individual lenses.

The description of Gawthern's diary could serve for Mary Woodforde's (d. 1730) diary too. The 1684–1690 record of this provincial clergyman's wife has just the sorts of entries attributed to Gawthern. It could serve for many other women as well; for instance, for Anne Lumb of Yorkshire (no dates available), whose extant country diaries of 1755 and 1757 are entirely domestic-social. Yet it will not serve neatly for provincial Mary Hardy (1733–1809), a prosperous farmer's wife. Hardy's diary is a domestic record, down to how much linen the maids and laundress wash at two- to four-week intervals, until finally Hardy rejoices, "We borrowed Mr. Davy's Washing Mill & washed 3 weeks linnen without a work woman" (19 April 1791).[26] But Hardy was fascinated by crimes, accidents, and disasters, which her 1783–1809 diary regularly reports with zeal from the weekly newsprints and local gossip. Londoner Louisa Bain (1803–1883) in her 1857–1883 diary shares Hardy's predilection for doom: bridges that give way under passenger trains, mass drownings in Regents Park, hangings, fires, attempts to blow up prisons, and like calamities dot her diary. Provincial Katherine Howard (1672–1765) includes some visits and a handful of weddings and births in her 1721–1764 diary (mostly the births of her dog's puppies, a litter a year). But her real interest is meteorological phenomena, to begin with, and then, with increasing momentum, deaths: local, national, international. Page after page records deaths. One learns, for example,

The Bills of Mortality were in ye Chester Journal at London 993. (18 November 1729)

Sir Henery Bunbury died. The King of Poland died. (12 February 1732)

My poor unfortunate neice Mary Hodgson I hear, died which proves a lie being alive still. (24 March 1741)

My neighbour Mrs. Ellen Bunbury died being elder than myself. (1 May 1763)[27]

Howard herself died at 93; hence she had ample opportunity to marvel at the vagaries of death and her own luck. Still, she is not the only diarist obsessed with mortality.

Women have also filled diary pages with other, more sanguine special interests, in addition to the usual daily records. Emily Shore (1819–1839), a devoted amateur naturalist, details her observations of flora and fauna in the part of her 1831–1839 diary she kept before 1835 and even provides an index to some of her lore. Mary Gladstone (1847–1927), an amateur musician, covers pages of her 1864–1920 diary with accounts of concerts, along with excerpts copied from the scores. Kate Russell (1842–1874), Viscountess Amberley, reports in her 1859–1872 diary on the sittings of Parliament, which she attended often, and on contemporary political issues. In her 1854–1882 diary, Lucy Cavendish instead scrutinizes the conditions of churches and follows current theological disputes. Beatrix Potter (1866–1943), still only a would-be artist, extensively catalogs exhibitions of paintings with her appraisals of them in her diary for 1881–1897. What a woman sees as repeatedly recordable depends on the woman, not just her time and station, though obviously they will influence her special interests. Englishwomen's diaries do continue Hoby's innovation, the personal domestic record; meanwhile, they are also unpredictable in the proportion of their domestic contents.

Because women's diaries have been written since at least the seventeenth century, with some preliminary excursions in the sixteenth, and have even evolved into increasingly more expansive and polished expression, one may speak of a literary tradition of women's diaries. Even without the evidence of commercial ventures like ladies' bound pocket diaries or all the extant pre-nineteenth-century diaries, one can tell that a widespread tradition of female diary-keeping existed by the early nineteenth century from Anna Brownell's (Jameson's) spurious *Diary of an Ennuyée*, published anonymously in London in 1826. A fiction—but "a very well written and interesting imposture," decided diarist Mary Shelley (1797–1851) in a critique for the *Westminister Review*—it was written to capitalize on such a tradition. It begins, moreover, with a telling question: "What young lady, travelling for the first time on the continent, does not write a 'Diary'?"[28] Encouraged first to keep devotional diaries, then, by the temper of the eighteenth century, to keep secular ones, women expected to keep diaries, and they could learn styles of diary keeping from other diarists.

However, the eighteenth-century novel also had some influence on the tradition of diary keeping by promoting self-expression and prompting verbal style. The novel of sensibility, such as Samuel Richardson's epistolary *Clarissa* (1747–1748), for example, showed its readers that outside the devotional diary a first-person narrator could intensively explore consciousness and vent emotion directly. The secular diary of the later eighteenth century probably became a more expressive form than its predecessors partly under the influence of the novel. Occasionally, diarists will duplicate the rhetoric of fictional characters for acts of self-dramatization. Witness, for example, Elizabeth (Webster) Fox (1770–1845), baroness of Holland House, lamenting her first marriage with all the grace of a Gothic heroine:

> Despair often prompts me to a remedy within my reach. . . . My mind is worked up to a state of savage exaltation and impels me to act with fury that proceeds more from passion and deep despair than I can in calmer moments justify. Oftentimes in the gloom of midnight I feel a desire to curtail my grief and but for an unaccountable shudder that creeps over me, ere this the deed of rashness would be executed. (27 June 1793)[29]

But she did not commit suicide; she took a lover instead.

More directly influential in the formation of a diary tradition, by the nineteenth century women were reading published female diaries (and male ones) and advice on diary keeping—though not all would-be diarists were readers and not all readers were uncritically receptive. Authentic diaries, followed by fictional ones like Brownell's (Jameson's), began to be published in the nineteenth century. After John Evelyn's diary had appeared in 1818 and Samuel Pepys's (abridged) in 1825, just before midcentury came Fanny (Frances) Burney's (Madame d'Arblay's). The first volume of Burney left her more reticent and modest great-niece, Fanny Anne Burney, Mrs. Wood (1812–1860), feeling that the editor should have pruned better. "As to six Volumes of these Journals, one yawns at the bare idea!" Nor did she like the way her honored relative became hardened to "the most insufferable flattery. . . . able to swallow apparently large lumps of the poisonous drug, without so much as wincing or showing any subsequent symptoms of mental indigestion" (7 February 1842).

35

Curiously, Fanny Anne Burney's own diary terminates in February 1842, the same month she has read her great-aunt's oeuvre.[30]

Not only family members were reading diaries. One also finds Brownell's (Jameson's) popular book listed in the diary of Clarissa Trant (1800–1844) among her annual summary of readings (31 December 1827). Although Trant was a young lady who prided herself on not reading anything so flimsy as fiction, clearly she did not read the *Westminster Review* either. Trant too apparently was not charmed by what she read, for she does not allow herself to be influenced by the sentimental Ennuyée, who presents herself as a woman literally dying of a broken heart in a Pyrrhic victory over a mysterious passion refused. Or in her purple prose, "Alas! what avails it that I have shaken the viper from my hand, if I have no miraculous antidote against the venom which has mingled with my life-blood!"[31] Quiet-voiced Trant refuses self-pity when her own love affair collapses, and in her annual stocktaking (of days as well as of books) reveals the same healthy-minded woman she was before reading the Ennuyée's woes: namely, one who has "felt the extremes of happiness and sorrow, but the former, thank God, has predominated" (31 December 1827).[32]

Brownell's (Jameson's) was not the only book of its type. By 1836 it had inspired Catherine Gore's also anonymously published *Diary of an Désennuyée*. Brownell and Gore's books purported to be contemporary records; but soon the two-volume *Lady Willoughby; or Passages from the Diary of a Wife and Mother in the Seventeenth Century* (1844–1848), actually by Hannah Rathbone, and then Harriet Skene's anonymously published *Diary of Martha Bethune Baliol, from 1753–1754* (1853) also tapped the past. In the same year and under her own name, Lady Charlotte Maria Pepys published *The Diary and Houres of the Ladye Adolie, a Faythfulle Childe, 1552* as a fully acknowledged fiction.[33] No matter; female readers welcomed any published diaries.

They would continue to have a taste for reading diaries—real, spurious, and admittedly fictional—into the twentieth century,[34] and would sometimes explicitly want to learn from them. Marie Bashkirtseff's authentic confessional *Journal of a Young Artist*, published posthumously in 1887, became an inspirational model for some women in the late nineteenth and early twentieth centuries much the way

Anaïs Nin's six-volume *Diary* (published 1966–1976) was to become a model during the later twentieth century. Lady Louisa Knightley (not a principal diarist; she intended to publish her diary) studied Bashkirtseff's diary to improve her own.[35] Katherine Mansfield (1888–1923), who quotes from Bashkirtseff in 1906 and reports putting aside her own writing to read Bashkirtseff (21 October 1907), was evidently influenced by her confessional mode. Yet Gladstone, who participates in the standards of Fanny Anne Burney (Wood), reads Bashkirtseff with some reservations, finding her "passionately self-centered and with little or no sense of duty" (13 August 1889). And though Lady Cynthia Asquith (1887–1960) records that reading Bashkirtseff makes her own diary "seem sadly insipid and impersonal" (29 December 1916),[36] she does nothing to change her methods thereafter. No necessary correspondence exists between what a diarist reads and what she writes. The reading becomes a possible model only when it matches the reader's predispositions. It is understandable that some diarists refused models like Fanny Burney, Brownell (Jameson), and Bashkirtseff; they violate female acculturation to self-abnegation, modesty, and silence. More ordinary diarists who fit in with women's socialization made better diary mothers. The great power that socialization wielded over women's diaries is suggested by the example of first diarist Margaret Hoby, who neither had nor needed female models to teach her to keep her marital problems out of her pages.

Potential influence on women diarists in the nineteenth century came not only from published diaries but also from conduct manuals, potent weapons of socialization. The 1837 *My Daughter's Manual* shows how public voices might encroach on the diary-keeping habits of women. The female writer of this manual, who borrows heavily from the account keeping of the journal of conscience, starts on a positive note in telling her readers to code their entries by signs designating sorrow and pleasure and health, for "at the end of a year . . . the crosses and the circles may be each summed up, and I am bold to say, the signs of good would immensely preponderate over the signs of evil." Unfortunately, however, that is not the only message. The diarist is also to keep track of personal causes for pain and pleasure, so that her diary will become "a kind of second conscience, permanently recording the dictates of our internal monitor" as "not only the register of *our actions*, but the remembrancer of our faults." [37] The power of negative thinking encouraged by such manuals fueled many women's diaries.

In any century, female family models too played their part in potentially influencing female diary keeping. For the Woodforde women who succeeded seventeenth-century Mary—Nancy, then Julia, then Ann—models were ready to hand in the family archives. Having lost her mother in early childhood, Trant reports longingly poring over her mother's diary. Other women may also have studied their mothers' writings, when available, even if they do not report doing so. Since Lady Louisa de Rothschild (1821–1910) explicitly continued her diary to help educate her two daughters, whom she encouraged to keep diaries as well, very probably she let them read parts of it too. And doubtless they were eager to do so.

For ample evidence across the centuries says that women like to read one another's diaries, familial or otherwise, that they are characteristically curious, even quite inquisitive, about other women's lives. Mary Frampton, for example, copied extracts from other women's diaries into her own diary in 1796 and 1805. [38] Lady Mary Coke (a letter diarist, therefore not a principal diarist) records in 1767 how "Lady Spencer came to see me, and found me writing my journal. She desired I wou'd let her read it. She wou'd be content with a single page." Though Coke decides "much as I love her I cou'd not consent," [39] other women were more openhanded with their diaries. Harriet Duncannon (1761–1821), countess of Bessborough, evidently shared some of her diary with her mother, Lady Georgiana Spencer (not Coke's petitioner), for the latter writes to her on 22 April 1786, "There are a few things I want to point out to you in your journal, but have not time." Florence Sitwell (1858–1930) obliges when her cousin Lucy "wanted very much to read my journal, . . . I let her do so" (3 May 1875). So too Elizabeth Barrett (Browning) (1806–1861) generously "read some of my diary to [sister] Arabel in bed! My diary is not meant to be read by any person except myself: but she deserves to be let behind the scenes" (2 January 1832). Woolf, who hopes that Mansfield will, as promised, "send me her diary," reports how her own cousin, Katherine Stephen, willingly granted Woolf's request for readings from the diaries Stephen had kept since 1877 (25 August 1920, 19 February 1923). Asquith remarks with some pride, "Gwendoline [Osborne] insisted on reading extracts from my diary: she said she would never be able to read anything else" (15 September 1918).[40]

Cynthia Huff, in her study of nineteenth-century female diaries, reports that, as the designated chroniclers of family records, women often copied out the diaries of family members, besides reading friends' and relatives' diaries or hearing them read aloud.[41] Only William Matthews contends that since diarists are solitaries, there can be no tradition for diaries: "Except for religious diaries and certain literary productions, diaries are mostly written without reference to other diaries and without influence from them, and so the form has no history except in the most general sense." Had he been a woman, he would have known otherwise.[42]

Englishwomen shared their diaries when they chose to and, given the limited contents of diaries, it was not difficult to do so. Emily Shore describes the usual state of affairs in female diary keeping in the past as she reflects on the first few years of her diary and finds it "meant . . . for little more than a journal of occurrences, deeds, occupations—not of the private state of my mind; consequently it has . . . been a journal meant neither merely for myself nor for any one intimate friend" (6 July 1838).[43] Female diary keeping, as evidenced by these English diaries, was much less introspective and frank than it is currently envisioned to be. The journal (*journal* is the preferred term) identified by feminist consciousness-raising, as by contemporary psychotherapy, is a willingly intimate outpouring, the result of an uncensored penetration of one's psyche. As American feminists Deena Metzger and Barbara Meyerhoff emphasize in 1979, journal keeping is a "process, in the course of which a Self may be constructed"; not "a record of what has occurred" but a record of "what is in the act of becoming in the course of the writing. . . . Its authenticity comes from the honesty of the writer and his/her willingness to embark on an uncharted course, with courage to allow the unknown to enter."[44] Such journalizing has affinities with the comparatively recent *journal intime,* some English practitioners of which are Ivy Jacquier (not included in this study) and, to some extent,

Mansfield. But it has little connection with the larger tradition of female English diary keeping. Women today in journal-writing workshops may "write of their private lives," as Metzger and Meyerhoff describe, "sitting with each other in supportive settings where 'confessions' of prostitution, abortion, maternal rage, sexual fear, rape, and similarly taboo experiences and emotions are . . . received by the group as a gift of sharing."[45] Women of the past wrote alone and kept taboo subjects hidden even from themselves. Their diaries are reticent rather than revealing—or rather, they reveal the very modes of censored thought that feminist consciousness-raising is attempting to wean women from.

Louisa Bain called her nineteenth-century diary "Dry Facts, no Feelings," and though her diary is not devoid of feelings, it does give them short shrift. Her label could be affixed to the large number of diaries that are bare-bones records. That quality is typical of early diaries, as Hoby's entries show, or the Civil War diary of Lady Isabella Twysden (1605–1657), kept from 1645–1651. Even when her husband, Sir Roger, has returned in 1647 after lengthy imprisonment, Twysden only notes, "The 5 of August my husband came to peckham where he had not ben in 5 yeare before having ben a prisoner most of that time by the parle [Parliament]." But not only the earliest diaries read thus, as 150 years later Faith Gray can illustrate. Though she may have expanded her memo book into her diary, her expansions, as shown by entries from a random page, are more like contractions:

> 1795 *10th* Sister Robinson, Jonathan, Margaret, William, Lucy and Edmund Gray myself and A. Burnett went to Filey.
> *Sept 3rd* Rode to Cayton first time. Mrs. Lofthouse with me. (on the 31st was thrown off the Galloway into the water!!)
> *8th* About this time the Sunday School was begun at Filey.
> *18th* Left Filey and got to York in the evening after a stay of 5 weeks. Mr. Gray with us part of the time.[46]

A pious Evangelical, Gray becomes expansive only when a close friend or relative has died. She details the last moments of the afflicted; she composes a eulogy for each Christian who has met death as a Christian should; she takes the occasion to review family history—but those are expansions about others, not about herself.

Many a diarist simply records how a day was spent. The entries could as well be letters, and in some instances essentially were. Mary Hamilton (1756–1816), for example, remarks, "I wrote a long letter to Miss Gunning after dinner on 7 sides of the largest uncut folio paper" (7 June 1783); whereupon her editors, Elizabeth and Florence Anson, having seen this letter of "pleasant doings for the past nine days," observe it to be "almost a facsimile of her diary." A recurrent comment in these diaries, as phrased here by Fanny Anne Burney (Wood), is "One day so closely resembles another in its occupations and pursuits that I have nothing to record in my Journal" (25 August 1853)—the letter writer's standard apology for not writing. She was on her honeymoon at the time. At an extreme, a diarist like Frampton all but gives up the burden of keeping a personal diary: "In default of personal narrative, I will give extracts from letters daily received by us" (1814).[47]

But even more ambitious diarists are inclined to be reticent and inhibited, candid neither about their bodies nor about their minds and feelings, neither self-reflective nor self-revealing, except minimally and inadvertently. Freely speaking diarists are the exception, not the rule. On the one hand, diaristic reticence is apparently neither gender-specific nor only a British national characteristic. Having studied nineteenth-century American and Canadian diaries, male and female—in this case almost all archival rather than published—Paul C. Rosenblatt concludes: "Diaries are most often not introspective. They are simply superficial, laconic memos." On the other hand, good reasons exist for reticence to be more typically female than male. Thus, even if Ponsonby feels that all British suffer from it, he also believes that "women seem to be more cautious and less prone to give themselves away. . . . English women diarists show that they are less morbid and introspective and fonder of objective narrative."[48]

Illness, pregnancy, and childbirth aside, the diarists in this study do not ordinarily discuss their physicality, and childbirth they treat most circumspectly, not as an experience (for routine births) but as an event. Lady Kate Amberly's husband, Viscount John Russell Amberley, who kept her diary for her when she was in childbed, may be able to record that he sucked her breasts to reduce the painful pressure caused by her inability to nurse (14 August 1864). She never duplicates his level of frankness, even though she is one of the rare Victorian diarists who can acknowledge a menstrual period. That is, her friend-cum-physician Miss Garrett has assured her she need not abandon a proposed trip to America "if I avoid fatigue at monthly periods" (9 August 1867)—an interesting caution since she was pregnant at the time. Menstruation and menopause are acknowledged as realities of female life by only two other diarists. Hester Thrale, always frank about the physical, notes her daughter Cecilia's *"particular Time"* because Cecilia's menses complicate an attack of consumption (for which Cecilia is bled!); she even acknowledges her own menses, "my oldest Friend," on the occasion of her menopause (20 October 1792, 9 April 1791). Likewise, Woolf sometimes (euphemistically) records her need to spend the day "recumbent . . . owing to the usual circumstances," as she says on 25 October 1917; and she later airs her fears of menopause (16 September 1929).[49] In life, the euphemisms for menstruation are unnumbered, and diarists may therefore be saying more than a reader recognizes. Rosenblatt found American and Canadian diarists using diary code to keep track of their menstrual periods,[50] but in these published English diaries either the writers do not do so, or their editors obscure the evidence inadvertently or possibly even deliberately.

As late as 1916, Cynthia Asquith, a woman with many male admirers, muses, "Not much Pepys about this part of my diary—I wonder if all diaries are as unrepresentative of their writers as this is of me" (4 September). They are: sexual relationships as such are also rarely a diary subject. Seventeenth-century Anne Clifford must be credited with being the first and almost the last diarist to report that her husband sleeps with her. She records, "My Lord lay in my chamber" on 7 April 1617, and two weeks later, on 24 April, "This night my Lord came to lie in my chamber"; whereas on 23 April, "My Lord should have lain with me, but he and I fell out about matters." By 2 August, however, she can report his lying in her chamber for all of his visit home.[51] Actually, Clifford is reporting on sexual politics, not sex. She and her first husband, Richard Sackville, second earl of Dorset, were at constant odds over her estates because he objected to her fight for the inheritance wrongly denied her by her father's will, especially since she refused to sign over any possible profits to him. When she was too stubborn about the estates, using time-honored methods Lord Dorset punished her via the marriage bed.

Aside from Clifford, only eighteenth-century and twentieth-century diarists show any frankness about sex. Elizabeth Raper (d. 1778), for example, coolly records the playing around she has done when

> Mr L[ipeat] desired to see the great room whither I attended him but found it was more for his sense of feeling than his sense of sight, Kissing being his chief business there. That over, we adjourned to the study, drank chocolate. (26 January 1758)

> At six A. went to bed, . . . by 11 Pompey [the servant]; soon after came Statue [her current boyfriend] and staid well past 3 Lord help's! (21 January 1759)

Thrale (Piozzi) upon remarriage dares still admit some facts of life, yearning, "Oh might *I* hope to be once more in that State [pregnancy] by the Man my Heart doats on" (1 January 1784). The nineteenth-century diarists usually try not to admit them. Late in the century, however, Beatrice (Potter) Webb (1858–1943), an unusually frank and introspective woman, acknowledges, and more than once, the pressures of her sexual desires—which she tries valiantly to suppress:

> You are really getting into a nasty and what I should call an indecent way of thinking of men, and love, and unless you take care you will lose all your purity of thought. (13 March 1874)

> I must check those feelings which are the expression of physical instinct craving for satisfaction; but God knows celibacy is as painful to a woman (even from the physical standpoint) as it is to a man. It could not be more painful than it is to a woman. (7 March 1889)

43

Nonetheless, unable to have the man she really desires, Joseph Chamberlain, she marries Sidney Webb, not hesitating to admit that theirs will be an asexual alliance "based on fellowship" (20 June 1891).[52]

By the twentieth century, a few candid diarists appear. In 1913, Great War diarist Vera Brittain at age twenty admits dislike for her sexuality and laments a gender role based on biology:

> On the way to golf I induced mother to disclose a few points on sexual matters which I thought I ought to know, though the information is always intensely distasteful to me and most depressing—in fact it quite put me off my game! I suppose it is the spiritual—& intellectual—development part of me that feels repugnance at being brought too closely in contact with physical 'open secrets.' Alas! Sometimes it feels sad to be a woman! Men seem to have so much choice as to what they are intended for.[53]

Mansfield, more open yet, is not only frank about her heterosexuality; she also records her lesbianism freely. Mansfield is so explicit, in fact, that although her editor-husband, John Middleton Murry, convinced himself that he could retain admissions such as "I feel more powerfully all those so-termed sexual impulses with her [Edie Bendall] than I have with any man"—expanded on in some impassioned detail—he suppressed and distorted others, such as this:

> Do other people of my age feel as I do I wonder so almost physically ill. . . . I want Maata I want her—and I have had her—terribly—This is unclear I know but true. What an extraordinary thing—I feel savagely crude—and almost powerfully enamoured of the child—I had thought that a thing of that cast—[two illegible words]—my mind is like a Russian novel—[54]

Woolf both acknowledges Ethel Smythe's amatory overtures and traces the emotional stages of her own lesbian relationship with Vita Sackville-West. Woolf can envision a diary as a means of diminishing self-censorship: "If one could be friendly with women, what a pleasure—the relationship so secret & private compared with relations with men. Why not write about it? truthfully? As I think, this diary writing has greatly helped my style; loosened the ligatures" (1 November 1924).[55] But the loosening for private matters, sexual or otherwise, remains only partial.

Editing may explain some of the censored quality of these diaries. All published diaries have been edited, and very few published women's diaries have appeared in unexpurgated or scholarly editions. Many editors undoubtedly deleted any sexually frank entries and anything else deemed improper for public consumption. It was standard practice to do so in the late nineteenth century, when diaries began to be widely published. Caroline Fox's editor, Horace N. Pym, for example, in 1882 reassures a reader that "nothing will be found in these pages which should seem like drawing aside the curtains that ought to be left covering the inner life of all." But as late as 1968, Asquith's editor, E. M. Horsley, cuts a diary that the writer herself has already censored with regard to her sexuality, because, he explains, "she wrote . . . very, very frankly." He later acknowledges removing "too personal and painful" references to her autistic child, John;[56] any other censored subjects remain his secret. Of course, like the diarist's family, whom the editor often represents, an editor must worry about any reputations that the diary might damage. As Middleton Murry shows, however, interested parties may go to inordinate lengths to protect their sense of the diarist's proper image. After Mansfield's manuscripts were purchased by the Alexander Turnbull Library in Wellington, New Zealand, in 1957, Philip Waldron discovered that Murry had cavalierly toned down and omitted material reflecting not just Mansfield's "less conventional sexual proclivities," but also, as Waldron bluntly puts it, her "tetchy, even bitchy personality" for the supposedly definitive edition of her diary Murry published in 1954.[57]

Editors aside, diarists themselves sometimes censor their diaries after writing them. Mansfield, for instance, destroyed a large portion of her early diaries; Beatrix Potter at twenty thinned the early pages of the diary she had begun at fourteen; and probably many a woman likewise removed from the record youthful sentiments to which she could no longer subscribe. And there are other reasons than adult consciousness to dictate self-editing. Mary Cowper was being practical when she destroyed a large part of her diary in 1723 because she learned that her husband, lord chancellor to George I, was accused of plotting with the Jacobites to restore the Stuarts by French invasion. The accusation was unfounded, but she took no chances. Claire Clairmont (1798–1879) obliterated words and tore out entries that perhaps testified to her brother-in-law Percy Shelley's rebukes of her excessive moodiness. Harriet Grove blotted out references to Shelley after their informal engagement foundered, besides tearing out two and one-half pages entirely.[58] Jane Carlyle (1801–1866) probably also had personal reasons for destroying most of her diaries, as had Webb, Thrale, and others for the pages they tore out. The 1820–1855 diary of Mary Bagot (dates unavailable) introduces yet another interesting possibility. Bagot's editor, Sophy Louisa Bagot, remarks on the introduction that her husband obliged her to destroy her own premarital diaries because "he had known so much unhappiness caused by such writings that he entertained both dislike and distrust of them."[59]

Editing of one sort or another has undoubtedly affected the diaries. Yet their reticence cannot be attributed solely to that. There is more justice in believing novelist Christa Wolf, herself a diarist, that "Anyone who asks about a person's diary must accept the fact more is concealed than said"[60]—whether about socially taboo subjects or about the diarist's inner life. Diaries published in full are rarely more open than edited ones, as the facsimile transcript of Elizabeth Barrett (Browning's) diary for 1831–1832, though incomplete, can illustrate. According to its editors, Philip Kelley and Ronald Hudson, the diary for 1832 lacks fifty-six pages excised by Barrett's brother George, who also partly excised eighteen others.[61] But the consistency of the remaining entries suggests that his excisions did not affect the tenor of the diary or disturb its controlling interest: Elizabeth's relationship with Hugh Stuart Boyd. George had no need to excise any references to Boyd; they are so circumspect as to still mislead some readers. He more likely took out remarks pertaining to the forced sale of Hope End, the family home in Herefordshire, an occasion of great grief for the family and of some rancor on Elizabeth's part.

Barrett's diary chronicles her intense, hopeless passion at twenty-five for her "friend," the blind scholar and religious controversialist Boyd. Boyd is fifty years old, married, and a close neighbor at Hope

End; Barrett reads classics and discusses intellectual issues with him and dreads losing him once her family moves. Ostensibly captivated with Boyd as a scholar-teacher, but actually infatuated with him as a man, she cannot admit her desires. Consequently, she does not call her frustrated feelings love; she only displays every anguished symptom. She hangs on Boyd's every word—"*If* he cared for me as I care for him, he could speak & act only in one way" (15 June 1831)—and is jealous of any attentions he pays to other women. She quivers for his regard: "Not that his regard and friendship are equal to mine. But as long as there *is* a reciprocity, I have no right to expect an equality,—and that he really has a real regard & friendship for me, I feel sure—at least today!—" (5 September 1831). The true situation is inadmissible in words, even though from the opening entry she has vowed to be honest in her diary:

> I wonder if I shall burn this sheet of paper like most others I have begun the same way. To write a diary, I have thought of very often at far & near distances of time: but how could I write a diary without throwing upon . . . paper my thoughts, all my thoughts—the thoughts of my heart as well as of my head?—& then how could I bear to look on *them* after they were written? . . . Well! but I will write: I must write. (4 June 1831) [62]

Two months later she reminds herself, "I have an oath in Heaven to be altogether sincere in this journal of mine" (5 August 1831). And up to a point Barrett can be honest. She can, for example, record her dreams, even if she cannot acknowledge the implications of them. Thus,

> I dreamt last night that I was married, just married; & in an agony to procure a dissolution of the engagement. Scarcely ever considered my single state with more satisfaction than when I awoke. I never *will* marry: but if I ever were to do such a foolish thing, I hope I may not feel as I did last night! (1 September 1831)

She repeats, "but I never will marry!" two months later (16 November 1831).

47

Barrett cannot admit any passional feelings for Boyd; she has re-fused to allow herself a lover. The best she can do is become uneasy when she realizes she is covering up something and remind herself, "Let me be honest, if I cant be wise!" (11 June 1831). But she is most honest only in a letter to Richard Hengist Horne some twelve years later, when she declares, on 5 October 1843, "Once indeed, for one year, I kept a diary in detail & largely,—&, at the end of the twelve months, was in such a crisis of self-disgust that there was nothing for me but to leave off the diary."[63] Maybe Barrett could not admit to herself her longing for a married man when she began her diary, but she certainly admitted it to herself as she continued writing—and suppressed it from her diary if not from her uneasy soul.

A wide range of deep feelings also may find no expression in di-aries. Wounded pride, for example, is common. Spinster Auguste Schlüter (1850–1917), to illustrate, alludes to a mysterious betrayer or two betrayers, probably a suitor or suitors, who evidently hurt her greatly (e.g., 14 April 1877, 27 June 1880), but she neither identifies the circumstances nor vents the sense of insult aroused in her. And only tucked away in a description of her delight at the generous birthday present given her by the Gladstones, whose maid she is, is there any indication that she has long been feeling herself misused: she admits now feeling "very small for allowing doubt to poison me lately more than once" (3 July 1887). A hundred years earlier, Lady Eleanor Butler (1739?–1829), in an unprecedented act for her era, refused to marry and ran away from home in 1778 with twenty-one-year-old gentlewoman Sarah Ponsonby to share a cottage in Wales. The scandal gradually died down, but after an attack on Butler and her beloved Sarah in the press in 1790 signaled a resumption of jour-nalistic hostilities, she wrote to Sir Edmund Burke demanding pros-ecution of the attacker, which he replied would be unfeasible. The only acknowledgment in her diary, however, of an issue so close to Butler's heart is the laconic "Writing to the Rt. Honble. Ed. Burke" (3 August 1790). Her bare-bones diary contains no mention of any of the slander she and Sarah endured, though Butler is a woman of waspish tongue and definite opinions who easily pens lines like "A large party from Wexham to see this place. Had the pleasure of refus-ing them. . . . All the family at the Castle [her relatives] well—as if

I cared" (8 July, 15 September 1789). Predictably, she reports her relationship with "My Sweet Love" Sarah, "the delight of my heart" and "my Better half" (7 December and 24 September 1785, 21 October 1807), only as reiterated claims of their perfect mutual contentment and kindness to each other. The intensities of their intimacy are not for paper.[64] Although Butler's extant diary (only a fragment of probably a much larger whole) has not been published in full, the mode of reticence is so marked that additional entries could not offset it.

However, the diary of Mary Shelley has been published in full, and it, too, is interesting in its reticence. Bisected by Percy Shelley's death in 1822, Mary's diary has two phases. The earlier portion consists of laconic, impersonal statements of daily activities and reading lists, though occasional circumstances such as her irritation with her half-sister, Claire Clairmont, who for a while shared the Shelley home, and her mourning for her first child, who died on 6 March 1815, sometimes impel Mary to more expressive entries, such as "Still think about my little baby—'tis hard indeed, for a mother to lose a child" (9 March 1815). Essentially, however, while Mary has Percy as confidant (and perhaps also because she prefers that he not have opportunity to read what she cannot tell him personally), neither joys nor griefs unlock her pen. Birth elicits only entries such as "I am confined Tuesday, 2nd" (which means that her daughter Clara was born) or "I have not kept my Journal all this time; but I have little to say, except that on the morning of Friday, November 12, little Percy Florence was born" (19 September 1817, 31 December 1819). Not until her later diary (5 October 1839) does one learn that she had a serious miscarriage on 16 June 1821, followed by deep depression. Likewise, though she has immediately acknowledged another son's death (4 August 1819), only belatedly does one learn that, when "four years ago, we lost our darling William; four years ago, in excessive agony, I called for death to free me from all I felt that I should suffer here" (31 May 1823).[65] Equivalent events, like the death of Percy's first wife, Harriet, are handled with the same terseness. Only when Mary is widowed does her diary become more expansive and introspective, especially on the woes of her widowhood. For most of her widow's diary, she is self-pitying and self-dramatizing, though she finally emerges as an admirably matured woman.

Lacking Percy as confidant, the widowed Mary resorts to her diary. She is now determined upon absolute candor and self-knowledge: "Above all let me fearlessly descend into the remotest caverns of my own mind, carry the torch of self-knowledge into its dimmest recesses" (25 February 1822). Yet, although she thinks of her diary as entirely private—"It has struck me what a very imperfect picture (only *no one* will ever see it) these querulous pages afford of *me*" (2 December 1834)—she cannot quite carry it off. She is both overwhelmed by her feelings—"But can I express all I feel? Can I give words to thoughts and feelings that, as a tempest, hurry me along? . . . This is too great an agony to be written about. I may express my despair, but my thoughts can find no words" (2 and 7 October 1822)— and unwilling always to say what she really thinks. Thus, for example, when she discovers that Jane Williams has been slandering her with tales about her inadequacies as Percy's wife, Mary expresses not her actual thoughts, but rhetorical formulae for grief. She retreats to the histronic style she uses for novels like her *Frankenstein:*

> Not for worlds would I attempt to transfer the deathly blackness of my meditations to these pages. Let no trace remain save the deep bleeding hidden wound of my lost heart, of such a tale of horror and despair. . . . What deadly cold flows through my veins; my head weighed down; my limbs sink under me. I start at every sound as the messenger of fresh misery, and despair invests my soul with trembling horror. (13 July 1827)[66]

The intent to be candid does not necessarily translate into the practice of candor.

Virginia Woolf's diary has also been published unexpurgated.[67] Woolf early envisions her diary as uninhibited: "What sort of diary should I like mine to be? . . . The main requisite . . . is not to play the part of censor, but to write as the mood comes or of anything whatever" (20 April 1919). And yet she does play censor, and is aware that she does so. Despite her frankness on many subjects, Woolf reserves a large part of herself for silence. When she boasts of

her diary keeping at Garsingon in 1917, Woolf discovers that Lady
Ottoline Morrell "keeps one . . . devoted however to her 'inner life':
which made me reflect that I haven't an inner life" (22 November).[68]
One can trace a path of her concern lest she let the inner life of her
own "soul" into her diary: revelations of her inmost personality and
intimate feelings.

Thus in 1919 she is surprised by her reactions to Mansfield, for "it
looks as if I had soul after all; these are revelations, self analyses"
(28 November). In 1920, "if this diary were a diary of the soul," she
could discourse at length on how humiliated she felt at the second
meeting of the Memoir Club, when she read a very personal paper to
an equally unresponsive audience—"What possessed me to lay bare
my soul! Still, the usual revulsion has now taken place" (18 March).
In 1923, albeit with some reluctance, she reaffirms her stand: "How
it would interest me if this diary were to become a real diary: something in which I could see changes, trace moods developing; but
then I should have to speak of the soul, & did I not banish the soul
when I began?" (19 February). By 1924, "I think its time to cancel
that vow against soul description" (21 June), but in 1929, she is still
only contemplating an "idea"—"to break my rule & write about
the soul for once" (15 August). And in 1932 she is still hesitant
about expressing "my mind—but is this [diary] to be a record of 'my
mind' . . . ?" (18 April). Meanwhile, to some extent she has been
revealing her soul all along, more and more as she comes to use her
diary as an emotional prop; and therefore she knows that "my soul
peeped out" (19 February 1923) from her pages. But it must peep, for
she refuses it full display. As she acknowledges ruefully in 1939, "I
never reach the depths; I'm too surface blown" (17 December).[69]

The reticence of women's diaries concerning body, mind, and
heart has certain obvious and some less obvious causes. Obviously,
for example, social censorship, to which women are very sensitive,
inhibits diarists' talking—sometimes even thinking—about taboo
subjects like sexual physicality. The mainly Victorian burden of prudery is a potent silencer and an enduring legacy. As late as 1918, a
woman who has attended a meeting of the Women's Cooperative
Guild at the Woolfs' tells how she had to enlist a friend "to explain
the period to her own daughter." "She still feels shy if the daughter

[twenty-three years old] is in the room when sexual subjects are discussed" (18 April), marvels Woolf. Before the Victorian and Edwardian eras, as already suggested by some diarists' ability to write of their own bodies and as one might expect, the diarists are generally less inhibited. Mary Hardy, for example, methodically records the many bastards conceived or born in her parish (e.g., 27 February 1775, 7 December 1779). Lady Elizabeth Northumberland gossips about the rarity of virtuous women at the Court of Bonn—"All have their Lovers and too often Those of their own Family" (9 April 1771)—and Hester Thrale, who tells shady jokes about castrati, speculates about whether particular women are those "unclean Birds," Sapphists (25 January 1794).[70] Because she is so frank about physical matters, Thrale even speaks of her own bodily functions after she has canvassed votes for her husband as M.P. for Streatham:

> I worked at Solicitation for ten Hours successively, without refreshment, or what I wished much more for—*a place of retirement.* this neglect, wch. was unavoidable, surrounded as I was with *Men* all the Time, gave me an exquisite pain in my Side—wch. tho' relieved at my return home of Course, has never quite left me since—(5 October 1780)[71]

Thrale may be frank about bodies; she is not necessarily so freespoken about feelings. She expands her own feelings principally when her amour propre is menaced or she feels frantic, but she is not, as a matter of course, given to analyses of them or to bouts of moods. K. C. Balderston, editor of *Thraliana*, attributes Thrale's restraint to her eighteenth-century rationalist training, intensified by a long tutelage under Dr. Samuel Johnson. That, according to Balderston, keeps even Thrale's intimate recordings detached and restrained, "supervised, as it were, by her wary intellectual censor," which abdicates only when her frustrated love for Gabriel Piozzi (eventually her second husband) drives her to speak like an "ordinary sentimental woman, carried away by emotion, and expressing it without restraint or distinction."[72] But is there such a creature as an ordinary sentimental woman with feelings that can flow from her pen? The diaries of women across the centuries suggest otherwise. They also suggest

52

that the Age of Reason is as inadequate to explain the lack of candor in women's diaries as is Victorian prudery, though each has had its effect.

More compelling explanations are possible. Novelist Jane Vaughan Pinkney, speaking in 1860, offers persuasive insight into why women may be so reticent in their diaries in observing a phenomenon that is not just Victorian, but, rather, indigenous to female acculturation at any time. "Women," she points out, "are greater dissemblers than men when they wish to conceal their own emotions. By habit, moral training, and modern education, they are obliged to do so. The very first lessons of infancy teach them to repress their feelings, control their very thoughts." So also does psychologist Jean Baker Miller in 1977 explain female silence in that "women have been so encouraged to concentrate on the emotions and reactions of others that they have been diverted from examining and expressing their own emotions."[73] Women have never been encouraged to accept, understand, or vent their own feelings. Habit, training, and expectations have historically combined to make them uncomfortable with feelings. Moreover, the very language they use may silence them. They have always had to articulate—even discover—their feelings through a male construct that disables, rather than enables, female speech.

The burden of male language has become a familiar issue in feminist thought. According to the formulations of anthropologists Shirley and Edward Ardener, seconded by linguist Dale Spender, women use a language encoded by the dominant male group to suit its own perceptions, not those of the subordinated (and hence muted) group of females. To be heard and understood, females may not speak spontaneously, but must instead monitor their expression and transform their meanings to conform to male requirements. Consequently, as Shirley Ardener asks rhetorically, "Are they able to think in ways in which they would have thought had they been responsible for generating the linguistic tools with which to shape their thoughts?" In the dominant-muted model, because men control meaning by controlling language, women must either internalize the "man made language" (in Dale Spender's term) and become alienated from the female experience it fails to encode, or else keep silent. Post-Lacanians such as Hélène Cixous, Julia Kristeva, and Luce Iragary concur from their own vantage point, at which formation of gender identity virtually coincides with entry into language and logic. Female repression is implicit in the linguistic and logical processes through which meaning is produced. "Language conceals an invincible adversary," says Cixous, "because it's the language of men and their grammar." If women are ever to speak a genuinely female text, they must, according to Kristeva, deconstruct the phallologocentric discourse that determines their perception of reality in the service of consciousness at the cost of the unconscious. They need "to break the code, to shatter language, to find a specific discourse closer to the body and emotions, to the unnameable repressed by the social contract."[74]

Because language mediates reality, it is a principal means of imprinting the patriarchal system of values on females. To speak of language as disabling a diarist is simultaneously to imply all the social formulations that might silence her. But *language* points also and immediately to words. Men have controlled not only linguistic but also metalinguistic processes such as education, and thereby have determined the very supply of words—hence, range of knowledge and concepts—that women have had at their command. As a young diarist, Caroline (Girle) Powys plaintively laments, during a sightseeing trip in 1760 when she cannot describe a fort, how

> the terms of fortification are quite out of female knowledge; and what with many other things the men would perhaps say, we should not endeavour to understand; yet I must own 'tis my opinion that women might be made acquainted with various subjects they are now ignorant of, more for want of instruction than capacity.[75]

Ironically, Powys provides the just metaphor for the whole. Those in power have indeed historically protected themselves against attack by keeping "terms . . . quite out of female knowledge."

The consequence of the various social pressures on women is inarticulateness in their diaries. An intense moment for a diarist is more likely to elicit silence than statement, especially concerning relationships with males. After a Mr. Dickenson has finally proposed to Mary Hamilton, for example, and been accepted, "the conversation was such as may be supposed between Persons who are interested in each other's future happiness" (18 June 1784). Elizabeth Wynne (1779–1857) agonizes that her lover, Captain Fremantle, lacks the money to marry; when he proves financially secure after all, "I could say much on this subject but what I must feel on this occasion is not easily expressed" (9 January 1797). It is not expressed at all. Mary Gladstone married only at thirty-eight. Her marriage-to-be is a momentous event that leaves her temporarily speechless: "All this time I have been unable to write anything, for it has been the great crisis of my life, and it was too absorbing, too full of wonderings, misgivings, doubts, fear, hopes, to write about. Now it is the last 10 days of my maiden life and I am . . . thinking it all over" (24 January 1886). There follows only a summary of prenuptial festivities. Writes Mary (Hardcastle) Collier (1849–1930), Baroness Monkswell: "On this auspicious day I became engaged to be married. . . . Being rather upset I felt a certain difficulty in writing my journal" (5 July 1873). "Rather upset" means that she is exultant; she has been hoping Baron Monkswell would propose. Woolf, on her nineteenth anniversary, muses: "How moving to find this warmth, curiosity, attachment in being alone with L[eonard]. If I dared I would investigate my own sensations with regard to him, but out of laziness, humility, pride, I don't know what reticence—refrain" ([April] 1931).[76] Embarrassment, perhaps?

Unaccustomed to putting deep feelings into words, some diarists are ashamed to do so. Hamilton cannot even verbalize to Mr. Dickenson. After their unrecorded conversation, she sends him away to take "this opportunity of telling him my *sentiments* on paper which I found easier to do on paper than by speech." Clarissa Trant's diary is instructive. On proudly hearing her clergyman-fiancé preach for the first time, she writes, "I must not now say all I feel and think about him because my journal like my heart will ever be open to his inspection" (3 December 1831).[77] Why need she be embarrassed that he might read of her pride in him, or of whatever response she had, since her response was complimentary? Because a display of emotions, it would seem, has been made to seem shameful to her. Actually, Mr. Bramston could as well have read her diary prior to their recent engagement, so circumspect is she when she thinks she is being frank, so little of her deepest self does she give away.

Whatever the subject, the women may sometimes be frankly puzzled by their feelings, like Mary Shelley, wondering how she can express all that she feels; or like Auguste Schlüter, candidly admitting, "I don't know what to write. Am I happy or unhappy?" (26 September 1880). Or, like Woolf, they may sometimes be defending themselves against their feelings. A diarist may have chosen not to unmask her inner self because, as for Barrett (Browning), there is a level of feeling she dares not confront. The self-protective impulse is a strong one. Thus, says Lady Monkswell, "I thought I would write my journal on a new principle, that I would put everything down pleasant & unpleasant. But I think on the whole I will stick to the old plan. Why should I remember the horrid things more than I am absolutely obliged?" (January 1889). [78]

Probably, fear of reawakening anguish regularly inhibits expression of pain and grief. Unspoken horror, even, lies behind Faith Gray's laconic entry on her two-year-old daughter's accident: "Margaret Gray was scalded with boiling starch on her head and face and was very ill and delirious at times for the first four or five days" (5 July 1784). The saddest statement in all the diaries is as terse as it is poignant. Mary Hardy's report of the death of her firstborn, nineteen-year-old son of an infection after she has nursed him for four months reads: "O how shall I write it. My poor Raven died this morng abt 5 o'clock" (12 February 1787). Jane Carlyle's diary is a notable example of a determined, if ultimately unsuccessful, attempt at self-protection. Aware of her tendency to depression, Carlyle resolves not to use her diary as a crying towel:

> Your journal about feelings aggravates whatever is factitious and morbid in you; that I have made experience of. And now the only sort of journal I should keep should have to do with what Mr. Carlyle calls 'the fact of things.' It is very bleak and barren, this fact of things as I now see it—very; and what good is to result from writing of it in a paper book is more than I can tell. But I have taken a notion to [it]. (21 October 1855)

Though she endeavors to keep to her resolve—"My heart is very sore tonight, but have promised myself not to make this journal a 'miserere'" (23 October 1855)—that resolve soon dissipates under the pressure of her need to express her despondency.[79]

Self-protectiveness guards not only inner frontiers but also outer ones. Even if women may sometimes share parts of their diaries with select friends, a significant impediment to diarists' expressiveness is fear of outside observers. Mansfield wrote freely in her diary, but with the assumption (whatever her unfulfilled promise to Woolf to share the diary) "I don't mean that any eye but mine should read this. . . . This is—*really private*" (14 July 1921). Likewise, the flyleaf of her 1915 book is inscribed "I shall be obliged if the contents of this book are regarded as my private property." Still, she had misgivings: "I am also an egoist of the deepest dye—such a one that it was very difficult to confess to it in case this book should be found" (1 February 1922). Hester Thrale wonders that "a Woman should write such a Book as this; put down every occurrence of her Life, every Emotion of her Heart, . . .—but then I mean to destroy it" (10 December 1780).[80]

Bibliographer Cynthia Huff, noting the frequent use of "we" in diaries, remarks that nineteenth-century diaries "were often written as family documents." No such diaries have been included in this study. But even if a diary is not intended for family perusal, women have to be cautious in any century. More women than Trant know that husbands may expect diary privileges. Cynthia Asquith, for example, during its first year records "fierce skirmishes with Beb [her husband Herbert] over my diary," and that he "read my diary nearly all day" (15 June and 18 September 1915). She seems rather to have enjoyed tormenting Beb with her diary's hints of amours. Nonetheless, though compared to many other diarists she is unusually candid, knowing that Beb (or others) might read her diary did check self-expression. By her editor's report on the manuscript, it contains "'space' indication when she could not trust herself to complete an entry fully."[81] That a wife's diary was far from untouchable is evident in the way some husbands continued their wives' diaries during the women's time in childbed: not only Lord Amberley for Kate in the nineteenth century, for instance, but also Percy Shelley for Mary. Percy wrote at other times, too, fifty-eight entries or partial entries between 1814 and 1816. In the eighteenth century, Hardy's husband and children were responsible for twelve entries in her book, and

57

Leonard Woolf made a few contributions to Virginia's contemporary diary at her specific request.

For younger and unmarried diarists, parents would have had inhibiting rights of access to diaries, and other adults might claim them. Emily Shore describes one such personally unforgettable incident, which occurred when she was writing her first diary at age eleven in the drawing room while a party of adults, including a family friend, were present: "Taking up the volume, he read a passage aloud for the amusement of the party" (11 April 1837).[82]

Fear of such adult prying into one's privacy drives some younger (and older) diarists to cryptography, a strategy in use from the start of diary keeping. Although family diaries may have existed by the nineteenth century, they were a development, not an original practice. The sense of a private self apart from the group is attested to not only by the emergence of the personal diary in the late sixteenth century, but also by the rapidity with which diarists took steps to keep their diaries from their families. Sara Heller Mendelson reports of the seventeenth century that most of the twenty-three Stuart diarists and writers of serial memoirs whom she studied actively tried to conceal their writing from other eyes by requesting its posthumous destruction. Alternatively, since women often acquired shorthand to take notes on sermons, they also employed it for their private writing, sometimes to the complete mystification of their families and the probable destruction of coded diaries no heirs could decipher.[83] Among later diarists, eighteenth-century Elizabeth Raper, who dangled many admirers simultaneously, kept her diary partly in cipher. Elizabeth Wynne also resorted to a code—easily cracked—for keeping her not very secret secrets. By transposing the last letter of each word to the beginning of the next one and incorporating some misleading capitals, she could hide such matters as her feelings about Baron Buohl, the suitor whom her parents were encouraging:

Wha/ tl/ feare/ dsinc/ es/ olon/ ga/tlas/ tarrive/ dan/dIhear/ dt Oda/ ytha/ ti/ ti/ shope/ dtha/ tth/ es/ odreade/ dmarriag/ ewil/ la/ tlengt/ hb/ epropose/ dbu/ tl stil/ lhop/ etha/ ti/ twil/ lno/ tsuccee/ d. (24 March 1794)[84]

Beatrix Potter's late-Victorian diary is written entirely in an elaborate code and is circumspect as well. Daughter of strict parents with whom she lived until nearly fifty years old, she took no chances at all.

That even in diaries intended as private, women are wary of the outside eye is understandable. The problem of possible observers is particularly acute for women because they are, as a rule, self-conscious about the image they cut, trained to believe that they must always create a good impression on others. Women are all the more likely, therefore, to inhibit their self-expression in their diaries, and even without recognizing or acknowledging it, to be like Asquith, who (she is self-aware) begins her diary with the admission, "I am entirely devoid of the gift of sincerity, and could never write as though I were really convinced no other eye would ever see what I wrote. I am incurably self-conscious" (15 April 1915). "Do I ever write, even here, for my own eye?" likewise speculates Woolf. "If not, for whose eye?" (17 August 1937). Self-consciousness leads Lady Charlotte Guest (1812–1895) to write that she has arranged to have her hair "made black again. What a thing for a woman not very old [forty-one] to own in her journal" (23 November 1853).[85] Where else?

Self-consciousness leads some diarists to make apologies to posterity. Lady Frances Shelley (1787–1873), for example, urges, "If, in accordance with my resolution to keep nothing back that might elucidate my character, I have betrayed a weakness, perhaps under the circumstances it may be pardoned"—even though "if these remarks are ever published, it will be long after my death" (1816). Self-consciousness—without awareness of it—leads some diarists automatically to defend their images in their diaries, painting one picture while the diary encodes another. Anne Clifford, for example, declares that she spends her lonely time stitching, "it being my chief help to pass away the time at work" (12 November 1616). In fact, however, she spends as much time relieving her boredom by gambling. She makes only seven other entries on her needlework; she makes ten entries for her gambling, occasionally identified as playing at Glecko—and usually losing.[86] But needlework has more moral resonance.

Unusually articulate, gifted young Shore comprehends the problem that self-consciousness poses for a diarist so well that her lengthy analysis is worth reproducing in full:

> I have poured out my feelings into these later pages; I have written them on the impulse of the moment, as well as from the coolness of calm deliberation. I have writen much that I would show only to a very few, and much that I would on no account submit to any other human eye. Still, even now, I cannot entirely divest myself of an uncomfortable notion that the whole may some future day, when I am in my grave, be read by some individual, and this notion has, even without my being often aware of it, cramped me, I am sure. I have by no means confessed myself in my journal; I have not opened my whole heart; I do not write my feelings and thoughts for the inspection of another—Heaven forbid!—but I imagine the vague fear I have above mentioned has grown into a sort of unconscious habit, instinctively limiting the extent of my confidence in ink and paper, so that the *secret chamber of the heart . . .* does not find in my pen a key to unlock it. (6 July 1838)

Shore is determined to combat her censorship, though only in "feeling certain that [my new journal] will never be seen by human eye, and let me take effectual means that this shall be the case."[87] Unfortunately, she was already dying of tuberculosis, so none of her plans could be carried out. Yet Shore's particular conception of her new diary is also significant, for it points up the moral burden in self-consciousness.

No diarist writes in a vacuum and, therefore, as Woolf says, "conventional morality always encroaches. One must not talk of oneself &c; one must not be vain &c. Even in complete privacy these ghosts slip between me & the page" (17 October 1924). Shore's conception of her new diary more specifically exposes the problem of moral valuation that keeps many diarists self-protectively cautious or even mute:

> I will continue this journal on my present plan, but I will commence and steadily continue another, into which I shall pour *all* the secret

60

feelings of my heart; my sins, my weaknesses, my progress towards goodness, or, if unhappily necessary, an occasional relapse or decline,—things known only to my conscience and my God—shall all be carefully and daily recorded there. Yes! I will endeavor to do so unshrinkingly. I know the task will be most painful and humiliating, I know I shall seem to be cutting across every sinew of my self-esteem with a blade of caustic; but do it I must.

Looking within, to Shore, means finding out her sins and lapses, at best only her progress towards goodness; and her assumptions about her innermost self are unfortunately only too common. Caroline Fox is quite right when she says, "A hearty sincere inlook tends, I think, in no manner to self-glorification" (26 April 1841). Faultfinding is the norm in these female diaries; religious and social training and a heritage of centuries of female devaluation have made these Englishwomen guilt-prone and self-critical. Consequently, many have probably preferred not to look within, not to inspect their thoughts, feelings, desires, thinking it safer, as Webb says (though she is perpetually looking within and excoriating herself), to keep the lid on:

There is much that goes on within one, which one, as a prudent mistress winks at and overlooks. To dwell on it even with disapproval might give it an ugly significance. It is not wise to stop the ruffianly-looking vagrant, and inquire from him whence he comes and whither he goeth. If thoughts and actions really run in the line of least resistance, we should be careful of enlarging with self-consciousness the channels in the wrong direction. (4 November 1882) [88]

The private image, Webb realizes, is as much a problem as the public one. "The thoughts of my heart . . . how could I bear to look on *them* after they were written? Adam made fig leaves necessary for the mind, as well as for the body" (4 June 1831), as Barrett (Browning) eloquently writes. Woolf knows that she can diminish her sense of impotent melancholy by writing about it in her diary. "Why then don't I write it down oftener? Well, one's vanity forbids. I want to appear a success even to myself" (25 October 1920). [89] Diaries are a form of self-presentation through language well before they are

61

records for posterity, and self-presentation can be a powerful silencer. Even if women do not glorify themselves in their diaries, they also take care not to condemn themselves irrevocably, not just before a possible reader, but also before themselves.

Because so many female English diarists have consciously or unconsciously been careful not to leave themselves vulnerable to attacks either by others or by self, a wide difference exists between the liberating journal of self-encounter envisioned by contemporary feminists and almost all these past diaries. Rosenblatt has found that for both males and females, "diaries rich in words about the inner life are rare."[90] The tendency is not limited to women. Yet even if people rarely are introspective, women have a special handicap to introspection, as to any sort of candor, in their diaries. As is true for any other sort of writing, the nature of the female diary existing since the sixteenth century has depended on the preconditions for its composing. Women's historical circumstances—their socialization, their lesser role in society, their ambivalent moral-sexual status, their burden of restricted and inauthentic language, their lack of privacy—have clogged the pen of the female diarist and made her more likely to be circumspect than spontaneous and more often reticent than communicative. Nonetheless, women's circumstances, the next chapter will suggest, may be the very reason they have for so long been attracted to keeping diaries.

TWO

PERSONAL TIME
Motivations and Justifications
for Diary Keeping

MIDDLE- AND UPPER-CLASS Englishwomen have been persistent diary keepers. Why? As the diarists claim or demonstrate, they have found their diaries helpful repositories for their memorabilia and records. When they have allowed such personification, their diaries have even become treasured confidantes or useful consciences. And yet more compelling, unacknowledged reasons than wanting to store up treasure, pour out woes, or chastise lapses may have motivated them to keep diaries. In various ways, diaries support and reinforce the female sense of self, whereas patriarchal societies do not. The nature and terms of women's lives have made the practice of diaries not only feasible and appealing, but probably even inevitable.

Starting a diary may be a response to external influences. In some families in the past, as may still occur, women undertook diaries because they were a family tradition. Among the Woodfordes, for example, both men and women had the habit from the seventeenth century on. In the Wynne family, the practice began in the eighteenth century with two young sisters, Elizabeth (b. 1779) and Eugenia (b. 1780), who started diaries simultaneously on 17 August 1789 while living abroad with their parents. They probably did so at the direction of their tutor, Monsieur Benincasa, for on 18 August Elizabeth reports, "He brought me ['us' scratched out] the book for the ['our' deleted] diary which I ['we' erased] began as Monday's journal describes." M. Benincasa also apparently reviewed their diaries after a suitable interval. As the Wynnes' editor, Anne Fremantle, remarks parenthetically, not only do both sisters give the same account for 31 August 1789, but it constitutes "a sudden and enormous improvement . . . ; the handwriting would have adorned a copybook; the sentiments grow strangely smug." A decline in the writing, however, suggests that he soon ceased his surveillance.[1] The Wynne sisters then passed on the diary habit to a younger sister, Harriet (b. 1786). Subsequently, Elizabeth's children and daughter-in-law also kept diaries (as did her husband).

Many a female parent or governess instigated diary keeping. Bibliographer Cynthia Huff reports it "common to read" in nineteenth-century female manuscript diaries that young children were instructed to keep a daily account in order to recall past action so that they could correct their mistakes and learn to use time more wisely.[2] But whatever the century, females, and not only young ones, were encouraged or inspired by both women and men to begin diaries. Harriet Grove's two extant diaries (1809, 1810), for example, are inscribed as New Year's gifts from her mother. Since Grove (b. 1791) herself bought the diary that succeeded them, those two gifts may have been the actual start of her diary keeping habit. But Caroline (Girle) Powys (b. 1739) began her long career of diary keeping in 1756 with a travel journal, which she labels "Journal of Caroline Girle, kept by desire of her father." After Katherine Howard's father died in 1719, she resumed his record-keeping diary in 1721 to keep track, as he would have done, of the sums involved in rearing her brother's children, before converting her book to a more personal diary. Friends, too, have inspired diaries. Cynthia Asquith, for example, began her diary by way of an impulsive "absurd compact" with a male friend that they would initiate diaries simultaneously (5 April 1915).[3]

Yet familial and equivalent personal influences certainly are not enough to explain diary keeping, for neither do all family members start nor do all diarists persist in the venture. When Asquith and her friend made their compact, both also pledged to each other to keep writing, a device that was at least partly successful; Asquith honored it whereas her friend did not. Pledges might well be necessary because without strong motivation, zeal diminishes before a daily task.

Annie de Rothschild (1844–1926) illustrates admirably how much easier it is to be an enthusiastic starter than a persistent diarist. Her mother, a diarist herself, encouraged fourteen-year-old Annie to keep a diary, and Annie was receptive—if overwhelmed, for "I must work and read and reread and look over and correct and be busy from morn till night. It is a source of anxiety to me, whether I can continue you my dear journal, there will be singing and playing and drawing. Good-gracious!" (1858). Nonetheless, with missionary zeal she records in 1859: "Had a dispute with Connie [her fifteen-year-old sister, Constance de Rothschild] about journals[.] Connie does not think them a good plan. I do, and said I wondered why she did not give it up, she made no answer and looked cross, I became angry, A journal is good."[4] Annie then kept her journal for only a few months more; Connie (1843–1931, Lady Battersea), for the rest of her long life. Why women keep diaries demands more cogent answers than the influence of family or friends.

The diarists often give conventional justifications for their diary habit, and those can be taken seriously as statements of conscious motives, though conscious motives are not necessarily the most potent ones for behavior. Until the eighteenth century, the main conventional justification for English diary keeping was self-improvement; then it became memories.[5] That shift both parallels the increasing secularization of the times and makes memory the more frequent claim. Diary critic Brian Dobbs has said of the memory motive that "the journal fundamentally arises out of a desire to capture a moment or a day of time which would otherwise be lost; lost to the diarist in later life, and to posterity. . . . the diarist has his [or her] journal as an *aide memoire* and souvenir rolled into one. The souvenir or the photograph can help us imperfectly to recall an occasion, a full diary entry enables us to relive it. Not only does the entry tell us what we did, it tells us how we felt about the action."[6] Diarist Caroline Fox illustrates Dobb's contention when, after a severe attack of bronchitis has induced heightened closeness to God, she observes, "I write all this now, because my feelings are already fading into commonplace, and I would fain fix some little scrap of my experience" (18 March 1866). Likewise, Beatrix Potter regrets that "I wrote this much, soon after I came home, but being busy, laid it aside and can

65

now only piece out from a rough note, which I am sorry for, for a diary, however private, brings back distinctly the memory of what in this case seemed like a most pleasant dream" (1894).[7]

Although in fact fully developed diary entries are not as common as Dobbs makes them out to be, and the diarists have a proclivity for keeping records as much as for storing up meaningful memories, still, many diarists show that they assume a diary serves as an *aide memoire*. Caroline Powys, for example, describes Stonehenge in 1759 "as a help to memory should time obliterate the idea of these very striking ruins from my mind." Mary Hamilton has visited Mrs. Garrick and (with a conventional flourish) "passed too pleasant a day to need to make any Memorandum to remember it by, [other] than by saying that I spent it there" (9 June 1783). She does, however, take care to list the distinguished names of the rest of the party because being in their society constitutes a precious memory. Lady Elizabeth Holland, after 148 (printed) pages of diary keeping, contemplates why she is bothering to resume her record: "Having a very bad memory, and many odd irregular half-hours, it has occurred to me to assist the one and occupy the others by writing down any events, conversations, anecdotes, etc., that may interest me at the moment" (July 1797). Eleanor Butler often follows the eighteenth-century practice of designating matters for later attention as memoranda, as in this tart reminder: "Sent him [the joiner] to Mr. Edwards . . . about the Mason's opening a quarry in our View. Received a Saucy answer in return. *Mem.*—to recollect it in proper time and season" (26 April 1790). But Frances Shelley gives a more gracious illustration of viewing the diary as a guide to future behavior: "Since I laid down my pen a week ago, I have been very seriously ill. I suffered agonies; but as pain is so soon forgotten, I make note of it that I may not forget to be thankful for having escaped from the dreadful disorder of quinsey" (1833). Likewise, Virginia Woolf, in her recurrent battle to rise above criticism, tries out a reassuring list of reasons for feeling secure, "please to remember it on Friday when the reviews come in" (7 March 1937).[8]

The diarists may want a memory aid to control attitudes or command facts, but they do not necessarily seek to relive an experience. Oftentimes they simply want a record. Accordingly, they conserve their labors when records such as letters already exist. Powys, for instance, though impressed while traveling, intends to "say nothing of this place . . . as in a letter to my father, I've given a description of it" (1781); and Lady Kate Amberley, whose father is dying, "wrote to Amberley every day of all that happened while I was in London . . . so I will not re-write here" (7 June 1869). Out of the record-keeping motive comes the inclusion of recipes and remedies, data important to women. Nancy Woodforde includes the recipe for a fascinating "Diet Drink" composed of senna, sassafras, guiacum, jalap, saffron, rhubarb, maidenhair, sweet fennel seed, aniseeds, and cream of tartar (24 March 1792). Eleanor Butler has an ingenious remedy for accidents—a "poultice of Bread and Milk and sweet oil as Hot as he could bear it"; when dispatched to a neighbor run over by his wagon, fortunately the "poultice had an immediate effect." She has an even more interesting "receipt to preserve the Teeth recommended by Lady Fortescue—wash the mouth with Tobacco water" (19 January 1789, 10 February 1788). Diana Astry (1671–1716) copiously preserves menus. As the eldest daughter of a country gentry family, who would have been responsible for helping her mother plan meals, she had reason to be attentive to food. For seven years her small vellum pocket book enumerates all the interesting meals she has encountered at home or dining out. In 1705 she also comments on her own weight as "4 score and 14 pound" (8 October)—6 stone and 10 pounds, or 94 pounds—which seems wonderous little considering the meals she describes; for example,

At Bristol for diner a dish of fish, a boyld tunge, coleflowr.[,] a bread puddinge, a venson pastey. Ye. 2d. cose a copple of rost turkeys, a dish of partgeas [partridges], a dish of french beans, a dish of larkes . . . : Ye. 3rd. cose a saluer of dri sweetmeats, a chainey [china] plate of apricote preserue, another of sitrens & limes, another of crudes [curds], another of crame, another of codlins. (31 July 1706)

Eighteenth-century Elizabeth Raper and Elizabeth Freke (1641–1714) specialize in recipes; the latter, in fact, preserves not only 250 food recipes but also 446 home remedies. Claire Clairmont even affixes a recipe to an end page of her 1820–1822 journal with wafers.[9] Whether hurried or lazy, she wanted the facts.

Not just recipes and remedies betray the record keeping urge, but also a miscellaneous assortment of contents (of memorabilia quality and otherwise). Women have been called sentimentalists, but they show a penchant for facts as much as for nostalgia.[10] Among the miscellanea in their diaries, women have cataloged pictures seen at exhibitions, the treasures in their Christmas stockings, the books they have read; partners at balls, and even a diagram for a quadrille; party guests, cabinet officials, mourners at funerals, neighbors deceased; personal expenses, gambling losses, and records of their work and travels. They have included line drawings of ground plans and illustrations for their diary entries; they have copied in or inserted newspaper columns and clippings, letters to and from themselves, to and from members of their families, ambassadors' speeches, lengthy passages from books, published and unpublished poetry, song lyrics, epitaphs, jokes, and anecdotes. An inveterate record keeper, Powys itemizes, among other things, the miles traveled on trips, the marchers in George II's funeral procession, the casts of plays, the toasts at a feast, the paintings at Strawberry Hill, and the nobility attending Mr. Tyson's ball. But Elizabeth Freke is queen of recorders. Among plentiful other lists, her diary itemizes the contents of her "upper Closett over the hall" and "Greatt Haire Trunk" and "Great Black Trunk by the fire side" (not to mention her other chests and boxes); directions for painting on satin and where to buy the paints; and a detailed grudging "accountt of whatt I Laid outt on the sickness, death and Buriall of my Deer Husband" (1711, 1713, 1707).[11]

As record keepers, the diarists worry about accuracy. Elizabeth Barrett (Browning), for example, explains that she has written only "a brief account of . . . my happy visit . . . to Malvern, because not having my [pocket] Diary with me, I was obliged to trust my memory" (22 October 1831). Diarists keep notes to ensure correct recall. Cynthia Asquith, for example, bemoans having let her diary lapse for nearly a month, for "it will be a grim grind to write it up from my mere jottings on odd bits of paper" (6 June 1917). And Woolf regrets the way "life piles up so fast that I have no time to write out the equally fast rising mound of reflections, which I always mark down as they rise to be inserted here" (19 March 1919). The expansion a diarist can effect from brief notes may be impressive. Frances Stevenson composes entries filling large pages from notes, which for one day (12 January 1917) look like this:

Speech.
Greatness of a P.M. [Prime Minister]
Altered constitution of Gov.
Mrs. Asquith—back in 6 weeks. [12]

When ill (nineteenth-century Emily Shore, for instance, who was tubercular), diarists may have others keep notes for them. Some are punctilious about omissions, like Mary Hamilton, who "forgot to mention that I yesterday recd. a Present" (25 May 1784). Some are punctilious about accuracy, like Mary Gladstone, who prefers a blank to an error in reporting that a "Pianoforte trio in ——— opened the Concert" (1 April 1879). Lucy Cavendish, too, must amend an entry about the Duke of Edinburgh's marriage: "(No; it was not the Eucharist Cup, but a simple seremony)" (24 January 1874). As Cavendish indicates, the diarists reread and correct or update if needed, sometimes years later. Thus Lady Mary Monkswell, for example, in 1916 finds she must add to her earlier record of two friends the bitter present-day truth that "both Douglas and Arthur's poor bodies now lie in Flanders Fields" (15 August). [13]

When diarists justify their writing as useful, as they often do, their frequent rationale is that it will produce a record for others. They write for the eventual edification of others or for their own children; they write for posterity, near or remote. Mary Cowper, to illustrate, claims in 1714 that she has begun her diary upon becoming a lady of the bedchamber to Princess Caroline because of all the lies circulating about the court of George I; presumably she will leave a truer record. Her court diary in reality tends to gossip, scandal, and rumors. Meanwhile, however, she is also observing some of the ugly actualities of her environment for the sake of history, and dissociating herself from them, as when

I carried the Gag which was brought from Preston by Mr. Carter to Court, by order of the Princess. A great Number of them were found at the House of one Shuttleworth, a Papist. . . . The Gags are really frightful. They go down the Throat a great Way, with a Bend, and under that there is an iron Spike that runs into the Tongue if it is stirred, and the Ends have Screws that screw into the Cheeks. (23 February 1716)

Posterity shall know from her disapproval that she was a participant in important events but not a partisan of evil. Spinster Elizabeth George also writes for posterity, claiming that it is not for herself but for her familial descendents that she pens her lengthy account of the coming-of-age celebrations for the Marquis of Chandos:

> I thought I should like to leave a record of the manner in which this important Event has been celebrated, more to be read by the young people amongst our kindred who may come (perhaps fifty years hereafter) than for any of them who are now living—I know I should have been highly delighted had I ever found a book of this sort (that had been written by an Aunt or Cousin of our family) descriptive of events that had occurred at Stowe or in the neighborhood before we were born. (1847) [14]

This diarist feels that a personally vouched for account has more pith and moment than a historian's. Actually, the account she writes is as much about the modest but hardworking part she played as tenant of the duke of Buckingham in boarding some of the distinguished guests who came for the celebration as about the celebration itself, much of which she missed because she was busy working. That her account also attests to her own value by reporting on her industriousness gives it significant commonality with Cowper's account and even more so with the plaintive conclusion to Auguste Schlüter's diary, terminated when she left the Gladstone family after twenty-two years of devoted service as maid, then housekeeper, to return to her native Germany: "I now will end my journal, but add a copy of Dear Mr. Gladstone's letter [of recommendation] to it. For perhaps I might sell it some day when I am in need" (20 November 1890). [15] She includes the letter lest she forget what it says when she has given it up. Meanwhile, masking her action under the guise of utility, she expresses her pride at meriting such a glowing letter.

As these diarists suggest, whatever the lure of memorabilia, memoranda, and the like, be it nostalgia or the urge for accurate data, assisting memory is not really the most basic motive for diary keeping. The truth is rather that diarists, even in public diaries, are taking an interest in self—in their own affairs and problems, in their own perceptions and times; in their own images. A self, a center of subjectivity, is an operative illusion for the women, and their sense of life seems important enough to them to record because it issues from and validates that self. Diary scholar Paul C. Rosenblatt puts it otherwise: "Diarists need a certain amount of egoism, enough to be interested in recording some aspects of the world they experience." [16] Beatrice Webb succinctly explains such diaristic egoism, as it might be called, when she decides that she may never "again take that interest in myself to make me much care to tell my thoughts and feelings to this . . . diary" (15 October 1884). However, even if interest in self may be an acceptable conscious motivation for a Beatrice Webb, it is not an acceptable one for most of the women. Even Woolf, who to a casual eye might seem to be wrapped up in herself, cannot accept her self-interest. She placates herself by acknowledging her diaries' therapeutic value. Rereading the books leaves her "now . . . much refreshed. This is by way of justifying these many written books" (7 July 1933). Hester Thrale 150 years earlier is not so different when, knowing that her first husband is mortally ill and his business is decaying (or so she presents it to herself), she bursts out, "& I! writing in the Thraliana! I do not do it often tho', & am always ashamed when I do" (1 January 1781). [17]

Diaristic egoism smacks of simple vanity and self-assertion, which go contrary to female training; it implies selfishness when one has been trained not to do for oneself what one could be doing for others. As feminist-psychologist Jean Baker Miller explains,

> The organization of one's life around serving others is . . . a central factor for women. . . . They have developed the sense that their lives should be guided by the constant need to attune themselves to the wishes, desires, and needs of others. The others are the important ones and the guides to action. . . . Women are taught that their main goal in life is to serve others—first men, and later, children. . . . It is true

that women, like everyone, are motivated out of the well-springs of their being. . . . It is also true, however, that women feel compelled to find a way to *translate* their own motivations into a means of serving others.[18]

So diaristic ego usually retreats behind justifications that are entirely self-acceptable: utility and need—a memoir for posterity, a record for my children, a self-improving discipline to make me more acceptable to others.

The process of erecting acceptable justifications is readily observable in these women's diaries, whatever the period in which they live. For example, in old age, Mary Berry (1763–1852), who has let her diary lapse, decides, "As I am now fast failing every day, I have a mind to recommence a journal of my feelings, mind and body. . . . it may amuse myself, and may in future be curious or interesting to some other old woman aware, like myself, of her situation" (18 September 1836). Her concern for other old women like herself is unusual, though understandable because Berry never married. Many more women claim it valuable to leave a record for their children. They may even, like sixteenth-century Grace Mildmay, almost first diarist, and nineteenth-century Clarissa Trant (Bramston), rewrite portions of their diaries for their children. Louisa de Rothschild began a cursory diary at sixteen, then dropped it for five years after her daughters were born. But she resumes it in expanded fashion, as she explains in 1847, because she wants a record of "my thoughts and feelings, the progress of my inward life and that of my children. It will be most interesting to me and of use to their education." Likewise, her younger contemporary Emily Shore speculates, "Should it hereafter happen that I should be married and the mother of a family, I think that much of these records of my own early life may be very interesting and instructive to *them*" (6 July 1838). A depressed Ellen Weeton (1776–1844), abused by her husband and cut off from her child, decides to continue her diary—and her life as well—for her daughter's sake:

I leaned over the side of the vessel, . . . considering whether I should any longer continue this Journal; for I always feel my own littleness in the world, and can assign no reason why I have continued it so long; but—the thought of my darling Mary shot into my mind—I will continue it for thy sake, my little one; those expressive eyes of thine will one day perhaps read a mother's thoughts with eagerness; thy warm and tender heart will enter into all a mother's feelings; and to delight my child, I will continue it. (19 May 1825) [19]

Weeton, in her anguish, is the most candid. *Interesting, useful, instructive* are polite fictions; "I keep a diary for my children's sake" is likely to be a justification screening another motive. A diary is an *apologia pro vita mea*. Reading their mothers' diaries, children will learn what their mothers were like as individuals and, mothers may hope, come to understand and admire or, if necessary, forgive.

But diaries provide yet another service to self. Rereading their own words, so too will the diarists learn what they are and have been like. Many women, less self-deceptive about their diary habit, declare their desire for a record because they anticipate retrospecting in older age to recapture their former selves. Frances Shelley, for instance, intends jotting down "les pensées qui me traversent l'esprit" because "Si je ne puis maintenant les distinguer et en approfondir la vérité, je pourrai dans quelques années d'ici me retracer un portrait de moi-même, de ma vivacité naturelle, avant que mon âge soit trop avancé" (2 April 1818). (That is, I will jot down my passing thoughts even if now I cannot sort them out or see any profundity in them because in a few years, before I am too old, I will be able to trace through them a self-portrait of my more youthful vitality.) Webb, too, assumes, "As it may be interesting in future years to know what my religious convictions were at nineteen, I might as well state roughly" what they are (31 March 1877). Woolf decides at intervals that she is writing for a future self—whose age keeps advancing. In her thirties she envisions that she will "build . . . memoirs out of these books" at fifty; by her forties, her diary "is to serve the purpose of my memoirs. At 60 I am to sit down & write my life" (20 January 1919, 8 February 1926). Whether or not Woolf actually intended to write her memoirs from her diaries—in 1938 she is still not sure she intends a memoir (17 August)—she did want, as she casually puts it, to be able to "waste an idle hour reading them" (3 February 1927). And she did expend those hours, finding that she thereby regained an active sense of her past (see, e.g., 17 December 1933).[20]

The diarists are rereaders. They do not only use their diaries as a focal point for reminiscential reverie, like Shore, beginning the eighth volume of her diary. She muses: "It seems but the other day I began the first. I was writing in the drawing-room of Brookhouse; papa, mamma, poor Miss Hall, Lady Malkin, and Sir Benjamin were in the room. Alas! such a party shall never meet again on earth." (11 April 1837). They also review their diaries to take stock, like Beatrix Potter, contemplating how "it is a year today since I wrote I had got the dumps. How are my prospects compared with last year. I am not, not in high spirits tonight" (18 January 1884). Sixty years earlier, in a common pattern among the diarists, Trant finds that rereading her diary reveals her weaknesses: "Je suis restée dans ma chambre où j'ai parcouru mon journal et j'ai pensé au temps passé. Je voudrais bien pouvoir méditer sur des sujets plus profitables, mais mon esprit léger et frivole ne peut guère s'élever au dessus des vanités de ce monde" (21 March 1824). (That is, I remained in my room and read over my journal and thought about the past. I would prefer to be able to meditate on more profitable subjects but my shallow, frivolous mind can scarcely raise itself above worldly conceits.) A quarter-century earlier, young Elizabeth Wynne also finds rereading no source of pride: "I have been reading today some of my journals and indeed find them so horribly stupid that it do[es] not encourage me to continue them" (26 January 1796). (Nonetheless, she continued her diary for the rest of her life, never missing an entry until the day her husband died.) At the other end of life, an elderly Webb, typing out the back volumes of her diary preparatory to writing her autobiography, instead finds it engrossing to watch "the development of my own thought," "of my own inner emotional and intellectual life, which I had completely forgotten" (22 December 1918, 25 February 1920). But Charlotte Guest, rereading the journals of fifty-four years past, is surprised by what she finds, for "I speak several times of being tired, and once of having a headache. I did not think I ever had one, and have no recollection of such a thing" (4 April 1887).[21]

The diarists' concern with balance is noteworthy. Anticipating rereading, Mary Shelley takes care to equalize her entries: "As I have until now recurred to this book to discharge into it the overflowings of a mind too full of the bitterest waters of life, so will I to-night . . . put down some of my milder reveries; that, when I turn it over, I may not only find a record of the most painful thoughts" (19 March 1823). Likewise, Woolf deems it "unfortunate, for truths sake, that I never write here except when jangled with talk. I only record the dumps & the dismals" (28 February 1939). Other diarists share the worry over imbalance.[22] A desire to be fair to their days reflects the women's sense that they are actually writing more than day-by-day records: they are also reconstructing their lives through words. For women, that is an important action, an opportunity for the self to see its individual nature and assert its intrinsic importance. The matter is worth pausing over.

Rereading makes it possible to rediscover the self one once was and perhaps to discover a self that endures. Although anthologist Vincent Waite mocks the inveterate diarist as possessing the "'juvenile sentimentality'" that envisions looking back with a thrill at seeing what one once wrote, the practice is neither juvenile nor sentimental nor thrilling—it may be painful.[23] Even if the impulse to attach to the past is not gender limited,[24] it is exacerbated for women because most female lives occur in discrete stages, each with social repercussions. The wife and mother is someone who was once, but can never again be, the virginal daughter. The widow has lost her role as wife, and the grandmother that of nurturer of her own children; both slip into the limbo of the aged. Although each stage may bring a sense of gain or loss, depending on the stage and the woman, discrete stages create a sense of discontinuity, and the balance tips more to loss than to gain as life advances. As Woolf says, to be middle-aged means that to the world one is "not a woman, but an elderly woman" (31 May 1929).[25] Because, as these diarists well know, society values only their youth, it may become the era to cherish and, at least vicariously, recapture through rereading.

If the ongoing writing reinforces a sense of one's importance as an entity, reading back helps piece out the design in that entity and re-declare its value. Rereading, as Woolf says, "composes. Why? I think shows one a stretch, when one's grubbing in an inch" (28 July 1939). The dual process of writing and rereading may allow the writer to discover what her sense of essential identity is. Thus Webb, being an introspective diarist, speculates, "It would be curious to discover who it is to whom one writes in a diary. Possibly to some mysterious personification of one's own identity, to the Unknown, which lies below the constant change of matters and ideas, constituting the individual at any given moment" (15 October 1884). Or, as Katherine Mansfield more eloquently ponders, perhaps "the rage for confession, autobiography, . . . is explained by our persistent yet mysterious belief in a self which is continuous and permanent; which, untouched by all we acquire and all we shed, pushes a green spear through the dead leaves and through the mould" ([April 1920]).[26]

The diary is a potential source of deep self-knowledge, and some diarists recognize it as such. Many more, however, envision it in terms of self-improvement—an acceptable, even laudatory motive for diary keeping, claimed or implied as their reason for starting their books and demonstrated as their motive for continuing them. Because of Puritan devotional diaries, moral self-improvement is a motive present from the start of diary keeping, though the habit outlives the Puritans. Even if she also strayed into other matters, Margaret Hoby, who mothered a tradition of self-mortifying diaries, initially intended her book to keep track of her devotions, catch out her omissions and sins, and earn her blessings. Thus she writes contritely,

> I . . . neclected my custom of praier, for which, as for many other sinnes, it pleased the Lord to punishe me with an Inward assalte . . . and, if I had not taken this Course of examenation [her record keeping], I think I had for gotten itt. (10 September 1599)

> At Night I thought to writt my daies Iournee [Journal] as before, becaus, in the readinge over some of my former spent time, I funde some profitt might be made of that Course from which, thorow two much neccligence, I had a Longe time dissisted: but they are vnworthye of godes benefittes and especiall fauours that Can fine no time to make a thankfull recorde of them. (1 April 1605)[27]

Hoby finds she learns her lapses by reading back. However, a diary is not only a vehicle for retrospection but also a prospective commitment to growth. Hence it answers naturally to intentions of self-improvement and therefore appeals to the young. When Lucy

(Lyttleton) Cavendish begins a new book of her diary at fifteen, she looks ahead with great moral fervor: "Well! I wonder how many things will be in this book when I finish it. . . . I wonder whether when I end it I shall be able honestly to say that I have mounted Higher, come Nearer. Excelsior! My own motto" (1 September 1856). At the same age, her contemporary Constance de Rothschild echoes her: "This journal I begin with the resolution to try and write in it nearly every day. . . . I hope that when I come to the end of this book I shall be able to say that I am improved" (1858). But not only the young look to their diaries for self-reform. Webb at thirty-one inscribes "Best wishes to you, Book 13 of my life! May you be fuller of interest, less egotistical than former volumes" (8 January 1889), even as Lady Elizabeth Eastlake (1809–1893), half a century earlier, begins her journal at thirty-three with the hope that "'it may become, the occasion for good, for self-examination, and for self-correction'" (1842). Her contemporary, Barrett (Browning), may be frightened of starting a diary at twenty-five, but she views the undertaking as a cure for her pride: "I will write: I must write—& the oftener wrong I know myself to be, the less wrong I shall be in one thing—the less *vain* I shall be!" (4 June 1831). Twenty-five years earlier, in middle-age, Berry begins the new diary that in old age she would let lapse, then resume for the edification of other elderly women (as she claims). At forty-four she decides to leave off writing merely descriptive travel diaries and reform by keeping a personal diary:

> I have hitherto avoided it, because I felt ashamed of the use, or rather the no-use, I made of my time—of the miserable minute duties and vexations which at once occupied and corroded my mind. . . .
>
> But now that *no future* remains to me, perhaps I may be encouraged to make the most of the present by marking its rapid passage, and setting before my eyes the folly of letting a day escape without *endeavouring*, at least, to make the best I can of it, and, above all, without making impossible attempts to mend or alter anybody but myself. (18 August 1807)[28]

Berry was to become a distinguished writer of social history and an editor of other women's writings. Her major work was the two-volume *A Comparative View of the Social Life of England and France*

(1828, 1831). She also edited the letters of Mme. du Deffand (1810) and of Rachel Wriothesley, Lady Russell (1819), besides publishing assorted essays and even attempting drama.[29] But she was disappointed in her hopes of marrying and lacked the male connections she needed for any sort of sustained public role. Frustrated ambitions lie behind her sense of waste, of "'all the life of life' certainly gone forever!" as she goes on to say. Significant is her sense of needing to discipline and improve herself, an assumption many women make when the world has betrayed their expectations. Pertinent here, she believes her diary will aid her to do so.

Changing intentions and mixed motives are, however, characteristic of diarists, and though self-improvement, like utility for others, may frequently be a declared intention for inaugurating a diary, the desire for self-help and relief is more often what keeps it going. Berry's new diary keeping was in time to become a much-anticipated pleasure, but she begins it as a painful chore. "An effort it must always be, and, therefore, the sooner it is got over the better," she prefaces her new book (21 August 1807). Two centuries later, Mansfield also finds the Puritan urge to keep a diary for self-correction disagreeable. Using hers to catch out her laziness about her writing—"I must keep this book so that I have a record of what I do each week"—renders it "a vile little diary. . . . damning little note-book" (13 November 1921, 1 January 1915, 4 July 1922).[30] Yet both Berry and Mansfield persisted in their diary keeping. They also rendered it more agreeable by relying on their diaries for emotional support rather than scourging.

Aside from record keeping, the most frequent recourse to diary writing is for some sort of emotional sustenance. Weeton, the diarist who conquered a suicidal impulse by thinking of her daughter, at one point intends starting a new diary "marking a few domestic events, but more particularly the religious state of my mind." However, "so painful and heart-rending have been the occurrences of the [last] few days . . . that agitation, anguish, and despair, have driven all thoughts of religion away" ([January] 1818). She writes of her marital woes instead. The history of Hester Thrale's diary shows a similar response to need. In 1776, shortly before her thirteenth marriage anniversary, her husband presented her with six calf-bound blank books stamped *Thraliana* in gold on their covers, in which to collect "all the little Anecdotes which might come to my Knowledge, all the Observations I might make or hear; all the Verses never likely to be published, and in fine ev'rything which struck me at the Time" (15 September 1776), as Dr. Samuel Johnson had long since advised her to do.[31] For two and one-half volumes she collected, though she also included a brief autobiography and personal diary entries. Midway through her third volume, however, her *Thraliana* became essentially her personal diary instead of a collection of discrete jottings. She had by then ceased to keep a diary for her children, which also served to a degree as an outlet for herself, and troubles had come upon her: a dangerous miscarriage; her husband's stroke, decline, and death; her business worries as a widow; and her problematical love for singing master Gabriel Piozzi, whom she desperately wanted to marry over the objections of her friends and daughters. Increasingly she had need of her diary and made it, as she acknowledges in retrospect, "my Confident, my solitary Comfort, and Depository of every Thought as it arose" (3 January 1791).[32]

Creative writers' diaries readily become their emotional resources because they are accustomed to translating feelings into words. "Nothing affords me the same relief" (14 July 1921),[33] Mansfield pronounces of the diary she uses not only as a rod, but also as a confessional for her personal problems and a trying ground for creative ideas. A combination of dated entries and writer's scrapbook, Mansfield's diary records her ongoing interior struggles with problems both as a woman and as an artist and briefly accounts for her activities; it also sweeps in notes for stories and story critiques, excerpts from her reading and commentaries on them, and unmailed letters to friends. When the diarist is a creative writer, the line between diary contents intended for self and those intended for the self's work is likely to be shadowy; in Mansfield's case it cannot even be located because John Middleton Murry chose to publish her scrapbooks and her diaries as a single journal. Yet the heterogeneous journal is unified by the personality of the writer, so that reading Mansfield's journal is, as Virginia Woolf says of it, like watching a mind that, "in its loneliness" can "divide into two and talk to itself."[34]

Such colloquy occurs most poignantly—and productively for

Mansfield's future career—as she slowly assimilates her grief over the death of her younger brother, Chummie (Leslie Heron Beauchamp), in a military training accident in 1915. Cutting across her suicidal despair ("not only am I not afraid of death—I welcome the idea") comes the self-protective impulse first to write for him; "then I will come as quickly as I can." She envisions recreating the world they shared in their New Zealand childhood, "to make our undiscovered country leap into the eyes of the Old World. . . . because you, my little sun of it, are set. You have dropped over the dazzling brim of the world. Now I must play my part." Yet she cannot write at all until she has projected his presence—"To whom did I always write when I kept those huge complaining diaries? Was it to myself? But now . . . I see you opposite to me. . . . Yes, it is to you [I communicate]"—and full creativity is restored only when "in every word I write and every place I visit I carry you with me" (29 October 1915, 22 January and 14 February 1916).[35] Communing with the brother she resurrected in her imagination was to empower Mansfield's best realized fiction, the New Zealand *Prelude* and "At the Bay."

Virginia Woolf's own diaries are most instructive about how the creative writer's diary may become more a sanatorium than a workshop. Her earliest diaries (kept in 1895, 1904, and 1913 and still unpublished)[36] are starts at diary keeping while recovering from serious mental problems and breakdowns. Critic Marie Gabrielle Siganto conjectures that those diaries were intended as therapeutic, Woolf "seeing an inherent healing power in the diarist's process of self-analysis."[37] Woolf's published diaries were begun in 1915, though the first of them was silenced after six weeks by another breakdown. She resumed in 1917, "on the impulse given by the discovery in a wooden box in my cupboard" of the 1915 diary (8 October) and continued keeping them for the rest of her life. Woolf refuses to pin herself down as to why she is so diligent a diarist. As late as 1938 she reminds herself "I . . . have half a mind one of these days to explain what my intention is in writing these continual diaries. Not publication. Revision? a memoir of my own life? Perhaps" (17 August). Meanwhile, in the course of writing her diary—ostensibly for the sake of memoirs or as a "chart of my progress"—she discovers her diary's additional functionality for her art: "It strikes me that in this book I *practise* writing; do my scales; yes & work at certain effects" (17 October 1922, 17 October 1924).[38] She finds herself perfecting her style, contemplating a new form, using her diary to articulate her intentions for particular writings.

Even more important, her diary becomes her invaluable confidante, through discourse with whom, to the extent that Woolf will allow it, she discovers and even savors her emotions:

> And why do I write this down? I have not even told Leonard; & whom do I tell when I tell a blank page? The truth is, I get nearer feelings in writing than in walking [sic]—I think: graze the bone, enjoy the expression; have them out of me; make them a little creditable to myself; I daresay suppress something, so that after all I'm doing what amounts to confiding. Why did Pepys write his diary after all? (5 August 1929)

She can rely on her diary for maintaining her equilibrium, both personally and professionally. When "it becomes a necessity to uncramp," then "once more, as so often, I hunt for my dear old red-covered book" (17 December 1939). When she can concentrate on nothing else, she can still write in her diary: "Unable to settle in [and read]; therefore I write diary. How often I have said this!" (3 December 1923). Woolf uses her diary to work off her angers, upsets, and anxieties and to counter repeated failures of nerve, both immediately and by reassuring herself through rereading. Or as she says at one point: "I may as well wreak my temper, write out my fidgets, in this book. . . . I shall write down the reason why I can't [write]—this diary being a kindly blank faced old confidante. Well, you see, I'm a failure as a writer. I'm out of fashion; old, shan't do any better" (26 May and 8 April 1921). As she is most unwilling, however, to accept failure, her diary must not just receive her despondency; it must also challenge her habitual despair upon completing a book: *The Years*, for example,

> such feeble twaddle—such twilight gossip . . . ; such a showup of my own decrepitude, & at such huge length. . . . [L.] said This always happens. But I felt, no it has never been so bad as this. I make this note should I be in the same state after another book. Now this morn-

ing, dipping in, it seems to me, on the contrary, a full, bustling live book. (16 January 1936)[39]

Less expressive than Mansfield's or Woolf's, George Eliot's Victorian diary too is both sounding board for ideas and recourse for problems. Eliot (Mary Ann Evans, 1819–1880) uses her diary to declare her intentions for her writings, as if to see them written down would make them even more certain to her. But she uses it even more to register and master her agonies over her writing and her self-doubt. Prone to depression, Eliot finds it as curative to be able to retrospect as does Woolf. Thus, for example, Eliot writes of how "I have been continually suffering from headache and depression, with almost total despair of future work. I look into this little book now to assure myself that this is not unprecedented. . . . I have often been helped, in looking back in it, to compare former with actual states of despondency from bad health or other apparent causes. In this way a past despondency has turned to present hopefulness" (27 October 1870, 31 December 1877). Other women also find retrospection therapeutic: Webb, for instance, declares, "So often have I found strength in turning over the back pages of my life" (1 November 1887). However, mid-Victorian Jane Carlyle is determined not to retrospect during depression. "My journal, let us renew our daily intercourse without looking back," she insists, in fear of becoming sentimental. "Looking back was not intended by nature, evidently, from the fact that our eyes are in our faces and not in our hind heads" (24 March 1856).[40] But she does turn to her diary for help. She unburdens herself of her marital troubles; she may even, unawares, be revenging herself for them by leaving a posthumous record of her sorrows to torment husband Thomas.[41]

A diary provides opportunities for purge and self-justification for any of those with a long-standing problem: Webb, for example, in her self-torturing relationship with Joseph Chamberlain, whom she desperately wanted to wed after having rejected his proposal; or Hester Thrale (Piozzi) in her struggles with the daughters who repudiated her when she remarried; or Ellen Weeton in her battles with the husband who abused her and denied her her child. At an extreme, like Woolf and Eliot some diarists have even relied on their diaries for maintaining their ongoing mental equilibrium. Webb's editors, Norman and Jeanne Mackenzie, are convinced that her "lifelong colloquy" with her diary even kept Webb, whose problems extended well beyond Chamberlain, "sane and helped her to cope with the self-destructive impulses that punctuated her career." Webb repeatedly proclaims the value of her diary, "a blessing when one has no companion . . . no one with whom one is intimate. . . . Sometimes I feel as if I must write, as if I must pour my crooked thoughts into somebody's heart, even if it be into my own" (3 July 1878). Keeping a diary allows her to articulate what is ordinarily suppressed—expression most other diarists refuse to allow themselves—and she recognizes the advantage: "What a blessing I can write in this little book without fearing that anyone will ever read and ridicule the nonsense and half-sense I scribble. . . . the great benefit one receives from keeping a diary is that it . . . is a vent for one's feelings, for those feelings in particular that one cannot communicate to other people" (6 March 1874, 25 November 1882, 11 December 1874).[42]

The introspective Webb is more self-critical than self-pitying. Not so a much earlier Elizabeth Freke, who announces her emotional problems when she subtitles her diary "Misfortunes . . . in My Unhappy Life" and uses it to vent her bitterness against a husband who, according to her increasingly paranoic account, has repeatedly defrauded her of her money and threatened her well-being. But Freke also uses her diary against everyone else who has insulted or wronged her (besides confronting them in person), and to her the list is long. It embraces, for one, the hardhearted sister who has not only preferred to go off on a jaunt to London rather than nurse her, but made it an expensive trip, too:

> Nor would Itt have Troubled mee soe much to have Left me soe, had she Gone to A House of her owne, but Itt was to goe & board att Wye Coledge Which I Could not butt Resent most Unkindly from her, Affter I had pinched myselfe for these several yeares . . . to serve her & hers by these guifts for her following [an itemized list of gifts and their costs, plus the coach fee to London, follows]. (9 September 1710)[43]

The lengthy lists in Freke's diary probably bespeak her fear of anyone's making off with something of hers. Freke's diary is the accommodating receptacle for an increasingly disturbed personality, whose diary apparently did not keep her entirely sane.

For any woman who feels lonely or isolated by her circumstances, the diary provides a needed listener. As Clarissa Trant reflects in a discouraged moment in 1826, "But why should I waste my time and temper committing to paper all these discontented reflexions. I talk to my journal because I must talk to something or somebody and by this faithful and accommodating confidante I am sure of being listened to with silent indulgence." "The only friend I had to confide in was my journal," her contemporary Charlotte Guest (29 July 1833) says of the time when she has appalled her family by affiancing her bluest of blood to a Welsh dissenter twice her age, and worse, "in trade." Separated from her native Germany and family while in service to the Gladstones, Auguste Schlüter for years even projects an intimate in her diary to whom she addresses letters:

Dear friend, I am no longer alone. (19 May 1878)

Here I am, dearest. You will be surprised to find me at the seaside. (10 October 1878)

You must pardon me, I don't know why I did not write last week. (30 January 1881)

Fool I was, I did not take pencil and paper. I want to let you have a share of it, and now . . . nearly all is gone out of my head. (2 July 1882)

But finally she drops the fiction. More usual is for a diarist to go directly to addressing herself, if addressing anyone, as does Webb agonizing over her sexuality: "And now, my dear friend, I want to tell you something seriously" (13 March 1874). Or Mansfield, in an attack of conscience over her idleness, summons "my unseen, my unknown, let us talk together" (13 November 1921). As Mary Berry eventually acknowledges, being a diarist is in fact a form of self-communication, "having a litte colloquy with myself every day" (19 September 1836). [44]

Nonetheless, for the lonely Mary Shelley her diary replaces her late husband as confidant. She sees herself for at least part of her widow's diary as addressing him: "I have no friend. For eight years I communicated, with unlimited freedom, with one whose genius . . . awakened and guided my thoughts. . . . now I am reduced to these white pages. . . . As I write, let me think what he would have said if, speaking thus to him, he could have answered me" (2 October 1822). Since she is only keeping her loss fresh, resurrecting Percy in her diary solves nothing, so that at her most frenzied she bemoans how "writing this is useless; it does not even soothe me; on the contrary, it irritates me by showing the pitiful expedient to which I am reduced: (26 October 1824). [45] And yet it seems to have tided her over her lonely anguish.

Both widows and wives may rely on their diaries for some sort of emotional sustenance and unburdening. Shelley becomes much more communicative after her husband's death. Like her, Katherine Howard keeps only a bare-bones diary until her husband's death in 1724, then becomes expansive. Until 1886, Mary Gladstone keeps a nearly continuous diary, which, after her marriage that year to the Reverend Harry Drew, reduces to fewer and shorter entries and finally ceases altogether for seven years. But the diary recommences with fullness in 1911, after Drew's death. Possibly such diarists before widowhood feared for their secrets, but possibly also they felt their marriages removed the need for a diary-confidante. As Shelley says, she once had Percy to communicate with unreservedly. Yet Guest, upon marriage, resumes her girlhood diary even if "now, every care and every joy, every sorrow and every delight is shared and sympathized with, and henceforth my only friend, my only confidant is my husband" (29 July 1833). [46] And Lady Kate Amberley keeps a detailed diary only after marriage, though her marriage is close and companionate. Whatever the human companionship available, women have needed the emotional resource of keeping personal books too. An important potential is inherent in the activity.

From record book to confidante, the diary is functional. Its peculiar value for women, however, lies not in its application but in its nature as a personal record, a book of self. The diarist who has inscribed herself in its pages has claimed time for herself and momentarily freed herself from being an object in a male-dominated world rather than a subject in her own right. She has, of course, also shown why diaries continue to exist: the tenacity of the human desire to matter personally. Human beings, female or male, develop a sense of self-worth that the energetic reflect by undertaking to keep more-or-less daily accounts of their being—it is a chore, as so many diarists complain. But there may be a peculiar urgency about the activity for women.

When critic Dobbs identifies "self-interest"—diaristic egoism—as a motive for diary keeping, he explains: "There are occasions when the temptation to make some sort of unique record, to impose something of ourselves upon an apparently heedless world before we are gone forever, is irresistible. Secretly, we all feel we have something unique to contribute . . . but sometimes it is necessary to convince others too. . . . as long as man retains sufficient individuality to believe that he is not exactly as other men are, it is unlikely the time will come when there are no diarists."[47] Some women diarists would agree with him. Existential anxiety shadows Claire Clairmont's diary when she declares herself "long resolved to recommence my Journal. . . . My life flows so swiftly away and so unobservedly that I have need of a Journal to mark a little its progress" (12–24 May 1825). Likewise it broods over Woolf's when she decides that she is continuing her diary keeping "partly . . . from my old sense of the race of time. 'Time's winged chariot hurrying near'—Does it stay it?" (7 October 1919). Much earlier than Woolf, Emily Shore combats a sense of mortality through her diary as she lies dying of tuberculosis. For even if she complains fretfully on 7 November 1838, "Journalizing has lost its interest with me. I am dreary, dispirited, ill," nonetheless she continues writing until 24 June 1839, a fortnight before her death, because though "I suppose I am beginning to sink; still I can at times take up my pen" (27 May 1839).[48] However, because not only man, but also woman feels unique, Dobbs's explanation again (as with memory) asks amending.

The diaries of women suggest that they think less in abstract and universal terms than in concrete and personal ones and less of convincing others of uniqueness than of reassuring themselves. Scaling

Dobbs's large abstractions down to the concretions of life in patriarchal society exposes a credible reason for women's so-frequent diary
keeping: a reaction to leading restricted or subordinated lives that
make some personal, more-or-less private, self-assertive act necessary
or valuable or appealing. Even Webb, whose marriage was an egali-
tarian working partnership, discovered that "in writing I am parasitic
on Sidney; I never write, except in this diary, in my own style, always
in a hybrid of his and mine. But I *must* speak my own words and
sentences" (8 December 1913).[49] If, as critic Margaret Willy says,
"there is something in the activity [of diary keeping] which strongly
appeals to female instinct and inclination,"[50] the appeal may lie in
the sorts of lives most women have historically led. Caroline Fox's
diary, for example, reveals what they had to contend with by mid-
nineteenth century, because she regularly and dispassionately reports
the pronouncements of her admired friend John Sterling, who is
given to representative male attitudes and so

> thinks it is the greatest mistake and perversion to educate them
> [women] in the same manner as men; they have a duty equally clear
> and equally important to perform, but quite distinct. (29 February
> 1840)

> [Sterling said that under Catholicism,] women became superstitious
> because, in conformity with their nature, they must prostrate them-
> selves before some higher power. (13 February 1840)

> Sterling considers the female authors we have lately had very credit-
> able to this country, though they have produced nothing that the world
> could not have done very well without. . . . Sterling remarked that
> [Sara Coleridge] shows the limited nature of a woman's mind in her
> "Phantasmion." (1 March 1840, 30 October 1843)

From the second half of the century, Webb provides a debate with
Professor Marshall during a visit to Cambridge:

> He holding that woman was a subordinate being, and that, if she
> ceased to be subordinate, there would be no object for a man to marry,
> that marriage was a sacrifice of the masculine freedom and would only

be tolerated by male creatures so long as it meant the devotion, body and mind, of the female, and no longer. Hence the woman must develop in no way unpleasant to the man: that strength, courage, independence were not attractive to women, that rivalry in men's pursuits was positively unpleasant. Therefore masculine strength and ability in women must be firmly trampled upon and 'boycotted' by men. *Contrast* was the essence of the matrimonial relation: feminine weakness contrasted with masculine strength, masculine egotism with feminine self-devotion. (8 March 1889)[51]

"Naturally enough," she adds, "I maintained the opposite argument."

Critic Fothergill speculates that "the need to project an ego-image does not appear to be a leading motive in diaries written by women. . . . One simply does not find in past centuries women diarists who strut and perform and descant on their own singularity"; conspicuously absent is the extreme interest in individual development "at the centre of male diaries for centuries." When he explains why, inadvertently he explains as well why women may be impelled to keep diaries:

> The position of women in society has tended to preclude the assertion of individual ego. The drive to become Somebody, to establish oneself as *the* Robert Fothergill (for example), and the conception of one's personal history as 'My Development', have been masculine traits. Egotism in men and preoccupation with an effective self-image have been accepted and rewarded; in women they have been discouraged. A woman cannot easily cast herself as protagonist, when society and the controlling personal relationships of her life demand proficiency in exclusively supporting roles.

Because a woman would not have had expectations of ego gratification, Forthergill adds, she would not be inclined "to project a more rather than less assertive ego" in her diary to compensate for what her ego has been denied in life.[52] He may, however, underestimate the female ego.

All egos expect gratification. Keeping a diary, even without descanting on one's singularity, is arrogating an importance to oneself that compensates for societal devaluation. At the simplest, keeping a diary says, some time each day belongs to me. More complexly it says, what I know matters; I am and I matter. Women accommodate themselves to male demands and expectations, but they also make adjustments for their own comfort. Whether or not they complain in their diaries about the pressures of a male-centered ethos, they are opposing it in the very act of diary keeping. In diary activity, ironically, women uncover the enabling potential of language, for all that patriarchal language may disable female expression by encoding inhibitory male symbolic systems. The self's sense of itself—reflexive consciousness—is most keenly present in the act of using language about oneself.[53] And therefore a woman's diary enables her to sustain her sense of selfhood: having made her moments, whether of activity or of observation, the subject of discourse, the diarist feels that she exists and matters. The female private diarist here at least parallels the female author of public autobiography, as critic Nancy K. Miller has presented her:

> The cogito for Sand, Stern, and Beauvoir thus would seem to be: I write, therefore I am. Writing—for publication—represents entrance into the world of others, and by means of that passage a rebirth: access to the status of autonomous subject. The textualization of a female "I" means escape from the sphere inhabited by those "relative beings" (as Beauvoir has characterized women) who experience the world only through the mediation of men.

Although Miller speaks of publication, the fact of public declaration is less significant than the act of inscribing one's own "I." As Domna C. Stanton succinctly says of "autogynography" (autobiographical writing by women and hence diaries, too), "The *graphing* [writing] of the auto [self]" has been "an act of self-assertion that denied and reversed woman's status."[54]

Writing her own words may not cure the diarist's feelings of inadequacy or destroy habits of self-deprecation. Nonetheless, it provides the diarist, however subliminally, some escape from the sense that a woman's life is lived only through and for others and that her existence is justified only through providing a reference point for me—or, as

Simone de Beauvoir's classic statement goes, "she is the incidental, the inessential as opposed to the essential. He is the Subject, he is the Absolute—she is the Other."[55] Liminally escape is possible too: witness Beatrice Webb's declaration that she must write in her own style. Even if the self a woman lays claim to may constitute a variable fiction subject to context and relationships, even if her ego may have rather fluid boundaries, a woman does assume she has a personal identity and wants it to speak autonomously, asserting its importance by articulating its quotidian existence. Fearing posterity less than exposure to a contemporary intimate, the many diarists who did not destroy their diaries (when circumstances allowed) must have wanted to leave their own words as concrete memorials to the significance of that societally disprized, but to them important, self.

Feminist critics have endeavored to explain women's diary keeping by the lives they have historically been obliged to lead. They have taken an intimate connection between being a woman and keeping a diary as a given; they have assumed, as Suzanne Juhasz puts it, that there are "deeper relationships between the diary form and women's lives." Possibly women have had an affinity for a form so akin to their own fragmented and limited lives. Mary Jane Moffatt first articulated the assumption: "The form has been an important outlet for women partly because it is an analogue to their lives: emotional, fragmentary, interrupted, modest, not to be taken seriously, private, restricted, daily, trivial, formless, concerned with self, as endless as their tasks." Estelle C. Jelinek observes a consequence:

> Surveying . . . various countries and periods, one is struck by the number of women writing diaries, journals, and notebooks, in contrast to the many more men writing autobiographies proper. From earliest times, these discontinuous forms have been important to women because they are analogous to the fragmented, interrupted, and formless nature of their lives:

Juhasz develops the details:

> In their form, women's lives . . . show less a pattern of linear development towards some clear goal than one of repetitive, cumulative,

cyclical structure. One thinks of housework or childcare, of domestic life in general. . . . Dailiness matters to most women; and dailiness is by definition never a conclusion, always a process. . . . The classic verbal articulation of dailiness is . . . the diary.[56]

There is some truth, stated and implied, in such formulations. Because women have not typically worked towards career goals until very recent history, dailiness has been their mode of being. Moreover, given the form of their lives, diary keeping has long been a feasible activity. Conducted daily or nearly so, it is not excessively time-consuming; it will fit in at home along with other responsibilities and bear interrupting; it requires but moderate literacy; it will admit any level of contents; it is a socially acceptable pursuit. Form aside, it is also a psychologically valuable pursuit. Such circumstances go far to explain the appeal of the diary for women. However, they do not make it somehow an inherently female form, as the critical formulations imply it is.

The preponderance of male autobiography is explicable without analogizing diaries to women's fragmented and formless lives. The women who composed brief autobiographical sketches (usually of their origins and childhood) along with keeping diaries, but did not attempt full autobiographies, would seem at first to corroborate that women have felt it fitter or more temperamentally agreeable, rather than simply more practical, to pursue fragmentary-entry diary keeping. Diarists Mary Berry, Mary Frampton, Faith Gray, Katherine Howard, Countess Frances Russell (1815–1898), Frances Shelley, Hester Thrale, and Ellen Weeton are a few such women. But other diarists composed both diaries and full-length autobiographies: for instance, Cynthia Asquith, Anne Clifford, Marie Belloc Lowndes (1868–1947), Constance de Rothschild, Frances Stevenson, and Beatrice Webb.[57] They all, however, had something other than humdrum existences to write of, the reason for most male autobiographies. Moreover, men have not been discouraged from writing books (a public activity implying publication), whereas women have been. As late as 1923, Constance de Rothschild writes that her autobiography "is selling wonderfully. . . . Dear Mother would have been delighted—Cyril [her husband, Lord Battersea] less so. He never encouraged me to write, and thought very little of my literary capacities" (1 January).[58] Cyril never discouraged her diary keeping, however.

Critic Dale Spender has put the historical case most forcefully in observing that since patriarchal culture could not entirely prevent women from writing, it has instead secluded their productions, "permitting women to write for private audience . . . but discouraging them from writing for a public audience, that is, men. . . . women have been permitted to write for themselves (for example, diaries) and for each other." And conventional-minded women have reinforced male teaching. Diarist Weeton, a would-be author, laments her inability to write even her autobiography because her mother so discouraged her literary aspirations: "'Should you become a wife, think what a ragged, neglected state your family would be if you gave up much of your time to books'" ([1809]).[59] Historically, women have had neither outward encouragement nor inward impetus to write autobiographies. Moffatt's "not to be taken seriously" is a telling claim. Like their male-dominated society, most women have not thought themselves bookworthy. Until recently, most of them have not even assumed that their diaries would be of interest to the world at large, except when their private lives have somehow brought them into public spheres.

Autobiographies aside, moreover, the suggestion that women historically have felt their diary keeping to be an extension of female life, a parallel to its formlessness and frustration, is suspect because it assumes women's having the heightened feminist consciousness of recent times, when their diaries show that they do not. As historian Nancy Cott has observed, "The more historians have relied on women's personal documents the more positively they have evaluated women's sphere."[60] For these English diarists, well-defined roles and routine tasks provide a form and meaning to life that they usually accept as valid, however unappealing to restless or intelligent spirits that life may be, and however much their sense of self may simultaneously need reinforcement. Diarist Margaret Hoby rationalizes her task-bound life as a blessing, for "buseneses hindereth wanderinge Coggetation" (19 March 1599);[61] and the habit of rationalizing, like the willingness to accommodate self to what is expected of women, long outlives her.

Women undoubtedly felt the irksomeness of their domestic responsibilities, even if they do not complain about them in their diaries.
Precocious diarist Emily Shore (b. 1819) at thirteen wrote a short
drama, "The Interruptions," which has been published as an appendix to her diary. In Shore's play, Mamma tries to hear Emily's lessons
(no less than Sir Joshua Reynolds's *Discourses*), only to be interrupted
by the housemaid, a manservant, the cook, the nurse, a maidservant, and her other child, in turn. The lesson is forestalled. When
Emily protests, "I have not read a page," Mamma responds, "Well it
can't be helped, you know."[62] Even an early nineteenth-century girl
could see that females' services were provided for, not their minds,
and that their time was fragmented and preempted. But "it can't be
helped," as Mamma says; it is the way of the world. Their lives may
have been vexatious, but these women's diaries say that the women of
the past usually did not feel their lives to be formless. The sense of
formlessness, along with the sense of unlimited possibility, may be
more of a problem today. Juhasz, indeed, suggests that the diary form
appeals to women nowadays just because its inherent lack of direction allows the writer to find her way by indirection:

> It is because the nature of meaning itself in women's lives is right now
> such an unclear and open issue that, finally, the diary model for wom-
> en's autobiography seems most appropriate and helpful. One can fling
> there a "mass of odds and ends" without preconception as to their
> meaning; if one allows the collection to sort itself, and coalesce. . .
> the writer is in a position to achieve new insight, based on the smallest
> units of daily experience, into her life as a woman.[63]

The diary form has always had such potential, of course, but that potential has not necessarily been exploited.

Sister A. Martha Westwater has inspected the manuscript diary of
a nineteenth-century woman who did have a sense of formlessness to
her life—Elizabeth Wilson (later Bagehot)—but only to reveal how
Wilson refused to use her diary to authenticate her existence. Her
diary, in Westwater's terms, is a "casebook of Victorian female passivity." Wilson, who lived the emptiest of genteel Victorian lives, at
least in her youth twice faced up in her diary to the limitations of her

own quiescent personality and her moribund life. "Literally, she was ashamed of her 'self.' If she saw little meaning in her day-to-day life, if the actions which consumed her 'busily-idling brain' were trivial, then in some way she must make them meaningful. . . . she must set about redeeming her existence." But although Wilson realizes in 1853 "I cannot spare any longer the benefits arising from a regular registering of the thoughts and reflections called forth by daily life," she procrastinates, unwilling to scrutinize her own self-consciousness. She knows that "whenever I have vigorously set to work, this feeling of emptiness and indefinite longing has left me," but there the theme of self-salvation ends. Instead of making purposeful use of her diary, Wilson, as Westwater phrases it, merely "unveils her vapid subservience to authority, her innate desire to please, her acceptance of those stultifying influences blocking any entrance into deeper self-understanding."[64]

Wilson provides an informative historical illustration. Finding female selfhood or, in Juhasz's phrase, "new insight into [one's] life as a woman," requires some will in the diarist to do so, plus her sense that such discovery is a function the diary is well suited to perform. Contemporary women see their diaries this way, but most women of the past did not, even though they may have reread their diaries for a sense of continuity and self-worth and may have strengthened their very sense of self just by keeping their personal records of the process of time. Expanded diaries may reflect inner growth. One can sometimes observe in diaries kept over long periods, especially when the years have included sustained suffering, the growth of a less shallow or less self-pitying personality—as, for example, with Berry, Mary Shelley, and Weeton. But those changes reflected in the diaries are not necessarily caused by them, nor are they the usual sort of growth in awareness nowadays called for.

Cynthia S. Pomerleau has found that in seventeenth-century English autobiography women reveal a widespread satisfaction with their lives. She speaks of largely upper-class women, for whom "the old traditions of order and female subordination were still workable" and who "could engage fairly comfortably in conventional relationships and submit to a subordinate role without being overwhelmed by a sense of oppression."[65] The description largely holds for seventeenth-century to early twentieth-century English diaries too, with most middle- and upper-class women continuing to accept a male-dominated culture and adjusting themselves to it, though later nineteenth-century feminism and the Great War at least partly cracked the mold. Among the principal diarists, the main dissidents are the few active feminist sympathizers, the few who were grossly wronged by men, and the few whose intellectual ambitions were frustrated by their gender. They may complain overtly, but even they usually accept more arrangements than they want to change. Objections to the patriarchy otherwise are very sporadic and indirect. Ironically, as an activity of language, the diary is and has always been a sanctioned form of expression for women. Unlike the authors of novels and poetry, the diarist has not had to avoid direct confrontation with male prerogatives by using disclaimers or a code for hidden communication through a rebellious or subversive subtext.[66] Especially in diaries intended to be private one might therefore expect women to express rebellious sentiments directly, eschewing protective screens. But these diarists respond to the opportunity to be freely captious about patriarchal ways largely by ignoring it, whether because they have not the habit of rebelling against the norms for female attitudes and behavior or because they never feel really free to do so. Some diarists do covertly encode rebelliousness, but only minimally in extent and import. Sotto voce resentments and restlessness may murmur then; nonetheless, apparently for most women dissension could coexist with essential satisfaction. The proof follows in the next chapter.

Rather than women's having gravitated to diary keeping as an extension of their lives, the more intellectual ones appear to have seen it as a corrective to them. In his funeral eulogy for Anne Clifford in 1676, the Bishop of Carlisle conjectured that Anne, a lifelong diarist, thought "she was better so employed, than in tattling or paying visits."[67] So too Weeton, who alternated between a diary and a letter diary, explains to a friend that her letter diary provides diversion more valuable than the usual female occupations of the mid-nineteenth century: "'My only reason for undertaking such a piece of work is, that it has been a great amusement during many a solitary hour when I had no other employ, when I should only have been engaged in

some fine, tedious piece of needlework or other.'" Emily Shore likewise writes: "I find it [keeping my journal] such an useful practice,
and so entertaining, that I am fully resolved to continue it all my life.
. . . I have been long convinced that . . . the use of the pen is
amongst the most valuable means of improving the mind" (30 April
1836).[68] The way in which so many women carefully record the
books they have been reading, with their critical estimates, also suggests that, instead of identifying their diaries with the limitations of
their task-ridden lives, some women were rather envisioning them as
a partial refuge from those lives.

The escape value of diary keeping has been noted in feminist criticism. Deena Metzger and Barbara Meyerhoff, for example, contend
that "in the past, women utilized the journal because it was an appropriate form in which disdained individuals could clarify and observe
their concerns. . . . allowing them a measure of that freedom and
responsibility in the personal domain which was lacking in the public
sphere." The problem in Metzger and Meyerhoff's approach lies in
the possibilities for unhistorical exaggeration. As they continue,

> Women have long kept secret journals, commonplace books, and dia-
> ries locked in hope chests among the linens. There was too often no
> other verification of an authentic existence apart from roles, and obe-
> dience to social functions, for women whose traditional bare poignant
> question was not "Who am I" but "Am I?" . . . critical speculation
> assumes that the journal served women in the past in the same way it
> served other marginal people (madmen, prisoners, slaves) as a means
> for holding onto some core of Self, holding at bay anonymity, trivi-
> ality, and madness.[69]

Such claims violate the evidence of these Englishwomen's diaries.

On the basis of that evidence, female diary keeping was not a clan-
destine activity. More crucial, most women were not using diaries to
conduct an intensive search for a hidden identity that would redeem
their lives, though their diaries could and sometimes did serve them
as revelations. Women did use their diaries to some degree as a means
of self-discovery and justification. In usually an ad hoc fashion, they
did rely upon their diary writing for a relief or a stimulus or a sense of

accomplishment. Those are all sufficiently good reasons for the frequency of female diary keeping. These women, though they did not necessarily see their lives as inauthentic, nonetheless lived in a world in which female selfhood was thwarted and female egoism discouraged. But they could assert themselves as individuals through their diaries, and they did feel their particular lives to be important enough to record for themselves or their progeny and posterity. The very nature of the diary as a personal record counters the limiting and devaluing of the female self entailed by accommodation to a male-dominated culture. Keeping a diary is not a peculiarly female habit. But it has been especially useful to female being.

THREE

ACCOMMODATION AND DEFIANCE:
On Women's Rights

"Butt I was Bound, & must obey" (9 June 1702), Elizabeth Freke explains her marriage. Married or not, however, women have historically been bound by a male power structure subordinating them to men and subjecting them to greater restrictions on behavior, and they have largely accommodated themselves to it. If Englishwomen wanted more equality, power, and freedom, not until the mid-nineteenth century did they begin agitating in numbers for such rights. After a scattering of protests in the 1830s and 1840s, a women's movement emerged in the 1850s, arguing for married women's rights to property and for better educational and employment opportunities. By the 1860s, attaining the suffrage to gain the power to change laws also became a goal. Before the nineteenth century, however, dissatisfaction with the patriarchy was but a low background rumble. During the latter half of the seventeenth century and the early eighteenth, speaking individually, not as a movement, a small number of bookish women wrote of the need for increased respect and independence for females, based on improved education. These early expressions of feminism, which had little influence on the general thought of the period, found one significant voice in Mary Astell, who became the center of a circle of like-minded women. Astell's *Serious Proposal to the Ladies* (1694, with several eighteenth-century appendices) urged upper-class women to greater use of their rational powers in serious study and Christian service. Attacking the negative impact of culture on women's lives, Astell proposed a private women's college to train upper-class females in exercise of their minds so that they could cease to be duped by roles that led them to cherish looks and fortune.[1]

The voice of dissension became most resonant, however, at the end of the eighteenth century with Mary Wollstonecraft, who would eventually become an inspiration for a women's movement, but whose contemporary followers were few. Wollstonecraft's *Vindication of the Rights of Women* (1792) attacked women's enforced ignorance and unjust subordination to men, but more important, with a keener sense than Astell's of the damage incurred by cultural conditioning, Wollstonecraft addressed women's need to develop more self-respect. It was not so much men, she saw, as women who must change their sense of women's being. To give women power over themselves, she sought, as she explained in her introduction,

> to persuade women to endeavour to acquire strength, both of mind and body, and to convince them that . . . soft phrases, susceptibility of heart, delicacy of sentiment, and refinement of taste, are almost synonymous with epithets of weakness, and that those beings who are only the objects of pity and that kind of love, which has been termed its sister, will soon become objects of contempt.[2]

Women must themselves want to become rational, independent-minded moral beings who refuse reduction to sexual objects and delicate dolls. Yet it would take until the twentieth century and require the incremental effect of the social upheavals caused by two world wars, plus the stimulus of a liberation movement, for any significant alteration of consciousness among the mass of women. Edwardian diarist Katherine Mansfield is in advance of her times and anticipates the 1960s when she explodes, "Talk of our enlightened days and our emancipated country—pure nonsense! We are firmly held with the self-fashioned chains of slavery. Yes, now I see that they *are* self-fashioned and must be self-removed" (May 1908).[3]

Although objection to the patriarchy became more vocal and activist as the nineteenth century progressed, to reach a climax in the agitation for the vote in the early twentieth century, the nineteenth-century British women's movement was less extensive and forceful than its American counterpart. As David Bouchier explains, "The contradictions in women's lives were less keenly experienced" in more traditionalist Britain, where females were historically granted less independence and had less engagement in "consciousness-raising public struggles" like the abolitionist movement.[4] Equal rights feminism met plentiful opposition from women, who, in the mass, had learned their subservience to men and relegation to their own domestic sphere very well and handed the lessons on to their daughters. The tenor of such indoctrination is apparent in early nineteenth-century conduct manuals written by women, such as Mrs. West's 1806 *Letters to a Young Lady*, which instructs:

> If we wish our girls to be happy, we must try to make them docile, contented, prudent and domestic. Man must range abroad and forage for his family; woman 'must look well to the ways of her household,' and 'bring up her children in the nurture and admonition of the Lord'. The passive virtues and the Christian graces, are her natural dowry.[5]

But women's diaries over the centuries also show how conservative women were of the male power system and its values, how inclined as a rule to keep themselves and their sisters in check. One might like to believe otherwise. Historian Patricia Branca, however, is right to caution against distorting the past, in this case the nineteenth century:

> Almost all the studies on Victorian women have one theme in common—the theme of discontent. It is the generally accepted position that more and more women, bored with their life of genteel uselessness, sought more meaningful roles outside the home. In other words, the feminist movement was a reaction against boredom, while the eminent women achieved their position by defying the common norms. . . . feminism and the eminent women alike may fit our standards of significance, but they . . . depart from the situation . . . of middle-class women during most of the nineteenth century.[6]

Her caveat against projecting the present onto the past applies to other eras as well.

The context for the diarists' conservative behavior is a male-controlled and male-centered society, which was and became even more spiritually restrictive for women during the seventeenth, eighteenth, and nineteenth centuries. Already designated inferior to men in intellect and virtue in the seventeenth century and enjoined by the Scriptures and subsequent Christian teachings to humble obedience to their betters, women were subjected to increased domination as the century advanced. A massive body of contemporary political theory and Puritan theology encouraged men to take their authority as husbands and fathers more seriously. Under common-law practice, moreover—without substantial modification until the nineteenth century—a married woman was subject to the concept of the *femme couverte:* the total dependence upon her husband, in whom all legal rights were vested, so that she could not administer her own property, make a contract, sue or be sued in tort. Nor had she any legal right over her own children. To illustrate briefly, aristocratic diarist Anne Clifford's husband could remove her child because Anne had quarreled with him, while she, though desolate, did not even contemplate redress (instead, she bided her time and eventually he brought the child back). The Court of Chancery, it is true, allowed a proprietary capacity to women of wealthier families concerning marriage settlements and trusts. Diarist Elizabeth Freke's proud report of a marriage portion given by her father in 1673 and held for her by five trustees demonstrates that women were not entirely constrained. Though her money-hungry husband managed to bilk her of a portion of it, "the Rest I Took for my own use. . . . I sould it quite outt of the bank of England, Itt then bearing a greatt price. I thought I could nott Doe better, the bank Running high" (3 June 1703). Moreover, clearly in some circumstances women could control their own property even when it was not part of a marriage settlement or trust, for Clifford personally owned and administered her belatedly inherited northern estates during the lifetime of her second husband.[7] Nonetheless, women's circumstances were bad and would worsen. By forces operating from several directions, they would become confined to a separate domestic sphere and mentality.

The Restoration contempt for women of learning, which extended even into the Enlightenment, and the continuing exclusion of most females from all but superficial education reinforced women's restrictive situation. The devaluing of the female mind also fed into the conceptual and circumstantial demarcation of a smaller world for women henceforth. When Enlightenment writers such as Rousseau presented a view of female nature as inherently different from male nature and thus governed by feeling, not reason, by sensation and imagination, not logic, and with moral qualities that required a domestic setting for fulfillment, they encouraged the growth of the separate-sphere ideology that dominated the late eighteenth century and especially the nineteenth century.[8]

Nonetheless, it required the Evangelical movement for moral reform after the 1790s to propagate the creed that public and private spheres—even activities within the home—should be rigidly split between the sexes because of the absolute differences between male and female; also, to tout the "doctrine of true womanhood" (in historian Olive Banks's phrase) for the common good.[9] Separate spheres narrowly defined woman's nature and reinforced her traditional role. Her distinctive qualities—variously construed as fragility, simplicity, purity, gentleness, kindness, patience, affection, and the like—meant that she belonged only in the home in service to family, for whose members—and by extension, for society—she would be a morally redemptive force.

Describing the family in an earlier period (1450–1700), historian Ralph Houlbrooke observes that the wife "was conventionally supposed to occupy a separate but subordinate sphere in the family economy." But husband and wife had overlapping responsibilities, and the arrangement did not necessarily imprison women spiritually or bodily in domesticity (as Margaret Hoby's extensive estate work testifies). It would do so, however, after the onset of the agricultural and industrial revolutions by the later eighteenth century, when home and workplace increasingly became separated and a burgeoning middle class made it economically feasible to enshrine the female at home. "Men in the middle strata of society," as feminist Sheila Rowbotham puts it, "who had to make themselves in a competitive market . . . looked to women for the sensibility and feeling impossible in the world of work. The ideal of the helpless languishing woman of leisure replaced the puritan yokefellow."[10] In the upwardly mobile society, females were expected to be "ladies" with social graces and accomplishments, not laborers.

Encouraged by Evangelical reformers to do charitable work, but ordinarily largely excluded from education, business, and politics (though aristocrats might serve at court), eighteenth- to nineteenth-century Englishwomen of the moneyed classes willingly accepted home and family as the proper focus of their lives. Thus they paralleled American women. Having studied American women's personal documents (1780–1838), historian Nancy Cott concludes that New England women also voluntarily identified with a women's-sphere ideology affording them a gender-specific role to play. Suggests Cott, women did not need to be coerced into women's sphere because they esteemed the concept that their domestic influence and maternal duties constituted a positive social role; it gave them a unique defense of their integrity and dignity.[11] Simple respect as men's equals might have made them feel much better about themselves. Nonetheless, not until the late nineteenth century would the confinements of the separate sphere be actively challenged by equal rights feminists, and the ideal of women's domestic moral influence played a role within the women's movement itself.[12] The more insidious gender assumptions also lingered on into the twentieth century, even after Victorian ideology wore off.

The essential conservatism of most of the diarists, who, for better or worse, accept the patriarchal system of power and values, is evident from the earliest diarists on. Among the five seventeenth-century women, Puritan Margaret Hoby; Isabella Twysden, a moderate who kept a bare-bones civil war diary; and Mary Woodforde, an Anglican clergyman's wife, write as model wives, though Hoby by contemporary accounts was wed to a surly and abusive man. All three are pious women living at a time when religious duty precludes marital insubordination, nor do they seem to contemplate it or any other form of independence. The other two women are only moderately more spirited. Clifford actively challenges both her first husband and the king over a contested inheritance, yet she is otherwise docile, even to suffering in silence when her husband invites his mistress home for a visit so that Anne can entertain her (the home as yet was no sanctuary). Though Freke complains incessantly of her husband's expenditures and neglect, she also blames herself because she dared marry "withoutt my deer Fathers Consent or knowledge, In A most dreadfull Raynie day, A presager of all my sorrows and misfortunes" (14 November 1671). An even more instructive example of conservatism, however, comes out of the 1791–1811 diary of Lady Elizabeth Holland. An aristocrat by marriage who is not confined to home and in her own way a courageous woman, Lady Holland, though a victim of the power system, is nonetheless its defender. It horrifies her to discover that a woman friend has learned "to exclaim against institutions, especially that of marriage, to which she says she has been a helpless victim. If I were to see much of her she might perhaps be benefited. . . . A little mild reproof and disapprobation of some of her doctrines might possibly rescue her from the gulf" (11 March 1801). To Holland, fortune has favored the English-woman (a notion shared with several eighteenth- and nineteenth-century sister-diarists), whereas "all the institutions in Southern countries are very degrading to the sex. Morally and physically we are treated [there] as beings of an inferior class" (1797).[13] Yet Lady Holland herself experienced a highly incompatible English marriage and a degrading divorce.

A Jamaican heiress in an era still of arranged marriages for the wealthy, Elizabeth Vassall (Lady Holland) was married at fifteen to Sir Godfrey Webster, twenty-three years older and, by her account, a violent-tempered bully. Their marriage brought him the money he needed as an inveterate gambler while uniting her to a respected English country family to which she did not wish to belong. Subjected "in the bloom and innocence of fifteen, to the power of a being who has made me execrate my life since it has belonged to him" (27 June 1793),[14] she not only contemplated suicide. She also escaped her unhappy marriage through an affair, starting in 1794 or 1795, with Lord Holland (Henry Richard Fox), whom she married in 1797 after Webster divorced her for bearing Holland's child. In the last decade of the seventeenth century, divorce with the right of remarriage had become possible by private Act of Parliament for husbands who could prove their wives adulterous. Such parliamentary divorce, as historian Roger Thompson succinctly comments, was not only "a purely male prerogative" but "only the rich need apply."[15]

Webster kept his wife's fortune, except for an annual living allowance; of course he also kept their children. Total rights over legitimate children were still vested uncontroversially in the father. Not until the 1839 Custody of Infants Act was a formal legal link established between mother and child. But even this limited reform—which gave a mother access to young children if she could prove her good character—would not have applied to Elizabeth.[16] As an adultress, she was not permitted to see her children, and Webster's will expressly enjoined their guardian to forbid them any communication with their mother. Consequently, upon Webster's suicide over his gambling debts in 1800, she had no access to the children, nor in 1801—when she is praising the institution of marriage—could she get any satisfaction from the courts to which she had applied for visiting rights. Eventually her children were restored to her, her second marriage was a happy one, and she became a celebrated hostess at Holland House as center of a Whig political salon. But one is left with the reality that a woman who had suffered from patriarchal institutions, then suffered again for asserting herself, upholds the system nonetheless. As such, she serves as a good illustration of the situation one largely finds in these Englishwomen's diaries until late in the nineteenth century.

However, if the diaries of most of these Englishwomen are not the diaries of rebels, neither are they the diaries of slaves. Instead, the diarists' attitude to the male power structure sanctified by law, religion, and custom is both acquiescent and rebellious. It is acquiescent in that the women not only yield to the necessity of male domination; they make a virtue of it, accepting the power structure as their source of good and deriving their satisfactions from fulfilling the roles assigned them. It is rebellious, nonetheless, because, as will later be demonstrated, the women also reserve some rights to themselves and increasingly see the structure as inimical to their welfare. Yet until the later nineteenth century, it is more acquiescent than not. For an immediate instance, Hester Thrale accepts the terms of her first marriage in 1763 with equanimity. Like Holland's, hers is an arranged marriage, for the custom died out only slowly during the century. Says Thrale:

> Why do the People say I never loved my first Husband? 'tis a very unjust Conjecture. *This day* on which 24 years ago I was married to him never returns without bringing with it many a tender Remem-

brance: though 'twas on *that* Evening when we retired together that I
was first alone with Mr. Thrale for five Minutes in my whole Life. Ours
was a Match of mere Prudence; and common good Liking, without the
smallest Pretensions to Passion on either Side: I knew no more of him
than of any other Gentleman who came to the House. (11 October
1787)[17]

By the nineteenth century, arranged marriages were no longer
customary. But the rigid separation of the sexes that accompanied
separate-sphere mentality and the ever more vigilant concern to protect female purity meant that blind unions persisted among the prosperous and their imitators. Less complaisant than Thrale, Lady Mary
Monkswell in 1874 objects to women's being expected to cast their
lot with virtual strangers: "In the present ridiculous state of society
the chances are as in my case that I literally only beheld Bob twice in
morning costume, i.e. not at a party, before I was engaged to him. I
will not complain of the bridge that has carried me over, but absurd
& mistaken in the extreme are the laws of the intercourse between
men & women" (29 June 1874).[18] One can observe in these diaries,
however, that even if there is more criticism of patriarchal ways as
the nineteenth century advances, they are still well imprinted on female minds. Some twenty-five years later, Edwardian Lady Monkswell
sounds like diarist Clarissa Trant in 1829. When Lady Monkswell attends the first Parliament of Edward VII, "Most glad I was to have a
kind good husband to look after me & put me in my place, or I certainly could not have ventured" (14 February 1901). When Trant
while out walking chances to encounter a former suitor who has de-
ceived her, she "clung close to my dearest brother's arm and turned
my head away. Thank God that I have a Father's and a Brother's protecting arm to support me" (9 May 1829).[19]

Partly on the evidence of diaries, Barbara Schnorrenberg and Jean
Hunter report "discontent with prevailing standards of female behavior" among eighteenth-century women. "Even in the diaries, letters,
novels, and other writings of seemingly conforming women, implicit
or explicit criticism of the standards of English masculine society can
be found. These women wanted change, and they wanted to unite
the women of England in pursuit of this change."[20] Eighteenth-

century published diaries suggest otherwise. Up to a point they show explicit criticism (leaving aside for now the implicit possibilities). Witness again, for example, young Caroline (Girle) Powys resenting masculine contempt for female intellect: "But is it anything surprising the [female] sex should amuse themselves with trifles when these lords of creation will not give themselves the trouble (in my conscience, I believe for fear of being outshone), to enlarge our minds by making them capable to retain those of more importance?" (1760). Mary Berry, moreover, looking back in 1823 to her twenty-first birthday in 1784, recalls "what regrets I felt then at having been born a woman, and deprived of the life and position which, as a man, I might have had in this world!" (16 March).[21]

Yet such explicit criticism is uncommon in eighteenth-century published diaries. It is not even common in Girle's diary; after her few youthful outbursts, she grows up, marries, and becomes staidly conservative Mrs. Powys. Faith Gray's diary captures a much commoner strain in the eighteenth-century diaries. There is no repining in it for a room of her own when she reminisces about her childhood: "I never saw a happier Family. The days were occupied in active employment and the evenings in a way calculated to improve and gratify the mind. My Brothers were engaged in the study of languages, in reading History, learning geography, or in music. My mother[,] sisters and myself were sewing or reading" (13 September 1787).[22] Like Gray, Powys, and Lady Holland, other women have left behind them eighteenth-century diaries accepting of the status quo: Diana Astry, Elizabeth Byrom, Mary Cowper, Lady Lucy Fitzgerald (1771–1851), Elizabeth Freke, Mary Hamilton, Mary Hardy, Katherine Howard, Annie Lumb, Lady Elizabeth Northumberland, Elizabeth Raper, Nancy Woodforde, Elizabeth and Eugenia Wynne. Even intellectual women conform. Thrale, like author-editor Mary Berry, may be a bluestocking sort with an independent spirit in some matters. But she is also, as already suggested, a submissive wife who would "never offer to cross my Master's Fancy . . . unless on some truly serious Occasion, nor do I think any Occasion serious enough to excuse Contradiction unless Virtue[,] Life, or Fortune are concerned. [W]as I to dye tomorrow I could swear, I never oppos'd his Inclination three Times in the fifteen Years we have been married" (10 February 1779).

Even Berry, though her heart rebels against the restrictions on women, has internalized her gender role. Thus, challenged at the Swiss border by an insolent official, "for once in my life I rejoiced at the helplessness of my sex; for . . . this young man . . . did so make my blood boil in my veins, that nothing *but* my sex could have prevented me being guilty of the signal folly of chastising him" (20 July 1803). More important, she takes it for granted that a man will decide what her writing is worth. She may have discussed with the publisher the format of her edition of Mme. du Deffand's letters, but "as to the price he would give me for the *Manuscript,* we agreed he should speak to my friend Edwards, and that I would be satisfied with whatever he arranged for me" (7 January 1809).[23]

Most women in the eighteenth century accepted subordination of their being to men's, as women also would do in the nineteenth. Although conduct manuals may diverge from actual conduct, Mrs. West's blunt advice in hers, at the turn of the nineteenth century, on mastering repression—and doing it gracefully—appears to reflect what females did more or less learn the trick of doing. They learned to maintain what she calls "a disposition that can yield to the desires of others, not only without *apparent* reluctance, but without enduring pain," one of "the qualities which a young lady should endeavour to obtain who determines to become a wife." Nineteenth-century Charlotte Guest, inspecting the family foundry with her husband, illustrates nicely how well that principle could be internalized:

> I walked to the [iron] Works with Merthyr. He took me to the top of the Yard and to look at the new Blast Engine. . . . Having no door, I was obliged to enter it by a ladder put against a window, and as the flooring was still wanting, my only way of going over it was by climbing along the rafters and machinery, and in one instance walking along the arm of a fly-wheel. Blind as I am, I thought the experiment rather perilous, but Merthyr wished it, and I suppose my neck is at his disposal. (9 August 1837)[24]

The imposition of male will is not the issue. Rather, it is induced male-dominant attitudes that persist though times may change: deference, for example. Even in the privacy of these very personal diaries, women honor the formalities of male dominance by not referring to a husband by his given name until well into the nineteenth century. Social historian Lawrence Stone cites male letters using given names for wives to prove his claim that more companionate marriages had developed by the early eighteenth century. He should rather have looked at women's diaries.[25] As Cynthia Asquith rightly observes upon reading *Pamela,* "They always cried and swooned when conversing with their husbands, but never neglected to call them 'Sir' or 'Mr. B'" (16 April 1915).[26] Though first names are sometimes used for other males, including suitors and even fiancés, only formal appellations or surnames are used for husbands (Mr., Sir, Lord, my Master, and an occasional my Husband or my dear Husband) until in 1833 Guest speaks of "Merthyr" (John Guest). Of course, descriptive labels may also slip in; Lady Holland's first husband is not only "Sir G. W." but also "my tormentor."

Male power is most forceful not as an imposition of will but as determinant of values. A relevant pattern in the diaries that transcends time is women's self-consciousness of gender in situations in which women are few. When a diarist is the only woman or one of few women present, she will remark it, whatever the century, eighteenth to twentieth. The women are perhaps reflecting their uneasiness about being solitary females among a number of men, given the custom of separate spheres; but something else is also impelling them to tell their diaries they are the only ones. To illustrate the pattern, there is not much to choose between Lady Holland dining with the duke of York at the English army camp near Dunkirk, though "I felt odd being the only female among such a party of men" (22 August 1793); Beatrice Webb at a meeting of dock laborers, though "I was the only woman present" (27 November 1887); and Frances Stevenson accompanying Lloyd George to the international ministers' conference at Rapallo, though "rather out of place here, being the only woman" (6 November 1917).[27] Doubtless the three are self-conscious at entering such male precincts, but they also feel proud.

Other entries across the years strongly imply women's pride at being honored by inclusion among a group of males. When as a young woman Powys has accepted an invitation to see the Royal Hospital at Haslar, she names all the party, then adds gratuitously in parentheses, "We three were the only ladies" (1760). In similar fashion, Mary Hamilton reports, upon dining at Sir Joshua Reynolds's, "There were no other ladies besides Miss Palmer & me; the men were: the celebrated Dr. Beattie & his son . . . the great Dr. Johnson" (27 June 1784). Or when Berry dines at Mr. Whitbread's, the august party included fourteen guests, "Lady Elizabeth and myself the only ladies" (15 March 1814). Margaret Jeune's self-satisfied description of attending an important lecture in hall as wife of the Master of Pembroke College memorializes finding that "Dr. Williams and Harington were there, but no other woman than myself" (21 February 1850). Mary Gladstone makes a revealing decision upon being asked to choose her ideal list for a dinner party; she chooses nine men and one woman: herself (5 April 1877). Lady Monkswell treasures the dinner party her husband has given for "9 distinguished men, at which I, the only woman, had the honour to dine" (6 May 1904).[28] And novelist Marie Belloc Lowndes announces proudly (although it is irrelevant to her account of events) that when Alice Warrender was founding the Hawthornden Prize for Literature, "she and I were the only women present, but there were six or seven men, all of them distinguished writers" (12 February 1919). For those women like Asquith who enjoy being the unchallenged center of male regard, remarking their own solitary female presence assuredly reflects self-satisfaction, as in "We had a very comfortable journey and I quite enjoyed . . . being the only member of one's sex" (28 October 1916). There is something to be said for being the only female present. One can place higher valuation on self when selected from among other women to associate with the dominant group. As Lady Monkswell says of her husband's dinner party, "How much I enjoy to talk to these clever men, & how pleased & complimented I feel that they should rather like to talk to me."[29]

Women may have always had a sense of female community concerning childbirth and have participated in female social networks. Nonetheless, to borrow a term popularized by feminist Adrienne Rich in another context, the diarists over the centuries are largely (even if not perfectly) male-identified: they have internalized the values of their male-directed society and behave accordingly. Male identification, as Rich explains, "'is the act whereby women place men above women, including themselves, in credibility, status, and importance, in most situations.'"[30] Diarist Hamilton, having been invited to the Prince of Wales's ball, consults Lady Stormont for advice, but refuses her urgings to accept the invitation because Hamilton herself wants neither to incur the expenses involved nor to attempt the social connections. But Hamilton also asks her Uncle William's opinion. When he says go, she attends the ball (5 March 1784). Guest behaves comparably when she not only comments on Lady Londonderry's speech to her workmen with "No man could have done better," but also denigrates her own compassionate feelings for her workers. Managing her first husband's Welsh mines after his death, she initially refuses to league with other mine owners (male) to break a strike, then yields, for "I suspected my objections might arise from a woman's weakness" (16 March 1856, 1 July 1853). Or Webb decides: "It is always so much easier to get on with men; they seldom criticize a girl who is willing to make herself pleasant to them. And then their wider knowledge of human nature makes them more interesting as companions" (21 November 1880). Male identification means that women assume men, not women, are the fountainhead of wisdom and values. It follows then that having male approval is the summum bonum, never to be jeopardized. Hester Thrale too is male identified when she opines, "She who would please the other Sex must certainly not encroach upon its privileges" (19 September 1797).[31]

The diarists are inclined to see the world through male-tinted spectacles: not with a sense of women's actual value or potential but with a vision learned from their culture. They need not declare their belief in the superiority of men in order to be recognizably male identified, since they constantly demonstrate their loyalty. Still, sometimes they do so declare; Frances Shelley, for example, upon hearing Samuel Romilly speak in Parliament, "felt so proud of the manly, energetic character of my countrymen, and reverently bowed my head in acknowledgment of their pre-eminence over my weak sex" (19 April 1818).[32] As the rest of her diary shows, she does not mean that she subscribes to a natural male superiority. Rather, with an attitude common among the diarists of her time, she accepts it de facto: men have achievements and power and the superiority vested in them by society, therefore meriting identification. Like the mass of women, Shelley has made a pragmatic adjustment to what Mrs. West's conduct manual describes as "the original institution of Providence, respecting the subservience of our sex"—which means, as West explains, "Though I stoutly deny, that this injunction originated in our natural inferiority, I believe it to be . . . expedient to the welfare and happiness of both parties." [33]

Caroline Fox's 1849 description of Clara Balfour's lectures shows what it meant in mid-nineteenth-century terms to know that women are not innately inferior. Clara (Lucas) Balfour was a popular temperance lecturer who branched out into other subjects such as the influence of women on society, the theme of the talks Fox attended. Fox finds that "there was nothing to annoy by its assumptions for our sex" (25 October) in Balfour's presentation, with its separate-sphere premises and Evangelical fervor. Touting women's responsibility to serve as moral forces and therefore their right to a decent education, Balfour restates the doctrine of de facto subordination, coupling it with the Enlightenment-inspired male image of female nature: intellectual incapacity. Fox recalls her saying "that the one sex is essentially inferior to the other has yet to be proved. Officially subordinate she undoubtedly is, but subordination does not imply inferiority of mind and character. The one [sex] has powers of abstraction and concentration which are most rare in the other; but woman has acuteness, accuracy of observation, quickness, play of fancy and taste, as a compensation." [34] Nineteenth-century women may have known that they were not categorically inferior to men, but such knowledge hardly constituted raised consciousness of female nature and worth. Nor do most of the other diarists do much better than the nineteenth-century ones, for they view women essentially as do men.

These diarists often evidence very masculinist preconceptions. Mary Shelley, for example, envisions woman as the passively adoring pupil: "There was much in me—the woman's love of looking up, and being guided, and being willing to do anything if any one supported and brought me forward" (21 October 1838). Amelia Opie (1769–1853), originally an admirer of Mary Wollstonecraft but by the diary period become a Quaker convert, subscribes to the notion of female docility. "I almost dread the idea of London, but 'such is the sweet

112

pliability of woman's spirit' that I dare say when I get there I shall be pleased" ([1834]). More analytical but no less misguided, Webb considers it characteristically feminine to be unobjective, adoration hungry—and dangerous: "If there is a moral flaw in [Miss Souvestre's] character it is the intensely personal aspect in which all things clothe themselves—her judgment warped by the opinion of her, the treatment of herself. She is in fact supremely *feminine* in her character, with a grand capacity for self-devotion *in return for adoration;* but also latent capacity to be a 'nasty enemy'" (22 May 1891). Cynthia Asquith is certain of the sway of male regard over female vanity: "It is amazing how open to suggestion I am in the way of looks: the mere vicinity of Basil is more effective than all the cosmetics in the world. I suppose all women are like that in varying degrees" (1 February 1916). Canards extend even to Lady Monkswell's certainty that women cannot tell jokes effectively (19 August 1881).[35]

That what the diarists have assumed to be female nature may instead be male myths or the result of nurture does not occur to most of them. They accept the myths as truth and do not think in terms of cultural conditioning. Nor is that surprising. Rousseauistic notions of women's different nature were too embedded for Mary Wollstonecraft to dislodge at the end of the eighteenth century, and they received powerful reinforcement afterwards when Darwinian science derived women's presumable traits, such as tenderness, generosity, intuition, and so forth, from biology. The result, as historian Jane Lewis says, was that "the pervasive belief in the natural, biological difference between male and female characteristics formed a framework within which feminists and non-feminists alike thought and lived" in the latter half of the nineteenth century.[36] Occasionally a diarist is alert to conditioning. Webb, for example, at least recognizes that the question of acculturation may exist: "How subjective women are," she says. "Does it belong to their education or their nature?" (4 November 1882). But she does not attempt to answer the question. Meanwhile, her own sense of the female is a product of Webb's nurture. Her description of a rebellious Margaret Postgate Cole's progress—"Courtship and marriage have increased her womanliness and self-restraint" (4 November 1918)—is indicative.[37]

Webb's valuation of Cole also implies the diarists' expressed sense of appropriate female behavior in the eighteenth and nineteenth centuries. (The few seventeenth-century diarists do not address the subject explicitly, and most Edwardians still subscribe to the same code.) A woman should be unassertive, complaisant, ladylike. Thus Faith Gray is perturbed to see in her daughter "a too great independency of spirit," and regrets "the absence of that kind and affectionate manner which renders the female character peculiarly engaging" (15 January 1813). Even so, Mary Bagot admires a Mrs. Somerville because her talents and knowledge "are all veiled under the most feminine, natural, and conciliatory manners" (July 1823). Fox enjoys Clara Balfour's talks not only for their sentiments but also because "even in the perilous act of lecturing the lady did not unsex herself" (25 October 1849). Lucy Cavendish decides that she approves of Newnham College for women because "the tone of the girls [is] feminine and unaffected" (18 March 1877), and it upsets Louisa Bain to watch a woman skate in a manner that is "not lady-like," and "hardly decorous" (3 January 1871). A hundred years earlier, Mary Hamilton is affronted that the duchess of Devonshire should canvass the Strand for Mr. Fox: "What a pity that any of our sex should ever forget what is due to female delicacy" (27 April 1784)[38]—precisely the objection that would later be directed at the aggressive Edwardian suffragists. The notion of appropriately refined female behavior has been durable among women, who have even supervised one another's performance for conformity.

For women of achievement and learning, the eighteenth- and nineteenth-century diarists show admiration, yet not without direct and indirect evidence of some ambivalence until the later nineteenth century. By then, well-educated women had become more usual, even if major advances awaited the last quarter of the century.[39] Hamilton is worried in 1784 about a highly educated young Miss Boyle, not only because men will "shun" her for showing that females can be as smart as males (and Hamilton believes they can be) but also because "though I think Miss B: will reap many advantages from having received so very superior an education, I fear it will prevent her enjoying the innocent pleasure of Society, for every other female will not only envy but be *afraid* of her" (10 July). Learned women, especially before the latter part of the nineteenth century, make the less intellectual diarists uneasy, even when those learned women have the acceptably feminine manner. At an extreme, educated women may make them as defensive as Margaret Jeune, bearing out Hamilton's suspicions a hundred years later. Jeune cuts down to a size she can handle "Madame Blaise de Bury, said to be the cleverest woman in Europe. She seems to have intimate relations with the Court of Austria for whose Policy she writes. She is brilliant (very much dressed) but vulgar and swallows any amount of flattery. . . . We remarked the exceedingly small quantity of sleeve she wore" (11 June 1861). Another possible response is simply to doubt female intellect. Thus Mary Frampton is offended by what she construes to be women's pretensions: "This is an age when every woman talks on every subject, and the prettier and younger they are, so much the more foolishly do they talk, or at least, so much the more are they listened to, on subjects far beyond their comprehension" (23 February 1832). Frampton actually is not so different from male-identified Mary Gladstone describing (ironically) "a wonderful argument . . . between A[rthur] B[alfour] and Mildred [Hope] on the difference between prejudice and bias. She argues well for a woman . . . but the clearness of understanding, the precision of language, and rapidity of thought were most striking on his side" (8 July 1871).[40]

Against female authors, the diarists have no animadversion. Female authors, largely ostracized earlier, had gained some respectability during the eighteenth century as their numbers and those of their female readers increased. Still, if all the diarists accept the idea of female authors, not all the diarists during the mid-Victorian era have an ideal sense of female authorship. Charlotte Guest may find *Jane Eyre* a "singular novel" and a "striking book," but she is "glad no unmarried daughter of mine wrote it" (28 December 1850). Elizabeth Eastlake, herself an author of belles lettres, has the distinction among the diarists of having published an article in the December 1848 *Quarterly Review* (*"Vanity Fair—Jane Eyre*—and Governesses") in which she proves that *Jane Eyre* was written by a man. But then, six years earlier she writes in her diary, "How little the female writers of the present day seem aware of their great responsibility: eager to show what they can do like men, they disregard the fact that they are capable of much more as women" (23 December 1842)—an objection not to women's being writers, but to their choice of unladylike subject matter. (George Eliot also reports on two women who are "*sure*" and "confident" that *Scenes of Clerical life* was written by a man [28 February 1858].)[41]

Women may write—but they *should* marry. With few exceptions, the diarists see marriage as the bright goal of life, "the greatest happiness of a woman's life," as Webb conventionally puts it (15 March 1886), echoed by Beatrix Potter: "A happy marriage is the crown of a woman's life" ([June] 1894). It is the nineteenth-century diarists who most often explicitly identify wife and mother as epitome roles, doubtless because of the entrenchment of separate-sphere ideology. In 1848, for example, Louisa de Rothschild is certain that it is "far better for women to occupy themselves more exclusively with their own family and for men to go and work abroad." As late as 1881, Cavendish is skeptical about any other arrangement: a Mrs. Palmer "is the head of the new Cancer Hospital. . . . How this goes with married life I know not!" (30 July). The implied threat to marriage as a career caused by gradual expansion of white-collar opportunities during the latter half of the century encouraged defending the system. The ethos, however, is certainly much older, so that when Mary Cowper, who dislikes gambling, "told my Mistress [Princess Caroline] . . . having four Children, Nobody would think ill of me if for their Sakes I desired to save my Money . . . she commended me, and said she thought the principal Duty of a woman was to take care of her Children" (15 November 1714). Most of the diarists, moreover, at least as a precept, assume devotion to one's marriage, whatever the hardship. "She conducts herself like an angel as the French would say," opines Clarissa Trant of a misalliance, "but in other words as an English Wife with a religious and well regulated mind ought to do" (27 May 1829).[42]

With marriage the accepted goal for respectable females and viable careers closed to them until well into the nineteenth century, spinsterhood is not only socially reprehensible; it seems a dreadful fate. "It is a great pity," says Elizabeth Wynne unequivocally of her maiden aunts, "they did not make a better use of their charms and refused the many good offers they had in England to lead a single & miserable Life in Italy" (2 February 1806). Seeing a procession of novices at St. Peter's in Rome, Trant is hopeful that, as two of the youthful ones "were both extremely pretty it is not impossible that they may change their minds" (11 December 1825). The diarists are as prejudiced as pitying, however. Thus, when Eastlake reads *Madam de Maintenon,* she "can't fancy the old maid [not just woman] of fifty-two attractive" (3 July 1845), and Jeune bewails the boredom of company made up of "fat old couples and spare old maids" (17 September 1859). That prejudice, moreover, extends into the twentieth century, when Cynthia Asquith is repelled by the "somewhat oppressive" atmosphere generated by all-woman households (16 August 1916), and Woolf dislikes the "dulness & flatness which generally exist in these self effacing unselfish old maids" (3 September 1918).[43]

The unwed eighteenth- and nineteenth-century diarists are ordinarily eager to escape spinsterhood, not just to flee from want but also to honor a sense of self shaped by a male-dominated culture. Of course the unwed woman was sorely disadvantaged once she could no longer be absorbed into the work of the family at her appropriate social level, as occurred when family industry declined because of the industrial-agricultural revolution. There was little enough a lower middle-class female could do to support herself honorably but marry.[44] However, because almost all these diarists are more prosperous women, they highlight another configuration: the psychospiritual need to marry when living in a patriarchy. Writer Mary Berry provides a good illustration because her broken engagement to General O'Hara so discolored her life. He left her because she refused to follow him to Gibraltar immediately upon marriage in order not to distress elderly Horace Walpole, whose protégée she was. Eleven years later she still laments the "fair prospects" lost, "Alas!" (21 August 1807), and perpetually she speaks of her life—despite her successful career as a writer and salon figure—as a failure. Prime minister's daughter Mary Gladstone, who married only at thirty-eight, may not repine at her singleness later in the century. But she betrays her yearnings nonetheless by noting a place that would be "nice" for a "honeymoon," a churchman's letters that make her feel she "shd. rather like to have married him," and, most revealing, "Today is the wedding-day of my last unmarried friend" (18–19 September 1879, 5–18 December 1881, 18 January 1883). It is painful to identify oneself with the unchosen; spinster (Rigby) Eastlake therefore does not do so. Instead, at thirty-seven, she looks to God for help for *other* unmarrieds, proposing that in a "state of society where many women must necessarily remain single," they "should make an offering of their singleness to God, instead of keeping it only because they have no opportunity of getting rid of it" (5 January 1846).[45] Men actually were in short supply at the time: the 1851 census revealed 405,000 more women than men in England. Accordingly, there were those who advised surplus women to emigrate.[46] But Eastlake is not planning any desperate course of action for herself, only venting frustration. Three years later she will marry. Most illuminating, however, concerning repugnance for spinsterhood is Beatrice (Potter) Webb.

A spinster *malgré elle* because she has felt she must refuse autocratic suitor Joseph Chamberlain, Webb has a successful career but is not consoled by an article on spinsters in *Macmillan's* for 1888 that describes "'a new race of women not looking for or expecting marriage.' 'Self-dependent, courageous, and cool-headed.' Ah, poor things" (3 September).[47] Historians have noted some change in attitude toward spinsterhood in the period 1870 to 1920, when the "New Woman" made her increasing appearance to meet the burgeoning demand for white-collar workers. They point to enhanced self-confidence and conviction that single life has advantages over married life, and to greater feasibility, in terms of transportation and housing, of carrying out the conscious decision not to marry.[48] However, even if the "revolt" of the spinsters may have earned the blessing of *Macmillan's* and become a feminist plank for some women, it plays no explicit part in these diaries, though probably it is implicit in the histories of some of the unmarried Great War diarists and may be pertinent to the two anonymous spinster diarists. It carries no weight with Webb, even if, in the spirit of the times, she tries dreadfully hard to accept spinsterhood.

In 1886 Webb debates unmarried life with friend Frederick Harrison, he "taking the extreme contrast view that marriage was absolutely essential to the development of character. . . . I maintaining that if unmarried women kept their feelings alive, did not choke them with routine idleness, practical work, or with intellectualism, though they must suffer pain, they were often for that very reason more sympathetic than married women" (24 May). In 1887, she counts her blessings: "I have liberty to follow [my interests] as far as the tether of faculty and strength will allow me. Surely this is a great privilege, more than the ordinary lot of unmarried womanhood?" Clearly, however, her blessings are not enough, for she continues, "God give me strength!" (25 December 1887).[49] Social conditioning makes marriage seem crucial to self-respect and happiness (though Eleanor Butler and her beloved Sarah Ponsonby provide notable exceptions to the rule). Although the diarists will not necessarily accept marriage at any cost, as Webb's and Berry's behavior suggests, they also ordinarily cannot see life as fulfilled without it. Their behavior during marriage is equally instructive of their internalized values, but the large subject of marriage is reserved for more detailed discussion in the next chapter.

Women's concern with appearance is worth considering here instead, for it is a topic that permeates these diaries, in some occupying inordinate space. After Eastlake, for example, has attended Mme. Alboni's concert, she writes, "Her appearance engrossed me as much as her voice" (31 August 1848); indeed, Eastlake gives only one sentence of a long passage of description to that voice.[50] Yet she is less appearance conscious than some other women. Very few diaries do not reveal a concern of some sort either with beauty of face and body or with dress and fashion or with both, although far less appears in the few seventeenth-century diaries than afterwards. A sure sign of the diarists' acculturation, their concern issues finally from a commitment to the conception of woman as sex object. The diarists rarely forget that beauty is an attractant in the mating game; they regularly reckon females in terms of their allure. So, for instance, having met Mrs. Bingham, Elizabeth Wynne "really was struck with her ugliness, and cannot imagine how any man could marry her" (25 July 1807); and to Lucy Cavendish, Mary Gladstone is "still so handsome it's wonderful she is an old maid," while Millicent Fawcett's "pretty fresh face [is] rather a waste for a blind man!" (28 October 1880, 10 May 1867). Woolf in a perceptive moment asks an easily answered question about Miss Matthaie, who has applied for work with Hogarth Press: "Why should a woman of her sense apologise all her life long because she is an unattractive woman? She looks up sidelong, like a child who has done wrong. And yet she has more in her head than all the cropheads put together" (7 December 1918).[51] The diarists know that, pragmatically, looks matter more than brains. Good looks earn male and female regard and therefore encourage self-esteem. (Looks of any sort earn female notice because women keep track of the competition for self-reassurance.)

Besides inherent beauty, comprising youth as well as pulchritude, dress enhances the female object. As Simone de Beauvoir says, woman is "required by society to make herself an erotic object. The purpose of the fashions to which she is enslaved is . . . to offer her as prey to male desires."[52] Though the concern with appearance may become divorced from its initial inspiration in woman as sex object, may become (so far as a woman knows) a fascination in its own right or a device for recording status, as the interest in dress regularly becomes, nonetheless concern with appearance is not trained into women for its own sake. In being extremely concerned with appearance, the diarists both reveal and reinforce the bars of their patriarchal prison. Beauty may be power, but reliance on it, as critic Patricia Meyer Spacks has pointed out, is dependency, for "beauty has value only by controlling others' perceptions."[53] These diarists yield themselves to that dependency.

Although some few diarists rarely remark a woman's appearance, more typically the diarists do so often. It seems to be almost an automatic reflex to evaluate a woman's looks. Reporting the sights in her travels, for example, Claire Clairmont includes "the only beautiful girl we have seen since we parted from Paris" (4 September 1814). Or when Quaker Caroline Fox has visited Coldbath Fields Prison for Women, she has "met the Duchess of Saxe-Weimar . . . , her two pretty daughters, and Lady Denbigh. The survey of the prison was exceedingly interesting" (11 June 1842). Appearance usually precedes other attributes. To Margaret Jeune, thus, "Mrs. Mansell is neither young nor pretty, but pleasing in manner," and Lady Barrington "is a blonde, not precisely handsome, not quite young, but most pleasing in countenance and manner" (19 October 1855, 19 June 1860). The 'pleasing manner' is but a secondary matter. Young Florence Sitwell observes the same sort of sequence describing her cousins Edith and Aggie—"both very plain (*I* think) but remarkably nice girls"—and a Mademoiselle Eugenie: "She is very plain, but has such a sweet expression" (29 June 1875, 4 June 1876). So too Harriet Wynne, much earlier in the century, can see that "both the Duchess and Lady Euston's daughters are ugly, but very good humoured" (16 August 1805). Even Woolf does not escape the pattern, despite her sometime contempt for looks as a criterion. Miss Matthaie, when Woolf first meets her, is "a lanky gawky unattractive woman" and ill dressed, too, though with a "quick mind" (9 April 1918).[54]

When the diarists write about a couple, they almost always see only the woman's looks. Thus, for example, Caroline Powys: "Major and Mrs. Plunket there. . . . an extremely plain woman" (6 February 1804). And Mary Berry: "Mr. and Mrs. Wilmot dined . . . ; she is a very pretty woman" (25 September 1810). And Harriet Grove: "Mr. & Mrs. J. Bastard & Mr. Snow dined here. I think Mrs. J:B: rather pretty" (3 December 1810). And Louisa Bain: "Mr. and Mrs. Frederick Macmillan came. . . . She is small, pretty and pleasant" (21 September 1878). Although the diarists do not entirely ignore male appearance, what they see is customarily attire and sometimes size, about which they are summary rather than detailed. Emily Shore's description of coach passengers can illustrate: "We took up a lady in green silk, who presently doffed her gloves in order to display a finger quite manacled with gaudy rings. She was a tall woman, with a brown face and large features. . . . A gentleman of great size . . . came inside for one stage" (3 September 1836). Even male attire they are likely to scant, as does, for example, Lady Elizabeth Northumberland, who takes a long paragraph to describe Queen Charlotte's wedding garb but needs only a sentence for George III (8 September 1761).[55]

Accepting the flesh market as a given of life, the eighteenth-century to twentieth-century diarists know that good looks are the way to success. As Frances Shelley succinctly explains, "In regard to the beauty of women, it is better to be a 'has been,' than a 'never was.'" Since she reasons by the logic her culture teaches, "Lady Catherine is young, and beautiful, she is consequently much admired" (10 December 1816, 8 July 1819). "A hideous woman is such a mistake," opines Elizabeth Eastlake (20 May 1846), and Webb agrees: "personal charm" is "the most precious gift of womanhood"

(14 September 1888). So too in Cynthia Asquith's estimate, Adele Essex's "legs are poems and, if I had such knees and feet, I feel I should be safe from all the 'slings and arrows of outrageous fortune.' They would be an unfailing source of consolation" (22 August 1915). Without looks, the diarists assume there will be no romances. Lady Northumberland accordingly discounts gossip about Voltaire and Mme. Denis, "for she is very short & fat & her Complexion & features exactly like [M.P.] Simon Fanshaw's" (13 May 1772). And Asquith speculates about the women among whom she does volunteer work, because "the women workers are not attractive. One wonders what on earth they do when there is no war" (6 November 1916).[56]

At social events, the women are critical appraisers of looks. But not only balls and dinners excite their observational skills. When Cavendish and a friend attend the opening of Parliament, they amuse themselves "greatly with finding out the few beauties among the fat and wizzy peeresses opposite" (7 June 1859). About the looks of others, the diarists can be candid indeed, like Lady Northumberland at a reception, where "Madame Sister to the Dauphin is as round as a Ball. I dare say her Circumference considerably exceeds her height. . . . Her Aunt Mme. Sophie is as remarkably lean & Horridly ugly" (16 May 1770). And Edith Lytton attends a dinner at which the Princess of Wales "looked lovely . . . she is so wise to put even a little help to give her a good colour" (12 October 1896). As a subject they know well and like to study, female looks fascinate the diarists. Lady Monkswell betrays as much when, though she enjoys being the only female present, she objects to attending a "'man-dinner' . . . to my mind its faults are obvious—too many clever men & no pretty women to look at" (6 May 1904). Any masculinity of look or manner catches the diarists' eyes, possibly because it is a reassuring reminder of their own more feminine appearances, and certainly because they assume the sexes should be distinct and different. Thus, for example, Clarissa Trant must comment of a Lady Hippesley: "Elle est une espèce d'homme manqué—une femme grenadière—versed in horseflesh and agriculture and more inclined to sit with the gentlemen than to retire with the ladies" (17 October 1832). And Lady Monkswell can see that Lady Selborne "looks *like a man*, & probably has a man's mind like her clever mother" (13 April 1907).[57]

Before real beauty, the diarists have a certain reverence—and the urge to find a flaw. To illustrate, Asquith—herself a beauty painted by McEvoy, Sargent, and Augustus John—reports on Mary Curzon, who "certainly is the perfect fairy princess, exactly like the conventional description of them—gold hair, deep blue eyes, jetty fringe, peach complexion. It may not be a very ambitious or imaginative type of beauty, but it is perfection in so far that it absolutely achieves what it attempts" (10 July 1915). Likewise, Lucy Cavendish describes Mrs. Preston: "*The* most fascinating beauty I have ever seen: shady deep eyes, all expression and grace; and such a lovely classical mouth; figure and manners most winning and refined. All this in spite of a strange impediment in her speech" (2 October 1858). And Shore comments on an unknown woman: "I never saw a beauty that could be compared to her. She is exquisite, perfectly beautiful; her features are all but faultless, the only defect being that her nose (though very well shaped) is a little too large" (25 July 1836). Beautiful women, observes Lady Monkswell, "certainly are a different race to common mortals. Whatever they do is right, they are not judged like other people" (2 January 1890)[58]—which may be why there is a nagging desire to reduce them to size.

If beauty fascinates the diarists, so does dress (fashion) and like looks forms part of their automatic response system. Any woman a diarist has met or seen is as likely to be ranked on her dress as on her pulchritude, or on both at once. Fashion for shallower women may even become a yardstick for merit, as with Jeune, who accordingly finds Mrs. Gladstone acceptable: "I don't think her manners are particularly pleasing, but she is a fine fashionable looking woman" (28 January 1853). The diarists' concern with dress—others' and their own—is almost inevitable. Dress is a social symbol. Therefore, as Beauvoir has remarked, fashion consciousness may be an index to conformity: The "social significance of the toilette allows woman to express, by her way of dressing, her attitude toward society. If she is submissive to the established order, she will assume a . . . stylish personality."[59] The many diarists who are conscious of fashion do not question its dictates; they aim only to keep up. That dress modes can be destructive to women's health and constrict their movements is an awareness which, except for a small handful of diarists—so few that they can be reviewed in a paragraph—women do not yet have. Only Mary Frampton protests against high heels, in the course of explaining their provenance: the marriage of the duke of York to Princess Frederica of Prussia, who had "a remarkably small foot."

> Consequently, it became the fashion for everyone to squeeze their feet without mercy, in order to be like her Royal Highness, and as she wore heels to her shoes, so did the rest of the world. I was very short, and of course wore high heels, raising my heels from the ground about two inches. The position, I think, made the ankle thinner and neater than the flat sole which after some years succeeded, but the high heel is perfectly unnatural, and gives a bad movement in walking. (1791)

Likewise, Shore scorns "the horrible (for it is no less) effect of tight-lacing, and want of exercise. The whole body is diseased, and every function depraved by this fatal practice" (26 February 1833). No other diarists criticize the burdens of high heels or corsets, though Beatrix Potter (probably in a burst of irritation at her secluded existence in her parents' home) does acknowledge the burden of fashion in her ambivalent yearning for it: "How is it these high-heeled ladies who dine out, paint and pinch their waists to deformity, can racket about all day long, while I who sleep o'nights, can turn in my stays, and dislike sweets and dinners, am so tired towards the end of the afternoon that I can scarcely keep my feet? It is very hard and strange, I wonder if it will always be so?" (6 May 1885). (Some ten years later, however, when new pastimes have become allowable for ladies, she sanely favors the freedom of movement possible in knickerbockers for cycling and gymnastics [31 August 1894].) Even if not alert to the disadvantages of high heels and stays, Hester Thrale a hundred years earlier expresses herself on a related matter when observing that Miss Sophia Pitches "died of a Disorder common enough to young Women[,] the Desire of Beauty; She had I fancy taken Quack Med'cines to prevent growing fat"—personally, Thrale condemns such "vile purposes" (July 1779). Caroline Powys (but only in old age) fears that the young women at Bath are destroying their health by thin clothing and late hours (28 January 1805).[60] For the rest, the diarists object only to the aesthetics of particular fashions, or their

124

indecency (almost invariably in France), not to the necessity for fashion.

Instead, whatever the century, fashion intrigues them. At important events, they regularly scrutinize who is wearing what, often down to the smallest particulars. Lady Monkswell shines at such reporting (see, for example, 22 June 1896), possibly because, as historian Leonore Davidoff has pointed out, in Victorian society every nuance of dress to the smallest furbelow symbolized a status category so that "girls and women of all classes were preoccupied with dress."[61] But the preoccupation has both wider causes and a longer history. The diarists also note their own garb for special events and the outfits they deem especially fine; Anne Clifford, for example, who "sayed [essayed?] on my sea water green satin gown and my damask embroidered with gold, both which gowns the Tailor . . . from *London* made fit for me to wear . . . W. open ruffs after the French fashion" (13 June 1617). They also keep track of what is officially or unofficially a la mode, like Caroline Powys, who notes the precise colors and trimmings allowed during the mourning for George III's mother (8 February 1772); or Mary Hamilton, who finds that "in ye Spring it is *allowable* to go to Assemblies in a Hat; indeed ye *Balloon* hat has been much worn all Winter" (20 May 1784); or Thrale, who notices how "the women wear seven Handkerchiefs at a Time now[:] one upon the Head[,] one upon the Hat, one round the Throat[,] one upon the Neck, one loosely thrown over the Shoulders & one in the Pocket" (25 January 1794). Space precludes illustrating all the other new fashions reported. Interestingly, Eleanor Butler may have chosen to flout convention by eloping with Sarah Ponsonby to a cottage in Wales, but she remains extremely particular about her garb, regularly returning garments to her tailor as ill-made. Nor does any woman who comes to her door escape careful scrutiny; for example, as when she "saw two Ladies (one in a black capotte, the other, in white muslin short dress, Each with large straw bonnet) coming up the lane" (28 July 1788). Even statuary does not go unnoticed by the diarists. The duchess of Suffolk, as depicted on her tomb, Powys timelessly observes, wears a ring "very like an old one I have of Lady Twysden's, and much resembles some I've latterly seen made this year 1789, so generally do fashions come round in a course of years" (9 July 1789).[62]

The women are so fashion conscious because dress is a dreadfully serious business for them. It is their allowable, expected profession, through which they not only endeavor to enhance their looks and reaffirm their social being, but also exercise their aesthetic sensibilities and their individuality. As Beauvoir points out, "By means of [dress] the woman who is deprived of *doing* anything feels that she expresses what she *is.*"[63] In a life of limited opportunities for individual self-expression, dress can take on heightened importance, become a little world of its own that may have nothing to do immediately with men or status. Nancy Woodforde, a provincial spinster keeping house for her bachelor uncle, a parson at Weston-Longville in Norfolk, as she did from her eighteenth year, shows how the socially sanctified little world of dress may become both an outlet for energies and a mode of social intercourse among women, a form of women's culture.

Nancy is thirty-five and chronically lame and stout in 1792, the only year for which an expanded diary of hers survives; she is thus no longer in the marriage market. But her diary shows her to be a keen observer and imitator of what other women are wearing. If, for example, Lady Bacon "was dress[ed] in a Dark Chintz Gown and a Muslin Petticoat, a very smart Bonnet," then, too, "I have made myself one very like it" (19 March). Woodforde's diary entries, moreover, form a scenario showing commerce in fashion become social activity and link among women:

> Mrs. Bodham lent me a Tucker and Ruff all in one by which I intend to make myself one like it. (20 June)
>
> Very busy all Day making a Tucker like Mrs. Bodhams which I accomplished. (21 June)
>
> I shewed her [Mrs. Custance] my new Bonnet with which she was so much pleased that she begged me to send to my Milliner for one exactly like it only . . . all White. (7 August)[64]

Dress, which registers in the eyes of a beholder, is also a means of validating one's importance or invalidating another's. Thus, Lady Elizabeth Northumberland finds it odd the ladies of Antwerp should be so elegantly and expensively adorned if "there is nobody to see them" (9 June 1771). Turned into an adorable object by society, a woman seeks, through securing envious or admiring approval of her dress, says Beauvoir, "to gain an absolute affirmation of her beauty, her elegance, her taste—herself." Therefore, for these diarists the wrong clothes become an ordeal. Even Woolf, however liberated a woman in some respects, suffers agonies over the problem of her clothes for public appearances. Being awarded the Femina Prize is a trial, for "afterwards there was the horror of having looked ugly in cheap black clothes. I cannot control this complex." For years she has known that she has "my clothes complex to deal with. When I am asked out my first thought is, but I have no clothes to go in. . . . there is the eternal, & insoluble question of clothes" (4 May 1928, 9 May 1926, 10 December 1918).[65] Entries on her clothes problem are characteristic enough to be indexed in her published diaries.

The validation by an important male is especially valuable to self-esteem. As unmodish a woman as Jane Carlyle must have a new dress to impress a former admirer: "I had been fretting over the need of a *new dress* for the Bath House affair; but now I went after it with alacrity. George [Rennies] should see that the smart girl of his Province wasn't become a *dowdy* among London women of 'a certain age'" (28 April 1856). Husbands constitute very important males. Clifford does not dress during her husband's absence. "All this time since my Lord went away," she writes, to emphasize her isolation, "I wore my black taffety night gown [i.e., afternoon and evening garb] and a yellow taffety waistcoat" (20 November 1616). Likewise, Nancy Woodforde's houseguest, Mrs. Jeans, affronts her because upon Mr. Jeans's arrival she "dress'd herself in a White Gown and Coat for the first time since she has been here, having appeared in nothing but a shabby coloured Gown . . . before." As Mrs. Jeans's attire signifies that the Woodfordes' sense of her does not count, though her husband's does, Nancy knows how to deal with Mrs. Jeans: "I was even with her in that respect for did not dress in anything smart during her stay with us" (4 November). Women are sensitive to the protocols of dress, with their implications of respect due. Annie Lumb, another middle-class diarist, records a comparable but earlier eighteenth-century social drama:

Mrs. Milnes, Mrs. Hawood, her son, Miss Bett Milnes, Miss Slater, Mr. Robert and his lady, with sister Sally, drank tea here. There visitt was intended to sister H., but her parlor was fresh painted, so I was obliged to entertain them in our hall. They was all much undressed, although Mrs. Robert made the visitt in return for one we paid her as a bride the first day she saw company, and dressed in our best damasks, so that it was very rude in her to come in that manner, undressed, and not sending us a word. (20 May 1757) [66]

Diarists are also affronted if their own dress does not properly register. For some nineteenth-century examples, when Beatrix Potter has asked at Kew Station for the ladies' waiting room, a young woman directs her, "who came a step after me to add that I would not have to pay anything. It is a great shame of railways to charge, but it made me wonder if I was wanting new clothes" (3 December 1896). Ironical though she may be, Potter is almost as insulted as Lady Monkswell, who wonders when she visits in Utah "what I have done that, dressed in a black gown made by Miss Winter, I should be taken for a Mormon immigrant??" (24 September 1881).[67] Having been taught to believe that appearance matters, the diarists expect their own displays to carry some weight.

The diarists' concern with appearance and dress is significant because it entrenches the women in a way of life women have always known. But these women are not eager for change. They are no more conservative in their regard for appearance than in their attitude to feminist sociopolitical change. The nineteenth-century diarists are inclined to be wary of or even hostile to such change—if they remark it at all. Historian Olive Banks justly says that "women as a whole have not been enthusiastic feminists."[68]

When Wollstonecraft at the end of the eighteenth century argued the need and right of women to become enfranchised socially, morally, even civically, she did not attract numerous followers. The history of women, as Cynthia Pomerleau remarks, "has always been retrogressive"; in women's autobiography in the years soon after Wollstonecraft, repudiating her became a public way of declaring the writer's respectability, partly because of Wollstonecraft's unconventional sexual life, partly because of her ideas. In the privacy of their diaries, women keep the peace as well. Even though Wollstonecraft's daughter, Mary Shelley, like her half-sister Claire Clairmont, reports reading her mother's writings, she finds she cannot quite commit herself to "'the good cause'—the cause of the advancement of freedom and knowledge, of the right of woman, &c." because

> I do not feel that I could say aught to support the cause efficiently; besides that, on some topics (especially with regard to my own sex), I am far from making up my mind. I believe we are sent here to educate ourselves, and that self-denial, and disappointment, and self-control, are part of our education; that it is not by taking away all restraining law that our improvement is to be achieved; and, though many things need great amendment, I can by no means go so far as my friends would have me. (21 October 1838) [69]

It might have been otherwise had Wollstonecraft survived Mary's birth.

Like Shelley, albeit less articulate, Elizabeth Eastlake some fifteen years later would also conserve the status quo as somehow more right for women:

> If woman, in addition to all the charms and graces she has had hitherto, is to have a depth and solidity she never had before, she must remove to another planet to show it in. Those advisers are all dangerous who try to make women seek for something which they have not yet possessed—for something, consequently, out of which they have been kept. Let us be satisfied, that what a woman does not attempt to gain she is not qualified to use. (3 February 1846) [70]

As nearly as one can tell, Eastlake may want to argue for a change in woman's status and treatment; meanwhile, she is dubious about woman's right to lay claim to any abilities (and changes contingent upon their acknowledgment) other than woman's accredited "charms and graces." It is not only "dangerous" to stir women up to attain "depth and solidity"; they have not proved that they really want such qualities anyway.

The movement for women's rights is not yet really underway when

Eastlake speaks, though by the mid-century decades, there clearly existed, in historian Jane Rendall's precise summary, "the cause of feminism, the explicit assertion of the individual autonomy of women, against their husbands, against the state and against prevailing stereotypes."[71] Nonetheless, even if the debates about extending the franchise for males in 1832 had stimulated isolated demands for emancipation of females from their sphere apart, it was only the decade from 1850 to 1860 that brought significant developments in group action. The cause that first brought together a group of active campaigners in 1855, reform of the married women's property laws, failed of its goals in 1857 (though successful in the 1870s and 1880s),[72] but was supplemented by a wide range of campaigns from the 1850s to the 1870s: the movement to achieve higher education and more occupational opportunities, the suffrage crusade, the campaign for repeal of the Contagious Diseases Acts (which permitted forcible detention and examination of prostitutes) and for an end to the operation of a double moral standard. After decades of ferment, however, forty years after Eastlake, women's ability to benefit from change still arouses female doubts, even if now the skepticism is expressed in different terms. In 1889, Webb has clearer but even less flattering reservations than Eastlake, as she reveals when she distrusts Maggie Hackness because "she is typical of the emancipated woman who has broken ties and struggled against the prejudice and oppression of bigoted and conventional relations to gain her freedom but who has never been disciplined by a public opinion which expects a woman to work with the masculine standard of honour and integrity" (14 November).[73]

Webb's personal revolt against the Victorian domestic ideal vies constantly with her male identification. She neither thinks of herself as a feminist nor—though one can trace progress in concern with women's condition and rights in her diary—in some respects is she ever one. Meanwhile, she was unusually liberated for her times and did pursue a career. What about the purely domestic woman of Webb's day and station? Lady Monkswell's ambivalent yet conservative feelings about women's rights are probably typical. Her abortive desire for that something missing from her life as the conventional wife of a successful lawyer and M.P. is coupled with passive acceptance of the circumstances that weakened such desire.

The occasion for a significant entry in Lady Monkswell's diary is her vicarious pleasure in the triumph of a Miss Fawcett, who has surpassed the Senior Wrangler in the Cambridge Mathematical Tripos. She undoubtedly was Philippa Fawcett, daughter of the feminist agitator Millicent Garrett (Fawcett) and Henry Fawcett, who encouraged his wife's activism (even if Lucy Cavendish thought the match a shame because Millicent's good looks were being wasted on a blind man). Philippa was the first Cambridge woman student to be placed above the Senior Wrangler in the Mathematical Tripos. The "memories" Lady Monkswell speaks of probably allude to studying art at the Slade before marrying:

> This success of Miss Fawcett's awakened old memories in me before I learnt that only the *one talent* had been committed to my charge, & my very unimportant business was to see that I did not hide it in a napkin. I used to care so very much for the "Women's Cause". Whether it is that the women who endeavour to lead it sicken me, or that my interests & joys are bound up in one man & three boys I do not know. Anyhow, like the Englishman in Ireland, I seem to have become more Irish than the Irish. The real reason why I have ceased to care for it is that I have lived surrounded by stronger characters than myself *who have not cared,* &, being reduced for so many years to less than half rations of health & strength, I have kept any small energy I might possess for more immediate use.

Proving herself indeed most Irish, she does not wind up with only a declaration of sisterhood—"Every woman feels 2 inches taller for this success of Miss Fawcett, aged 22." She also appends a defense of Fawcett's looks: "I heard from Mr. Evelyn Ashley that she is not attractive any way. [She] is *very* nice looking, with a white face & a profusion of red hair beautifully arranged" (13 June 1890).[74] Conditioning clings. However, Lady Monkswell at least is aware of the forces that severed her sympathies from the women's cause; not all the diarists' objections are held up to such scrutiny.

Active campaigning for the suffrage began in 1865 with the formation of a women's suffrage committee under the aegis of Barbara Leigh Smith (Bodichon), which undertook petitions to the House of Commons, and whose activities soon inspired similar groups. Yet women's suffrage found difficult passage among the mass of women, as the diarists reflect. Most of the Victorian diarists do not mention the suffrage at all. Cavendish does mention it, but only to damn it summarily: "The subject of female suffrage (odious and ridiculous notion as it is) is actually beginning to be spoken of without laughter, and as if it was an open question. I trust we are not coming to that" (15 January 1867). For her, the whole matter is too unladylike. That widespread Victorian attitude intensified after the formation of the militant Women's Social and Political Union in 1903. By 1905, suffrage agitators were creating disturbances not only offensive to Parliament but also repugnant to many women. Lady Monkswell is repelled by the "shocking sight" of militancy. Faced with the effrontery of a suffragist's interrupting a lecturer on (ironically) "Democracy" during a meeting in the House of Lords chaired by (another irony) the secretary of war, "I was indeed ashamed of my sex," she says, "& so were the other 300 or so women present." The protesters are only nuisances to her; she is uninterested in their plea for justice and relieved when the last one has been carried out, for "we then proceeded to business & settled down to listen to Professor Masterman" (surely the name is yet another irony) (22 May 1909).[75]

Even when the suffrage bill is finally passed, some major female figures damn it with faint praise. Webb, for example, initially opposed to extending the vote, along with 103 other women, signs the infamous "Appeal" against national suffrage for women, published in the *Nineteenth Century* in 1889. Soon, however, she decides the cause is valid; she can tolerate it, but she will not advocate it, and for tortuous reasons—"I have as yet accomplished no work which gives me a right to speak as representative of the class [it] would enfranchise: celibate women." Besides, she is reluctant about exposing women to politics when she has a "strong prejudice against political life and political methods" (29 June 1889). Finally, she acknowledges the extension of the vote to women in March 1918 tepidly at best. "I note with interest," she observes on 16 June, "that not once

132

in this diary have I mentioned . . . the passage of the Representation of the People Act," having been "wholly indifferent to my own political disenfranchisement." She is much more interested in what the extension of the franchise may do for the Labour party than for women. Woolf is equally casual about the vote, speaking in terms only of "another sedentary day, which must however be entered for the sake of recording that the Lords have passed the Suffrage Bill. I dont feel much more important—perhaps slightly so. Its like a knighthood; might be useful to impress people one despises." And a victory rally in March arouses her contempt, for "the pure essence of either sex is a little disheartening" (11 January and 9 March 1918).[76]

Yet Webb's and Woolf's disdain for the suffrage issue is deceptive. Webb is also reluctant to devote herself to female labor questions, being "not in the least interested," she declares, "in the relation of men's and women's wages" (18 December 1918). Yet (according to her editor Margaret Cole) she made out an excellent case for equal pay for women in the minority report she wrote for the government during the war. And Woolf sees the need for "the feminists who will drain off this black blood of bitterness which is poisoning us all" (17 February 1922). Both are concerned about women's issues and rights. Moreover, if they are fainthearted about the suffrage, some other diarists are not. Mary Gladstone, for example, otherwise a very conventional woman, anxiously discusses its possibilities with her father and worries whether prosuffrage women can make their cause prevail, for after having heard a debate, "I felt strongly what amateurs we were and how shallow seemed our arguments" (12 March and 29 May 1884). Thirty years later, Frances Stevenson, Lloyd George's secretary, queries him about its current chances (30 October 1914). Stevenson is not an activist and personally dislikes Lady Nancy Astor, but she is nonetheless proud in October 1918 to see the first woman M.P. take her place in the House, once the House, as a natural consequence of the extended suffrage, has passed a bill making women eligible for membership:

It really was a thrilling moment, not from the personal point of view, but from the fact that all these hundreds of years, this was the first time that a woman had set foot upon that floor to represent the

people—or a certain number of them. I had a lump in my throat as I
saw her come in. (1 December 1919).[77]

In the early days of the women's movement, Lady Kate Amberley
works hard for the acceptance of the Married Women's Property Bill
as well as the suffrage. Her understated diary is interesting as a record
of one Victorian woman's growth into activism. Daughter of Liberal
politician Lord Stanley of Alderley and, more important, a mother
(Henrietta Maria Stanley) who advocates education for women,
seventeen-year-old Kate Stanley nonetheless enjoys listening to the
chauvinistic talk of Thomas Carlyle, who often visits the family
home. Carlyle declares that woman "had better not meddle with
those things [like writing books] but be quiet with darning stockings," a sentiment which, she observes, is "a very different idea from
Mrs. Mill's in her Enfranchisement of Women." But Carlyle "talked
of her & said she was a silly woman." "I always like to listen to him,"
young Kate comments, "one always learns something" ([29 September 1859]). Nor does she indulge in irony here; it is not her style. By
1866, however, Lady Amberley is standing up in her heart to no less
than Benjamin Jowett of Oxford. When he advises "not going against
the world & doing as every one did, and he strongly urged it in every
thing that was not positively wrong, & said for instance a woman
shd. never have the character of an esprit fort," "I did so disagree
with him . . . —I may change but now feel a strong inclination to go
against the world" (20 January).[78]

In the seven-year interval between the two entries, two significant
events have occurred. She has married John Russell, Viscount Amberley (in 1864), who encourages her to activism, and she has met
the Mills—John Stuart, his wife, Harriet Taylor, and Taylor's daughter Helen—and been drawn into feminist circles. She can go on to
support her heart with her deeds. When Lucretia Mott and Elizabeth
Cady Stanton come to lecture in England, Kate is sufficiently impressed that, over her mother-in-law's protests, she later names her
daughter Rachel Lucretia after Mott. She also adopts Elizabeth Garrett (Anderson), the pioneer female physician, as family doctor. Active in circulating petitions for the Married Women's Property Bill,
Kate regrets that mourning for her father precludes her also accepting
the chair for the Committee on the Bill, for "Amberley wished me to

[accept] & I should not have minded" (1 November 1869). Instead, she goes on to campaign industriously for the vote. Her diary records not only the discouragements, but also the satisfactions for her, as when "nine women & one man came at 5 to hear me speak about Women's Suffrage. I spoke for an hour quite easily & fluently & all who came signed the petition" (20 January 1871). Although disinclined to argue the women's cause in her private writing, she pens an eloquent statement of 1860s feminist goals in a letter to a Mr. Crompton (3 January 1869), published with her diary.[79]

Diarists such as Lady Amberley reflect that Englishwomen's attitude to women's lot was not simply acquiescent. The other face of the coin shows that Englishwomen never had the mentality of willing slaves. Thus, though the diaries may reflect widespread acceptance of a male-dominated society, they also show conscious and unconscious defiance of that arrangement of power and its ramifications. The women are aware that female lives are constrained; and their deference before what is granted to be the superior power coexists with a not-so-deferential grumbling, outright complaining, undercutting, and manipulating of men, and even, under extreme duress or conviction, outright insubordination. While most of the diarists may scorn a more-or-less official women's cause, the diarists also insist on some personal rights. Lady Mary Monkswell is useful again, here commenting on Sir Richard Solomon and wife: "Solomon corrected her statements *in company* (this is not fair in a husband)" (15–17 May 1909).[80] She may not question his authority to correct his wife, but she cannot accept his tactlessness in shaming his wife publicly, for she also does not question woman's rights to have her dignity preserved. Plentiful diarists support her stand that women reserve some rights to themselves.

Male identification is not entire, and if the diarists accept male superiority they also compensate increasingly over the centuries by criticizing and minimizing males, so elevating the worth of women, at least indirectly. The simplest means suffice, like showing contempt for men's ways. Thus, for example, the sort of masculine image a man may pride himself on evokes Lady Northumberland's scorn:

Men that are fond of Horses generally prefer the Stable to good Company & occupied with the Conversation of Jockeys Coachmen Grooms

& postillions they contract in such Company a rude coarse manner of speaking which destroys that politeness so necessary in the Society of Ladys by which means they come to neglect them & often become swearers & Brutes[.] And the Ladys in return always reckon them to have little wit & much ignorance. (27 September 1771)

Clarissa Trant likewise mocks her manly new neighbor: "Oh what a specimen of a Co. Limerick foxhunter! What a melancholy attempt at being *irresistible!*" (12 September 1824).[81]

Male egotism is a frequent target of scorn. Jane Carlyle is contemptuous of how vulnerable it makes men to female manipulation: "When I was young and charming, men asked me about *myself*, and listened with interest real or pretended to whatever I pleased to tell them. Now they compensate to themselves for the want of charm in my company by using me as a listener to *their* egotism. A woman who will *accept* and exploit that role may still exercise an influence" (1 June 1856). (Carlyle, however, is also contemptuous of women who want that role.) Cynthia Asquith mocks the sexual egotism of males who, if one refuses their advances, always talk "as though the alternatives were between 'se donnering' to *him* and a nunnery. . . . They always . . . attribute a woman's refusal to love of abstract chastity, rather than to lack of love for them" (22 June 1918). Wrestling with the same problem, Frances Shelley earlier decides that Englishmen are singlemindedly intent on their own pleasure (2 April 1818); and Lady Holland even earlier concludes that they are hypocrites about it too (14 February 1794).[82]

As for the male intellect, her contemporary, Mary Hamilton, knows why men shun learned women: "The men in general are so jealous of our sex as being as wise as themselves" (10 July 1784). Woolf even more energetically slashes at the supposed objectivity of male scholarship, after having read "a stout life by Neale of Q. Elizabeth which pretending to impartiality emphasises the double chin & the wig of Mary at the critical moment: a fig for impartial and learned historians! All men are liars!" (14 February 1934).[83] An anonymous spinster forty years earlier probably would have agreed with her. That spinster's diary collects unequivocally antimale anecdotes and limericks. To illustrate, for their full flavor:

Talking of Mrs. Harrison . . . and her book *Colonel Enderby's Wife,*
Mrs. Meynell said that no woman could be so absolutely heartless as was
Mrs. Enderby—that therefore the character was unnatural. "Surely,"
she had asked Mrs. Harrison, "you did not take that from the life?"
"Well, yes, I did," was the reply; "but I drew it from a man." (11 July
1891)

Here lieth the mother of children five,
Two of them died and three are alive;
The two that died preferred rather
To go with their mother than stay with their father. ([1889])[84]

The arsenal holds yet other weapons. Diarists also undercut male
superiority by condescending to men as out of touch with reality and
helpless to manage in practical matters without them. Thus, for example, for Margaret Jeune, caring for her husband's library is "a
matter I generally contrive to effect in F's absence, as men always
seem to expect that the ugly process of cleaning must be done by
magic, and not by visible agency" (27 October 1848). Carlyle, in
turn, goes to tax court for her husband with a strong sense of his in-
eptitude and cowardice:

If Mr. C should go himself he would run his head against some post in
his impatience; and besides, for me, when it is over it will be over,
whereas he would not get the better of it for twelve months—if ever at
all. . . . Mr. C. said 'the voice of honour seemed to call on him to go
himself.' But either it did not call loud enough, or he would not listen
to that charmer. I went. (20 and 21 November 1855)

Lady Monkswell makes sure her presumably helpless husband dresses
right when he has to attend a public function in uniform "& could
not for the life of him remember whether he ought to take his white
sword or his black sword—so like a man not to know" (22 June
1896). Some diarists are rather proud of how well they manage their
men, not just their men's affairs or goods. When Lady Holland, for
example, travels to Europe with her first husband, she sees to it that
she stays abroad while he returns home: "My health did not allow me

to engage in travelling, and to say the truth I made as much as I could of that pretext. . . . In May Sir G. W. set off to England, as he affixed an importance to his own appearance there that I own I did not strive to convince him against" ([1795]).[85]

More significant, because direct, objections to the patriarchy lie in diarists' balking at the notion that they may be treated like slaves or beasts at male disposal. "Is a wife no better than a sheep or a horse?" asks Ellen Weeton (15 June 1825), bitter that animals are protected by laws acknowledging their value, while women are not. Frances Shelley, twenty-five years later, may be awed by the superiority of men as she listens to Samuel Romilly from the ventilator room of Parliament (women were not then permitted in the gallery), but their superiority does not, in her mind, entail the exploitation of women. She is very critical of a ducal friend who "was the slave of her boys. . . . I have seen her carrying their fishing-nets, their bats, balls, and stumps, apparently not perceiving how bad it was for them to regard a woman, far less their mother, as a simple drudge, fit only to minister to their pleasures" (14 September 1852). Actually, here Shelley echoes the advice given in Mrs. West's popular conduct manual that a mother must train her son to proper respect for women:

> Let him be taught (and he cannot imbibe this notion too early) that nature has designed him to be the protector and friend of women: and let every attempt to tyrannize over or insult the females of his family be *reprobated*. . . . If mothers would but consider themselves, as they really are, the guardians of the future generation of wives, the germ of domestic tyranny might be crushed in its bud.[86]

Thus did women persuade themselves that they were keeping some control over the conditions of their lives.

The diarists who have traveled to the United States, such as Lady Monkswell and young Beatrice (Potter) Webb, are offended by the male supremacism of the Salt Lake City Mormons. Lady Monkswell may soon declare herself antipathetic to the women's cause, but in Utah she cannot believe "that women should be such arrant fools as to marry a man on the understanding that he may discard them when he pleases & leave them unprovided for. I don't know what the women can be made of" (22 September 1881). Webb is struck by "particularly the dejected look of the women, as if they had continually on their mind their inferiority to their lords and masters" (1 November 1873). Cutting closer to the quick, Woolf is furious at the picture she gets of Jack Squire's marriage, where the despot rules by the power of the purse:

> I record Mary's telling me last night how she loved cigars but Jack refuses to let her smoke them—against his idea of what his wife should do— . . . or to let her dress in a dress cut low at the back. Cant go out with you in that frock. Go & put on another. Its indecent. . . . "I threw everything out of the window once" she said. "He treats us— Barbara & me—as if we were tame leopards—pets belonging to him". As indeed they do, since neither has a penny except of Jack's earning & giving. (11 February 1932) [87]

Occasionally diarists even move right to the heart of the matter of sexual politics by objecting to woman's status as body. Mansfield, in her Edwardian youth, when such ideas were circulating among feminists, rejects the "doctrine that love is the only thing in the world, taught, hammered into women, from generation to generation. . . . We must get rid of that bogey—and then, then comes the opportunity of happiness and freedom" (May 1908). Earlier, even Webb becomes annoyed that her good looks have smoothed her way—"Are all women 'nailed to their sex'?" (1 December 1890)—and earlier yet, Claire Clairmont, offered some verses by an admirer, "knocked them out of his hand and would not read them for I am tired of learning that I am charming." She also attacks the double standard, men's "usual nonsense about infidelity being unpardonable in women but very pardonable in men." So much more important to Clairmont is "the necessity of Women's being free that Man may walk, unencumbered by his fair clog, more freely towards a noble destiny" (8 January 1827). [88]

Knowing that they have little societal power, the eighteenth- and nineteenth-century diarists expect men to respect their situation and be their protectors, not their oppressors. Hester Thrale thus is indignant at how the theater managers abuse the "female Wits: the poor Girls are so easily brow beaten, & dare not tell how Mr. Such a one treated their Piece with Contempt . . . so then Mr. Such a one lays it by as worthless, & in a Year or two . . . brings out a Play of his own upon her Plot" (21[?] January 1780). Having been offended by Jefferson Hogg, Mary Shelley "cannot forgive any man that insults any woman. She cannot call him out, she disdains words of retort; she must endure, but it is never to be forgiven; not, indeed, cherished as a matter of enmity . . . but of caution to shield oneself from the like again" (12 February 1839). Shelley temporizes with an admonition to herself. Not so Weeton (Stock), who accepts her resentments unashamedly, uttering an early, impassioned, radically feminist outcry:

> If man injures man, the injured has a great portion of power to defend himself, either from natural strength of body, of [or?] resolution, of [or?] the countenance of many of his fellows, or from the laws; but when man injures woman, how can she defend herself? Her frame is weaker, her spirit timid; and if she be a wife, there is scarce a man anywhere to be found who will use the slightest exertion in her defence; and her own sex cannot, having no powers. She has no hope from law; for man, woman's enemy, exercises, as well as makes those laws. She cannot have a jury of her peers or equals, for men, every where prejudiced against the sex, are her jurors; man is her judge. . . . This is the lot not merely of a few, but of one half, if not two thirds of the sex! (8 June 1825)

The lower-middle-class Weeton rages with cause. Her husband, Aaron Stock, was a scoundrel who married Ellen for the pittance she had saved up as a governess and then abused her with insults, starvation, and beatings. When she left him after seven and a half years, he secluded their daughter, Mary, in a private school. The deed of separation he forced on Ellen (with the help of her brother Tom, who had engineered the marriage and got a bonus from his mother's will for it) allowed her to see Mary only three days a year in the presence of witnesses. Ellen defiantly persisted in seeing Mary clandestinely nonetheless. Not an activist, but become a spiritual feminist out of her ordeals, Weeton inveighs in her diary against the abuse of women through wife-beating and desertion, and, anticipating the Edwardian feminists, male-transmitted venereal disease (e.g., 8 and 15 June 1825).[89] Weeton's style of attack is rare in these diaries, however. Few other of the women are writing out of sustained, male-induced misery, nor do they generalize from their personal distress to the plight of women.

Nonetheless, the diarists do not express perfect contentment with the system. The constrained style of life deemed appropriate for ladies does arouse rebellious feelings.[90] Women want more freedom of movement and, in small ways, take it. Moved to Malaga for her health, Emily Shore marvels at how "no Portuguese lady is ever allowed . . . to walk anywhere by herself, whether she be married or unmarried, which I should think a very disagreeable restraint" (19 January 1839). Yet such restriction and its equivalent was increasingly the Victorian lady's fate. Young Lucy (Lyttleton) Cavendish is not permitted to waltz in 1859 or to view an opera in 1862 because it has a ballet attached (see 21 June 1859, 10 May 1862). In 1877 Florence Sitwell, age nineteen, goes walking and driving only if attended by a maid (27 March). Cavendish designates her sister Lou's daring to drive her fiancé to the station unchaperoned "a very improper proceeding" (20 July 1865). But as Lou shows, females took pleasure in evading petty restrictions when they had a mind or a need to do so—Cavendish does so herself. And women did complain, at least privately. Sitwell describes such a complaint by a young woman who "seemed to think her greatest trouble was not being able to go about without an escort, which often prevents her doing things. 'I am just allowed to go as far as the bridge, by myself,' she said in a mournful voice" (27 March 1877).[91]

The social round expected of women becomes a sore spot. Although diarist after diarist records without complaint the rounds of tea drinking dear to the eighteenth century and the formal social calls that, especially during the nineteenth century, became an elaborate ritual for the prosperous, some diarists cavil at the frivolity and tediousness. "Mama took me to make visits, which I hate," protests Lucy Fitzgerald, for instance ([17??]). Mary Berry notes the satisfaction provided by a "sort of blue-stocking assembly, misses and their mamas without end, so pleased to carry them to a rational house, and unite pleasure and wisdom together" (8 February 1811). She herself occasionally rebels against the vapidity of purely social gatherings. Shore rejoices when a flu epidemic curtails afternoon rounds (24 January 1837), but evening parties are no better to her contemporary Elizabeth Barrett (Browning), who cannot endure "curling hair & dressing to meet a crowd of people whom I know nothing of, & care for less than I know" (30 December 1831). "Oh, how debasing is the existence of fine ladies" ([1860s]), pronounces young Constance de Rothschild, happiest herself when she has work to do; and Webb seconds her: "Ladies are so expressionless. . . . Could it be otherwise with the daily life of ladies in society? . . . How can intelligent women wish to marry into the set where this is the social regime?" (1 March 1883).[92]

Dissatisfied with a life-style for prosperous women that, in the eighteenth and most of the nineteenth centuries, channels female interests and energies narrowly into domesticity, society, and philanthropy, a few diarists want better education for females. Complaints about typical female education in the eighteenth century have their best spokesperson in Thrale, who not only sees how "exteriors are . . . dearly purchased by the utter darkness with regard to . . . 'daily Life' . . . that surrounds a Ladies Boarding School." Wiser yet, she also objects to the accepted purpose for educating a female, who is "heaped with Accomplishments which She ought to disdaine, when She reflects that her Mother only loads her with Allurements . . . to decoy & catch the unwary Traveller" (29 December 1780, 15 March 1784).[93] Thrale gave her own daughters a thoroughgoing education at home, more intense even than some of them preferred.

Occasionally a diarist betrays insecurity because of inadequate education: Lady Elizabeth Holland, for one, who "should be *bien autre chose* if I had been regularly taught. I never had any method in my pursuits, and I was always too greedy to follow a thing with any *suite.* Till lately I did not know the common principles of grammar, and still a boy of ten years old would outdo me" (14 November 1791). She insists that parents should train a child's mind, as hers did not. Seventy-five to one hundred years later, it is not just some sort of intellectual training for females that diarists want to see, but higher education with all that it implies about possible careers. Impressed by

Emily Davies's campaign to secure equal education for females, Lady Kate Amberley (whose mother had been a founder of Queens College) gives a founder's donation to the future Girton College for Women in 1873 (as does her mother) and a three-year woman's scholarship at Edinburgh (7 May and 14 August 1869). Another fifty years and Woolf is protesting the financial poverty of women's colleges like Girton (27 October 1928). Because the course of study at Girton and Newnham comes without the baccalaureate degree, Mary Gladstone supports women's agitation for degrees at Cambridge (16 and 20 April 1880), just as Great War diarist Vera Brittain would do for degrees at Oxford after the war.[94]

Even if Gladstone herself does not aspire to matriculate and does not contemplate any sort of career, she shows how Victorian women could feel the need for the kind of structure that a job may add to existence. Given some work to do for her father, she reports having "started my new life . . . ; felt I should like it very much, because of the definiteness supplying some little backbone to one's life" (6 February 1882). Berry even earlier also wants such structure, though she declares her yearnings in a letter rather than her diary. Both are spiritual ancestors to Brittain, furious when her father must be forced into letting her attend Oxford and treats her schooling as a mere whim. When, on the occasion of her brother's going to college, her father explains how important it is for his son to have a career, "I asked if it were not equally important that I should have a career too. He answered very decidedly 'No, Edward was the one who must be given an occupation & the means to provide for himself.' The secondary sex again! It makes me feel very angry that I, the more intellectual of the two, should be regarded in this light because I happen not to be a man" (8 October 1915).[95] The issue that Thrale identifies—undervaluation of the female mind—well outlived her day.

Diarists may carp and criticize, but such behavior is only a weak indicator of rebellious spirit. If women are not spineless expressions of the patriarchy, they should perform indicative and significant deeds, aside from joining a women's movement. Ellen Weeton, for example, refuses to stay with an abusive husband or away from a beloved child. Even so, in the seventeenth century, second diarist Anne Clifford defies not only the Crown but also her own husband—

defiance at close quarters is harder—for what she considers rightfully hers. Clifford refuses to give up the extensive estates that her father bequeathed to his brother, the next earl of Cumberland, even though they were already entailed upon her as an only child. When James I, seconded by her husband, wants Clifford to put the matter in his hands for adjudication, she reports proudly, "I beseech'd His Majesty to pardon me for that I would never part from *Westmoreland* while I lived upon any condition whatsoever." Nor did she. Her spendthrift first husband, Richard Sackville, earl of Dorset, had no better luck than the king. It was because she refused to renounce her rights to any part of the estate for a cash settlement that Dorset, "on a very grievous and sorrowful day," removed their infant daughter to break Clifford's spirit (18 January 1617, 9 May 1616).[96] But that worked no better than his isolating her in the country or depriving her of sex or quarreling constantly with her. He returned her child before the end of the year; and she persisted in her lawsuit until 1643, when the estate reverted to her on the death of Cumberland's sole heir. Thereafter, she ruled her vast domain with great skill. Clifford, however, was a noblewoman besides being a woman of indomitable will. More normative examples of defiance are the middle-class women who refused to marry just to escape spinsterhood.

Repugnance for spinsterhood takes on different shading when diarists are personally faced with the wrong man as potential spouse. Eighteenth-century aristocrat Eleanor Butler, who eloped with her beloved Sarah, wants no man. But Elizabeth Raper, her middle-class contemporary, is eager to marry though constantly disappointed in her expectations. Nonetheless, she is thankful when her parents trip her most likely and captivating prospect into admitting he is a fortune hunter. "I could have *loved* and *valued* him, but upon my soul . . . I am *off* without a *pang*," she exults (16 March 1761), and even if her sanguine reaction may be partly bravado, she does not repine afterwards. Early nineteenth-century Clarissa Trant provides an even better example. At twenty-three she has an express aversion to spinsterhood and prays glibly, "If I do live to be an old Maid let me not resemble any of the Bath Sisterhood," still quite confident that theirs will not be her fate. Four years later, however, she is much more uneasy, for "my maiden friends are dropping off one after another, and I shall soon be left like the 'Last Rose of Summer' to bloom alone" (31 December 1823, 14 July 1827). Yet, though copiously courted— at least twelve suitors are identified in her diary and others implied— Trant constantly rejects proposals and the intimacies that could encourage them. Not wealthy, sometimes even in financial difficulties because her widower father is only a retired army officer, she refuses to marry for security. She holds out for a spiritually compatible mate and finally marries her choice, a clergyman, at a dangerously late thirty-one.[97]

Later nineteenth-century Beatrice (Potter) Webb's repining at her spinsterhood may be sustained. Nonetheless, in 1884 she creates her situation when she rejects the advances of Joseph Chamberlain, the Radical politician who would later become prime minister, because she fears that this male supremacist will dominate her and trivialize her life. As she works it out in her diary,

> I shall be absorbed into the life of a man whose aims are not my aims; who will refuse me all freedom of thought . . . ; to whose career I shall have to subordinate all my life, mental and physical, without believing in the usefulness of this career. . . . I hate every form of despotism. . . . If I married him I should become a cynic as regards my own mental life. . . . I should become *par excellence* the mother and the woman of the world intent only on fulfilling my practical duties and gaining practical ends. (16 March)

Her reasons are excellent, but because Webb belatedly decides she wants him after all, wants him desperately, no other man can woo her. Consequently, she has also created years in which to lament her single state. Only in 1892, with Chamberlain long married, does she accept Sidney Webb's promise of a marriage that will be a working partnership. Most of the diarists want to marry, but they also reject marriage at any cost. "I may be lonely," as Beatrix Potter avows of her enclosed life in her parents' staid household, "but better that than an unhappy marriage" (7 September 1885).[98]

On the evidence of these women's diaries, English patriarchy was never entirely successful at indoctrinating women to accept inferior roles and restricted lives. However self-critical, the diarists also retain some sense of woman's instrinsic value and of her right to a personally acceptable life. Some are keenly aware that female lives, or their own lives, have been diminished by the roles and behaviors deemed appropriate. Yet typically the diarists do accommodate themselves to male intentions for them and even become male identified. Except for a few, they live out their lives without directly attacking the system; they find their satisfactions in it and even promulgate it. What is asked of women may put great pressure on their instincts, aptitudes, and individual preferences; yet although ultimately they may avail themselves of their diaries to counteract that strain by reasserting their individual importance, more immediately most of the diarists accept their lives in a male-dominated culture. Either they ignore any serious strain when they write or they do not see it as a strain at all.

FOUR

WOMEN'S WORLD
On Marriage and Motherhood

"AND THUS ENDS the most eventful year of my life—the year that has decided my fate for ever!" (31 December 1831), says Clarissa Trant of the year she married; "my fate in life is fixed" (3 February 1834), echoes newlywed Charlotte Guest understandably. Marriage and its attendant motherhood have traditionally structured female existence and determined its quality. Both these diarists speak from a period when women's sphere had become securely established, but diarists before and after the early nineteenth century share the same decisive sense of marriage. To read what they say about its stages, from courting through marriage and motherhood to widowhood, is to experience their most usual lives. It is also to discover that most of the diarists paint a flattering picture of female fate as marriage and motherhood. Before marriage, the diarists are eager to wed, "wondering whether I should ever be in the same happy position," as young Constance de Rothschild says of a bride (26 November 1858). Retrospectively they may be less sanguine. Some diarists betray a sense of bitter wisdom when they meet newlyweds. "One could only hope that the girl's light-heartedness may continue," reflects Margaret Jeune (5 April 1861). They "were so happy in each other's company that it made me both sad & envious," Lady Monkswell admits (18 November 1890).[1] Yet there is scarcely widespread repining. Though many of the diarists have observed the marital distress of others, and

147

some few are eloquent about their own, most declare the happiness they have experienced in marriage, or propose nothing to imply that they are discontent. Nor do they complain about the burden of motherhood. The women affirm the roles in which their culture has taught them they matter most and from which usually, even if not invariably, they do derive satisfaction.

The terms under which these diarists and other women undertook marriage varied over past centuries. Personal attraction, for example, was not yet an essential attribute of a match in the seventeenth century, nor even much of the eighteenth century. Among gentlefolk, money, property, and familial status were deemed more significant than love, a duty, a form of behavior expected of those already married. The incompatible arranged marriages of Margaret Hoby, Lady Holland, and Hester Thrale show the limitations of the arrangement. After the Restoration, and especially in the eighteenth century, among the "quality" folk and the higher aristocracy, marriage came increasingly to be based on prior personal affection or loving attraction.[2] Elizabeth Freke's disastrous elopement with her cousin Ralph in 1671 is an instance; a hundred years later and a little lower on the social scale, comes the more successful choice made by Faith Gray in 1777. But even if the selection process in mates changed so that women might gain more choice, an underlying principle did not. As writer Dorothy M. Stetson laconically says, "According to English custom, all women are wives, potential wives, or former wives."[3] Culturally bred for marriage, Englishwomen wanted to wed—more than ever by the Victorian era, at least until the advent of the defiant "New Woman" spinster of late Victorian and Edwardian times. Even after the First World War, despite a temporary increase in unwed females, marriage remained a normative expectation of women, whatever their class.[4] For the diarists of this study, marriage is the goal toward which their mothers have directed them and toward which they themselves aspire.

Being already married, the seventeenth-century diarists offer only indirect evidence of their personal goals, but given that during the Stuart era the spinster was considered a family burden and a "living confession of failure,"[5] one can assume they wanted to marry. Anne Clifford even personally chose to remarry, though she made a very poor choice of mate. The twentieth-century diarists set wider sights than just marriage, but all of them do marry. The most frequent illustrations of the marital goal come from the late eighteenth century to past mid-nineteenth century, the heyday of separate-sphere thinking, when Eugenia Wynne recalls of her girlhood how the message at home from "Mama" was "marriez vous mes filles" (17 January 1805). Trant sees right through a woman who has "announced her determination of not allowing her girls to marry until after her death. *Tell that to the Marines.* . . . it is evident that her whole heart is set upon their disobedience to this precept" (5 October 1829). A female at seventeen has come to "an age of peculiar interest for a young girl, in which she enters first on life as a young woman," reflects Jeune of her daughter (6 May 1856), meaning that she views the girl as marriageable. Then and later, some conscientious mothers have scruples about marriages that answer only to worldly ambition. Florence Sitwell's pious mother, for example, "cannot bear the talk we continually hear, nothing but marriage and dress, and such a solemn thing as marriage spoken of so lightly; really one would think to hear it, that it was to be the one aim in every girl's life to get soon and well married" (27 March 1877). Nonetheless, mothers (like fathers) hope that, in suitable fashion, their daughters will wed. "This is one of those rare days in my life, to which a white mark may be affixed. My dear daughter Fanny is engaged to be married. . . . There is not a cloud in our hearts, or in the sky!" exults Frances Shelley (1 January 1834) with representative delight.[6]

For the affianced female, in turn, an engagement is so momentous an achievement (at least by the nineteenth century) that it may create a sense of unreality. "I often feel inclined to ask myself 'Is it really you, Clara, who are going to be married?' It seems to me as if it were some other person," marvels Trant (16 December 1831). "I sat up with Agnes and Helen talking it all over and trying to believe it was true," echoes Mary Gladstone fifty years later (24 January 1886). That these engagements were long delayed may intensify the feeling of too good to be true; it does not create it. Lucy (Lyttleton) Cavendish becomes engaged young, but only receiving her first letter from her fiancé "makes it all very real to me" (26 April 1864). So significant is an engagement that its anniversary may afterward be noted, as Cavendish solemnly does (21 April 1865). Lady Monkswell knows precisely that "today by the days of the week & tomorrow by the days of the month" her proposal came the year before, and her feelings upon being proposed to remain a touchstone for intense emotion (29 June 1874, 16 March 1880).[7]

An engagement signifies Here beginneth a new life, arriving at which point occupies plentiful space in many diaries. From the eighteenth to the twentieth centuries, diarists like to record their various suitors (sometimes even after marriage). To be courted flatters the ego; it creates a satisfying sense of self-worth and power. So too the opportunity to pick and choose does, when the modest female is otherwise expected, especially by the nineteenth century, to be passive about love. Eugenia Wynne even notes the anniversary of a proposal she refused (1 March 1798). Entries about rejected suitors betray pride in the diarist's discriminating taste and superior value: Wynne's contemptuous "Captain Birch . . . very nearly *popped the question*. He is hideous" (27 April 1803), for example; or Constance de Rothschild's "to think that an old Russian monster should have proposed to me. . . . It was almost laughable" (14 February [187?]). Diarists take pride too in their strategies for removing unwanted suitors without creating a bad impression. Gladstone, for instance, adroitly disposes of a Mr. Sala, a "rum man. . . . Have had the 'inferior' subject out. A beautiful crucifix as a farewell offering" (11 June 1881). Trant, fifty years earlier, deflects a Mr. Burgess most competently, she preens herself, because experience "has been enough to teach me how to carry on that kind of warfare without losing one iota of my self-possession." Trant is especially proud of her skill at effecting amicable partings: "My candour and sincerity did not offend [Mr. Lloyd's] feelings and in losing a *lover* I have gained a friend" (5 October 1829, 30 August 1824)—one of many such "friends" she believes she has made.[8]

For the maidens, disposing of male admirers is a game; for the married, a more serious problem—and yet also a game agreeable to the ego. Diarists dare talk about it before and after Victorian days. Thus Lady Holland commends herself for her skill in warding off a Mr. Tierney when "I was in an eloquent *veine,* and happily conveyed all I intended to express without the rigorous exterior of forbidding prudery." She is equally proud of how she earlier discouraged a Mr. Adderley by presenting to him forcefully the dreadful consequences "were any officious person to suggest to [Lord Holland] that [your] visits did not proceed from friendship to him, but from love to me" (10 and 6 July 1799). She has reason to admire her skill because her diary shows that she has already gained Holland's sympathy by telling him herself that Adderley is pursuing her (see 4 July). Cynthia Asquith, on the other hand, finds herself incapable of warding off any of her numerous too-persistent admirers while her husband is off serving in the army. She is "helplessly tongue-tied" and must resort to letters, does not "know how to cope," and finds it "impossible to give the plain, brutally truthful negative answer to, 'For God's Sake, tell me you do care a little for me!'" (30 December 1915, 8 June 1917, 19 November 1918).[9] She in fact prefers to keep her admirers.

For the unwed, the serious problems are the men they do want who are lost to them. But the diaries are regrettably skimpy about several of these sad stories. Harriet Wynne loses her love to treachery, after her diary has shown her growing up into love for a childhood playmate. When she is nearly twenty, her Tom departs for Ireland, leaving her afraid that "a boy of seventeen can never retain his same sentiments for four years" (30 May 1806), and yet he does. He sends back a proposal in a letter she never receives because his sister destroys it. However, the denouement is part of the editor's notes, not Harriet's diary. Lucy Fitzgerald's fragmentary diary charts the waves and troughs of an intense adolescent crush, but there is no telling what happened to the mysterious "he" because of whose loss of interest "I often wish I were quiet in my grave. . . . agitation . . . is not so distructive to the health as the cold stupor of despair" ([178?]). Circumstances plus editors' choices of extracts curtail both accounts. Diarist Julia Woodforde herself curtails another. Her memobook diary reduces the story of her love for John Power, a former Trappist whom she helped return to secular life, largely to wishes for his good health and notations of how long he has been gone since he emigrated to Sierra Leone to make his fortune. She has no entries at all when he dies there of fever in the fall of 1819, though her sister Ann does, who has "wept more this year than all the rest of my life" (13 November).[10]

There are, however, other, more expansive eighteenth- and nineteenth-century accounts of disappointed expectations, often over marriage portions. Hapless Elizabeth Raper, for example, has no luck with her slippery suitors, so that her life falls into a pattern:

> Had like to have been in possession of the grand secret but [he] escaped, however not without an assurance that I should hear it another time, and when I told him about his being fixed he repeated 'that he looked upon himself as engaged while a certain young lady was single.' . . . Kissed and hugged me, think I am gratifying my present inclination at the expense of (perhaps) my future happiness. God knows how it will be in the end. . . . I imagine he will never speak plain, and hints can never come to anything. (25 September, 8 and 21 October 1759)

The only suitor who does "speak plain," fortune hunter Samuel Horsley, reveals himself to her parents so clearly that they refuse him present gain and test him with vague promises for the future, a contretemps that obliges her to acknowledge his caliber: "If he had chose to say the handsome thing, or to have made any reserve for hereafter—but he was mute *as a picture*" (16 March 1761). Unwilling to consider herself less desirable than money, she puts him out of mind and eventually marries another. Trant needs the same strength when Colonel Cameron, whom she has set her heart on, stays mute while her father spurns her inadequate marriage portion. Cameron remains a sore spot, however, an embarrassment every time they chance to meet until with implied relish she finally writes, "Colonel Cameron was married at Bath to [word illegible] to the disgust of his family" (1 December 1831). To record that the man is married is also a way of declaring the matter settled, but Beatrice (Potter) Webb attempts such closure without success. On the day of Joseph Chamberlain's marriage she records, "It must be over: and they are man and wife," yet her stubborn passion for the man she first rejected, then longed for, still elicits "a week of utter nervous collapse. . . . intense pain" (15 and 24 November 1888).[11] Her obsession persists for two years more, until she finally accepts Sidney Webb.

The successful courtships begin without thunderclaps. Faith Gray, indeed, goes back in her diary to underline and so give one *"Thurs-day.* Drank tea at my Aunt Mortimer's, met . . . Mr Gray" (4 January 1775) its belated significance as day of first meeting. A few other dia-rists magnify that day by giving it an anniversary entry: Lady Kate Amberley, for example (17 September 1865), and Cavendish (4 De-cember 1864). Cavendish's diary shows a typical situation. The dia-rist is unaware that she is meeting fate in person when "At dinner I got into an argument with Lord Frederick Cavendish on the Church, which excited and interested me. I don't think I was wrong, as I did not introduce the topic on purpose; but I wish I had been somebody who could have convinced him!" A few more weeks, and "if it were not for my trust . . . in the Heavenly Guidance, I shd be full of rest-lessness and excitement. And as it is, I fear I shall be, sooner or later." So she is, by April, when her life has "this wonderful under-tone running through it, and I am in a new life" (4 and 31 December 1863, 15 April 1864). By 21 April, she is engaged.[12]

For wealthy women like Cavendish, courted by also wealthy men, finances are no problem, but wealth is not necessarily the only con-sideration. Frances (Elliot) Russell must think hard before accepting Lord Russell bcause he is a widower with six children. For other dia-rists—the middle-class Wynne sisters, for example—money is a hurdle. Elizabeth's love follows upon a year of sustained, restless carp-ing at her life, until it chances that the Wynnes are evacuated on HMS *Inconstant* from Leghorn a few hours before the French revolu-tionary armies arrive. Whereupon, Captain (later, Admiral) Fre-mantle "wins every day more in my affection. . . . I should be the most ungrateful of beings if I did not feel more than friendship for a person that has behaved so uncommonly well" (5 and 12 July 1796). But until he brings in a prize ship, Fremantle feels he lacks sufficient fortune to maintain a family. Eugenia's prospects too seem almost dashed when her lover, Robert Campbell, refuses to marry unless he secures a lucrative diplomatic appointment. "How different is the Love of a Woman to that of a Man!—" wails Eugenia. "There is nothing that I could not give up for him but he cannot be happy on £ 1500 pr. annm leading an inactive life" (12 May 1806).[13] However, they wed two months later.

When finally the diarists are to marry, they feel the momentousness of the event. The change of names means assuming a new identity. "For the last time I shall write as Miss Wynne," says Elizabeth, for example; "what a day tomorrow is—I dread it" (11 January 1797). Thrale recalls her first marriage as the day on which "did Hester-Lynch Salusbury write her Maiden name—for the last Time— officially" (11 October 1804). Russell hardly "know[s] how to begin my journal again. I wrote the last page as Fanny Elliot; I am now Fanny Russell" (29 July 1841). For Webb, it is "Exit Beatrice Potter. Enter Beatrice Webb, or rather (Mrs.) Sidney Webb for I lose alas! both names" (23 July 1892). She is the only one, however, to object to subsuming her identity under her husband's name. If not the change of name, then the change of space signifies the new era— "This last day at home. The last time I shall sleep in this little room! . . . My heart is full," as (Lyttleton) Cavendish, for instance, laments (20 May 1864). Apprehensiveness at leaving the familiar is common. "This event makes me perfectly happy," worries Elizabeth Wynne, "yet I dread it and the idea of leaving so suddenly my Father Mother and sisters, distresses me[.] I can hardly make up my mind to it. . . . I wished it myself and now that what I desired must happen, it frightens me and I think the undertaking almost too great" (10 January 1797). Even so her sister Eugenia feels "very strange—I was afraid to reflect or to think least I should lose the courage which every Woman stands in need of on such an occasion" (22 July 1806). After the ceremony, Fanny Anne Burney (Wood) finds that "the parting with own dear family & so many kind friends was *very, very* painful to me. . . . when [father] gave me his parting kiss and *blessing,* . . . I felt so choked with many contending feelings that I scarcely knew where I was" (8 August 1835).[14]

Few diarists are expansive about the wedding day itself. The briefest marriage entry is Caroline Powys's businesslike "I was married to Philip Lybbe Powys of Hardwick Hall, Oxfordshire" (5 August 1762). Gray allots three sentences, but does (again) underline "*Married*" (9 October 1777). The most laconic, they are not alone in their inability or unwillingness to articulate their states of mind. "What I felt at the wedding is not to be described," asserts Elizabeth Wynne (12 January 1797). "If ever the mind is indisposed to enter into the details of satin and lace, and blonde and feathers, it is at such a moment as this, when the heart is full of thoughts 'too big for utterance,' when every feeling is absorbed in the *one* engrossing subject" (5 January 1831), explains Trant, though she does find words for her feelings of gratitude to God. "I cannot write about it," says Cavendish simply (7 June 1864), though she identifies place and minister. But Eugenia Wynne finds words, if few, for her bridal gown and her agitation during the ceremony (22 July 1806). Fanny Anne Burney (a bride who forgets to identify her bridegroom by name) lingers over the family's crying in the vestry—"I know nothing which could tempt me to endure that hour of excitement a second time!" (8 August 1835)—and her relief at escaping from the crowd of curious onlookers to the ceremony. And Charlotte Guest is proud of her self-control, since she has forborne to exacerbate the friction with her family over her marriage (29 July 1833).[15]

Still, these diarists on the whole give their wedding days, and invariably any remarriages, but brief entries. Historically, weddings per se had little importance until after the first decades of the nineteenth century. Not until mid-century did they become elaborate social rituals that might have long guest lists.[16] Yet even after weddings become more public events, evidently the diarists for themselves do not need the social details of the day, either the guest lists or the fashions. Lady Monkswell is singular in describing her wedding in close detail, including all the fine points of nuptial attire (21 August 1873). For this one event, other diarists leave dress to be a spectator's sport, and most of their ruminations go unrecorded, though Gladstone adds a noteworthy comment to her otherwise impersonal description of events: "The great wonder was to feel it all so natural and to feel I was I when I thought I was going to be somebody else" (2 February 1886).[17]

The feelings the diarists prefer to talk about come after the wedding day when the new life has been confirmed. As Burney (Wood) characterizes it, being newly wed is "my new situation and change of life, which at first appeared so strange that I fancied myself in a daydream" (20 August 1835). More significant, the diarists proclaim their bliss quickly and reaffirm it later. Because they do not know their spouses well, they rejoice in what they discover. "We are very quiet and happy," reports Trant the day after her marriage, for "every subject we discuss brings with it the delightful discovery of some new kindred feeling . . . we love—*each other*" (6 January 1832). "His kindness, his tenderness are the joy of my life," declares Russell a few months after hers, her frequent theme, restated even after twenty-four years because she is thankful for "happy, happy days, so full of reality. . . . When we sit together . . . and talk . . . my heart seems to leap within me from the sense of happiness" (2 November 1865). "The day month since our marriage," rejoices Cavendish, "a month of ever-deepening happiness" (7 July 1864). "I felt as if great changes had come over me in the great blessing I have now & the promise of still more happiness in the future," says Lady Amberley on New Year's Day; five years later, she reaffirms her delight in her marriage: "We are as happy as ever & fonder of one another each year" (1 January 1865, 31 December 1870). She does so on anniversaries and on random occasions as well.[18] Anniversaries and the New Year are typical declaration points, for then one takes stock of blessings, and the diarists repeatedly find theirs in their marriages.

On her third anniversary, Mary Hamilton, for instance, wishes, "*Oh may the next 3 years be as happy*" (13 June 1788), even as Caroline Powys on a much later anniversary declares, "We had been married now forty-one years, and I believe I may most sincerely say, as perfectly happy as 'tis possible to be" (5 August 1803). "My new record must commence by acknowledging with the deepest gratitude my present happiness, blessed as I am by my darling husband and surrounded by my children" (1 January 1856), declares Charlotte Guest (Schreiber), remarried—but she is happy with her first marriage too. George Eliot's more and more "blessed" "double life" with George Henry Lewes is always part of her annual reviews, for "In each other we are happier than ever. I am more grateful to my dear husband for his perfect love, which helps me in all good and checks me in all evil—more conscious that in him I have the greatest of blessings" (31 December 1858, 1 January 1865). So too Frances Stevenson says of her liaison with David Lloyd George, "It is just two years since [David] & I were 'married,' and our love seems to increase rather than diminish" (21 January 1915). Beatrice Webb can look back on "the memory of a perfect marriage"; even when she is seventy-three, the Webbs are "still a honeymoon couple!" (9 August 1922, 25 May 1931).[19]

Early in her marriage, Virginia Woolf declares, "I daresay we're the happiest couple in England"; and "after 24 years *cant* bear to be separate. . . . it is an enormous pleasure, being wanted: a wife. And our marriage so complete" (28 December 1919, 22 October 1937). Locating the "core of my life" in "this complete comfort with L." (14 June 1925), Woolf also, at an earlier time, articulates what other diarists may be less able to verbalize:

> One's personality seems to echo out across space, when he's not there to enclose all one's vibrations. This is not very intelligently written; but the feeling itself is a strange one—as if marriage were the completing of the instrument, & the sound of one alone penetrates as if it were a violin robbed of its orchestra or piano. (2 November 1917) [20]

A century before Woolf, Mary Shelley, lamenting all she has lost in becoming a widow, anticipates Woolf's intensity of feeling, even if she lacks Woolf's facility of expression. Not all the diarists are self-conscious about their marriage or articulate. Nonetheless, the evidence of the diaries is that, for most of these women, being a wife is not just an obligatory role but also an appreciated source of fulfillment, gratification, or emotional support. The remaining diarists, barring a few whose marriages were bad, convey the impression that marriage is no more unhappy a state than life itself. The diarists, moreover, apparently are not singular. Historian Sara Heller Mendelson found that fifteen of the twenty-three Stuart women's diaries and serial memoirs she studied showed a sense of loving, companionable marriages, and only six of unsatisfying ones. [21]

The husband, not the children of the union, is the pivot upon which the women's sense of marriage turns. Thus Lady Elizabeth Holland suffers the "*besoin* [need] I have to belong to something that I can cherish" (14 June 1793) while trapped in her first and unhappy marriage, for all that she has three children to love. But more indicative are happy marriages. Lady Monkswell's comment after visiting the home of the chief justice shows how one's husband may take precedence over one's children: "They are certainly a happy couple. . . . [But] I think on the whole I prefer being my *young man's*, indeed I may say my *young men's* [sons'] *slave*" (4 October 1887). Her exaggeration (she would never countenance anything like slavery) is rhetorical, but the precedence she gives to her "man" over the after-thought "men" is no mere flourish. On her thirty-first birthday, she likewise writes: "He [my husband] has no relation & no friend, who is a hundredth part so nearly related to him, or so much his compan-ion & friend as I, and I should be very angry if it were otherwise" (2 November 1880). Stevenson, whose thoughts about her long-term liaison with Lloyd George run parallel, does not miss children, for "I often think that if I were married & had children, then I should not be able to keep in touch with D.'s work to the extent that I do now, & perhaps should be less happy. At present all our interests lie to-gether; he does nothing but what I know of it" (8 February 1916). But Lady Amberley best articulates apportionment of loyalties when she has accompanied her husband to his campaign in Leeds while she is pregnant. Every time there is applause, "I felt it thrill through me," she says, "& having been told excitement was bad for me spe-cially . . . I feared to stay & tore myself away for the sake of the future, but for myself I felt no child could ever be to me what the husband was—" (31 January 1865). Likewise, Charlotte Guest, nine months pregnant, accompanies her husband to Wales despite her ap-prehensions about the heavy snows because "I always feel it my duty to be with him" (3 March 1837).[22]

Clarissa Trant describes her husband-to-be as "all that my heart could desire in the guide, the friend, the protector of my future life" (14 November 1831)—or what ideally the women probably envision their mates will be. Their own roles vis-à-vis such mates Frances Shelley suggests when, in her widowhood, she is thankful that, "though my great task is ended, my life is still of value" (1 April 1853). Wifeliness is service, whether marriage is the duty enjoined by religion earlier or the 'great task' that gives female life dedicated purpose according to separate-sphere thinking later. "May God bless him for all his kindness," as Fanny Anne Burney (Wood) says in the spirit of the latter, "and make me a solace and comfort unto him" (20 August 1835).[23] The separatist "cult of domesticity" and its corollary "cult of true womanhood" (historian Olive Banks's terms in *Faces of Feminism*), which assigned to females attributes of gentleness and loving kindness, taught women that marriage would fulfill their na-tures and verify their womanliness by giving them a mission to care for others. Here the heart of the matter beats for the diarists, who see marriage as the great opportunity to love and care for man and child—especially the man.

In her mid-twenties, Beatrice (Potter) Webb thinks, "It is almost necessary to the health of a woman, physical and mental, to have definite home duties to fulfil: details of practical management and, above all things, someone dependent on her love and tender care." At the time, because her mother has died and she has a father and four sisters to care for, Webb feels that she has "mission enough as a *woman*," though as yet unmarried and with the "restless ambition of my nature" also still to be provided for (5 November 1883). Psychologist Jean Baker Miller has identified the crucial aspect for personality development in Webb's attitude, and it still flourishes: "[Women] have developed the sense that their lives should be guided by the constant need to attune themselves to the wishes, desires, and needs of others," because "women are taught that their main goal in life is to serve others—first men, and later, children."[24] By the time Webb does marry, she is so well entrenched in the career forced on her by spinster circumstances, as well as by her restless ambition, that she fears "lest my work should be ended and I absorbed in the details of domestic life" (7 July 1891). She does not, however, fear the other part of womanliness: having "someone dependent on my love and tender care" (even if already long since resentful of her familial obligations). After all, "Was I made for brain work? Is any woman made for a purely intellectual life?" (29 March 1890).[25]

Womanliness in culturally approved terms carries the satisfaction of being needed, of having others dependent upon oneself for nurturance. Nonetheless, such womanliness is also dependency. As Lady Holland, who needs a husband to cherish, also says, "I strive to repress, but often feel, a strong desire to be dependent upon another for happiness" (14 June 1793). In the form of dependency, the doctrine of true womanhood carries great potential not only for victimization, but also for self-victimization. Margaret Jeune's diary can illustrate. It shows a woman fulfilling her role with entire wifely devotion to a man and to the children he has given her and finding it gratifying—"an inexpressible happiness to me to think that I have a share in contributing to his . . . 'happy, most happy home.' May I indeed be enabled to be a comfort to him" (29 February 1844).[26] There is, however, also a subtext.

159

Wife to Francis Jeune, dean of Jersey, in 1843 when her diary begins, Margaret is twenty-five and has been married for seven years. At the time, she has three children; two more are born at Oxford, to which the family removes because, to Margaret's great satisfaction, Francis has been elected master of Pembroke College. By 1858, he has advanced to vice-chancellor. Her children occupy her time and much of her emotional energy: her diary divides between her social activities as wife of an administrator and her concern for her children's growth, health, and schooling. But Francis is the center of her emotional life, as she captures well when she writes upon his return from a trip, "It seems that each time we are separated I am more and more rejoiced at our meeting again. How all one's feelings are changed in a few minutes. Now I am all joy and cheerfulness" (20 March 1844). She ministers to his well-being and is a helpmate in his career, so that if he has suffered a disappointment when serving on a university commission, "I . . . felt specially how one's place is by one's husband" (23 June 1854).[27]

Francis is a generous and considerate husband. Nonetheless, their relations turn on her subordination and docility. Thus she writes, when Francis leaves on a trip, "I am concerned to find that next week he leaves me again; but there is no help for it, and therefore I must submit" ([January] 1844). Her feelings and desires come second to Francis's. Francis, at one point, could leave on the next morning or on the same evening to visit the daughters they have sent to school in Paris; she is unsure which he intends. "If the latter he will reach Paris by 9 tomorrow morning. What a delightful surprise for our darlings—but I said nothing to induce him to undertake night travelling, though I should rejoice if he felt equal to it" (25 February 1854). Because Margaret's respect and admiration for Francis are unqualified, Conservative politician Goldwin Smith ranks only as "the most agreeable man of the company—my own dear gifted husband excepted"; and a man she dislikes possesses "*one* unsullied qualification . . . in my eyes, which is his cordial regard for my dear husband" (2 February 1853, 27 July 1846). She sees to it, moreover, that Francis can be proud of her; if he "gives me unlimited permission to fit myself out" for the initial move from Jersey to Oxford, "he may be sure I shall not abuse it" (22 April 1844).[28]

Jeune's diary is a portrait of a successful Victorian marriage, whose reverse side is only what Margaret inadvertently betrays as a sense of hollowness in her life. Or as she writes in a significant slip of the pen, "In a general way our life is so monotonous that I am often induced to give it up, (keeping a journal I mean) for long intervals" (18 June 1855).[29] Were she more self-aware she would speak of a degree of emptiness as consequence of living so much through others. Jeune decides that her life is not so boring after all once Francis has become a vice-chancellor and their social life more exciting. Whereupon she feels she has plentiful copy for her diary—which now becomes even more external than it has been from the start. In Jeune's marital portrait, the individual woman is a negligible personality and, though she assumes otherwise, not entirely a happy woman because she has suppressed her own being. There lies the pitfall in happy marriages like the Jeunes'.

However, not all women subordinate themselves and get in return a lurking sense of emptiness. Frances Stevenson's diary shows a woman who thrives on her devotion to a man and his career. An educated woman with a degree in classics from London University and mildly a sympathizer of the women's suffrage cause, Stevenson became David Lloyd George's confidential secretary and, beginning in 1912, his mistress; in 1943, she became his wife. She played an important part in his career, advising him, helping compose his speeches, and accompanying him on foreign missions. When he became prime minister in 1916, she was one of his two joint principal private secretaries, the first time a woman held such a position. Her diary reflects her hero worship of Lloyd George; not until the 1930s is she actively critical of him. More pertinent here is the gratification she finds in serving and tending him. "He tells me that he could not go on without me," she writes, "& I like to believe that that is true, for I love to think that I am helping him a little." She is well aware, however, that to help him even a little requires entire dedication: "D. needs so much someone who will not hesitate to give him everything, & if necessary to give up everything, & whose sole thought and occupation is for him. Without that it is hopeless to try and serve him" (1 February and 1 March 1917). Contending, as does he, that his wife neglects his welfare, Stevenson intends "to try my hand & see what I can do!" (26 May 1917).[30]

In her concern for his comfort, as otherwise, she sounds much like Jeune. For Stevenson too parting is an ordeal and retaining her man's admiration is essential, so much so that she wants even "to be really good at golf as D. has been so sweet about my learning & takes such a patient interest in my progress" (26 November 1919). If Stevenson and Jeune differ noticeably in that Stevenson will cross Lloyd George—though only for his welfare—still, it bothers her to address him "rather harshly" with career advice, for "God knows, I would not wound him" (12 October 1915). And his welfare, not hers, remains paramount: "I got quite alarmed about him last week, especially as he was not at all nice to me, which is always a sign that he is overworked or very worried" (28 May 1917). Likewise, though "I suppose I am only human and I get depressed," she reflects, "I feel as though I ought not to mind when he is busy & cannot pay me very much attention" (2 April 1917). Stevenson has opportunity to marry elsewhere, but "I can see that he would be unhappy if I left him, so I promised him I would not" (23 May 1919).[31] She herself, that is, would not be happy without him. Significantly, she feels neither guilt at her illicit relationship nor any sense of an empty life. Her active involvement in her lover's career and her occasional self-assertion apparently save her from the sense of hollowness shadowing Jeune.

Their husbands' careers may become a locus of meaning for any of the diarists. Most achieve their only public status through those careers, which become part of the women's own identity. Even Woolf, who will later say it "annoys" her "to be like other wives," lapses into a common mode of self-designation upon Leonard's appointment to the *International Review:* "Today I am the wife of an Editor" (11 May 1923, 8 September 1918). Some of the nineteenth-century diarists live vicariously through their men's political careers: Lady Monkswell, for example, who registers her disappointment very revealingly when she realizes after Balfour's resignation "that we should be left out altogether—offered nothing" in the new cabinet; "These were some of the most painful moments of my life" (10 December 1905).[32] Lady Kate Amberley; her mother-in-law, Frances Russell; and Lucy Cavendish also register the successes and disappointment of their husbands' political careers on their own pulses.

Their men's careers often bring meaning into the lives of the diarists by enhancing their self-estimates when they have the opportunity to assist in some significant way. Thus Mary Cowper, for instance, takes pride in her own generosity when her ailing husband decides to resign his post as lord chancellor to George I. She makes "a Resolution never to press him more to keep his Place. . . . I offered him, if it would be any Pleasure done him, to retire with him into the Country, and . . . what was more, never to repine at doing so, though it was the greatest Sacrifice that could be made him" (14 and 15 February 1716). Likewise, Hester Thrale preens herself on how she rushes home from Bath to canvass Mr. Thrale's borough for him, though "I shall be fatigued and never thanked—no matter—it is fit he who is ill should rest, & fit that I who am well should work—" (14 May 1780). So too does Lady Elizabeth Holland congratulate herself (meanwhile rationalizing her own pleasures) for helping Lord Holland by seeking "new acquaintances . . . not so much, however, for my own gratification, as from a notion that mixing with a variety of people is an advantage to Ld. H." (30 May 1799).[33] Nineteenth-century Charlotte Guest's skill at helping her first husband with his ironworks as secretary, bookkeeper, and even sales agent builds her self-esteem, besides all the advantages to him. Though their marriages may make them only secondary figures, one way or another the diarists contrive to effect gratification from them.

With marriage so central to female existence, the advent of widowhood is likely to be shattering, except when the marriage has been a burden. Women who matured in the Victorian era seem especially to lament a sense of closure to their lives. "And so ends my life on earth" (31 March 1884), grieves Guest (Schreiber) upon her second husband's death, though she was to live on for many active years. "What a gulf separates that time from this. An epoch of my life closed—a new, changed, sad one commencing," laments Louisa de Rothschild, certain that "—all, *all* is changed" (12 March 1876). "All is riddled and pierced with pain," later adds Mary Gladstone (Drew), sharing in another common widow's theme when she and Queen Alexandra "talked of the way men died and left the huge majority of women. 'If only women would but die more'" (1–10 December and 31 March 1912). The covert longing for death is a common response, though Cavendish instead makes her loss tolerable through a sustained rationalization, the only diarist to do so. When Frederick Cavendish, newly appointed chief secretary for Ireland, becomes a victim in the Dublin Phoenix Park murders, she convinces herself that his Christlike sacrifice has served the Divine purpose of bringing peace to Ireland (9 February 1883). [34]

Open longing for death extends from the nineteenth into the twentieth century. Mary Shelley insists that her child is "the only chain that links me to time; but for you, I should be free." "May I die young!" to rejoin Percy becomes her "usual prayer" (5 October 1822, 8 June 1824). At Lloyd George's request, Stevenson even agrees to kill herself should he, being the elder, predecease her; without that pact, "sometimes my heart would stop beating with terror at the thought of life without D" (23 April 1917). Although it is more usual for the diarists just to dread the thought of inevitable separation, diarist Dora Carrington (1893–1932) did indeed commit suicide upon the death of Lytton Strachey, to whom she had devoted her life, because "that there is nobody any longer to serve and love completely and entirely makes everything pointless" ([February] 1932). [35] Carrington's sense of closure points up the true source of distress upon widowhood: not the loneliness or the social negligibility of widows, and not the specter of need (a worry these largely prosperous diarists never express when their husbands or the equivalent die), but rather the felt loss of the center of meaning—someone to love and serve. Such a sense of loss may afflict even women with opportunities for a life of their own.

The wives fear widowhood and the widows mourn, but certainly all is not perfect love, as Thrale's widow-entries suggest. Thrale (Piozzi) declares that she rejoices in both her marriages—"I pass'd 17 years & a half with my first Husband . . . & never wished I had remained unmarried, or prefer'd any mortal Man to him: I have now spent 16 years & a half almost with Mr. Piozzi, & every Creature has Considered us a model of Conjugal Felicity." Nonetheless, this diarist's way of recording the advent of her widowhood is instructive. Mr. Thrale's death is reported in an abrupt two-sentence announcement in the center of an otherwise blank page, whereas Mr. Piozzi's elicites an outburst: "All is over; my second Husbands Death is the last Thing recorded in my first husband's Present! Cruel Death!" (10

October 1800, April 1781, 30 March 1809). Thrale truly laments only the man she really loved and herself chose, and with whom she was happier. For all her protestations of perfect contentment with Mr. Thrale, her diary records resentment of his negligent and unfaithful behavior;[36] and the loss of Piozzi, not Thrale, is what hurts. Like Thrale's, the marriages and long-term liaisons reported in these diaries were doubtless none of them without their friction points or worse.

Across the centuries, some of the marriages readily betray themselves as hardly close. Lady Northumberland, for example, may write, "Were it not that I have the pleasing hope of meeting my Dearest Lord at the end of my journey, I should have left Cologny with the utmost regret" (18 May 1772). This is but a conventional formula, and she does regret leaving. Her husband has been conspicuously absent from her diary. Likewise, Frances Shelley's husband remains a shadowy figure in hers. The real high point of her life is her conquest of the duke of Wellington, and she is irritated by the socially and personally inept Lord John Shelley, whose own real interest is horseracing plus gambling that burdens her with debts. Expressive of their relationship is her memory of an accident she had in 1825 when "My dear husband meant to be kind, but he knew not what to do with an invalid. The mere fact of my illness worried him; so I was glad when he went to Newmarket where I knew he was happy, and innocently amused" (14 September 1852). Her contention, in an autobiographical sketch, is "I made it a point never to interfere in any way with my husband's mode of life," which favor he apparently returned. Sixty years later, Cynthia Asquith's numerous entries on her admirers and her casual neglect of her husband when he is ill do not give an encouraging picture of her marriage either, and that she intermittently claims a renewed interest in him and an improved relationship bespeaks a less compatible past.[37]

Both weak marriages and strong ones with friction points existed; nonetheless, with a few exceptions, the diarists prefer not to discuss their own marital troubles, though they readily express their sympathy for others' plights. A few examples, from the superficial to the significant, will suffice to show the drift. Mindful of nineteenth-century standards of genteel decorum, Clarissa Trant declares, "Oh, how I pity that interesting and accomplished young woman in having sacrificed herself to such a vulgar man. . . . Oh, how I feel for her when her coarse-looking, vulgar husband half smothers her with kisses in company" (6 July 1829). A more thoughtful Eugenia Wynne pities a Mrs. Manners "most sincerely for being married to such a man—She talks cooly of riding hard to procure a miscarriage, and this because he hates children and beats her for having some" (5 March 1806). So too Lady Amberley is "very unhappy" for his wife and "much shocked" that Mr. Grote has had an affair (14 March 1866).[38] To acknowledge trouble at a distance is easy.

Meanwhile, about their own problems, most of the diarists have little to say—though even the first diarists obliquely evidence some marital discord. Margaret Hoby records on 18 July 1600 reading "ap-aper [sic] that wrought a . . . humiliation in me," then on 19 July that she "wrett an answer to a demand Mr Hoby had given me ouer night." Relations must have been tense at the time if the Hobys, living in the same house, felt obliged to write to each other. So Hoby's editor, Dorothy M. Meads, speculates, conjecturing that the 'paper' may have been Thomas's demand that Margaret make over her lands to him; there may have been additional friction over her chaplain, Richard Rhodes, frequently mentioned in her diary, or per-haps another man.[39] But Margaret herself has nothing more to say on the subject. Anne Clifford, also unfortunately wed, had more marital problems than her estate squabbles to contend with. Dorset also ne-glected her for an affair with a Lady Penniston and even obliged Clifford to receive his paramour at their home. On 24 August 1619, having recorded that Penniston and husband came to Knole with a party of guests who stayed until 26 August, Clifford remarks in a side note, "This coming hither of Lady *Penniston's* was much talked of abroad and my Lord was condemned for it"; one can only imagine Clifford's own feelings. Fortunately she is finally able to record in a side note, "The 29th of November [1619] was the last time my Lord came to Lady *Penniston's* at her Mother's lodgings in the Strand." The affair she never designates as such apparently had ended. Indirectly Clifford may imply resentments; for example, when "I wrote not to my Lord because he wrote not to me since he went away" (May 1617). But except for objecting to Dorset's behavior about her estates and his cancellation of a jointure—whereupon "I told him how good he was to everybody else and how unkind to me" (17–31 May 1619)—she does not criticize her husband any more than Hoby does hers, though outside the diary the latter distinguished himself through unneighborly quarrels as a intolerant, irascible, and suspicious man. Local legend accused Mr. Hoby of hastening Margaret's end by kicking her downstairs.[40]

Whether they fear prying eyes, or they do not wish to confront ugly truth, only in guarded fashion, if at all, do most of the diarists choose to admit to trouble under the domestic roof. Nor are they readily censorious of their husbands. Even when Guest's second husband (Charles Schreiber) takes out his disappointment over losing a parliamentary election on her by threatening to leave her, she writes not about his small-mindedness, but about her struggle to save her marriage (2 May 1859).[41]

Only the extremely unhappy diarists who suffered long-term distress, such as Lady Holland in her first marriage, vent their grief and animosity. Chief among them is Ellen Weeton (Stock), who may well say, "Bitter have been the years of my marriage." She endured Aaron Stock's abuse for some eight years, with only sporadic escapes, because she was uncertain before God whether she was "right in struggling to free myself from his griping hand" (1818). Yet he beat and starved her and otherwise tried to break her spirit:

> Turned out of doors into the street! In the anguish of my mind, I broke out into complaints; this only was my fault. . . . Mr. Stock wants me either to remain at home pennyless, as an underling to his own daughter [by a former marriage], or to be kept by anyone that will take me. . . . I am obliged totally to withdraw myself from any domestic affairs, in obedience to my husband's orders; to live in an apartment alone; not to sit at table with the family, but to have my meat sent to me; and amuse or employ myself as I can. (5 January 1818)[42]

Elizabeth Freke's diary alone matches Weeton's in the sustained intensity of its disillusionment with marriage; it is even subtitled "Some Few Remembrances of My Misfortuns Which Have Atended Me In My Unhappy Life Since I Were Marryed." Freke (the only diarist to sign her entries) objects that her husband, Percy, repeatedly cheats her out of her goods and money, besides periodically deserting her. But Freke's rancor is so randomly distributed as well over ungrateful relatives, lying neighbors, thieving and even murderous servants, and insulting acquaintances as to bespeak a sick mind, increasingly diseased over the years. Possibly Percy's frequent (and perhaps understandable) absences soured her; still, her account is suspect.

More to be taken seriously as neglected wife is Jane Welsh Carlyle, whose published diary is largely the record of her depression during an unhappy period of her marriage—though she will not agree that "'nine-tenths of the misery of human life proceeds . . . from the Institution of Marriage!'" as another suggests. "He should say from the demoralization, the desecration, of the Institution of Marriage and then I should cordially agree with him" (29 May 1856). She and Thomas have grown apart; he, she says, keeps "setting up always another milestone and another betwixt himself and me." Because he has become enamored of high society at Bath House, where Lord and Lady Ashburton hold court and where Jane, though invited, is not really welcome, she feels neglected and resentful. Maybe "it is not always . . . that unjust treatment, harshness, and disdain in her husband drive a woman *jusqu'au désordre* [crazy], but it drives her to something, and something not to his advantage any more than to hers" (22 October and 11 November 1855). Claire Clairmont, even more aggrieved, denounces her former lover Byron, whom she knows "too well to suspect he was ever sorry for the mischief he had done me. He planned that mischief in cold blood, executed it in cold blood and rejoiced at it in cold blood." She cannot forgive him for putting their child Allegra in a convent where "he left his daughter to the care of ignorant bigoted mercenaries and let her die for want of care" (28 January 1827)—it embitters her life.[43]

Certainly the diaries do not lack their measure of male-caused marital (or the equivalent) unhappiness. Yet, as Carlyle suggests, the diarists' quarrel is not with the institution of marriage, only with individual desecrations. They are more inclined to present marriage, especially their own marriages, as the source of female purpose and happiness than as the source of female misery. Although some may be exaggerating their marital bliss and others are most certainly covering up their distress, still, defiant spinster Eleanor Butler aside, the diarists are at peace with the values they have been taught; and many of the marriages were apparently happy ones. Of course, if some diarists protect themselves by knowingly censoring particular discords, so too all the diarists protect themselves just by accepting the status quo. Until the late nineteenth century, where else but marriage and motherhood could they go for decent financial support, personal status, and self-esteem?

The affirmation of motherhood in these diaries parallels the affirmation of marriage. Not only has marriage traditionally entailed the right and obligation to bear children—indeed, before the eighteenth century, procreation was the justification for marital sex.[44] Religion and culture have also solemnized, even glorified, female fruitfulness; and women have internalized the teaching. Even if, after 1877, English fertility began a long-term decline,[45] women were not so much refusing motherhood as limiting the number of their progeny; childless marriages remained few. Victorian and Edwardian women still took great pride in their biological function. The self-satisfaction (like the competitive spirit) is unmistakable in Lady Amberley's voice not long before 1877 when she can write that Lady Powercrest "is very anxious to have a child indeed. She was married 6 months before I was & not begun yet—She said she envied me my boy" (8 October 1865). It sounds in Lady Monkswell's much later too, as she gloats that the Rivett Carnacs "have no children, which makes her 100 years older than me" (11 September 1907).[46] But across the centuries legitimate conception is welcomed. Certainty of pregnancy because fetal movement has been felt (the surest prenatal test until the 1880s)[47] is an important event that merits recording. "I began to think I was quick with child so as I told it to my Lord, my Sister *Sackville*, and my Sister *Compton*," writes Clifford (2 October 1619). "I quickened today," writes Amberley (27 October 1867) with more assurance. Historically between the two, Fanny Anne Burney (Wood) more evasively, but no less proudly, predicts correctly, "Before another anniversary of this day comes round I shall in all probability have become a Mother" (25 December 1836).[48]

The diction for childbearing modifies over the centuries. The women report themselves as "with child" through the eighteenth century, and later, more euphemistically, as "in a family way" or, in one case, "in the encreasing" (Elizabeth Wynne, 11 February 1803); though Hester Thrale also speaks in 1778, in an autobiographical entry, of her 1764 "Pregnancy."[49] One (oneself or another woman) is next "in travail" or, later, "in labor" in the sixteenth and seventeenth centuries; and "lying in" or "delivered of" a child, or, more often, "brought to bed" of a child, in the seventeenth through early nineteenth centuries. My (her) child was "born" enters in the later seventeenth century as an alternate term, followed by I (she) was "confined" in the later eighteenth and nineteenth centuries, driving the older terms out. Historian Judith S. Lewis has suggested that, among the upper classes, "confined" may reflect an attitude of resentment: accouchements perceived as restricting one's life. More striking is that diary-scholar Paul C. Rosenblatt has found nineteenth-century Canadian and American diarists, until about 1865, commonly referring to childbirth as 'sickness' or 'illness' or being on a 'bed of suffering' because (he conjectures) of the dangers and high mortality rate for childbed.[50] These English diarists rarely use such language. The few instances include Harriet Wynne's referring to sister Elizabeth's labor as "her Misery" (7 September 1805)—for Elizabeth, it is more emphatically "my *miseries*" (25 July 1807)—and Guest's (3 July 1834) and Lady Amberley's (21 July 1865) using "taken ill" for giving birth. But even if the diarists' diction is neutral, they are well aware of how hazardous childbirth is. "May God grant me a grateful heart for His preservation . . . during the late delivery," Faith Gray says (28 May 1782), Burney (Wood) echoing her (2 January 1837).[51] Nor are they singular in such prayers.

The women know well what childbirth entails, not only from their own experiences, but also from others'. The childbirth ordeal, indeed, creates a sense of female community. Before the advent of routinely hospital deliveries, women expect to assist one another with birthing. Thus, Hoby "went to awiffe in trauill of child" (15 August 1599); and Mary Hardy has a long day when "Mrs. Neve sent for me morn. past 7, was brought to bed of a boy even past 1. . . . I came home even 6" (1 January 1780). Or Cynthia Asquith is called in to assist a friend, who begins hemorrhaging in "a nightmare of terror and horror" (10 August 1915). Responsive to the ordeals of others, the diarists often report on difficult and fatal deliveries: how, for some eighteenth-century examples, there "died in childbed, and likewise the infant, my sister[-in-law] . . . just sixteen years of age," as Caroline Powys learns (6 September 1764); or how, according to Eleanor Butler, a poor woman "was in labour three days and very little hopes of her life" (2 February 1789).[52]

By the eighteenth century, male midwives were replacing the traditional female ones. Hester Thrale gives an indignant account of one whom she construes to be an inept practitioner, too eager to extract the fetus piecemeal in her daughter Cecilia's difficult labor. The account is worth reproducing in full for the mingled attitude toward medical advances (forceps were introduced only in the late eighteenth century, though the hook was traditional); for the knowledgeable air with which Thrale speaks (she bore twelve children herself); and for her sense of horror at wasted lives:

> But I hate these Country Accoucheurs—these *Demi Savans:* They are so forward to produce their *Instruments.* A London Hospital would have saved this Child I doubt not, tho' the Birth *was* laborious. I find there was no wrong Presentation, only a Lentor [slowness] in the pains perhaps—With Opium & Encouragement, & not putting her too soon upon Labour, I verily do think that a skilful Practitioner might have brought the Baby forward with the *Forceps* at worst—but they are so plaguy hasty. —Either Doctor Denman or an old Woman would have waited—but since the horrid death-doing Crochet [hook] has been found out, & its use permitted—Oh! many & many a Life has been flung away. (19 September 1797)[53]

From the seventeenth to the late nineteenth century, puerperal fever raged; not until the second half of the last century did modern gynecological surgery exist; and not until the turn of the twentieth century was effective blood transfusion perfected—though in the twentieth century, for all the advances, maternal mortality remained a major cause of female death.[54] With good reason do the diarists express their sorrow for others and their fears for themselves. Thrale, for example, because of childbed, contemplates "the next Volume of This Farrago—should I live to begin the next" (May 1778); and Lady

Amberley, how "if should die I should like him [her husband] to have [the child] much with him" (3 August 1865).[55] The women who articulate their fears (and not all the diarists do so) differ significantly from the nineteenth-century American women trekking West, described by historian Lillian Schlissel, whose diaries hide their anxieties. "No diarist," she reports, "opens to another's eyes the doubt, the pain, or the uncertainties that childbirth must have held."[56] Was it prudery? Or the distressing circumstance of giving birth on the trail, too frightening personally to contemplate? Or that their diaries were usually intended for relatives who would make the same journey a season later and should be shielded? Whatever the reasons, they do not write of their pregnancies at all.

These Englishwomen, who write for themselves, within the limits of their characteristic reticence can admit their anxieties and ordeals when they so chose. Thus one learns how childbed brings Charlotte Guest and both Shelley diarists near death—so near for the latter two as to become a transforming experience. Mary Shelley conquers her fear of death through her belatedly reported serious miscarriage of 1822: "I had opportunity to look at Death in the face, and did not fear it—far from it. . . . Whether the nature of my illness—debility from loss of blood, without pain—caused this tranquillity of soul, I cannot tell; but so it was, and it had this blessed effect, that I have never since anticipated death with terror" (5 October 1839). Badly depressed Frances Shelley instead thanks childbirth crisis for restoring her faith in life: "Mes couches, qui m'ont mise au bord du tombeau, m'ont fait faire des réflexions propres à calmer mon amour-propre blessé, à recevoir avec reconnaissance les bienfaits dont je suis entourée, et m'ont remise dans mon état ordinaire" (2 April 1818). (That is, childbed, which brought me to the edge of the grave, also soothed my wounded self-esteem and made me appreciate the blessings that surround me, thus returning me to my more usual frame of mind.) Guest, with lucid recall, merely dispassionately records a singular aftermath to an easy birth, when suddenly,

I felt as if I were dying, and as though but one moment remained to put up a hasty prayer. The next instant I was senseless, or rather unconscious, and for four hours after I went from one swoon into another, being during the intervals delirious or wandering. I can remember feeling that my hands were numbed and had no circulation. I can remember thinking of my husband and repressing his name when it came to my lips as too sacred to utter at such a moment with none but attendants to hear me. This is all I can remember. But some of my visions must have been of beauty, for they say I used expressions of admiration and spoke of splendour and loveliness. They have told me since that my symptoms were those of great danger, and that I was very nearly dying of debility or exhaustion. (25 August 1847)[57]

Out of childbed experiences such as these come the intense dramas of women's diaries—though her particular sense of honor is noteworthy too. Even if public battlefields are lacking, biology ensures that women will become intimates of death.

Because death stalks the childbed, the diarists must also record disappointments. Elizabeth Freke, for example, among her tribulations "lay In of Annother son . . . which, by hard Labour & severall frights, was Dead borne, And Lyes buryed . . . In London, with one of my Ld haliffaxes, In the Same Grave" (2 May 1677). Some diarists have miscarriages to report. Thrale, whose account is the most graphic, blames hers on her husband, who, after sending her to do some business concerning his brewery though he knew she was in danger of miscarriage,

would not be hurried—the probable Consequences *did* begin to arise, I pressed him to order the Coach—he could not be hurried—I told his Valet my Danger, & begged him to hasten his Master: no Pain, no Entreaties of mine could make him set out one *Moment* before the appointed hour—so I lay along in the Coach all the way from London to Streatham in a State not to be described, nor endured;—*but by me:*— & being carried to my Chamber the Instant I got home, miscarried in the utmost Agony before they get me into Bed, after fainting five Times.—(1 August 1779)

Others may attribute Mr. Thrale's callous behavior to mental confusion caused by his stroke—she herself opines in a side note that that "would have been but a too fair excuse." Thrale's long entry for

1 August 1779 (actually covering many days), to which on 15 August she adds the story of her miscarriage, is arranged so that it climaxes in the venting of her resentment. She has already dispassionately announced the birth of a premature, stillborn boy before the coach trip: "Tis less a miscarriage after all than a dead Child: A Boy quite formed & perfect; once I wished for such a Blessing—now if my Life is left me no matter for the rest." But she deceives herself. Because two sons have died young (five daughters survived), she desperately wants a boy. Consequently, five paragraphs later her smoldering resentment has erupted in the belatedly penned description of the slow trip home that cost her her son.[58]

The diaries show amply that women know childbearing to be an ordeal and a hazard, but that does not preclude their wanting children. One of Freke's few admissions that she has anything to be grateful for is that one child was miraculously saved for her. Her vivid account of his birth probably for once is not unduly exaggerated:

> I were 4 or 5 days In Labour of him, And had for him Fowre Mid-Wifes aboutt mee when he was borne, the Man Midwife afirming he had bin Long dead to my husband And Aunte [and] sister Norton with my Lady Thinn, all who were with mee severall days in this my extremity.
>
> My Great & Good God . . . Raised me up a good Woman Midwife of My Lady Thinns Acquaintance, one Mrs. Mills, who Came in att this Juncture of Tiem, and, by my Gods Mercy & providence to mee, I was saffly Delivered, And tho' [apparently] of a dead Child, My God Raised him up to me soe Farr as the Same Night to baptize him of my Deer Fathers Name. (2–3 June 1675)[59]

She makes no mention of her pain during several, if not necessarily "4 or 5," days of labor.

In compliance with their social training, women may blank out a great deal when having children is the issue. Judith S. Lewis believes that childbirth pain even traditionally assumed a "transforming and purifying significance" for aristocratic women, completed their sense of womanhood, though they would also welcome childbed anesthesia when it became available. By 1847, Dr. James Simpson had discov-

174

ered the use of chloroform, although it took about thirty years for the benefits to be widely recognized, over the objections of the clergy and the English medical establishment.[60] Whatever their class, women favored anesthesia. And yet as late as 1916, Asquith's attitude to the new "'twilight birth,' a method of some sort of injection which renders childbirth completely painless," as she describes it, is instructive. She objects to eliminating "all that particular pain—it would take too much drama out of life." Besides, she contends, for women "the recollection of the pain of the actual birth never, or scarcely ever, acts as a deterrent. . . . I find most of my friends . . . commit treason to their sex by saying they found [the pain] less bad than they expected" (24 July 1916). That she recognizes 'treason' to her sex perhaps reflects the aggressiveness of Edwardian feminism, long since urging freedom from biological bonds.[61] Meanwhile, Asquith herself wants the 'drama' of the pain.

The pain does not matter because women know, as Frances Russell says, that children are an addition to one's "blessings" and a sacred commitment. "And now I am a mother," she exults when her first child is born, and prays God "enable me to be one indeed and to feel that an immortal soul is entrusted to my care" (6 May 1848, [1842]). "My Children's Souls are in my Care, & all I can do for them is indispensable Duty," Thrale anticipates her (14 July 1780). As Lady Monkswell, poses it, if a woman "has a contempt for children, & does not even desire any," then "could anybody be more 'madly with her blessedness at strife'?" (24 December 1896).[62]

Not to be able to conceive becomes the ordeal, rather than childbirth. Conjecturally, even childless Hoby reveals her desire for a child in her 7 October 1603 entry, in which "this day I fasted untill Eueninge, eatinge nor drinkinge any thinge, begging of the Lord that blissinge wch. yet I want." Some 250 years later, Lucy Cavendish's diary is an ongoing record of frustrated longing, with many entries like these: "Two pretty baptisms which brought tears to my eyes, so foolishly did I long to see a baby of our own christened. . . . There is actually a baby expected [by Cousin Louisa]—stupid of me to feel this a pang, but O dear! if it *could* but be me instead!" (18 February 1866, 22 September 1869).[63] She bore no children, despite her longing. Although childless marriages doubled in the years following 1914 (compared to the last quarter of the nineteenth century), such marriages were still comparatively few,[64] and motherhood remained a lure. Fifty years after Cavendish, another diarist longs for a child no less than she did.

Virginia Woolf was also childless, because her shaky mental health precluded attempting conception. Woolf blames herself for that: "My own fault too—a little more self control on my part, & we might have had a boy of 12, a girl of 10: This always makes me wretched in the early hours" (5 September 1926). Like Cavendish, she finds desire perpetually awakened by others' children, especially those of her sister Nessa (Vanessa Bell). So, for example, "I am in one of my moods. . . . And what is it & why? A desire for children, I suppose; for Nessa's life; for the sense of flowers breaking all round me involuntarily" (2 January 1923). No one could state better the inherent appeal of children. But more is operative, which is why, quarreling with Nessa on one occasion, Woolf "set out to prove that being childless I was less normal than she" (4 February 1922). Woolf attempts to console herself with writing as the greater form of creativity: "I had a day of intoxication when I said Children are nothing to this: when I sat surveying the whole book complete" (28 March 1930). And perhaps intermittently she does convince herself with her substitute fertility. She can, for example, speak of completing *Three Guineas* as "the mildest childbirth I have ever had" (5 June 1938). But her deepest feelings run contrary: "Years & years ago, . . . I said to myself, . . . never pretend that the things you haven't got are not worth having; good advice I think. At least it often comes back to me. Never pretend that children, for instance, can be replaced by other things." Thus, fifteen years later, morose and discouraged, she senses still "the old jealousy of Nessa's children" (2 January 1923, 24 November 1938).[65] Bearing children is too tightly implicated in traditional female identity for even Woolf, feminist at heart, to escape the sense that if barren, then not a woman.

Katherine Mansfield also endeavors to make her writing rather than her fertility her form of creativity, and speaks of composing as "the moment of delivery" and "my one *happy issue*" (July 1918). But Mans-

176

field both does not and does want a child, as her diary shows. At seventeen, she is determined to be a liberated woman. "'Me marier et avoir des enfants! Mais quelle blanchisseuse—je veux la gloire,'" she writes in 1906, borrowing a line from Marie Bashkirtseff, who says, "Me! Marry and have children! But what a laundress I would make—I demand fame." Mansfield nonetheless married twice (George Bowden and John Middleton Murry); more pertinent here, in 1909 she miscarried Garnet Trowell's child, a blow she took so hard that she temporarily took in an older child to care for. An alleged pregnancy in 1911 may have terminated in an abortion, or more likely never existed, for surgery in 1910 as a consequence of gonorrhea made future pregnancy very improbable: one of her fallopian tubes was removed.[66] Mansfield nonetheless continued to yearn for a child. Thus, on 3 April 1914, "I wish I lived on a barge with Jack [John M. Murry] for a husband and a little boy for a son." And in June 1918, "As I [turned down the bed cover] I thought of John as a boy of about 17. I had a sort of *prophetic vision* of doing just the same thing for my son . . . in years to come." She attempts to brush off her 'vision': "The moment had no emotional value at all—especially as it was all drowned in the smell of roast mutting." But it bespeaks something important enough to her so that in 1919 (21 June and [?] December) she is musing, "O, I'd like a child . . .—a baby boy" and envisioning a fantasy child—"Some days it was a boy. For two years now it had very often been a little girl." By 12 January 1920, she has returned to the start: "Oh, misery! I cannot sleep. I lie *retracing* my steps—going over all the old life before. . . . The baby of Garnet Trowell" (ellipsis in original).[67]

At one point Mansfield reveals that she sees a child as a means of escape from male-centered love, not just for herself but for all women:

I hardly dare give rein to my thoughts of J. and my longing for J. And I thought: if I had a child, I would play with it now and *lose myself in it* and kiss it and make it laugh. And I'd use my child as my guard against my deepest feeling. . . .

That's true, I think, of all, all women. And it accounts for the curious look of security that you see in young mothers: they are safe from any *ultimate* state of feeling because of the child in their arms. (January 1914).[68]

Whatever Mansfield may believe an "ultimate" state of feeling to be, she is right that women (but not all women) may find an escape from self in tending their infants, who have an intrinsic potential for focusing all feeling and regard on themselves. The mystique of motherhood—"The Sacred Calling," feminist Adrienne Rich calls it—[69] with its mythology of the joys of motherhood, expands that potential, exploiting its sentimental nuances. And Mansfield has assimilated the mythology despite herself. That may be why she, like Woolf, cannot be at peace with her childlessness.

Culturally conditioned, most women have traditionally felt they want children. Although Thrale (Piozzi), for example, has borne twelve children in her first marriage, remarried she still wants "a Child by the Man I so love—*that* only could add to my happiness" (27 January 1785). Earlier, when her first husband suffers a stroke, she is pregnant—but not penitent, despite her disclaimers: "Five Little girls . . . , & breeding again, & Fool enough to be proud of it! Ah Ideot! what should I want more Children for? God knows only to please my Husband, who now perhaps may be much better without them—" (11 June 1779). More likely it is herself she pleases; children prove her value. So right does it seem to desire children that even Asquith, self-involved as she is and distasteful to her as is pregnancy, convinces herself that she should have another child, besides her John and Michael, though

> I am in no immediate hurry—am anxious to do some strenuous war work and would like to have a baby born in the winter. But, in the circumstances [the war], I have a superstitious feeling that one ought not to postpone. I think it is largely the extraordinary delight Michael is to me now. I feel that, whatever happened, life could not be anything but thrilling with such a child. The nursery seems the only solution—I would so love to have a daughter. So, I really think I shall condemn myself, though it does require some strength of mind. (20 November 1916)

Likewise, "a blessed sentimentality envelops me" two years later when she assumes herself pregnant (18 February 1918).[70]

In the absence of reliable contraceptives and the presence of social and religious prescriptions to multiply, married women take pride in themselves as breeders. Elizabeth Wynne, a Catholic, had nine children, all of whose births she welcomes, recording each with a satisfied description of an effortless accouchement. But she is no different from Protestant Guest, nine of whose ten accouchements barely ruffle her day. Even the tenth, though, the one that belatedly proves nearly fatal, in the immediate event shows her typical sangfroid:

> I had rather suspected I might soon be confined, but I went to sleep and forgot it. In the morning when I woke I became pretty sure the event was not far distant. I merely told Merthyr I would breakfast upstairs, which I did. I suffered scarcely at all, and at half past 10 gave birth to another little girl, our 5th daughter and 10th child. . . . I sent for Merthyr, who did not even know I was indisposed, and showed him our new treasure. (25 August 1847)

Wynne too makes childbirth seem the easiest, most natural of functions. Her characteristic birth entry runs, "I did not feel very well all day, but took a drive in the afternoon with all the Children—towards ten o'clock I sent for Dr. Tookey, and was happily and safely brought to Bed a few minutes after twelve, of another Boy" (30 August 1810). Only her younger, unmarried sister Harriet, present at one accouchement, opines, "*I do* not think much of a Lying in," though she admits that Elizabeth "really had an uncommon good time" of hers (7 September 1805). Not until her fifth child does Elizabeth suggest that she might have been disappointed to find herself pregnant yet again: "I have not been at all well for this week past, being most wretchedly sick & sleepy—c'est un mauvais signe! [it's a bad sign]" (20 January 1805).[71]

Doubtless not all the women wanted every child they had, and perhaps some even wanted none. But the weight of public opinion and tradition have historically been against married women who would not breed. Until the interwar period of the twentieth century,

179

when women ignored the pronatalist propaganda to reverse the falling birthrate and instead severely limited family size, women endeavored to reproduce generously. Historian Patricia Branca has argued that middle-class Victorian women began controlling their fertility after mid-century by employing the improved contraceptive devices available by then (effective earlier contraception, coitus interruptus, was under male control). At the same time, she must acknowledge that during the Victorian era, "almost all middle-class women expected pregnancy at least once . . . and most became pregnant four or five times during their lives." Women continued to conceive children: perhaps they did not have as much control as Branca claims, and perhaps they still felt it wrong to limit a family too much, if at all. Even in the second half of the nineteenth century, when birth control (neo-Malthusianism) began to be publicly advocated by liberal thinkers, it met opposition from women. Diarist Beatrice (Potter) Webb finds it repugnant: "The open discussion of it is every day more permitted. I see it practised by men and women who are perfectly pure. I cannot see *reasons* against it; yet my moral instinct is not with it" (22 February 1888). No other Victorian (or non-Victorian) diarist comments on birth control, except Lady Amberley, who does so indirectly by supporting her husband when he publicly advocates it despite the risk to his political career. However, her discussion with female Dr. Sewell, who operates a women's hospital in Boston but could as well speak from England, captures a typically righteous establishment stance when Sewell attacks "the frequent habit here of procuring abortions to avoid the trouble of children" (8 November 1867).[72] A good woman accepts her duties and bears her progeny. Many women could feel that to be true.

On the other hand, abortion as a method of birth control, especially practiced clandestinely through abortifacient drugs, has always been a recourse. Though none of these diarists ever speaks of having resorted to it, some of the reported miscarriages of other women may be euphemisms for induced abortions, and some explicitly are. Eugenia Wynne is not alone in writing of induced miscarriages (as earlier noted: 5 March 1806). A century earlier, Mary Cowper's gossip about how Lord Strafford's wife, "who had fancied herself with

Child, miscarried as she had resolved to do . . . and as I had been told by her Mother-in-law (in Confidence) she would do" (2 February 1715), is clear enough. Likewise, Ellen Weeton in her letter-diary writes of a woman who "took something when pregnant of her little girl intended to fall on the child" (13 December 1807).[73] If any of these diarists did so too, they cannot mention it.

The children they have borne engage some space in all the mothers' diaries, though variably so. Children play little or no part in court diaries; as a rule, they play a lesser part in aristocratic than in middle-class diaries; and more space necessarily goes to daily minutiae about the young in the writings of women who themselves tend their children instead of servants' doing so. At least two diarists also kept separate books for their children.[74] Hester Thrale (as earlier indicated) kept "a Register of my Children's Powers of Mind and Body beginning with the first down to the last" (19 February 1788), but converted it to a general diary,[75] and twentieth-century Cynthia Asquith kept books for her first two sons, the record for the elder child intended partly as an aid to his doctors.

The diarists' maternal roles are as acceptable to them as their wifely ones. Rarely do diarists complain of the daily burden of child care—the women are more likely to complain of rude or inept servants—even when it largely devolves upon them rather than their servants. Some timeless situations are acknowledged, though. For example, Elizabeth Wynne's "brats," as she affectionately calls them, remain welcome but wear her down when "Charles is better, but Harry was very sick and did nothing but cry all night. My bed is so near the nursery I scarcely ever have a good night, and I have lately slept very little, wake at daylight." (25 January 1804). Also she discovers she must forego her harpsichord practice ([April] 1798), even as Guest, with her first child, must forego Persian lessons because "Baby leaves but little time for anything" (3 September 1834). Lady Monkswell complains that she could scarcely enjoy her brother-in-law's wedding because "My whole soul & body was taken up with endeavours to keep Bino quiet" (3 July 1879).[76]

Mothers typically record their children's growth, accomplishments, schooling; misbehaviors and illnesses (or deaths); courtships, engagements, and marriages. Seventeenth-century mothers also record rites of passage in dress. Thus Anne Clifford reports of her daughter Margaret (b. 2 July 1614) in 1617:

> The 28th was the first time the Child put on a pair of whale-bone bodice.

> Upon the 1st I cut the Child's strings off from her coats and made her use togs alone, so as she had two or three falls at first but had no hurt with them.
> The 2nd the Child put on her first coat that was laced with Lace, being of red baize. (April and May)

The proviso about the strings probably refers to a string at the back of a pinafore used to control a toddler. Thrale writes of her two-year-old daughter, Hester Maria, when the child can "walk & run alone" that "tho' the Backstring is still kept on it is no longer of Use" (17 September 1766). The *togs* are coats (according to the *Oxford English Dictionary*); that is, clothes. The whalebone bodice and laced petticoats that make the child a miniature adult signify that the infant is growing up female. The ceremony of breeching for boys, when the gowns of infancy are left off (for boys there was a public ceremony), is recaptured in Isabella Twysden's diary when "roger was put in to breches the 15 Octo: 1648 being somewhat above 6 yeare old, he was very littell of groweth."[77]

Across the centuries, mothers are concerned with their children's traits and behavior. A few illustrations of frequent themes will be indicative. Her daughter's progress and intelligence are Fanny Anne Burney (Wood's) great pride, for at age four "she promises to be a child of much intellect and of great observation, with the power of applying her little stock of ideas, and with a singularly retentive memory" (23 February 1841). For Margaret Jeune, it is rather her daughter's looks and popularity (though she is also pleased that the girl is levelheaded and good): "It amuses me to see the homage which dear Meggie begins to receive. She is certainly very strikingly superior to most of the other girls here, and has a fine bearing which distinguishes her" (14 January 1856). Charlotte Guest, however, is disturbed by her daughter's behavior, for Katherine "was very naughty and got into a pet, and I had a scene with her that unnerved me completely, and made me quite ill" (20 January 1858). Almost twenty-one, Katherine danced thrice with the same man at a ball, nearly a declaration of engagement by the etiquette of her contemporary social circle. The unruly schooldays of Mary Woodforde's sons (no girl's mother has to contend with such a problem) worry her constantly, as one of many similar entries may suggest:

> This evening I had the cutting news that my second boy was in rebellion at the College at Winton, where he and all his Companions resolved not to make any verses, and being called to be whipped for it several of them refused to be punished, mine amongst the rest. . . . God I beseech thee subdue their stubborn hearts. (6 March 1687)

Louisa Bain worries about her son's sudden engagement, though his fiancée proves pretty and pleasant "and will I hope make him a good wife" (6 April 1871). Some mothers establish their goals for their children: Louisa de Rothschild, for example, who wants "to lead them right and yet leave to them their individuality," and intends to see that they, "please God, shall be better instructed" in their faith than was she ([18??]). But Ellen Weeton hopes her daughter will resemble her and have "a great regard for personal modesty" and tend to her stockings: "I am not afraid to take my shoe off at any time, for I have no holes, or soil, to hide" (13 June 1825).[78]

Any of these particular motherly observations about traits, behavior, and aspirations might have been made recently (though the specific cause for Guest's quarrel with her daughter would change since such rigid social etiquette died in the Great War). But some diaristic content clearly is of another day. Twentieth-century conceptions of mother-child intimacy are violated in the older diaries. The earlier the diary, the less the concern for frequent close contact between mother and babe. Though Clifford, for example, loves her daughter and is proud when she has eighteen teeth and wears lace-edged petticoats, concerned when she is sick, and distraught when she is taken away, the child's company bores her—"the time being very tedious unto me as having neither comfort nor company, only the Child

(8 May 1617)—and their relationship is rather formal. Not until the girl's fifth birthday is "the child" named; she becomes (and thereafter is referred to as) Lady Margaret. And only when Margaret is three years old (and has achieved her new petticoats) does she come "to lie with me which was the first time that ever she lay all night in a bed with me since she was born" (2 July 1619, 4 May 1617). Before then, she sleeps with her nurse, Mary Hicken. Mary Woodforde's son (Woodforde was the wife of a provincial clergyman) leaves home very young by her account: "Dear little Willy [age four] went . . . to board at Mr. Wallace's, to go to School" (14 January 1687). The baptism of Mary Hardy's daughter Polly (Hardy was the wife of a prosperous farmer) occurs on 5 November 1773; and on Tuesday, 21 November 1775, "Polly began going to school"—presumably a dame school. But Hester Thrale's Susan Arabella (b. 23 May 1770) goes off to boarding school by 3 March 1774. Middle-class Faith Gray's daughter is taken away from home to be weaned (2 May 1794) in a common eighteenth-century practice, prosperous women having by then begun nursing their infants. (Earlier, those who could afford it, such as Isabella Twysden in 1645, used wet nurses.) [79]

Thrale prides herself that until her eldest daughter is past five years old, she has never left the child, when awake, to the care of servants (21 March 1770). But up through the nineteenth century, the infants of the wealthy were often entrusted to servants, a practice that not only diminished parent-child intimacy, but was also potentially hazardous. Elizabeth Freke includes a graphic, possibly exaggerated account of her son's crippling "by the Carlessnes of his Nurse, & Aboutt 14 of December [he] brok his Legg shortt In the Hackle Bone, which she kept pryvatte for neer a quarter of A year Til A Jelley was Grown between Itt; She keeping him in his Cradle, & everybody believed he was Breeding of his Teeth." Away in Ireland, Freke is recalled by her father to attend the child and "recovered him from his Cruches with my poor Weak endeavours," or so she claims (14 December 1675, 15 June 1676). Over a century later, Elizabeth, Lady Holland, reports being "brought to bed of a lovely boy . . . but owing to the neglect of the nurses he fell into convulsions and died'" (4 October 1795). Three-quarters of a century later, Lady Amberley discovers through her infant's wet nurse that his nursemaid has been neglecting and torturing him, though the details of his "brutal treatment" (21 October 1865) appear in a letter rather than her diary.[80]

Historian Leonore Davidoff observes that in Victorian upper-class society, "motherhood *per se* was not the most important part of the matron's life. . . . being a mother was certainly not expected to absorb all her time and attention. The physical and emotional care of young children was, in fact, considered to be a distraction from the more important business of wider family and social duties." But Judith S. Lewis, conversely, describes a changing attitude to motherhood during the period 1760–1860, which made it among the aristocracy "a moral, intellectual, and emotional pursuit" as "a woman's greatest source of dignity and emotional satisfaction," no longer just the achievement of having produced an heir.[81] The truth indicated by these diaries falls between both extremes, and the attitudes are not limited to a particular period or social class. The diaries show that parent-child bonding in certain significant ways is discouraged from the seventeenth century to the nineteenth, but they also show that mothers take active concern for their children's well-being, even with reliance on servant assistance.

One indication is that children's illness is a recurrent theme. The great fear of earlier centuries is smallpox and its attendant scarring. After inoculation became possible (1721 and after),[82] eighteenth-century mothers regularly record their children's fortunes with it, thankful when only a light case of the pox results. Faith Gray's diary affords a good sense of the course of smallpox in a household full of children:

1794 Jan. 2nd Mr. Gray set off on Horse back to London. . . .
24th Frances began to be ill in the small pox.
30th Mr. Gray arrived in London.
Feb. 2nd. Frances small pox at the height. She got well through them.
8th Edmund began in the small pox.
10th Lucy and Robert begun in them.
14th Edmund's small pox at the height.
22nd William began to be ill.
March Through the kind hand of our gracious God, all the five chil-

dren got well thro' the small pox, not one of them likely to be at all marked.[83]

Mr. Gray is well out of it. The burden of the sick children and the anxiety devolve on Faith.

Although she herself writes dispassionately, children's sufferings are crises for their mothers in any century. Margaret Jeune reflects seventy-five years later "how such an illness seems to endear a child to one!" (16 May 1854) after a violent croup has nearly been fatal to her son Fritz. (She reports him saved by the prompt application of a "mustard plaster to the spine, which we could only keep on by the use of Chloroform, and afterwards bleeding from the jugular vein"— a remedy one would think might rather have killed him.) Thrale panics when her daughter Sophia is afflicted with fits. She administers a dram of whiskey and when the fits recur massages Sophia "so as to keep the heart in Motion," then faints. Thrale self-dramatizes and implores Heaven to spare the child, taking "in Exchange the life of her wretched Mother!" (19 November 1783), but her anxiety is honest enough. Having watched her son Charles through a bad case of measles, Lady Holland cries, "My God, what anguish can equal the pang a mother feels who sees her infant struggling against death" (25 January 1801). As Louisa de Rothschild says when her husband has received bad financial news, "But after all, what is the worst in this case in comparison with so many other misfortunes which might befall one? The loss of eyesight; the loss, or even *the fear* of the loss of a child" (February 1848).[84]

The fear had to be very real for the diarists. Child mortality has historically been appalling. In the period 1730–1749, for example, as many as three-quarters of London children died by age five; even in 1810–1829 slightly under one-third succumbed. Although child mortality dropped markedly during the Victorian era, until the twentieth century, as historian Jane Lewis remarks, "it was not uncommon for women to speak in the same breath of the number of children they had raised and the number they had buried."[85] For the many diarists who lose children to death, great suffering ensues, whether or not they are the natural mothers and irrespective of time. As Mary

186

Shelley says upon the death of her four-year-old William, "To have won, and then cruelly to have lost, the associations of four years, is not an accident to which the human mind can bend without much suffering" (4 August 1819). Or, as Eliot grieves upon losing Lewes's son Thornie, "This death seems to me the beginning of our own" (19 October 1869), and as governess Claire Clairmont writes about her charge Dunia, "A sudden gloom falls upon all the senses, the universe . . . becomes black & dark" (25 September 1825). "My affliction almost overpowers me at the loss of such a darling and lovely Child," laments Elizabeth Wynne when her five-year-old daughter dies, but she has another young child to care for, so "I am obliged to exert myself in this severe trial" (24 October 1819). When pious eighteenth-century Gray's adored firstborn daughter, Lucy, dies, she cannot repine; that would be questioning God's will. But thereafter she keeps the anniversary of Lucy's birth even as her contemporary Caroline Powys (by her editor's report) does for her deceased firstborn.[86]

Historian Joseph E. Ilick suggests that because girls were taught to sublimate anger or aggression through religion, seventeenth- and even eighteenth-century women uncomplainingly accepted a child's loss as God's will. These diarists may not complain, but they do keenly mourn their losses, infant or older, not simply resign themselves. Much like Ilick, historian Lawrence Stone contends that, from the sixteenth to the early eighteenth centuries, because of high infant mortality, parents limited their psychological involvement with their young children; "it was very rash . . . to get too emotionally concerned about creatures whose expectation of life was so very low." In evidence, he quotes Hester Thrale, in the following manner:

> When in 1770 Susanna Arabella was born two months prematurely, her mother never expected her to live, and took an instant dislike to her, since "she is so very poor a creature I can scarce bear to look on her." When two years later another daughter, Penelope, died within ten hours of birth, her mother commented coolly, "one cannot grieve after her much, and I have just now other things to think of."[87]

187

Thrale's own entries suggest a different mentality. For premature Susanna Arabella, Thrale expresses her fear that the child will die after all. Her comment is not made in May, upon the child's birth, but in August, when Thrale reports anxiously,

> She lives . . . & Doctor Johnson comforts me by saying She will be like other people; of which however if She *does live*, I make very great doubt. —She sucks well enough at present but is so very poor a Creature, I can scarce bear to look on her; Evans says he never christen'd so small a Child before, & Bromfield said he never saw but one born so very little & kept alive to a Year old. (4 August 1770)

Susanna lived to be eighty-eight. Of Penelope, Thrale writes that she

> liv'd but 10 hours, looked black & could not breathe freely—poor little Maid! one cannot grieve after her much, and I have just now other things to think of—this has been a sad Lying In: my mother dying—& every thing going wrong. (September 1772)

The mother to whom Thrale is very close has died, and her husband is on the edge of bankruptcy. But Thrale certainly cares about her "poor little Maid" though she has much else to think of. The great number of children's deaths, newborn or older, reported in these diaries yields a wide range of grief reactions. Only one makes a reader question the diarist's real feelings—Frances Shelley's upon her granddaughter's death: "Poor child! only eighteen. This will, of course, prevent my going out into society" (16 May 1854).[88]

Thrale bore one brain-impaired child, but he died young. Cynthia Asquith must contend with another anguish than death. Her son John (b. 1911) proves to be autistic although Michael (b. 1914) is not (nor would be Simon, b. 1919, after the diary closes). Asquith's diary becomes her gradual discovery of John's abnormality. In 1915, the year the diary begins, only friend D. H. Lawrence thinks John "very abnormal. . . . He quite alarmed me about John;" Asquith herself assumes him to be merely a contrary child, "very challenging, just doing things for the sake of being told not to—" with a "peculiar, indescribable detachment" (12 and 11 May). By 1916, however, she is anxious, for "he is nearly five and must be taken in hand. Sometimes I feel miserably worried about his abnormality." A visit to a specialist brings "cold terror about John now more and more often. It is just because the word 'stupid' is so inapplicable and because of a strange completeness about him as he is, that makes one despair of any reason why he should ever change. Oh God, surely nothing so cruel can really have happened to me myself?" (17 April and 13 May). Thereafter, spells of hope alternate with growing hopelessness, climaxing in her recognition that she can never escape the "tragedy" of John, "a past, present, and future nightmare. I loved my idea of that baby more than I have ever loved anything—and it was just something that never existed" (24 October 1917).[89] She decides for Michael's sake, and probably her own as well, to think less about John (long since residing apart with a nurse, in any case, and fated to die in his twenties).

The ordeals of other mothers lie in enforced separations from their children. As it chances, the painful separations are from daughters. In the two instances in which the same mothers (Caroline Powys and Lady Elizabeth Holland) also have sons, their ties with their daughters are closer, even as psychologist Nancy Chodorow has suggested will occur. Chodorow observes that, from children's pre-oedipal stage on, mothers "normally identify more with daughters and experience them as less separate" than sons; their daughters are extensions, "more like, and continuous with" the mothers themselves.[90] More willingly do these two mother-diarists give up their sons. Powys's attachment to her daughter turns even Caroline's overnight stay with a friend into active suffering as "the first time I had ever parted for a night with my dear girl, tho' then fifteen" (2 June 1790). This closeness of Powys and her Caroline is duplicated by Powys's great-grandmother Thrale and her mother. Thrale writes, "My Mother & I had never been twelve *hours* apart from each other till I married, nor ever more than twelve *Days* afterwards" ([June] 1777). However, Thrale's mother did arrange for her to marry. When Powys' Caroline is to be married Powys is "so affected with the loss of my dear girl (who till latterly I had never parted with for even one night [her diary could have told her it was actually three years earlier]), that I dreaded how I should behave at the time" (14 March

1793). On the family's advice, she does not attend the wedding. And six years later, the young couple's remove from the neighborhood "was to me one of the most melancholy days I ever experienced, as it was to part me and my dearest Caroline" (13 September 1799). Parting from son Tom after his marriage is sad, but not unduly agitating (see 9 November 1799, 15 January 1800).[91]

Even more noteworthy is Lady Holland's attempt to keep her daughter, Harriet, when her divorce obliges her to return his children to her first husband, Godfrey Webster. From 1796 to 1799 she conceals Harriet, pretending that the girl has died in illness, because "the certainty of losing all my children was agonising, and I resolved to keep one in my possession, and I chose that one who, from her age and sex, required the tenderness of a mother." Maybe more important, Harriet "is so captivating. With her I feel amused, with my others I feel gratified at seeing them healthy and intelligent, but her winning manners convert the duty of maternal attention into a positive enjoyment. I delight in being with her, and think her society sufficient" (19 and 20 June 1799). Only the anticipation of discovery and fear of compromising Lord Holland induce her to surrender Harriet, and upon Webster's suicide in 1800, she endeavors to undertake the expenses of maintaining Harriet in absentia because Webster's will has made lesser provision for the girl than the boys ([11 June] 1800).[92]

In two other separations, the mothers have only one child. Claire Clairmont was persuaded by Mary and Percy Shelley to relinquish Allegra, the child she had borne to Byron, because (according to Clairmont's editor, Marion Kingston Stocking) they believed it would benefit Allegra to be the acknowledged daughter of a peer, not to mention silencing gossip linking Percy to Clairmont. Although Clairmont has found a peace of mind rare for her in her absorption in Allegra, she reluctantly agrees to have the child conveyed to Byron in the spring of 1818, then lapses into depression and mistrust of Byron. "If I recovered Allegra," it would be "as if I had come back to the warmth of life after the cold stiffness of the grave" (12 April 1821), she writes.[93] But her schemes to regain her child are unsuccessful, and in 1822 the five-year-old Allegra dies of typhus at the Convent of Bagnacavallo. Years of depression follow, for her mother.

The outcome is more fortunate for Ellen Weeton (Stock), whose diary records her ordeal to maintain frequent communication with her daughter Mary though legally forbidden it by her marital separation. She walks eight miles to see Mary at the school where Stock has sequestered her and is treated shabbily by the headmaster, but though she "almost despaired of accomplishing so long a journey on foot," she returns frequently nonetheless because "a mother's heart can do great things" (30 April 1824). When Weeton is forbidden to enter the school, she contrives to observe Mary walking on the grounds, then to meet up with the school crocodile and accompany Mary to chapel, even to enter the chapel and accompany the girl partway back to school. Warnings to desist only strengthen her determination, for "'the loss of a mother . . . is the greatest loss she can sustain, and it shall not be my fault if she is without one'" (15 May 1825). Happily, Mary was eventually returned to Weeton when Stock left the community, though that event lies outside the diary and is only reported by its editor, Edward Hall.[94] The diary is a moving account of a woman's growth out of self-pity and into strength as a result of her struggle to keep watch over her child.

For widowed Hester Thrale (Piozzi) and Charlotte Guest (Schreiber) the problem of separation is spiritual rather than physical: each confronts daughterly opposition to her remarriage. Schreiber and her eldest daughter, Maria, begin at loggerheads: "I believe she shuns me. . . . I am sure it is months since she has said one kind word. . . . How deeply I have suffered I can never describe" (11 March and 19 July 1856). But Maria capitulates; Thrale's five daughters do not. "They love not me. Is it my fault or theirs!" she asks rhetorically, certain that she is the most self-sacrificing of mothers. "There are none of them for whom I would not willingly give my Life" (1 September 1781, 30 March, 1792). Despite her manipulative exertions, her three eldest daughters break with her when she insists on marrying singing master Gabriel Piozzi; the younger child, Cecilia, whom she takes to live with her after remarriage, continues to ally with her sisters (a second young daughter dies). Because Thrale is never resigned to the separation—"We shall never more embrace like Parent & Child . . . Oh good God! how dreadful is that Idea!" (28 January 1788)—she rejoices when the three enemies make overtures of friendship after six years of animosity. When it emerges that their motivation is concern for their estate, not affection for their mother, she accepts the disappointment philosophically and persists in admiring their ringleader, her eldest daughter, "Queeney," for "I really delight unfeignedly in the Company of Miss Thrale . . . a person greatly to my Taste, independent of relationship or Vanity" (25 November 1795). This is not to say that she does not also resent Queeney's behavior, for finally, in another unsuccessful venture, she adopts a nephew of her husband's as heir to see "if He will be more grateful, & rational, & comfortable than Miss Thrales have been to the Mother they have at length *driven to Desperation*" (17 January 1798).[95]

For doughty Thrale, the choice between the man she loves and her daughters resolves in favor of the man, though she does not cease to love her daughters because of the contest of wills. Once she has the opportunity to do so, Thrale, whose first marriage was her mother's choice, while her second is her own, is determined to remain in control of her life. In fact, of course, she is not in control. The fundamental decisions have already been made for her by her male-dominant society, which has taught her that she wants to be wed and to bear children. Like most of her sister diarists, Thrale does not question those values. Instead, like them, she arranges her existence in women's designated world of marriage and motherhood, where sorrow pursues women unable to conform or unlucky as wives and mothers; but happiness is not precluded by conventional womanly roles, though self-development may be. That living in a masculinist culture amidst traditions handed down from mother to daughter may also cost women fair self-valuation is a matter the next chapter considers.

FIVE

"A VERY ORDINARY WOMAN"

On Female Psychology and Daughterhood

R EADING Englishwomen's diaries with sensitivity to their thoughts
and feelings on any subject, not just marriage and motherhood, one
gains a sense of pattern to their thinking about self. A dominant
motif emerges only too soon. Virginia Woolf captures it when she
writes, "Were it not for my flash of imagination, & this turn for books,
I should be a very ordinary woman. No faculty of mine is really very
strong" (3 August 1924).[1] While the self-estimate is ridiculous, Woolf
is quite ordinary in devaluing herself. Although the diaries contain
some position self-estimates, low self-esteem and confidence are their
more common bent, corroborating feminist Elaine Morgan's concern
that "the first of all things women need to be liberated from is their
chronic tendency to feelings (admitted, concealed, or aggressively
overcompensated for) of guilt and inadequacy."[2] The diarists are far
less happy with themselves and secure in themselves than ideally
they should be or existentially they deserve to be.

Diarist Frances Russell may be only a dispirited adolescent when
she realizes that "I require to forget myself in order to be happy" and
"I dislike myself more than ever. . . . If my manner is so bad must
there not be some real fault in me that makes it so?" (31 January and
24 December 1836). But the same distressing strain runs through
adult women's diaries too, in which Clarissa Trant at twenty-four is
"tired of *myself*" (12 November 1824); Cynthia Asquith at twenty-

193

nine is "beginning to tire of my own company. . . . Am not growing on myself" (22 September 1916); and Lady Monkswell at forty-one is "glad I went [on a visit] as it took me out of myself (a place I am very tired of)" (18 November 1890). Some spirit abroad, become a poison within, makes a Mary Shelley thankful for studies whereby she is gaining "a profounder knowledge of my defects" (19 March 1823) and gives a George Eliot at year's end "a more acute sense of my deficiencies" (31 December 1857),³ when they could be relaxing in their virtues, achievements, and perfections. Even if the diarists discover some praiseworthy qualities in themselves and extol certain of their accomplishments, they find much to criticize and condemn, doubt and despair of. They are also given to bouts of depression, and they dread aging, so providing the companion pieces to low self-esteem and confidence. Like the mothers whom they love and emulate and duplicate—remarkably few of the women are estranged from their mothers—these diarists are subject to pernicious habits of mind as well as inclined to merely conventional ones. Generation to generation, from the culture at large and from maternal example and precept, women diarists have ingested bases for self-disparagement.

Reasons women should be unimpressed by themselves, never far to seek in a masculinist culture, are implicit in Elizabeth Byrom's innocent description of the Pretender's march on Manchester in 1745: "The Presbyterians are sending everything that's valuable away, wives, children, and all, for fear of the rebels" (26 September). Centuries of appraisal as a superior kind of property, yet an inferior mode of creature, lead to male identification and self-effacement, not to deep admiration for women or high self-esteem and confidence. The historical devaluation of women is more conducive to a woman's assuming, as for example the adult Russell does, that she compares ill with her husband, "in whom I see all the strength and goodness that my weak and erring nature so much requires. . . . How often his strength makes me feel . . . my own weakness." (29 July 1841, 18 August 1867). Woolf too knows that "at the bottom of my mind, I feel that I am distanced by L[eonard] in every respect" (26 September 1920); and Eliot that her "worship" of George Lewes's fine character is "my best life" (25 March 1865).⁴

Cultural devaluation leads to Trant's delight at walking with her brother Tom, "leaning on his arm and feeling that he does not think me a plague" (15 May 1829), and to Elizabeth Barrett (Browning's) thinking it would be a pleasure to visit Mr. Boyd, "knowing that I was not in the way" (11 March 1832). It leads to Ellen Weeton's priding herself first that "my father was an African [ship's] captain; my brother is an attorney" and only last that "I have been a schoolmistress." It prevents her taking simple pride in climbing a Welsh mountain unassisted. Instead she hides her face from male climbers lest they recognize her, for "I should dread the being pointed at in the road . . . as—'That is the lady I saw ascending Snowdon, alone!'" (4 December 1808, June 1825). It shadows Elizabeth Eastlake, who will write an article for the *Quarterly Review*, though "to keep down the redundancy of mere word, and keep up the succession of real thought is a task beyond the usual strength of women" (2 February 1845).[5] Cultural historian Katharine M. Rogers has observed of eighteenth-century misogyny that it "implanted inhibitions and self-disparagement in women."[6] That consequence is scarcely limited to the eighteenth century. At any time, if one is a woman, "one does learn a little to mistrust oneself" (Lucy Cavendish, 7 November 1866).[7]

Psychologists have pinned down such manifestations of cultural influence to specific causes, in theories often borne out by the diarists' lived experience. As early as the 1930s, Karen Horney's pioneer studies pointed out that self-confidence in either sex requires the development of diverse human traits: the full human potential for behavior and achievement.[8] Yet woman's potential in a male-dominant culture is sorely circumscribed by the "overvaluation of love." Not only has the culture historically dictated that woman shall devote herself to love rather than develop her other inherent capacities; it has also assured her doing so by creating an economic, social, and emotional dependency on men. Direct access to security and prestige have been denied her; her status and accomplishments have come only through the male. Nor dare she risk loss of male approbation and love by rebellion. Katherine Mansfield is therefore a visionary when she assumes in 1922 that she need not allow her life to be male-dependent:

In fact, don't you yet know that the more active and apart you make your own life, the more content the other is? . . .

195

How badly, how stupidly you manage your life! . . . You are the
most stupid woman I have ever met. You never will see that it all rests
with you. ([June])[9]

The self-condemnation is as characteristic a female touch as her inability to act on her perception. Historically, moreover, most women
have not even contemplated the self-confident possibility that all
rests with them.

The overvaluation of love means women need to stifle ambitions
and behaviors that qualify as competitive and therefore invite rejec-
tion. Eastlake captures that spirit of social compulsion when she
turns down another offer to write a review because "my woman-
ish part, and it is a large one, has no share in ambition and applause"
(28 December 1842). At its simplest, the overvaluation of love means
that women practice unassertive, deferential, noncompetitive behavior like Lady Monkswell, listening to Lord Rendel talking "with
his usual freedom & brilliancy. I lay very low, as his views are not
mine." Or enjoying herself at the Trevelyans', where "the conversation was extremely brilliant," she "chiefly sat & listened and was well
amused" (25 July 1903, 16 June 1905).[10] But something else happens, more serious for the female psyche and already implied by her
protective behavior. Many women, as Horney points out, unconsciously solve the problem of maintaining acceptable femininity by
adopting weakened self-confidence, for "the conviction of one's own
incapacity affords an excellent protection against achieving anything
worthwhile, and thus ensures one against the dangers of successful
competition." A classic illustration is Lady Monkswell when Miss
Fawcett has bested the senior wrangler in the Cambridge Mathematical Tripos: "I never saw Bob more moved as one of his most intimate
beliefs is the inferiority of the female brain where mathematics are
concerned. He has a perfect right to this belief after having been
married for 17 years, for I can just get through the household accounts & the yearly budget & *no more* (13 June 1890).[11] Conscious
policy may keep her silent in society, but unconscious psychic ma-
neuvering appears to have taken its toll as well. Defensive postures
become a habit of mind for women in a patriarchy, affecting their
relations with themselves and other women, not just with men.

As a follower of Horney particularly interested in developmental psychology, Judith M. Bardwick has also observed how much females "perceive the world in interpersonal terms. . . . Notwithstanding occupational achievements, they tend to esteem themselves only insofar as they are esteemed by those they love and respect." [12] Thus their self-esteem and confidence are necessarily linked closely to the appearance and functioning of their bodies, the instruments that effect the sexual and maternal success requisite for the esteem of others—a linkage the diarists have already amply demonstrated. It makes aging, as they also show, an ordeal for their egos. More pertinent here is Bardwick's Horneyian sense of how role conflict can destroy the self-esteem of the maturing girl. Reared for affiliation, she may nonetheless be motivated to gratify a desire for achievement. But having perceived that achievement is male territory, she will stifle her potential. Denying her ideal self will cost her her self-worth. As Bardwick sums up, "Because role conflict is more likely to exist in women . . . women have lower self-esteem than men."

Beatrice Webb may offer a good illustration. As a young woman, Webb keeps under cover before family and friends, aiming "to appear commonplace and sensible" because "to be on the right side of ordinary is the perfection of prudence in a young woman, and will save her from much heartburning and mortification of spirit" (25 November 1882). Webb feels split within, not only because "my life is divided sharply into the thoughtful part and the active part, completely unconnected one with the other," but also because "the one ideal is hidden from the world, the truth being that in my heart of hearts I'm *ashamed* of it and yet it is actually the dominant internal power" (24 April 1883, emphasis added). Thus, by age twenty-three, she has come to "a due realization of the poverty of my intellect and its incapability of dealing with most of the problems that are continually cropping up" in her studies. By twenty-six, she is appalled by the "minuteness of my faculties" (12 September 1881, 24 October 1884). [13] And despite every evidence of intellectual ability, self-doubt plagues her, as it does so many other talented diarists, thereafter.

Approaching devaluation from a different direction, Jean Baker Miller focuses on the perpetual assaults made on female self-worth. [14] She points, for example, to the objectification of women intrinsic to male-female relationships, wherein the dehumanization of being treated like an object is psychically intolerable and contributes to "a woman's belief that there must be something terribly bad and evil about her. It must be true, since others, the important and worthy others, seem to think she deserves to be treated as an object." But equally pernicious to Miller is how "the sense of pleasing herself has been a very rare experience for most women" in their subordinated, servitors' lives. Margaret Jeune provides a fine illustration, while commenting on an outing: "A day in the open air was most refreshing, and I enjoyed my husband's enjoyment" (21 June 1860). Jeune doubtless did. Nonetheless, she resembles Eliot, probably deceiving herself in declaring the terms of her pleasure on receiving a bouquet from an admirer: "Happily my dear husband is . . . able to enjoy these things for me. That he rejoices in them is my most distinct personal pleasure in such tributes" (1 January 1873).[15] Eliot cannot accept the simple pleasure of a tribute to herself; to be acceptable, the pleasure must come through Lewes's pride in her achievement.

The sorriest effect of women's subordination that Miller points out is their inability to assert themselves without simultaneously attacking themselves. As she puts it, "Since women have had to live by trying to please men, they have been conditioned to prevent men from feeling even uncomfortable. . . . when women suspect that they have caused men to feel unhappy or angry, they have a strong tendency to assume that they themselves are wrong." Witness Frances Stevenson, for example:

> He [David Lloyd George] made an extraordinarily good speech in the House last night. I behaved very badly. I was feeling very tired & had a splitting headache, & D. had annoyed me over a trifling little thing, & I quite forgot to say anything to him about his speech, or to compliment him on it. . . . And when he came back to Downing St. after 11.0 he came up to me & said: 'You haven't said a word to me about my speech—not a word. And you know how I count on your words to me after my speeches.' I felt a perfect pig at once, & did my best to make up for it, & it ended quite happily. But I hate myself for having behaved like that. (23 December 1919).[16]

When women conflict with men, as Miller points out, they have no way to validate their contrariness, given the cultural disparagement of female experience and perceptions. But a woman can always soothe herself by denigrating her own opinion, as does Lady Monkswell: "I had some difficulty in restraining my feelings when [Mr. Mathew], thinking I must be a Home Ruler because Bob is, began talking to me very intimately about Dillon whom I consider a murderer. Fortunately *my* poor opinion is of *no importance*" (4 March 1896).[17] Her opinion, however, as her italics betray, is important to her, even if it lacks public status; and she resents her insignificance. What happens to such negative feelings? Women, suggests Miller, turn their cultural devaluation against themselves: "No person really experiences . . . effacement and denial . . . without simultaneously reacting to it. One is hurt. . . . One also becomes angry but has nowhere to go with this anger. . . . The anger adds further to the sense of being wrong. . . . not only wrong, but . . . *bad* and *evil.*"

Miller states the process at the extreme. It can operate as well on more middling ground, as Clarissa Trant illustrates. Trant must do something with her rightful anger when Colonel Cameron throws her over for her lack of fortune. She has a bitter pill to swallow because he evidently courted her knowing that as a retired army officer's daughter she had no fortune so that he would never have to commit himself to an engagement. And thus,

> What a little fool I was! With all my *fancied* cleverness and knowledge of the world, what a novice I was, how unprepared for that most insidious mode of warfare upon a silly girl's heart, that of showing every species of the kindest interest in all I said and did, and yet not saying a word which could commit himself. . . . But it is all over, and I forgive him. I only pray that I may never again be tempted to rely upon my own weak, erring judgment. (20 June 1829)

Played for a fool and her pride sorely wounded, Trant can neither simply admit her right to think herself someone special nor say that he is despicable and she is furious. Instead, with Christian charity she forgives him and condemns her own judgment. Better to call herself the fool than him the knave. She has already discovered that inexplicably it shames her to encounter him publicly, though "why should I fear to [meet his eye]? I have *nothing* to reproach myself with" (25 May 1829).[18] Nor does she—except for feeling herself the disesteemed object, which also makes her feel herself in the wrong.

The frequency and ubiquity of the women's self-devaluation argues against their merely mouthing social formulae and repeating rituals. Some conventional downgrading certainly does occur. Diarists at times denigrate themselves because it would not do to praise themselves before that possible reader someday; they continue their habit of modest self-presentation. But more persistent and typical is a genuine sense of inferior worth. It betrays itself when a diarist has no intention of being modest or unassuming, but something like conditioned reflex operates to make her minimize herself nonetheless—such as when Charlotte Guest has fears because, for the while being pregnant and ill, she no longer serves as her first husband's secretary-cum-accountant. "I hope I shall not be much less beloved because I am become useless" (18 May 1840), she writes, as if her only value were in the tasks she performs. Frances Russell echoes that sentiment from her sickbed when she is thankful she has strength enough to hear her sons' lessons and can show them how to be patient in suffering, "so that even in illness I may not be wholly useless to them" (8 September 1855).[19] Guest also provides an excellent, full-scale illustration of female self-image warped toward inferiority under cultural pressures.

She reveals herself as a woman who overcompensates for feelings of inadequacy; or, as she says, "Whatever I undertake I must reach an eminence in. I cannot endure anything in a second grade" (27 April 1839). During her first marriage she produces ten children, all surviving, in thirteen years; establishes the family in good society despite the taint of her husband's being "in trade"; becomes competent in the business affairs of her husband's flourishing ironworks at Dowlais; establishes six schools for workers and children; composes a book on the history of the iron trade; and masters Welsh, including medieval Welsh, to prepare a complete translation (published in 1846) of the *Mabinogion*. Concerning the last, very substantial achievement, however, one of the sources for Tennyson's *Idylls of the King*, she writes

ten years later: "He [Tennyson] talked a great deal about Welsh literature, and I, who have forgotten all the little I ever knew about that
and everything else, felt quite ashamed at my own ignorance." Moreover, though Tennyson "told me he considered my English the finest
he knew, ranking with Malory's *Morte d'Arthur,*" as she says on another occasion, "I am sure if he saw this scrambling journal he would
not say so of me now" (28 October 1857, 12 August 1859).[20]

Guest is never secure in herself. But then, she is also living out an
unacknowledged conflict between the separate-sphere female image
imbibed from her culture and the desires and valuations of her own
heart, complicated by her leading a more public a life than usual for
her class and time. The conflict betrays itself when her husband
sends her to negotiate concerning rails for the Midland Counties
Railway. "The Midland agent "seemed at first rather surprised at
seeing me, but we soon began discussing questions of freight, interest, etc., as comfortably as if I had not the mortification of being of
weaker sex and intellect than himself" (13 March 1838). It shows up
again when, despite her skill at business (or perhaps because of it; she
does not say why) her husband soon decides to move her out of his
office:

> Merthyr has weaned me from all my own pursuits and taught me to be
> fond of his business, and now that I have got into such habits that
> business is almost the only thing that interests me, it is put out of my
> reach and I cannot follow it without going perhaps further than I
> ought. I feel it rather hard to have now to try and take up again the
> occupations which I have been led to abandon. But everything is for
> the best and all these little mortifications are good for one who as a
> woman must expect suffering and humiliation. (20 March 1838)

The conflict shows up yet again when she withdraws from further
scholarship as the *Mabinogion* nears its close:

> And now that my dear seven babies are growing up and require so
> much of my time and attention, it is quite right that I should have
> done with authorship. I am quite content with what will have been
> done when the present work is concluded, and I am sure if a woman is

201

to do her duty as a wife and mother, that the less she meddles with pen
and ink the better. (6 February 1843) [21]

Having been born female, Guest, like other diarists, pays a price in
interior harmony and self-concept.

The price has one provenance, significant to these diaries, that female psychologists ordinarily do not identify, though others have
done so. Female self-concept before the secular-minded twentieth
century was painfully scarred by masculinist religion, whether directly as dogma or indirectly as moral force. "The misogynism of
Christian theology is deep-rooted," to quote feminist Mary Daly—
who might as well have said Judeo-Christian—and it legitimates sex-
ism, for "if God is male, then the male is God." Simone de Beauvoir
long ago pointed out how the Catholic church historically diminished woman by elevating her to symbolic status as a Mary who wor-
ships her own son and is herself without autonomous being. Although
medieval tradition fastened sexual licentiousness to woman, English
Puritan misogyny of the sixteenth and seventeenth centuries is even
more notorious. Puritan Pauline teaching, which insisted upon woman's subordination to man, emphasized the Fallen Eve, responsible for
Original Sin. The "insidious belittlement" (critic Rogers's phrase)
that replaced Puritan dogma in the less-religious eighteenth century
merely converted misogyny to new forms of expression. So did the
mainly nineteenth-century apotheosis of woman: her idealization as
purifier of the home and society propounded by Evangelical moral
reformers but also assimilated by the Church of England, [22] for that
"cult of true womanhood" was patronizing and premised on female
intellectual inferiority.

Granted, the Victorian religiosocial doctrine of woman's moral superiority made up for the lesser importance of Mary in Protestantism.
Still, it could not improve female self-image for at least two reasons.
First, English Protestantism, as Rogers points out, actually continued
to assume female moral inferiority, even if woman was no longer re-
proached for the sin of Eve or accused of destructive passions, and
Pauline strictures now were tactfully attributed to concern for her
welfare rather than need for her punishment. [23] Second, holding up
any image of perfection or near-perfection before women only exac-

erbates the problem of female self-concept because women can but feel their inability to match that image when every other force reminds them of their imperfection. And perhaps subliminally women even saw the hypocrisy of the image. At its heart is a glorified conception of motherhood. But, as feminist Sheila Jeffreys has remarked in another context, "the glorification of motherhood enhances the status of woman's reproductive roles and appears to give women respect for an activity which women rightly deduce as being a badge of inferiority under male domination."[24]

Even the conscious sense of the image, however, would be enough to cause trouble. Diarist Webb shows the socioreligious image of ideal womanhood in destructive operation when, in Cologne Minster, "I thought of the worship a man is giving me—not me—but Woman through me—and I prayed again that I might make my life a temple of purity wherein to receive it. And I, so vain, so impure" (31 May 1890).[25] Webb is not even a Christian at the time, yet that scarcely matters; she was reared as one and has internalized certain habits of thought. Nonetheless, the heart of the religious problem for women may finally be neither misogyny nor false images per se, but rather the socialization that renders women particularly vulnerable to the self-condemnation Judeo-Christianity encourages in anyone. Its emphasis on guilt has been women's bane and has transferred readily from their devotions to their life at large.

The diaries under study are not devotional diaries, but they were kept by women who, at least in past centuries, had religious training and faith, and whose entries include religious occasions. Such events directly summoned the diarists' self-castigation. The young diarists are especially condemnatory. Thus, for example, on Yom Kippur, the annual Day of Atonement for Jews, eighteen-year-old Constance de Rothschild questions herself "carefully on my sins and my faults," for "I have so many." *Many* proves to be a lack of moral courage and a general timidity but also a tendency to flirt—"A flirt! How terrible to think of" (1861). At seventeen, her mother, Louisa, was also berating herself, but for her engrossment in "worldly concerns" rather than "real piety" (2 June 1838). The young Christians find out their sins with even more painful regularity, though their lapses may be no less trivial. So, for example, Lady Amberley, on the anniversary of her confirmation is praying God "I may be a little less selfish & less sulky & less cold" (1859).[26] Yet not just the young engage in such faultfinding and not just special days summon it forth. The diarists, who largely have mastered castigation from their religious indoctrination, simply are inclined to see themselves as sinners. Nor when they do so are they performing empty rituals; the tone of their diaries says that they feel strongly the self-disparagements they indite.

Margaret Hoby's diary initially comes closest to a religious diary since she began it intending to catch out her sins. Hoby was a sickly woman. Doubtless to any sufferer pain may seem like punishment, but Hoby is convinced that her bodily tribulations are divine retribution for her moral lapses. So she writes, in a characteristic early entry, of how it pleased the Puritans' Lord,

> for a Iust punishment to corricte my sinnes, to send me febelnis of stomak and paine of my head, that kept me vpon my bed tell 5: a clock: at which time I arose, haveinge release of my sickness, according to the wonted kindnes of the Lord, who, after he had Let me se how I had offended, that so I might take better heed to my body and soule hereafter, with a gentle corriction let me feele he was reconsiled To me. ([17 August 1599])

Hoby's spirit lives on in pious nineteenth-century Auguste Schlüter, a Lutheran, who "sprained my ankle . . . being much too gay on a Sunday . . .—it was due punishment for my wickedness" (3 August 1880). The same spirit encourages the self-flagellation of devout Emily Shore, an Anglican clergyman's daughter, humbly admitting, as she often does, "I am liked and loved far more than I deserve. I hate—yes, I truly hate myself; for I see the depths of sin within me, which are hidden from all other eyes" (25 December 1836). Shore is echoed by Frances Russell, who also knows "how much better I am loved than I deserve to be." Russell's adolescent confusions and unreasonable depressions have long since signified to her the frailty of her emotions, how "wicked, sinful must be those feelings that make me miserable" (2 February 1845, 28 March 1836).[27]

Even Hester Thrale, a more worldly woman than any of these in a more rationalist eighteenth century, prays God's forgiveness for "my foolish repining Spirit" and His "Grace to be thankful for . . . the Blessings I do not deserve" (17 September 1780); just as Mary Berry appreciates a God to whom she can confide "all the weaknesses inherent in my nature" (19 September 1836). Nineteenth-century Clarissa Trant, like Berry, is thankful for the mercy of a God "whose commandments I am daily and hourly transgressing" (26 July 1825). Her contemporary Amelia Opie, who had been a freethinking radical, became a Quaker. But her diary is written in the old Puritan flagellant spirit and daily reviews failings that send her "to bed *not* satisfied with myself" and "so dissatisfied with myself, that I dare hardly ask a blessing on my labors. . . . I am, and was, vile" (1 February 1831, 5 January and 1 February 1827).[28] As this sampling suggests, religious faith for many of the diarists entails very active conscience.

One need not, however, be a pious Christian, or even a Christian at all, to be subject to Puritan conscience, that voice of duty, lapse from which into pleasure brings guilt. Similar entries by Hoby and by more worldly Margaret Jeune, 250 years apart, showing that Puritan conscience in action, differ only in what constitutes duty:

> This day I bestowed to much time in the Garden, and thereby was worse able to performe sperituall dutes. (Hoby, 6 April 1605)

> I enjoy being in the garden so much, that I find I seldom sit to anything like regular work. However I quiet my conscience by considering that it is a pleasure I can have but for a small portion of the year and that I am consulting my health as well as *inclination* by making the most of it. (Jeune, 8 July 1854)

A pervasive force in English culture, the Puritan conscience can erupt anywhere; no direct religious indoctrination is necessary. More important, being duty oriented to begin with, women can scarcely avoid it. "Women," as Annie de Rothschild knows by thirteen, "are put into the world to be useful" (17 December 1858).[29]

Puritan conscience shadows even the women's attitude to their diary keeping. That almost all the diarists give reasons (excuses) for falling behind or omitting days is not remarkable. But some diarists criticize themselves for being laggard with a vehemence scarcely warranted by the nature of their private activity. "I did wrong, and I am going to correct myself" (16 April 1825), promises Berry, one such sinner. "*Disgraceful! disgraceful! disgraceful!*" (11 June 1922), shudders Woolf a hundred years later. Likewise, Opie laments "What indolence and neglect! . . . Oh for the power to be more diligent in the future" (6 May 1827); and Florence Sitwell exclaims, "How truly *awful* to think how backward I am" (31 May 1876). When a diarist has made her book a moral commitment—and a superego audience, as it were—lapses require penitence. Woolf, who announces about her diary "My conscience drives me again to write" (22 July 1922), may offer some insight into why women make their diary keeping such a moral commitment. Curiously, she also finds that "I always have to confess, when I write diary in the morning" (when, that is, she should be at her professional work); "Isn't it shameful to write here first thing?" (22 August 1922, 22 June 1937). In this particular sense of guilt, stretching across Woolf's career as a diarist, she is echoed by Mansfield, for whom "this is sheer sin, for I ought to be writing my book and instead I am pretending here" (March 1916).[30] Woolf has a good sense of how she comes by her "internal, automatic scale of values; which decides what I had better do with my time. . . . Perhaps its the legacy of puritan grandfathers. I suspect pleasure slightly" (1 March 1921). Keeping a diary is, in fact, a form of pleasurable self-indulgence, being an expression of interest in self (not salvation, just self), though one may disguise that by turning the diary into a duty or moral obligation, as women so often do. Since Woolf actually is putting pleasure first, but has become addicted to her diary, she decides at one point to set aside a particular time of day for making her entries, because "Give it a name & a place, & then perhaps, such is the human mind, I shall come to think it a duty, & disregard other duties for it" (8 April 1925).[31] Duty is always acceptable to the female mind, which is also quite good at guilt.

Writers are particularly prone to attacks of conscience over neglected duty. The self-censure of other diarists over laggard entries is but mild reproof compared to the drubbing Mansfield gives herself for doing "no work. In fact I was more idle and hateful than ever. Full of sin" (3 January 1922). Her failure to fulfill her obligation (as she sees it) to be a perpetually productive creative writer is the leitmotif of her diary. She may hold herself in contempt for assorted lapses during the course of her life: for not being "good" or "brave" or truthful, or for "bad" temper and "personal habits . . . not above reproach" (17 March 1908, February 1921). But those are negligible problems to her. Achieving a "state of virtue" means having finished a story, and if she has "done no work," she is "not in an active state of grace" (12 January 1915, 13 February 1916). But "am I ever free from the sense of guilt, even? Never." As a dying woman, Mansfield still has "a sense of guilt" from resting from her labors (18 October 1920, 13 July 1921). Yet she was a productive writer.[32] Eliot, likewise prolific, also berates herself frequently for meager output, for "it is grievous to me how little, from one cause or other, chiefly languor and occasionally positive ailments, I manage to get done." If a "fortnight has slipped by without my being able to show much result for it. . . . I have done no *visible* work" (19 March 1871, 20 July 1856), she is blameworthy—for all that, during the interval, as she knows, she has been storing up ideas and strength. Webb, as industrious as she was, also regularly castigates herself for lack of application, early to late in her life and not only over her writing. She claims in 1874: "I have been extremely irregular in all my duties. . . . I have not worked as much as I ought to have done . . . been lazy about my religious duties . . . lazy in getting up." In 1914 not much has changed: "I have been idle and distracted. [I have] a bad conscience: I am neither doing my share of emergency work nor yet carrying forward, with sufficient steadfastness, my own work" (25 January 1874, 3 November 1914).[33] Once prey to Puritan conscience, then forever prey.

Although the moral training of women does not impress them only with the importance of duty, duty takes pride of place. Duty minimizes egoism, the trait that religion and culture alike teach women to repudiate, with two precepts. Neither should females be vain, seeking and glorying in admiration. Nor should they put their importance before others—a precept that returns them to a commitment to duty. The prohibition against vanity strikes directly at women's adjustment to life, for female self-esteem is largely a consequence of favorable reflection in others' eyes—for professional writers, acclaim is even the necessary goal. Nonetheless, these diarists struggle to respect humility, even if they evidently like receiving admiration, and they attempt to deny any show of vanity. Lady Elizabeth Northumberland, for example, conventionally apologizes in advance lest it "be deem'd an unpardonable Vanity in me" (11 October 1763) that she includes a letter of commendation in her diary; and Elizabeth Wynne hesitates to assume Captain Fremantle's interest in her lest it seem "too vain on my part to presume to have such ideas" (11 July 1796). In more revealing fashion, Trant writes cautiously, "Read in the papers an account of the death of one of my earliest—I may say admirers, as this is my *private* diary" (5 October 1824). And Opie "dare not be guilty of the egotism" (6 December 1830) of admitting that her father was grateful for her birth.[34]

To quote Annie de Rothschild's caution to herself in her youth, the diarists rebuke themselves for even "a little vanity which I will try to overcome" (December 1858). Shore considers herself a fallen woman for letting herself be "led astray by flattery and vanity" when she has visited friends by whom "I was considered a wonder, a prodigy of talents, goodness," because "all this awoke in me a new desire of admiration. . . . The load of remorse I had laid up for myself during those ten months has burdened me ever since" (17 February 1839). Elizabeth Barrett (Browning) constantly attacks the "narrow, narrow heart" that makes her value others only as they are fond of her and take incurable delight in praise of her writing—proof to her, she says facetiously, that she is "more difficult to be reformed than the House of Commons" (5 and 3 August 1831).[35] "Ashamed of my egotism"— "vanity! . . . how detestable it is—how I swear to crush it out—" Woolf excoriates that "crouching servile feeling which is my lowest & worst; the desire for praise" (2 August and 8 September 1920, 3 December 1923). When she laments "the curse of a writers life to want praise so much, & be so cast down by blame, or indifference" (3 November 1918), she knows whereof she speaks; the leitmotif of her diary is her struggle to transcend criticism.[36] Mansfield, who deems herself "an egoist of the deepest dye," reproaches herself that "even my being well is a kind of occasion for *vanity,*" when "there is nothing worse for the soul than egotism." But "there seems to be some bad old pride in my heart" which is ineradicable (1 February 1922, October 1921). "God keep me from vanity," prays Webb (27 March 1880).[37]

Yet however dreadful vanity is, to put self first is as damnable for a woman as to cherish praise. Therefore, only after her husband's death does Lucy Cavendish go in retreat at St. Mary's: "I had never gone to a Retreat before—never able to leave my own darling only for my own sake" ([1883?]). And therefore, a century earlier, Hester Thrale hopes "*I* have always been much more tender, of everybody's else Health than of my own" (5 October 1789). Shore debates abandoning her difficult studies, "but the thought that by cultivating my mind I might render myself some day useful to others finally decided the question; otherwise, had only my own gratification been concerned, I doubt whether I might not have come to a different determination" (27 January 1838).[38]

The alternative to willing subordination of self is guilt for selfishness. Thus Lady Holland must berate herself on the death of her son Stephen, for "perhaps if I had not left you in the summer, but stayed and watched with maternal care all your little ailments, I might have had you still" (11 March 1801)—even if the doctors told her that his tuberculosis was incurably advanced, his death unpreventable. Likewise, when Webb is "not willing to sacrifice my own interests" to her anorexic sister's, she invites self-conflict: "I am not at rest with my own conscience. I know I might have done better by Rosy" (3 December 1882). Although Barrett (Browning) dreads the sale of Hope End, which will part her from easy access to Boyd, the neighbor she loves, she is ashamed of her feeling because "I ought not to think so much of myself. Poor Papa! *He* is the person to be thought of, & felt for!—" Likewise, "I *am* . . [.] *quite selfish*" to be glad when Boyd's distracting daughter goes away, and "it was very wrong of me to be out of humour" when obliged to go visiting against her inclinations (6 June, 3 and 27 October 1831). How Woolf agonizes with "headache; guilt; remorse" over Leonard's "hobby—his peach tree—to be pulled down because of me. . . . Forget he says: but I shant" (28 July 1939).[39] Females may not always be selfless, but they do not forget that they have been enjoined to be.

The presumable moral failings already identified are the most constant personal criticisms in the diaries. Yet they by no means exhaust the long and varied list of attacks on self. The list also sweeps in diarists' distaste for their emotionality—"I feel vexed with myself that I am quite cheerful tonight, yet a week ago I was sad enough" (8 September 1892), Beatrix Potter complains; or Barrett (Browning): "My spirits werre so depressed this evening, that it was an effort for me to talk. . . . Write myself down an ass!—" (29 December 1831). "Why am I always cross?" ponders Clarissa Trant. "I hate myself for being so disagreeable" (9 May and 29 June 1824). Some censure themselves for reading the wrong books; Faith Gray even reproaches herself for being "given much to talking which I endeavoured to cure in my own strength[,] as might be expected, to no purpose" (1770). Mansfield criticizes herself for poor handwriting (February 1921). They denigrate themselves as clumsy—"I . . . was distressed" by " a conviction of my innate clumsiness" (5 September 1895), laments Potter because she has accidentally dropped a camera; "I felt very humiliated by my clumsiness" (1 November 1916), confesses Asquith when she begins her war work.[40]

The diarists often find themselves homely too: "It is impossible for anybody ever to admire my looks or think me agreeable" (19 March 1836), grieves Frances Russell; I have "an ordinary face" (6 June 1879), opines Mary Gladstone; "I feel a bit more cheerful to-day because I don't look quite so revolting (2 February 1915), decides Mansfield. "I . . . was struck by my own ugliness," declares Woolf; "I can never look like other people—too broad, tall, flat, with hair hanging. And now my neck is so ugly" (21 March 1927).[41] They likewise belittle their intelligence and their talents. If Mary Hamilton finds Akenside's *Pleasures of the Imagination* obscure, it is "more likely to be a defect owing to my want of comprehension" (27 July 1784) than to Akenside. Amelia Opie wants to write about politics, but "a sense of my inability to do the subject justice" (2 August 1830) restrains her; and Louisa de Rothschild finds that when "most anxious to appear least stupid" in conversation, "I often am most so" (1847). Elizabeth Wynne is considered a promising young harpsichordist in Italy, but only because "they never heard any good player upon that instrument . . . so they find me a prodigy" (26 March 1796). Repeatedly the diarists reveal their sense of insignificance, such as Frances Stevenson, when promised Clemenceau's autograph "on condition that I sent him one of my own for his grandson. Imagine the joy of the grandson on receiving my autograph!" (13 December 1919). Or Potter is happy to receive two mementos of her grandmother when "I should not have ventured to ask for either, but that they spoke of giving it to the servants!" (2 April 1884).[42]

The diarists who are, or would be, authors are particularly given to painful self-doubt. Though writing is irresistible to Ellen Weeton, for example, she writes only for private amusement because "what I write is not worth the showing" ([1809]). Woolf's need for reassurance from Leonard and her agonies over what bad reviews may imply about her talents are lengedary. Even she cautions herself in 1921, "For my own good, . . . I must get out of the way of minding what people say of my writing. I am noted for it" (10 September). Yet she cannot; the struggle goes on so that as late as 1937, bad reviews of *The Years* mean that "I'm found out & that odious rice pudding of a book is . . . a dank failure. . . . this pain woke me at 4 am. & I suffered acutely" (2 April). But one can go back in time among distinguished authors and find the same insecurity. When Mary Berry, for example, compliments Maria Edgeworth on her achievements, Edgeworth returns the praises, but "feeling that I did not deserve them, it had little effect upon me, and had hardly the power of raising me for a moment from . . . depression" (12 May 1813).[43]

Berry shares her shaky confidence, like her depression, with Eliot, probably the prime sufferer among the diarists from writer's doubts. For Eliot, "Flashes of hope are succeeded by long intervals of dim distrust. . . . as usual I am suffering much from doubt as to the worth of what I am doing, and fear lest I may not be able to complete it so as to make it a contribution to literature" (8 December 1861, 13 January 1875). Self-doubt, the leitmotif of Eliot's diary, brings on severe bouts of "the despondency that comes from too egoistic a dread of failure" (16 June 1861). Such depression, which impedes her work, thereby deepening her despondency, is a lifelong burden that has sucked away "the sap of half the hours which might have been filled by energetic youthful activity; and the same demon tries to get hold of me again whenever an old work is dismissed and a new one is being meditated" (19 June 1861).[44] However, as Berry implies, Eliot is not alone in her depression. Rather, depression is another frequent pattern in the diaries; nor is it, of course, only suffered by writers. Feminist Phyllis Chesler once observed that women are "in a continual state of mourning—for what they never had—or had too briefly, and for what they can't have in the present, be it Prince Charming or direct worldly power." Because depression is the companion to female devaluation and powerlessness, numerous diarists suffer sustained or intermittent bouts of depression. That women will repond to life's stresses with "odious fits of low spirits" (diarist Potter's phrase, 13 December 1884)[45] is inevitable when outwardly they are weak and disesteemed and inwardly they feel inadequate, imperfect, or wrong. Their social roles and status and the personality traits they foster conduce to depression.

Women may very well (as Chesler continues) respond to deprivation by "keeping a deadly faith with their 'feminine' role" and turning against themselves any angers they feel, converted into depression. Yet also they are vulnerable to just the depression-inducing feelings that Martin E. P. Seligman's "learned helplessness" theory has identified. Seligman says, "I suggest that what produces self-esteem and a sense of competence, and protects against depression, is not only the absolute quality of experience, but the perception that one's own actions controlled the experience. To the degree that uncontrollable events occur . . . depression will be predisposed and ego strength undermined. To the degree that controllable events occur, a sense of mastery and resistance to depression will result." In short, if one concludes that she is controlled by life, rather than controlling it, she is likely to become depressed. Women have reason to feel controlled. Silvano Arieti points to the gender discrimination and inequality they endure, which mean economic and legal helplessness and dependence on others, encouraging low self-esteem and aspirations and, in turn, depression. Because women have been trained to dependency and endured negative cultural images, they are "bound to feel despondent about their lot and more inclined than men to become melancholic."[46] So it would seem, for besides Berry and Eliot, an impressively long list of diarists confirms the assumption that women are prone to react to life's stresses with depressions.[47] At varying intensities, the other sufferers at one time or another include Asquith, Carlyle, Carrington, Cavendish, Clairmont, Clifford, Freke, Gladstone, Guest, Lady Holland, Mansfield, Potter, Louisa de Rothschild, Frances Russell, Schlüter, Mary Shelley, Shore, Stevenson, Thrale, Trant, Webb, Weeton, and Woolf.

The immediate causations they report or imply are diverse. Woolf, for example, self-described as "a born melancholiac" and liable to pathological depression, speaks of succumbing to any sort of threat to her amour propre: not only negative criticism of her writing, but even "because Clive laughed at my new hat, Vita pitied me . . . I sank to the depths of gloom" (23 June 1929, 30 June 1926). Berry's long life is punctuated by fits of deep melancholy over frustrated ambitions. In her fifty-first year, she takes stock eloquently, though

> I very rarely allow myself now these fits of despondency to which, even in my youth, I was subject; but sometimes, in spite of me, all these recollections return with irresistible force. I suffer from what I am, from what I have been, from what I might have been, and from what I never shall be. (24 August 1814)

Webb's identity conflicts subject her from childhood on to intense, even disabling, depressions, the "nethermost being of despairing self-consciousness" (28 August 1888). But it is marital problems that occasion deep, near-suicidal depressions for Carlyle, who cannot "see why, if I *did* die, I should 'regret the loss of myself'" (15 April 1856), and earlier for Lady Holland, even as widowhood does for Mary Shelley. Earlier yet, Clifford reacts to her husband's bullying and neglect by "being extremely melancholy and sad" and "sad and melancholy" (30 June 1617, 2 June 1619). Loneliness, however, scourges Weeton even before her unhappy marriage, so that "sometimes I sit . . . indulging in melancholy, weeping bitterly; for no one interrupts me, no voice soothes, advises, or pities" (1 May 1813). Likewise, because of her sense of loss, isolation, and meaninglessness, Clairmont's diary for 1822 and 1825 is a litany of frequent "low spirits," "miserable spirits," and "very bad spirits."[48]

The diarists' depression can be ascribed to no one immediate cause and described by no one symptomatology other than what attends bleakness. Their depression may or may not come accompanied by physical debility, though sometimes, as for tubercular Mansfield and Shore, it is immediately occasioned by illness or, as for Guest, by old age. But neither illness nor old age is part of most of the depressions—nor is there necessarily any immediate cause. For some diarists,

213

as for Louisa de Rothschild, there simply occur "strange moments of gloom and melancholy in which I feel as it were iced all over and cannot break through the frigid bondage. I have been liable from a child to these fits of desponding sadness" (1848). Or, in times of anxiety, as for Trant, "there are moments when all my efforts are unavailing and a feeling of depression steals over me which I try in vain to overcome" (5 April 1826).⁴⁹ Whereas chronic depression often has physiological origins, no immediate cause may be necessary for random bouts of depression when the social devaluation of women provides long-standing causes in female conditioning and self-concept. Although of course entries written during depression diminish that self-concept even more, not only in depression are diarists self-critical. Their depressions are sporadic; their self-devaluations, in one manifestation or another, are perpetual.

A sometimes contributor to depression is aging, a circumstance with constant potential for inspiring self-denigration. When Mary Gladstone has occasion to notice, "Yesterday was Valentine's. Got none—a sign of old age and wisdom creeping on apace" (15 February 1870), she points to another prominent pattern of self-disparagement in the diaries: the response to aging. Of the premium that Western culture puts on female youth, feminist Cynthia S. Pomerleau aptly says, "Earlier and more decisively than for a man, the curve of a woman's life is seen by herself and society to be one of deterioration and degeneration. Men may mature, but women age." That all men are mortal poses less problem for females than that all women who survive the perilous childbearing years must live out the days until death. As sociologist Jessie Bernard observes, "The identification of women with reproduction has led the male world to wipe women of fifty years of age or older out of existence or deprive them of identity as women." Constance de Rothschild articulates the specter that looms: "In the end I shall be a useless, helpless, old female" (29 April 1926).⁵⁰

An indomitable woman, she speaks on her eighty-third birthday. Most other diarists would say the end had already come; they find middle age much more trying to their sense of self than old age. Expecting to be disesteemed as they move out of their presumable prime years, the women disparage themselves. By old age they are accustomed to thinking little of their worth. Given a culture that makes no provision for respecting venerable wise women, Berry at eighty-two is thankful for her unusual circumstances, "aware how much better off than most or almost any women of my great age" she is. "Instead of neglect of the world and of friends, I feel myself more considered, more sought after . . . than ever I was when I might be said to have deserved them" (26 June 1845). But fifty-nine-year-old Caroline Powys expresses much the same self-deprecatory attitude fifty years earlier when she attends a dinner given by her brother-in-law, the dean of Canterbury, for Prince William: "Tho' the two beautiful ladies were very near us, politeness, no doubt, made [William] address most of his conversation to the Dean's sister, tho' an old grandmother!" (25 August 1798).[51]

Regretting the loss of her youth, Hester Thrale opines, "Youth was the only thing that the more it was out of Sight the less it was out of mind" (1 May 1779). Women, however, have cause to brood over the transiency of youth. At forty-seven, Woolf undergoes a common experience of the middle-aged female: "The oculist said to me this afternoon 'Perhaps you're not as young as you were.' This is the first time that has been said to me; & it seemed to me an astonishing statement. It means that one now seems to a stranger not a woman, but an elderly woman" (31 May 1929). The diarists dread passing over that line beyond which one no longer seems a woman. Cynthia Asquith records a younger version of the awful moment of recognition, when "Ettie and I agreed what a terrible jar it was the first time one was told . . . that one looked young." Herself thirty, Asquith is reassured when her friends "said I didn't look married and that they would take me for about twenty-four" (22 January 1917). Even approaching her twenty-ninth birthday she is "haunted by the sense of evanescence lately—feel the horizon shutting down on me"; and on that day, "Alas! I have entered my thirtieth year. Grim thought." She encourages herself not to think too much about having become that "*femme de trente ans.* It's sad" (16 and 27 September 1916, 27 September 1917).[52]

Thirty apparently has well-entrenched horrors as the gateway to middle age. In 1799 Lady Holland's lamentations begin even earlier than Asquith's, when "On Monday I was 28 years old!!! Alas! Alas!"

That she too dreads becoming the femme is equally evident in her earlier appraisal of another woman as attractive though "past thirty considerably" (25 March 1799, 10 June 1794). Likewise, her contemporary Eugenia Wynne marvels, "Good God how swiftly time passes and if now that I am only seventeen I complain of its rapidity, what shall I do when I am thirty?" (1 January 1797). Nineteenth-century Quaker spinster Caroline Fox ordinarily does not acknowledge her birthdays. However, she does recognize when "Twenty-nine years . . . [have come] to an end," reminding herself "May our Father's will, and that only, be done . . . whatever temporal suffering it may involve." Two years later, she admits "My birthday," now reminding herself to count her blessings: "My future life might well be spent in giving thanks for all the mercies of the past" (23 May 1848, 24 May 1850). Had she contrary impulses that required quelling now that her moment of womanhood was clearly passing and she yet unwed? The problem of thirty is that it anticipates forty. When thirty-nine-year-old Thrale has been "praised this Year for my youthful Look" (14 July 1780), she preens herself. On the "last day of being 35," Woolf "trembles to write the years that come after it: all tinged with the shadow of 40," though she does not "like thinking of the lady of 50" either. Being "in shadow," she observes, seems "the best light for women's nerves once they're passed 40. . . . my women guests of that age . . . move to have their backs to the window, on some excuse or other" (24 January 1918, 20 January 1919, 17 February 1922).[53]

The women's perceptions may be sadly askew when they scent decline prematurely, yet the cultural climate does encourge their notions. At forty, Mary Berry, who lived to be an octogenarian, assumes that all is over for her because prospects and hopes "at sober forty can *never* be renewed!" But she has long since formulated "clear ideas of what alone can make a woman loved and amiable after youth is past": she must become self-effacing and inconspicuous (28 May 1803, 23 October 1807). At thirty-four, Frances Shelley, another future octogenarian, decides that "nothing can revive the ardent spirit from which my greatest enjoyments have been derived; . . . henceforth . . . I must become [but] a spectator in the drama of life. Leaving the stage to be trodden by younger performers, I must now begin my descent . . . into [the] shadow" ([1821]. Even at twenty-seven, however, the "chief thing" Mansfield has been feeling "lately about myself is that I am getting old. I don't feel like a girl any more, or even like a young woman. I feel really quite past my prime" (2 January 1915). Just so, Mary Shelley at the same age, if a century earlier, can see that "My brow is sadly trenched, the blossom of youth faded. My mind gathers wrinkles" (26 October 1824).[54]

Not to be young is to assume oneself superannuated. Marie Belloc Lowndes's luncheon club of women remind themselves that "love goes in a man when a woman becomes middle-aged. I said that it often amazed me to see how love endured though I admitted that in . . . the prosperous commercial class, no man, whatever his age, has any use for a woman, even for her company, after she is, say, forty" (16 March 1912). The exaggeration betrays a valid anxiety, which keeps most women hypersensitive to their age. It even makes Clarissa Trant and Lady Holland more concerned about their years than are their mates. Trant wishes "I were younger for his sake" (20 November 1831) when she becomes engaged; and Lady Holland earlier laments the "horrid disparity"—"alas! two years and eight months" (July 1797)—that leaves her senior to her new husband.[55]

With decline presumably threatening them, diarists may anxiously compare themselves to younger women. "Young girls make me feel *forty*," says Mansfield, for example, at thirty, and adds defensively, "Well, one certainly doesn't want to look 21" (12 April 1920). Or Lady Monkswell finds that "the older I grow the more slave I am to [youthful] beauty," and that "as a rule I stand very much in awe of the handsome, sought-after girl of 20" (2–3 July 1874, 18 June 1890). But the diarists also keep track of older women. Thrale even methodically reviews her friends for how well they have weathered (see 11 March 1789). To be sure, the diarists are not necessarily, or even frequently, kindly about what they see among such women. "How pale these elderly women get! The rough pale skin of toads" (23 October 1917), Woolf, for example, clinically observes.[56] It especially bothers them to see older women claiming the prerogatives of the young. Says Elizabeth Eastlake, who dislikes youthful attire on elderly bodies, "Old ladies forget that the younger they dress, the older they look" (4 November 1846), even as Margaret Jeune nastily describes

217

a seventy-year-old on whom there is "not a gray hair to be seen, but unfortunately her dress accords with this youthful appearance" (20 May 1844). Lady Holland mocks a "superannuated beauty" who "has survived her *attraits* [charms] without perceiving their dereliction" (20 November 1798), and a hundred years later Lucy Cavendish deems it "utterly disgusting" that a woman of "66 or so" intends to marry a much younger man (16–22 August 1880). The decorum of aging applies to the diarists themselves too. Middle-aged Charlotte Guest is not only embarrassed to admit in her diary that she has begun dyeing her hair; when her daughters protest her rejuvenation, she can "quite understand their feelings about it" (17 December 1853).[57] Although the diarists may fear aging because it diminishes their worth, they also become partisans of the value system that consigns an older woman to lesser life.

The most personal and defiant responses to female aging are made by the two women who face their physicality directly. Refusing the censorship that keeps mention of one's menopause out of the other diaries,[58] Thrale and Woolf, 138 years apart, instead confront and resolve their fears of that significant stage in female life. Thrale does so while striving for a sense of continuity in her life by retrospection to when her cycle began:

> I believe my *oldest Friend* is at last going to leave me, & that will probably make a Change in my Health, if not induce the Loss of it for ever. an odd thing has been observable on the Occasion, & merits Notice.
>
> When I was a Girl of ten Years old perhaps, the Measles attacked & put me in some Danger—leaving at their Departure a small red swelling on my Cheek, which my Mother called the Measle-Mark, & it remained there till the *Change of life* [menstruation] took it quite away. That very Mark is now upon this second *critical Change* returned—nor do I, nor did I *then* feel any other *very material* Alteration from the coming or going of Youth.
>
> I am now exactly 50 Years old I think, & am possessed of great Corporal Strength blessed be God, with ability to endure Fatigue if necessary. (9 April 1791)[59]

Thrale is able to conclude that, after all, she is not a diminished thing; neither "the coming or going of Youth" has amounted to more than a measle-mark, and she is still healthy and strong. No longer being that socially valuable entity, a breeder, does not matter. Given lives fragmented into stages by female reproductive power, women have peculiar need to see their lives whole, upon menopause, and to remind themselves of their own enduring worth, as does healthy-minded Thrale. But if other diarists also did so, they do not record the act.

Woolf also finds a sane perspective, though not while directly confronting her menopause. At forty-seven, she dreads physical decline—her eyes are weakening—and "will there not be the change of life? And may that not be a difficult & even dangerous time?" But she succeeds in reassuring herself: "Obviously one can get over it by facing it with common sense—that it is a natural process; that one can lie out here & read; that one's faculties will be the same afterwards; that one has nothing to worry about in one sense." (16 September 1929). Her inability to have children strips menopause of most of its threat. Perhaps more important, she has already found an answer to the cost of the years: resist the stigma of aging with the sensibility of growth. For as she says staunchly, "Even if I see ugliness in the glass, I think, very well, inwardly I am more full of shape & colour than ever" (28 March 1929).[60] Woolf's finally sanguine sense of herself, like Thrale's, is significant. Even if low self-esteem and shaky confidence are so prevalent in the women's diaries, the female self-image is not just negative.

Female habits of mind have also their self-enhancing cast, and women find emotional sustenance and ego support within the confines of the lives allowed them. In general terms and as already discussed, these diarists derive self-validation from courtship, marriage, and motherhood. When assured that they perform valued tasks, the knowledge gratifies them. But their positive thinking also translates more specifically into the following sampling of self-affirmations, supplementary to the satisfactions of deeming oneself a good wife, a careful housekeeper, a devoted mother.

Their social skills and successes are also a source of pride and accomplishment, irrespective of century. Many diarists are delighted with their social abilities. Thus Mary Gladstone, for example, is proud of how in one hour she has set a table prettier than the one "the great Mentmore gardener took 8 hours over" (20 May 1880). And Lady Monkswell deems herself quite sharp for having "carefully thrown" two of Mark Twain's books "in a careless manner" onto a nearby table before Twain came to tea, to make him feel "at home" (15 February 1897). Eastlake, very much a Mrs. Dalloway, relishes the sense of herself being the source of a social event (21 April 1845). But diarists also take pride in being a success at other's events. To be engaged rapidly for every dance at a ball as Cavendish is, at twenty is predictably gratifying (10 June 1862), though no more so than to be the toast of Vienna, as Frances Shelley believes she has been. She prides herself that she triumphed without compromising her virtue and meanwhile vindicated "the character of my countrywomen, who . . . had through their prudery and vulgarity contrived to leave an unfavorable impression" before her advent (1816). Nor can Hester Thrale disguise her satisfaction at being "all the Mode this Winter; no Parties are thought highly of, except Mrs. Thrale makes one of Them: my Wit, & even my Beauty . . . is celebrated" (1 December 1782).[61]

Recognition is important. When they receive the validation of special notice or cordiality from some distinguished personage, diarists feel particularly good about themselves. So, for example, Mary Hamilton at court finds "myself gratified by the manner wth. wch. the Queen, Lady Charlotte Finch, & Miss Goldsworthy [court governesses] treat me," and by how the king "takes every opportunity to make me feel at ease by his flattering notice" (28 June 1777). Very satisfying to Caroline Fox is that Lord Northampton "acknowledged the force of my arguments!" and that John Sterling has read with pleasure Talfourd's Lamb "in consequence of my recommendation— Hem!" (16 September 1837, 29 February 1840). Diarists not only bask in compliments on their appearance, as Thrale shows; they sometimes even admire their own beauty. Young Mansfield decides at one point, "I look *perfectly charming*" (17 December 1907); and when Cynthia Asquith, inclined to be narcissistic, finds herself "in best looks," she is certain that "today I could really pass a great deal of time very happily just looking at myself in the glass" (6 January 1917).[62]

The diarists derive a sense of achievement from a range of possible sources and may admire themselves for any job well done, whether it be serving as Queen Victoria's lady-in-waiting—for Cavendish it is "pleasant indeed to think I have gone through my first waiting and really without a rub" (14 September 1863)—or caring for the guests of the lord of the manor. When unexpected guests descend during the shooting season, tenant's daughter Elizabeth George exhausts herself but is proud of managing so efficiently on such short notice. Charitable and other humanitarian endeavors are rewarding (and especially when acknowledged). Philanthropist Amelia Opie beams when fellow coach passengers "overwhelmed me with thanks and praises for the good derived from my works. I was fool enough to be pleased" ([1834]). Lady Northumberland, glows to think "that it should please God to make such a Weak Being as myself the Instrument of saving the Life of this poor Creature" (27 November 1772) when she has obtained King's Pardon for a convicted woman while Lord Northumberland is lord lieutenant of Ireland. Jane Carlyle grumbles at how others dump their woes on her, but meanwhile congratulates herself for her rescue of a lost child and succor of a fallen woman (April 1845). Throughout her life, Constance de Rothschild cherishes her work for her people, whether in the London free schools or in rescue missions in the Jewish community (see, e.g., April 1861, 1885). Young Florence Sitwell likewise is gratified to be teaching poor girls (e.g., 24 August 1874).[63]

The diarists take pride in their artistic talents—Beatrix Potter, for one, appreciates her teachers but is "convinced it lies chiefly with oneself" (21 November 1883)—and their academic achievements. Auguste Schlüter, who "had much to study, for examinations of ambulance and nursing classes" but "passed both *first* class" (3 July 1887), is no less delighted with herself than Frances Stevenson, who recalls her "sense of exhilaration" and her "marvellous sense of achievement and satisfaction" (10 April 1934) on earning a first in her matriculation examination. However, the diarists also pride themselves on unusual physical accomplishments: Ellen Weeton, for example, for her successful (if embarrassing) ascent of Snowdon (15 June 1825), and

Lady Monkswell for accompanying an experienced mountaineer on what proves a more strenuous walk than anticipated and "raised me in my own estimation at least 50 degrees" (1 September 1891).[64]

If their lives have brought them before the public, the diarists extol their poise and aplomb. How well Webb manages on such occasions brings her many fine moments in her long career, but even Cavendish is gratified to have named a ship "and made a splendid smash of the champagne bottle" (19 October 1873). Constance de Rothschild brags that she successfully addressed an international conference of women in Berlin without feeling "in the least shy" (16 June 1904). When their creativity earns public recognition, it brings a great sense of accomplishment. Being accepted by the *Penny Magazine* seems agreeably like the start of a writing career to eighteen-year-old Emily Shore (3 January 1838). After a long, successful writer's career, Marie Belloc Lowndes congratulates herself for having a "plot mind," which is "curiously rare, and does secure for its owner a kind of immortality. . . . long after the writer is dead, the books go on being reprinted" (9 March 1923).[65] For the great writers like Eliot, Mansfield, and Woolf, self-doubts abate at least temporarily with every successful review.

The later diarists feel special pride in knowing that women can be achievers. Webb confidently offers her services to inquire into female labor because that will "give me an opportunity of showing that a woman can do thorough work" (17 April 1891); and Woolf thrills at being invited to give the Ford Clark Lectures, for "this, I suppose, is the first time a woman has been asked; & so it is a great honour—think of me, the uneducated child reading books in my room at 22 H[yde] P[ark] G[ate]—now advanced to this glory" (29 February 1932). Stevenson feels great satisfaction because "people have just woken up to the fact that . . . the Sec. of State for War has a lady Secretary. I have people calling to interview me, & I have my photograph in the papers!" (26 July 1916). Potter, on the other hand, is delighted but amused that her designs for cards are accepted by a commercial company that sends "a very civil letter under the misapprehension that I was a gentleman" (May 1890).[66]

Achievements aside, diarists admire themselves for personal traits such as loyalty, integrity, honesty; forbearance, circumspection, prudence; resourcefulness, industriousness, determination. Although such a list may appear gender-free, combined with the diarists' valued achievements it is not. The composite image formed by the diarists' thinking about self is distinctly female. Their pride in self and sense of accomplishment derive not (except incidentally, for the few women with careers) from public lives and career ambitions, but from relatedness to people and from private talents; and not (except minimally) from aggressiveness or competitive drive, but rather from skills and interests that ease survival in the human world as women have historically known it. That adaptability alone might well be a source of pride. However, the persistence of the diarists' tendency to self-devaluation suggests it cannot be source enough. The women do not gain so full a sense of accomplishment from their private spheres as to make them glory in their female selves. Too many negative feelings pursue them; such self-esteem as they allow themselves perches precariously on the edge of their doubts, distrusts, and need for praise in their assigned roles to reassure them of their personal worth.

The patterns of positive thinking in these diaries comprise the diarists' daughterhood as well, not because the women are proud of being good, loving daughters, but because they are just such daughters. Since, moreover, they have learned how to exist in the world primarily from their mothers, who gave them their initial sense of female existence, their positive sense of filiality is significant: it implies perpetuation of maternal attitudes. Adrienne Rich has written of the potential for "the deepest mutuality and the most painful estrangement" in the cathexis between mother and daughter,[67] but it is mutuality that resonates in these diaries, where estrangements are few and sometimes even convert to mutuality.

Thrale sets the tone when she declares: "How falsely did She [mother] use to say that when I had a Husband & Children I should forget my Mother! No! No! No! Two husbands, two young Sons and ten Daughter's Lives & Deaths have not eras'd her Image from my Mind" (17 May 1790). Although Thrale thinks that "for true Love of one's Mother & real preference of her to all human Kind, I believe I am a singular Example" (December 1778), in fact she is but one of many. Her biographer, Mary Hyde, attributes Thrale's maternal closeness to the absence of her father, John Salusbury, who not only went to Nova Scotia to repair his fortune, but also died young, so that Thrale's mother had the care of her and could become the decisive influence in her life.[68] Yet Thrale's relationship with her mother is only an intensification of the widespread pattern that Nancy Chodorow postulates for daughters, for whom the primary tie to the mother supersedes any later ties formed. "Men tend to remain *emotionally* secondary to women," declares Chodorow. "The mother remains a primary internal object to the girl, so that heterosexual relationships are on the model of a nonexclusive, second relationship for her."[69] Diarist Constance de Rothschild, a hundred years later than Thrale, may also show Chodorow's claim in operation.

Mother Louisa is central to Rothschild's life. As Constance says, "With her, sunshine; without her, cold shade. Her love transforms me, her delicacy refreshes me. God be praised at having given me such a Mother!" (23 September 1882). Sometime after 1877 she writes, "My Husband declares that I only care for my Mother"; and, in fact, when fifteen years later she faces conflicting loyalties, Constance chooses her mother over her husband, Lord Cyril Battersea. Because Louisa is seventy-two and inseparable from her daughter, Constance urges Cyril to turn down the governorship of New South Wales, which he very much wants. Though her behavior rocks her marriage, so that Constance must "most profoundly regret my decision," she cannot change it, for "had it been otherwise, it might have killed my mother" (21 February 1893).[70]

The maternal tie is strong in many diaries. Like Rothschild, Shore cannot imagine life without her mother: "If she died I should never be happy again." Shore's mother too is "quite sunshine; I am generally altogether dull and gloomy without her" (28 January 1833, 27 August 1838). Asquith's mother is "a blessed being—a witness to God if ever there was one" for her help with autistic John, but Asquith values her mother more than for her services and empathizes with her personal problems (22 August 1918, 1 May 1917). To care for her "dearest mother, no heart like hers in this world" (22 July 1833), Schlüter leaves her job with the Gladstones. Newlywed Elizabeth Wynne is mortified that her mother should think her unfeeling, for "I know how much I am indebted to so indulgent so good a parent. I shall ever have regard and love for the best of Mothers and ever

224

be thoughtful for all she has done for me" (29 January 1797). Caroline Powys's mother "made us all happy" by coming to live part of each year with the Powyses; "we could not reconcile ourselves to her being at so great a distance" (1782).[71] And so it continues throughout most of the diaries, irrespective of when they were written. Even if the diarists do not always directly articulate their love and respect, they demonstrate it by sharing their personal lives with their mothers and taking direction from them.

Rather than chafing at ties to their mothers, the diarists are inclined to strengthen their attachments. Diaries aside, Elizabeth Eastlake, according to her editor, Charles Eastlake, for sixteen years after marrying wrote three times weekly to her mother and sister, apologizing for any letter less than six pages long. Within the diaries, though Mansfield's mother has repudiated her for errant behavior, Mansfield keeps her mother vividly present in spirit after her mother's death: "My little Mother, my star, my courage, my *own.* I seem to dwell in her now" (19 May 1919). In moments of stress, diarists turn their thoughts to their mothers, seeking comfort and reassurance. Thus Carlyle, out of her marital unhappiness, apostrophizes, "Oh, my mother! nobody sees what I am suffering now . . . 'All to myself.' From 'only childless' to that, is a far and rough road to travel" (7 November 1855). Or Clarissa Trant, uncertain that she has been right to refuse an attractive marriage proposal, ponders, "Have I acted as my beloved mother would have done in my place?" (6 September 1824). Trant often uses her deceased mother as a reference point for behavior; so does Lucy Cavendish. When, for example, Cavendish accidentally pulls off her wedding ring, she has her husband put it on again "as I remember Mamma used to make Papa." She perpetually uses her mother—"the thought of her [shines] in all that happens"—to validate and solemnize family events (30 June 1867, 29 July 1859).[72] Marie Belloc Lowndes likes to refer back to her mother's long-distant pronouncements (e.g., 3 March and 7 December 1939). Weeton feels she must pass on to her daughter the training her mother gave her (14 June 1825). Thrale's mother is her standard for excellence: "I can do nothing like her; Would I Could!" ([December 1778]). Carlyle's is hers for beauty (24 June 1856).[73]

The deaths of their mothers, as Trant and Cavendish imply, come hard for many of the diarists, who feel that such deprivation has diminished the quality of their lives or natures. They lament whether or not they and their mothers were actually intimate. How Elizabeth George, for example, regrets that "I have never even had the happiness of seeing a letter of my dear Mother's—I should have considered one quite a treasure, as I had the misfortune to lose her during my infancy, and consequently have no personal recollection of her" (1847). Or Webb, in her anguish over Joseph Chamberlain, moans, "If I had only been guided by some strong perceiving woman. If I had had a mother or a sister to whom I could have confessed all!" (28 February 1889). Her sisters are alive but not close; her mother is dead and was never a confidante; yet Webb participates in a common longing for an intimate female presence. So does Thrale, out of more actual ties, when she fears that the child she carries is dead, but she has "nobody to tell my Uneasiness to, no Mother, no Female Friend—no nothing: So I must eat up my own Heart & be quiet" (20 December 1777).[74] Trant, who pores over her mother's diaries and letters, ponders "what a different being Clara would have been had she lived to realise her views on education. . . . The loss of a mother and such a Mother can *never* be replaced" (24 October 1824). Trant's longing, Barrett (Browning) shares, and knows why:

> How I thought of those words *"You will never find another person who will love you as I love you"*—And how I felt that to hear again the sound of those beloved, those ever beloved lips, I wd. barter all other sounds & sights—that I wd. in joy & gratitude lay down before her my tastes & feelings each & all, in sacrifice for the love, the exceeding love which I never, in truth, can find again. (13 August 1831)

For devoted Frances Russell, simply, "the world is changed for me for ever. . . . My dear, dear Mama has left it" (3 August 1853). A century before, Faith Gray is too pious not to be thankful that her adored mother has been received among the saints, but her sense of loss nonetheless pervades the long biographical eulogy she composes (13 September 1787).[75]

Yet certainly not all the filial-maternal relationships were idyllic. Claire Clairmont, for example, whose mother had married Mary

Shelley's father, William Godwin, in 1801, ran off at sixteen by joining Mary and Percy's 1814 elopement; after her mother pursued them to Calais, Clairmont refused to return home. Eighteenth-century Eleanor Butler, who also fled from home to settle in Wales with Sarah Ponsonby, had no love for either of her parents. But Butler's impersonal diary has nothing to say about her parents, except for indicating how little they interest her, and Clairmont does not discuss her mother—though she does continue to write to her mother, years later.[76] Possibly (as with marital discord) a few other diarists also preferred to maintain silence over deep difference with their mothers or long-standing antipathies. Beatrix Potter, for example, is plainly fonder of the father with whom she shares interests in photography, natural history, and art than of her domineering mother, against whom she must have stored up plentiful resentments. But almost never does she admit them. On one occasion she declares herself provoked "because my mother will not order the carriage in the morning or make up her mind, and if I say I should like to go out after lunch I am keeping her in," and so on. Nonetheless, as she remarks later on the same frustrating day, she also endeavors to keep "my feelings private" (11 September 1894)[77] and so leaves them only to inference. More explicit and serious rumbling comes from Nancy Woodforde, obliged to become her uncle's housekeeper because of parental improvidence. After her father's death, she records writing to her brothers about selling the reversion of the children's estate because "our Mother has not the goodness to allow us a Single Shilling. . . . Pray God make her a better Mother to her first born Children who have never offended her and who have been cruelly used by her" (5 October 1792).[78] The Thrale daughters, according to their mother's diary, were unrelenting in their opposition not only to Hester Thrale's remarriage, but also to her person. The diaries are certainly not tension free.

But the disagreements revealed are almost all either petty or short-lived or both, when daughters themselves are the diarists. They are inclined to be yielding in disagreements with their mothers and eager to keep their love. When Sophia Fitzgerald, for example, affronts her mother by failing to wait upon her before attending a ball, she quickly apologizes for her rudeness; the reprimand she has received is grievous to her, for "God knows I did not mean to do it, and it all proceeded from want of thought. . . . I have not forgiven myself as soon as my Dear Mother has" ([17??]). Though Lady Kate Amberley quarrels with her mother over John Stuart Mill and storms out of the house without farewells, she returns the next week "and made it up with Mama" (6 July 1868).[79]

Men provoke some of the most serious temporary rifts, for daughters can be unyielding about their choices of mate. At her mother's deathbed, Charlotte Guest (Schreiber), whose own eldest daughter is yet recalcitrant about her mother's remarriage, must ask "forgiveness for any trouble or sorrow I have ever occasioned her [my mother]" because "I know that she fretted much about my marriage" (22 November 1858). Yet even though her mother did not approve of Charlotte's choice of Charles Schreiber, there has been no permanent estrangement. Frances Stevenson is forced into the most sustained maternal conflict reported because of her affair with Lloyd George, to which her mother predictably objects. But Stevenson "can't help *hating* myself for making Mamma so miserable. The thought haunts me all day long, and I would do anything to prevent it" (11 March 1915)[80]—short of terminating the affair. However, as the relationship proves durable, her mother yields, and daughter and mother remain friends.

If men do not permanently estrange most of these diarists from their mothers, neither do personality clashes. Even Beatrice Webb, for example, resolves the tensions and trials of protracted filial animosity of which she writes in her girlhood: "a kind of feeling of dislike and distrust which I believe is mutual" (24 March 1874). The divided personality of the mother, Lawrencina Heyworth Potter, a frustrated intellectual of puritanical bent who wanted the life of the mind but instead found herself with nine daughters to rear (her one son died), is relived by the daughter, who feels a "duplex personality" in herself. To her mother she attributes its negative side, the "*nether* being in me; the despondent[,] vain, grasping person—(the Heyworth)—doomed to failure. Linked to this nethermost being was the phantom of Mother, the gloomily religious" (10 December 1886). Yet the two women briefly approach intimacy as Lawrencina on her deathbed confides some of her marital problems to Beatrice, and, in a classic situation, the daughter comes to appreciate her mother after Lawrencina's death. "Looking back," says Webb, "I see how bitterly she must have felt our want of affection and sympathy. . . . I never knew how much she had done for me. . . . I now feel the presence of her influence and think of her as an absent friend. . . . her intellectual strivings . . . will be the originating impulse of all my ambition, urging me onward towards something better in action or thought" (27 August 1882).[81] So even Webb, existentially always her mother's daughter, finally becomes willingly that person. Either by statement or demonstration, almost all the diarists are willingly their mothers' daughters. They affirm their mothers, they cherish them, they accept their guidance and seek their approval.

Thus they are all the more likely to carry their mothers' imprint—complete with any ambivalences it may contain or conflicts it may generate—as Webb also illustrates. Webb's tribute to her mother is not a passing thing, and fifty years later when Webb is elected first woman member of the British Academy, she thinks of her achievement foremost in terms of her mother, who

> would have been . . . gratified by my F[ellow] B[ritish] A[cademy] and triple doctorate. Her daughter the perfected *Blue Stocking!* And her own lifelong absorption in book learning amply justified—her ambition brought to fruition in one of the ten children whom she had, at the cost of her own career as an intellectual, brought into the world. Bless her. (28 April 1932)[82]

The blessing is generous, for Beatrice, too, has paid the "cost of [Lawrencina's] career." Lawrencina's unresolved conflict between her intellectual strivings and contemporary role expectations turned her into a shrew and made her instrumental in Beatrice's neurotic condition.

Ellen Weeton, however, because she is a less-tortured person than Webb and the child of a very ordinary, nonintellectual mother, is a more representative example of destructive maternal influence. Although Weeton is among the very talented diarists as a writer, she derides her skill and laments her inability to undertake a large-scale piece such as an autobiography. Some mysterious impediment stays her pen: "Whether it proceeds from indolence, or some other undefinable motive, I cannot say; but whether I have a letter to write, a journal, or an account, it seems to task me; and yet the activity of my mind perpetually urges me to it. It is a strange contradiction!" (2 February 1824). It proves not so strange after all, however. Fifteen years earlier, in an autobiographical essay incorporated into the diary in 1809, Weeton's self-estimate runs: "too ignorant to dare to commence author, and too aspiring for a mere domestic character. . . . the automaton of accident, sometimes moved by one spring, and sometimes by another; and fixed to nothing." Lying behind her precarious self-image, she recognizes the mother who thwarted her "inclination to scribble . . . so powerful, I feel it next to impossible to resist" with the maternal wisdom that "'a *wretched* subsistence do they obtain who have it to earn by their literary abilities! Or should you become a wife, think in what a ragged, neglected state your family would be if you gave up much of your time to books.'"[83] Although Weeton persisted in "scribbling" clandestinely, the harm to her self-concept had been done ([June] 1809).

Masculinist cultures prosper as such because women promulgate their doctrines. Bred to accommodation, they indoctrinate their daughters in turn, consciously and unconsciously, even as daughters so respond. Closeness intensifies teaching. Losing male regard is not all that women dread; they also fear their losing mothers' approbation. Without it their self-esteem lags, though with it, as it is male-centered, their self-esteem is scarcely enhanced. The pervasive sense of mother-daughter love in these diaries is consequential. Moreover, it is not unusual. Historian Carroll Smith-Rosenberg also uncovered a world of close female relationships by studying the diaries and correspondence of American women of the late eighteenth century through the early nineteenth century. At the "heart" of the female world, she found, lay "an intimate mother-daughter relationship," with "closeness and mutual emotional dependency," rather than "that mother-daughter hostility today considered almost inevitable to an adolescent's struggle for autonomy."[84] Affection, gratitude, respect, and a conscious willingness to take their mothers (and sometimes compatible diary mothers) as models and mentors, not to mention what they take in without conscious will—these one finds true of the diarists. If such responsive ties are characteristic of Englishwomen prior to the recent past, as their diaries suggest, then of course certain habits of mind, behaviors, and values will have been perpetuated (reinforced from outside the family), so that the same sorts of statements, reflecting not just self-estimates but entire adjustments to life, appear in diaries from the seventeenth to the mid-twentieth centuries. The conservatism of the diaries suggests that many such statements might persist beyond the mid-twentieth century as well.

Because by example and precept mothers customarily have taught daughters to fit in, Englishwomen such as these diarists have historically been traditionalists, not revolutionaries: *ordinary* women in that sense too. Yet women could respond to opportunities for change. As the Afterword will demonstrate, the Great War provided a heady and revealing experience of liberation for middle- and upper-class women, who could escape the confines of home by doing wartime service and otherwise participate in the upheavals in social standards brought by the war—and were eager to do so. But that is not the period of the diarists in the main study. For them, life largely flows in conventional currents, and they are very much their mothers' daughters. They adjust themselves to a male-run world, finding their gratifications within its limited possibilities; they protect themselves from impolitic revelations, even in the ostensible privacy of their personal diaries; and much too readily they disesteem themselves. It should have been otherwise. However, the lost history of women lies not only in recoverable documents, but also in untried talents, undared rebellions, and denial of joy in self. To read Englishwomen's private diaries is not only to experience their lives in process, but also to confront such habits of mind, remarkably persistent over long periods of time. Even the Great War, for all its opportunities, could not entirely disrupt them.

AFTERWORD

CHANGE
AND CONTINUITY
On Diaries of the Great War

Because they look both to past and future, the diaries of the
Great War period provide a fitting afterword to this account of women's private diary keeping over the centuries. Retaining old habits of
mind alongside new ones encouraged by that disordered time when
"our good solid world, on which we have walked so safely all our
lives, has broken up," to quote diarist Mary Houghton in 1914
(5 August),[1] the wartime diaries reflect both women's conservatism
and their capacity for change. The published diaries drawn on here
were written by twenty-five middle-and upper-class Englishwomen
who were waiting out the war in England, or in one case in Africa;
serving in or near the combat zones; or living temporarily or permanently on the continent. Six diarists reappear from the main study;
all but three of the nineteen new diarists themselves published their
books or intended them for publication,[2] usually having rewritten
them with hindsight and an eye to effect. Collectively the twenty-
five wartime diarists return a reader vicariously to the moments when
Englishwomen were in process of exulting, suffering, and sometimes
changing because of the war. The reactions in the first two instances
parallel men's, but certain liberating changes are more distinctively
women's own.

Aside from the few who were pacifists, these women's initial response to the war was to welcome England's entry as "a matter of national honor . . . we went out to fight like gentlemen," as diarist Sarah Macnaughtan puts it (August 1914).[3] Like their men, they want England to fight. That the decision is not neutrality means "Joy at last!" (30 August 1914), even for Lady Harriet Jephson, inconveniently become an enemy alien because she has been caught abroad taking the waters at Altheim. By mid-August 1914, women's prompt eagerness to serve, reports nurse Violetta Thurstan, has brought "an endless procession" of females to the Red Cross in London, whether "anxious for adventure and clamouring 'to go to the front at once'" or "willing and anxious to do the humblest service that would be of use in this time of crisis." Maintaining conventional passivity came hard. "I cursed Providence," chafes Vera Brittain after a year of war, "because I was not a man and in it all (28 September 1915)."[4]

Since "even when one is not skilful it is better to proceed slowly than to do *nothing* to help," Brittain has already laboriously attempted many women's first recourse, "the only work it seems possible as yet for women to do": knitting (6 August 1914). But eager knitters had no certainty that their efforts were appreciated. Kathleen Isherwood, mother of novelist Christopher Isherwood and wife of a regular-army officer, ruefully records her husband's warnings against sending any more superfluous knitted goods (19 and 20 December 1914). Expatriate Houghton (who lived abroad with her husband), scenting busywork concocted by the doctors to pacify women, is dubious about the eighty-centime bandages the women in Geneva knit when better bandages can be bought for threepence (19 August 1914). Since this imaginative woman nonetheless wants "to do something myself," she instead enlists other women's help to send an optimistic petition to the New York *Herald* requesting that the heads of the great powers order their generals to avoid great churches in their paths (19 August 1 September 1914). Later she would publish part of her diary to give the profits to the Serbian and Montenegran Red Cross funds.[5]

Initially, even the trained nurses among the diarists record difficulty getting their services accepted for more productive and active work than knitting or otherwise ladylike schemes. The untrained, like the irate Macnaughtan, who recognizes "boundless opportunity"—"we are in luck to have a chance of doing our darndest"

(27 September 1914)—discover that the women who respond to calls for volunteers are "frequently snubbed, which left them wondering why they had been called" (August 1914). Macnaughtan, who assisted the Red Cross in South Africa during the Boer War, resents the notion that her "'duty is to give to the Queen's Fund . . . and to get properly thanked,'" nothing more (28 October 1915). Like many other women, she wants to get near the front, and though comments in her diary suggest she may have been in or near her seventies at the time,[6] by becoming an orderly she succeeds in doing so. A resourceful, determined woman whose efforts suggest a certain spirit that prevailed, she first joined Mrs. St. Clair Stobart's all-women Red Cross unit, which established a military hospital at Antwerp; and then after the fall of Antwerp, Dr. Hector Munro's ambulance corps at Furnes. There, having independent means, she set up the first of her soup kitchens for the wounded at railway junctions.

Novelist May Sinclair became treasurer, reporter, and nursing assistant for Munro's corps. Several other diarists got to the front as Red Cross nurses. Nurse Grace McDougall, using another possibility, joined a First Aid Nursing Yeomanry unit (a FANY), a women's ambulance corps; and Brittain, who served both at home and abroad, became a VAD: member of a Voluntary Aid Detachment. Still others, such as future novelist Enid Bagnold and Cynthia Asquith, served as VADs in England or did other volunteer work.[7] Wealthy diarists like Lady Kate Courtney, sister of Beatrice Webb, and Constance de Rothschild (Lady Battersea) lent their country homes as military hospitals. Closer to the seat of power, Frances Stevenson exerted personal influence behind the scenes by her advice to Lloyd George.[8]

As the war dragged on, women (like men) made more sober assessments. "How can such things be endured by women?" reflects Asquith, faced with news of yet another death. "We have all been caught up into a Greek tragedy and are but gradually beginning to realise it" (27 May 1915).[9] Over 600,000 of England's younger men were killed in the course of the war and 1.6 million wounded, many severely mutilated.[10] "Oh why was I born for this time? Before one is thirty to know more dead than living people?" laments Asquith (11 November 1915), echoing Vera Brittain, who has begun "to feel I shall soon have no male acquaintances left" (14 June 1915). In 1918, Webb scorns celebrations of peace when "every day one meets saddened women, with haggard faces and lethargic movements, and one dare not ask after husband or son" (17 November). The diaries reveal not only the strategies survivors relied on for coping with their grief, but also how hollow those rationalizations could be. When, for example, Asquith's younger brother Yvo dies, she spurns the usual "high-faluting platitude . . . that they were not to be pitied, but were safe, unassailable, young, and glamorous for ever." She moves on to a rationalization more tolerable to her: refusing the "treachery involved to the very ones we love, were one to allow oneself to be in any way the worse" because of them (20 October 1915, 8 July 1916). But in West Africa, Laura Boyle, wife of a district administrator, tries a comparable approach much less successfully: "At such moments for us, left behind, life seems to stand still, there is neither past nor future, only a kind of suspended stricken present. But we must go on, and be brave and happy, for that is what they would tell us to be if they could speak. Only it is almost harder to go on living than to die as they did" ([26 October 1916]).[11]

The cessation of time that Boyle feels, is Isherwood's experience too upon confirmation of her husband's death, when "time seemed to have stood still" (25 June 1915). Losses were not always transcended. Thereafter she dates her life by the length of time that has passed since her Frank disappeared, missing in action: "Two years ago today. . . . It is four years today" (9 May 1917 and 1919), and so on. Likewise the death of Brittain's fiancé, Roland, becomes a reference point in her life: "Always at 11 p.m. on the 23rd day of the month I mean to pause in whatever I am doing & let my spirit go out to His" (25–26 January 1916).[12] For Katherine Mansfield alone does an insurmountable war death—her brother's—become, ironically, a source of good, by motivating her New Zealand stories.

The women at home, as Stevenson realizes, were comparatively fortunate: "Sometimes one sees a woman sobbing, coming from the War Office, and then one realises with a pang what war means. But the dreadful scenes of desolation . . .—these it has not been our lot to witness, and so the grimness of war in its reality has passed us by" (3 December 1915). The women at the front, less fortunate, also endured personal losses, and (like the men) under the additional horrors of battle conditions, military hospitals, and refugee suffering, they soon rejected their idealistic preassumptions about war. Repeatedly the war-front diarists catalog the miseries they have seen and register the shocks of their disillusionment at the "wanton destruction, rapine, murder," in nurse Kate Finzi's words (18 February 1915). The military nurses quickly learn that war does not necessarily bring out the best in people. "I think everyone (every woman) out here has noticed how indifferent and really 'nasty' people are to each other at the front," complains Macnaughtan, for example, of her hospital at one point (spring 1915).[13] Equally upsetting is fear of one's own hardening. The "battle," as Bagnold reports, is not limited to the front; it is also "the struggle to feel pain, to repel the invading familiarity." The constant need to anesthetize their sensibilities in order to perform their duties makes the nurses dread themselves. "One hears, one feels, but in a numb, apathetic sort of way—as though all the edges of reality had been smoothed away," writes Florence Farmborough, serving with the Russian Red Cross. She agrees with a sister nurse: "'I would rather feel the most intense pain . . . than that I should grow callous and indifferent to human suffering'" (11–17 July 1915).[14]

Even from the start, pacifists like Courtney, Virginia Woolf, and Lady Ottoline Morrell have nothing good to say of the war. "Nothing can convert me to feel that war is right," insists Morrell ([January 1916]). Mary Houghton is sure, within a month, that "war is ruinous" to neutrals and combatants alike (5 September 1914). More significant, those who witness war on the continent come to repudiate it as male-engendered destruction exacting an exorbitant price from women. Direct experience of war polarizes attitudes. In 1914, McDougall voices the establishment view—"pride" in "my men" who have gone out "to fight for *me* and all the women of the Empire"— sounding much like Finzi, who hopes that 1915 will bring "the strength to play our parts in the great game worthily of our men!" (31 December 1914). Even in 1917, Brittain asks only "that I may fulfil my own small weary part in this War in such a way as to be worthy of Them, who die & suffer pain" (18 April).[15] Yet a growing resistance has its spokeswomen too.

Gladys Lloyd, a journalist in German-occupied France, is arrested as a spy and entrusted to a burgomaster's wife, who complains that her husband will leave his family unprovided for when he goes to the front. Lloyd declares, "On the just or the unjust side, in war as in life, it is always the woman who pays." ([1914]). Likewise, Houghton, when her maid's son has been called up, acknowledges "the great truth that underlies the pomp and glory of war. . . . So much of youth and manhood is being cut down every hour. And the mothers pay" (7 September 1914). If, in advance of events, Macnaughtan can identify with the "gentlemen" who go to fight, after Antwerp she knows better: "At present women are only repairers, darning socks, cleaning, washing up after men, bringing up reinforcements in the way of fresh life, and patching up wounded men, but some day they must and will have to say, 'The life I produce has as much right to protection as the property you produce, and I claim my right to protect it.'" By 1915 she reports, "Women are asking many questions now," for "there comes a moment when [woman] stands protesting passionately that she has had no voice in the making of war, and she rebels utterly and absolutely against having to pay this unthinkable price for it" (16 October 1914, June 1915). Whereas Webb sees the enemy of future wars in manual workers, Macnaughtan foresees the abolition of war as "one of the tasks which will in the future belong" to women (June 1915). The sentiment is shared by Courtney, one of those who fought for the right of Englishwomen to attend the Women's International Congress for Peace at the Hague in 1915, over Lord Haldane's objections that "we could do no good, and might do harm" (18 April 1915).[16]

With reason to challenge the cost of war, some women did so. Yet though in 1918 Woolf finds it "difficult to see how even a jingo can now believe in any good from war" (17 December 1918), the Great War was actually contemporaneous middle- and upper-class women's gain, for it freed them in ways subtler than the political enfranchising of 1918 by affording them an honorific impetus to action and self-expression. Although women's initial sense of the war as an occasion for patriotism may have matched men's, their recognition of the war as a liberating opportunity was a response more particularly their own. The war could free privileged women from overprotected lives of sustained triviality centered in pleasing males through faithful domestic service while suppressing the women's own inclinations and talents. Princess Daisy of Pless (Mary Fürstin von Pless, an English-woman married to a German noble) captures the cost of such an existence. Before the war, "I was quite sorry not to die, and I asked . . . what on earth I was to live for if my life was to be a continuation of parties and society." But she must "thank God I am myself so well now" when she is needed to nurse British prisoners of war (16 August 1914). "I have always felt," remarks Sarah Macnaughtan perspicaciously of the determined competition for heavy work among the women of her Antwerp hospital unit, "that zeal has a right to expend itself like any other form of energy, and that it can be expended wholesomely if it has an outlet, while assuredly it will not make for peacre if that outlet is denied it" (September 1914).[17] She seizes on precisely the problem the war was peculiarly fitted to solve for middle- and upper-class women.

Whatever their heroic desires to live up to their highest ideal of themselves, women wanted foremost to escape the cotton-wool confinement of privileged lives that forbade them (unless liberated "New Women") to walk unaccompanied or to cultivate friendships outside their class, and largely limited them to superficial interests. The commonest note sounded by women who made it to the continent is eagerness to partake of "reality." "No wonder everyone who can afford to be is in France," Finzi, for example, exults. "It is the Real Thing; one is no longer a looker-on, but a moving factor of things" (10 April 1914). "Here we were, girls of the twentieth century in this atmosphere of storm and war," rejoices McDougall, "living what surely few women ever dreamt in their wildest fancies until this war began. This was life!" ([1914]). Obviously some women enjoyed the sheer excitement of being near battle. May Sinclair, for example, feels "a steady thrill" once she arrives at the Belgian war zones, and she recognizes in her speech "the voice of someone enjoying herself" (26 September 1914). Violetta Thurstan calls her own dangerous departure from Lodz under heavy fire "thrilling"—"I must say I have rarely enjoyed anything more." Yet Sinclair bristles when a Belgian opines that the women in her group "looked on the whole thing as an adventure." No. They think rather of duty: "We certainly were not out for amusement" (11 October 1914).[18] But the truth lies on both sides of the conversation. Along with the satisfaction of doing one's duty, the war enabled that gratifying quickening of pulse accompanying danger and independent responsibility that these economically privileged women so lacked. It was not only a commendable outlet for stifled energies, but also a welcome stimulant.

That Sinclair can admit to women's pursuit of duty, but not of pleasure, is understandable. She respects "the greatest of all joys—the joy of service," as Finzi puts it (12 November 1914). Edwardian conditioning inculcated the traditional female service to others and self-abnegation, not self-gratification. The women's intense eagerness to be useful to the war effort betrays their acculturation. So too does their tendency (despite a growing assertiveness) to efface themselves, not presume on their importance as individuals. "Oh, I do hope that I have the luck to live through this war," says Lady Dorothy Kennard (who came to Rumania with her husband for unexplained reasons), then quickly retreats: "It is really only an impersonal desire to be in at the finish, not the wish to live, that prompts these words" (August 1916).[19]

The women's sense of guilt at expressions of self-gratification and self-advantage likewise betrays their heritage. If Farmborough on leave in Moscow enjoys herself at a party, "a sense of deep shame" overcomes her for enjoying while others are grieving. "I knew then that I should always—all my life—regret that I had given way to my own selfish wishes and sought my own selfish pleasure" (10 November 1917). If the women do not serve others before self and suffer when men are suffering, they have violated the rationale for their existence and are blameworthy. Even pacifist Morrell berates herself because her convictions have precluded her being of any substantial help with the war (20 February 1918). May Sinclair condescends to a British nurse who justifies herself obsessively for leaving Ostend to seek a safer post. But Sinclair herself is guilt-ridden for leaving Ghent because elsewhere, she laments, "I have been something, done something that absolves me. But for these . . . I have not done anything." (11 October 1914). H. Pearl Adam, an expatriate in Paris, finds it "humiliating to think that, while our men were facing desperate odds, we sat in cellars and shivered for our precious civilian skins—skins that can't even be tanned to any useful purpose" (1918). And how guilty Enid Bagnold feels to be free of pain when her soldier-patients are suffering, for, she apologizes, "there is a sort of shame in such strength. 'What can I do for you?' my eyes cry dumbly." [20]

Edwardian women assumed they existed to serve and gratify others. Therefore the war was in fact a rare opportunity, for while it commandeered altruism, it could simultaneously accommodate needs of very different sorts. In the personally acceptable guise of service to others, women's wartime service, wherever pursued, allowed them not only to use their energies and satisfy their curiosity, but also, as they candidly admit, to feel involved and important. They could genuinely want to serve and suffer for others—and meanwhile strengthen self. High among the results of their involvement is enhanced self-respect because of their new roles. "In spite of constant contact with suffering . . . to us . . . there was a great share of happiness," reports an anonymous nurse, for example. "It is a great thing to feel you are fighting death and saving heroes" (fall 1914). Working voluntary two-hour factory shifts making respirators, Cynthia Asquith "simply loved" her new role, but her nursing is even more rewarding: "Directly I stepped into the ward I felt an entirely new being—efficient, untiring, and quite unsqueamish. . . . I loved hearing myself called 'nurse' and would certainly go on with it if I were free." In 1918 she writes: "I *am* glad I decided to do this. My self-esteem is much reinforced" (31 May 1915, 26 December 1916, 9 May 1918). The women treasure recognition of their skills, and they are astonished at their own resources. "Was it *I*—really *I*—who did that?" marvels Florence Farmborough, for instance, in retrospect. "From where had the strength come to endure those ghastly moments?" (1918). Likewise, Kennard "sometimes . . . can hardly credit the fact that this woman, indifferent to blood . . . is myself. I had been inside one hospital in my life, and that when I was the person who was ill" (October 1916). [21]

The diarists are not only proud of themselves. They also take a new pride in womanhood out of a dawning respect for women's capabilities. The war encouraged a sense of community among women to replace identification with men. [22] By releasing women like these diarists from domestic seclusion and allowing them to associate closely with other women and men, it temporarily enabled, in Violetta Thurstan's words, "the joys of comradeship to the full, the taking and giving, and helping and being helped in a way that would be impossible to conceive in the ordinary world." It also encourged mutual concern. Thus Macnaughtan, for example, bristles at men's complaints over gear lost during the flight from Antwerp: "They got an immense reception [at Folkestone], which I, for one, do not grudge them; but women—the nurses and the orderlies and the staff—were adding up the value of the things that they had left behind, and I am sure no one ever knew when or where they landed in England! They came back unnoticed, and began to save up out of their little salaries money enough to replace their caps and aprons" (October 1914). Equally important, the war gave women reason to admire one another, especially at the front. "This at least the Great War has done," brags Grace McDougall, "—it has proved to men that women can share men's dangers and privations and hardships and yet remain women." Indeed, the women at the front have a sense not just of how much individual women are doing, but also, as Kate Finzi says, of "how much devolved on us as representatives of our countrywomen" (29 December 1914). And in fact they were becoming inspirational models. On leave in Paris, McDougall reports how two well-dressed women nearby in a cafe "talked of us and smiled in our direction, and at length one came over and said to us cordially: 'I must tell you how we admire you and your work. If I were twenty years younger I would come with you myself.'"[23]

Many of the war-front diarists published their books very quickly, and the zeal with which they focus on women's achievements rather than on men's suggests some didactic desire to raise sights at home. Diarists may occasionally grumble at competitiveness, pettiness, and ignorance,[24] but they are also lavish with praise: variously, for women's efficiency, determination, altruism, endurance, heroism, aplomb, responsibility, loyalty—and skill with motor vehicles. "Oh, give me intelligent women to do things for me!" insists Macnaughtan, for one. "The best-run things I have seen since the war began have been our women's unit at Antwerp and Lady Bagot's hospital" (spring 1915). Thurstan, for another, praises her nurses' spirit and stamina, for "never were Sisters so loyal and unselfish as mine. . . . They were overworked and underfed, and no word of grumbling or complaint was ever heard from them. They worked from morning till night."

Macnaughtan herself comes in for comparable praise from Sinclair during the siege of Antwerp when "she looked as if she could not have held out another night. . . . Miss ——— may drop to pieces at her post, but it is there that she will drop" (4 October 1914). She is also praised by the anonymous nurse for her soup kitchen at Furnes ([1914]). Diarists take special notice of all-women endeavors, proud that they manage entirely without male help, and they are enthusiastic about the intriguing possibility of women soldiers. "The extraordinary fact remains that they really *were* there" (13 March 1915), rejoices Finzi upon hearing the rumors. The women in Florence Famborough's Russian unit are "thrilled to the core" to learn of Yasha Bacharova's women's battalion, even if later to be disillusioned by its rout (19 August 1917).[25]

The diarists also reveal a new independence in their relationships with men. Vera Brittain, for example, finds herself communicating more frankly to her lover because "the nearness of death breaks down the reserves & conventions" (17 April 1915). More consequential, women are no longer obliged to have intimates at all. As nurses or attendants, they can escape for a while from the mating game. Although Enid Bagnold cannot quite adjust to her "convent" of a hospital (the royal Hospital at Woolwich) with its "strangely unsexed women," she nonetheless finds it "wonderful to talk to men affectionately without exciting or implying love." To Asquith the possibility is liberating: "the *only* human relationship in which I haven't been bothered by self-consciousness" (20 June 1918). McDougall likes the sanctity of role protecting war nurses, who, "alone in the midst of the Belgian army," are "as safe as in a London drawing-room."[26] Whether nurses, drivers, reporters, or travelers, these diarists are not hunting for sexual partners during their war work. Or, if they are, they keep it well hidden from their diaries. They want to see themselves—or given the self-published diaries—to be seen in other terms.

It had become possible, sometimes even essential, to be assertive: to challenge male, and male-engendered, authority. Kate Finzi, for example, reports the Boulogne nurses' effective protest at salary cuts in their measly pay: "Let their stand," she exults, ". . . be recorded as one of the first women's trade unions" (31 December 1914). By

1915, Princess Daisy of Pless declares herself not only no longer the emperor's 'obedient servant'—"I am nobody's servant; neither shall I play the role of dressed-up housekeeper" (5 May 1915). After a contretemps with her head nurse, Bagnold ponders what she herself recognizes as a significant question: "Is to be 'liked' the final standard?"[27] Although in a masculinist culture it is, and renders women docile, the women at the front think it more important to be treated well. Moreover, women reared to be submissive and proper find themselves delighting in becoming lawbreakers and antagonists. Sarah Macnaughtan, "amazed at the pleasure that wrong-doing gives," regrets "my desperately strict past life" (19 May 1915) after entering the British lines illicitly. McDougall flatly refuses a German order to leave Ghent, chortling, "and I swanked out . . . as if khaki had never before been fittingly worn!" ([1914]). When Brittain wants to become a nurse, she goes "off for the first time on my own account," without asking her family's permission (10 April 1915). When Dorothy Kennard (December 1916) and Farmborough (10 October 1917) cannot get transport for essential supplies, they unashamedly and effectively lose their tempers in public, even as the anonymous nurse confidently challenges a surgeon's order for a needless amputation.[28] Some of the reported defiance, especially in the self-published diaries, is doubtless posturing, but the particular postures chosen are noteworthy.

Critical of male attitudes toward women, the war-front diarists want what May Sinclair describes as the "New chivalry, that refuses to keep women back even from the firing line." "The modern woman," says she, "does not ask to be protected" (1 and 9 October 1914). The anonymous nurse objects when she overhears "one of our men say 'I wish we had all these women safe in England.'" "They all funked having a lot of women in their charge" (1914), she complains. The women at the front like to think of themselves as equivalent to the men, not their charges. Though only Farmborough directly refers to herself as a "soldier, going to war" (30 January 1915), others apparently view themselves as soldiers—in fact, officers—too. The diarists have little patience with chauvinism at home either, grumbling at how men take women's labors for granted and demean their being. Macnaughtan, for example, mocks the romanticizing of women's lives in the mystique of "'the woman's touch.' When a woman has been down on her knees scrubbing for a week, and washing for another week, a man, returning and finding his house in order, and vaguely conscious of a newer and fresher smell about it, talks quite tenderly of 'a woman's touch'" (7 March 1915). Only half-jokingly does Mary Houghton complain about how an Englishman views his wife: "Once married, she doesn't exist any longer as a thinking animal—why should she think? Can't he do it lots better for her?" (3 August 1914).[29]

Diarists abroad enjoy the relaxed and more comfortable garb that wartime allowed: shorter, fuller skirts and sometimes even trousers. Princess Daisy thinks it "a relief not to have to put on something *fashionable*" (3 November 1915), even when on leave; and Dorothy Kennard, at least for a while, believes that war has "brought home to us women how utterly absurd is fashion" (February 1917). But significantly, though wartime conditions may have modified women's relationships with men, the diarists also cling to the insidious traditional concern with personal appearance, consequence of their conditioning as sexual objects. Even near the battle lines, they require an attractive appearance for self-esteem. When her illness at the Russian front necessitates shaving Farmborough's head, for instance, she feels ludicrous. "[My head] was a dreadful sight," she says. "But," she quickly adds, "I took care to have it well-covered when any male member of the personnel was at hand" (December 1916). With half an hour to evacuate Brussels before the German entry, Violetta Thurstan hastily collects her nurses, "looking," in her words, "more like a set of rag-and-bone men than respectable British nursing sisters." But "Mercifully no one took much notice of us." Kate Finzi is unhappy with Red Cross uniforms, "so effective *en masse*, so unbecoming to the individual" (October 1914).[30] However much the women treasure the opportunity to serve their country, native or adopted, they would prefer to cut a nice figure while doing so.

While Bagnold is busy at her nursing, she realizes sadly, "My ruined charms cry aloud for help. The cap wears away my front hair; my feet are widening from the everlasting boards." She recalls, "I was advised last night . . . to marry immediately before it was too late." But she demurs: "A desperate remedy. I will try cold cream and hair tonics first."[31] However facetious her tone, Bagnold captures the transitional quality of these war years. A new world not dependent on male validation was forming for women; indeed, the defiant spinster already existed before the war in small numbers. Nonetheless, the sort of feminist movement that would radically change the female sense of self, not just legal and civic status, was still some fifty years and another world war away. The Great War effected no major feministic upheaval of attitude. Like more than three centuries of women before them, these diarists are characteristically service oriented, guilt-ridden at self-concern, and appearance-conscious. Most of their rebelliousness belongs to women who served in war zones and who were probably independent minded to begin with, though the war enabled them to express their spirit. Critic Sandra Gilbert has spoken of women's postwar guilt, anxiety, and doubt in the face of intensified misogyny;[32] they were predictable reactions. The women of this wartime period, the diarists show, still assumed, reflected, and accepted a male-dominant society. The postwar diaries are mildly suggestive of change, but not strikingly different from prewar ones, and not only because the few postwar diarists had already matured before the war. Yet if the brief burst of war did not entirely undo centuries of role conditioning, nonetheless peace also could not mean simply a return to the prewar status quo. As diarist Helen Adams contemplates in 1918, "We are different people. The people we were in 1914 . . . we have lost sight of" (June).[33]

Englishwomen in particular not only lost too many of their men and much of their innocence; they also gained some personally enfranchising awareness. Having known a new self-respect and pride as women, having tasted a measure of very "real" life and freedom of expression, women who had served in the war in some capacity, especially abroad, had to have a different sense of what being female could encompass.[34] Quite a few felt so much at the center of things that they published their diaries for others to read. The number of published diaries is itself significant. Moreover, as David Mitchell says, "Thousands of ex-VAD's joined the fight against humbug and lunatic tradition" in the twenties.[35] Diarist Vera Brittain was one of them. Immediately after the war she became an activist for women's right to degrees at Oxford; during the twenties, writing regularly for the feminist journal *Time and Tide,* she advocated extensive legal and social reforms.

For women like these diarists, circumstances precluded simple resumption of prewar habits. Not only was there substantial civic gain, even aside from achieving national suffrage,[36] but women were forced into less conventionally feminine roles by the shortage and disablement of males. Historian Jane Lewis notes how "World War I had a dramatic effect on the marriage expectations of women, and it may be hypothesized that there were concomitant changes in attitudes towards the desirability of careers for daughters of middle-class parents. Of those women who were single and in their late twenties in 1912, 50 percent remained unmarried a decade later." Moreover, the old pattern of social life was no longer an attraction for the very privileged and their imitators. Given a reduced standard of living for most of the middle class and a new freedom for girls, as historian Leonore Davidoff says, "the 'career' sequence of schoolgirl, deb (or provincial variant), daughter-at-home, matron and dowager wielding power in the social/political world, had ceased to have much cogency."[37]

A way of life was over. Women did marry, however, and husbands remained the dominant marital partners, while women believed stoutly in their domestic roles and worked even harder at mothering than ever before. Yet middle- and upper-class women also participated in the steady decline of marital fertility until the Second World War, and they expected their marriages to be companionate and sexually satisfying. By the interwar years, to quote Lewis, married women "were no longer regarded primarily as ornamental and sexually innocent creatures."[38] Nor, then, would they regard themselves that way.

Something attitudinal was instigated for middle- and upper-class women by the Great War period: a different sense of female being. It was by no means fully developed, for simultaneously with any postwar advances came reversions like the supplanting of equal-rights feminism by a type of welfare feminism with separate-sphere premises.[39] Moreover, women were likely to feel torn between home and career rather than invest themselves freely in careers.[40] But there remained embers that could ignite during the upheaval of another war and its aftermath of a women's movement, neither so far away in time. Mid-twentieth century women would become more resistant to

247

male controls over their lives and less accepting of marriage and motherhood as women's only functions and fulfillment; more convinced of inherent female worth and abilities and less tolerant of abuse.[41] By the sixties, the contemporary liberation movement, which was to accelerate changes in female sense of self, could begin. That, however, is not the era of the Great War diaries; only what they tentatively anticipate.

Expressions of an earlier age, the Great War diaries themselves point both forward and back. Long-engrained habits of mind, such as characterize most diaries before them, persist in their pages alongside a new sense of release and confidence. A lesson from the past for the feminism of the present is perhaps inscribed in these women's diaries: patience. Centuries of female days cannot be undone in one brave new day.

APPENDIX

PAGES FROM LADY ANNE CLIFFORD'S FINAL DIARY, 1676*

At the time of her death Clifford was "Countess Dowager of Dorset, Pembroke and Montgomery, Baroness Clifford, Westmoreland and Vesci, Lady of the Honour of Skipton in Craven, and High Sheriffess of Westmoreland," as the stone slabs she had affixed to each of her castles announced. For thirty-three years she had been the active ruler of her domain.

[January] The 24th Day. And this day there was none that dined here nor visited me, so I spent the day in hearing some chapters read to me and in preparing myself to receive the Holy Sacrament of Bread and Wine which I intend, God willing, to receive with my family.

The 25th Day. I remembered how this day was 52 years, in the withdrawing Room Chamber at Knowle House in Kent as we satt at dinner, had my first Lord and I a great falling out, when but the day before I came from London, from being Godmother to his Brother's youngest son. Deut., c. 23, v. 5.:—"Nevertheless the Lord thy God would not hearken unto Balaam, but the Lord thy God turned the curse into a Blessing, because the Lord thy God loveth thee." And this Morning about eight o'clock did Mr. Samuel Grasty, our parson, preach a good Sermon in my Chamber to me and my family and a little after he administered the Sacrament of Bread and Wine to me and my family, viz., to Mrs. Frances Pate and Mrs. Susan Machell

*Diary quoted from Williamson, *Lady Anne Clifford*, 270–280, and inscription from *The Diary*, edited by Sackville-West, iii. See Clifford.

(my two Gentlewomen), Dorothy Demain, Margaret Dargue, Anne Chipen-
dale, and Jane Slidall my four Laundry Maids, Isabella Jordon my Wash-
woman, Mr. Edward Hasell [Estate Steward], Mr. Henry Machell [Appleby
Estate Steward], George Boodion [valet], Edward Forster, Allan Strickland
[Chief Steward], William Dargue, Jos. Hall [Chief Groom], Abraham Fitter
[Postillion], Isaac Walker [Stable Groom], Richard Raynolson, William
Buckle, Richard Lowes [House Steward], Cuthbert Rawling, Jacob Murga-
troids, Arthur Swinden [Under Butler], and George Lough, the Clark,
which I nor they received since the third of November last, and Parson
Grasty dined here with my folks and then he went.

I went not out of my House nor out of my Chamber to-day. Psa. 121.

The 28th Day. And this morning by letters I received from my daughter
Thanett and by the packet of this week from London I came to know that
she herself my said daughter was well and most of her generation and posterity in their several places and homes.

The 29th Day. And yesternight late did John Bradford come from Skipton
and over Cotter and Stake afoot hither, but I did not see him till this morning and he brought the news of Mrs. Sutton's death, the Mother of my Almshouse at Beamsly.

And this morning about six o'clock before I got out of my bed did I pair
the tops of my Nails of my Fingers and toes and burnt them in the fire after I
was up, I went not out of the House nor out of my Chamber to-day.

The 30th Day. Being Sunday I considered how this was 86 years, then
Friday about seven o'clock in the Evening was my blessed Mother with very
hard labour brought to bed of me in her own Chamber in Skipton Castle,
my Brother Robert, Lord Clifford, then all lying in that Castle, but my
Noble Father then lay in Bedford House in the Strand at London.

The 31st Day. And this day did my family keep as a fast the Martyrdom of
King Charles the 1st, tho' he was beheaded the day before, the day being
commanded by Act of Parliament. And this day about three o'clock in the
afternoon did John Twentyman, Gardener, to the Lord Bishop of Carlisle,
came from Rose Castle in Cumberland hither to this Brougham Castle to
look after and order my Garden here, so he lay in the Bannister Room five
nights together, during which time he worked in my Garden here, upon
Saturday the Fifth of February, in the morning, he went home again, and I
sent by him a Bottle of the Pulp of Pomcittron to the Bishop of Carlisle.

February of 7th Day. Being Shrove Monday, and to-day there dined without
with my folks, Dorothy Wiber, the woman of my Almshouse at Appleby, and
after dinner I had her into my Chamber and saw her paid for five dozen yards
of Bonlace, but I was very angry with her for bringing so much and told her I
would have no more of her.

I went not out of my house nor out of my Chamber to-day. Psa. 121.

And this afternoon about one o'clock, after I had taken my leave of them in my chamber, did Mr. Edward Hasell and Christopher Rawling ride out of this Brougham Castle, towards Rose Castle in Cumberland to his Uncle and Aunt the Bishop of Carlisle and his Lady, when he and his Man, lay three nights, and on the 14th day they came back again hither.

I went not out of my house nor out of My Chamber to-day.

This afternoon, about one o'clock, did Sir George Fletcher and his lady and her daughter by her first husband, and Mr. Fleming and his eldest daughter, come hither, so I had them into my chamber and kissed the women and took the men by the hand, and Sir George delivered to me sev-erall letters of my ancestors, which were sent me by order of my Lord Marshall, and after I had talked with them and given the women each of them an emerald gold ring they all went away.

12th day. In the morning did I see mr. Robert Willison of Penrith, paid for a rundlet of sack, but I was very angry with him, because I thought it too dear, and told him I would have no more of him, and then he slipt away from me in a good hurry.

The 14th Day. And this day did John Webster come hither into my cham-ber so I took him by the hand and talked with him and then he retreated into the Dining Room, and dined with my folk.

And this 14th day early in the morning did my Black Spoted Bitch called Zurmue [the word may be "Quinne"] pupp in my Bed and Chamber four little puppies but they were all dead.

I went not out of my House nor out of my Chamber to-day.

The 15th Day. And came hither this afternoon about one o'clock my Cousin Mrs. Anne Howard, sister to Mr. Francis Howard of Corby and her cousin Sir Charles Howard's daughter and two other Gentlemen with them, whose names I know not, so I had them into my Chamber and kissed the women and took the men by the hand and talked with them a good while, and a little after they rode away on Horseback to the said Corby Castle in Cumberland.

I went not out of my house nor out of my Chamber to-day.

17th Day. I remember how this day was 60 years when I and my first Lord lay in Little Dorsett House in London Town in the afternoon in the best Gallery in Great Dorsett House did George Abbot, Archbishop of Canter-bury and many others come to my first Lord and mee and did earnestly per-swaid mee both by fair words and threatings to stand to the award of the four judges, wou'd then make betwixt my first Lord and mee on the one part and my Uncle of Cumberland and his son on the other part concerning the land of mine inheritances and thereupon it was agreed that I should go to my

Blessed Mother In Westmoreland and begin my Journey the 21st of that month, which I did accordingly. Eccles., c. 3; Pro., c. 20.

And this 17th day in the afternoon about three o'clock did my Cousin Mr. Richard Musgrave oldest son to my cousin Sir Philip Musgrave, and his Lady and their daughter, who is their only child, come in their coach hither from Edenhall, and I had them into my Chamber, and kissed my said Cousin and his wife and the child and also their gentlewomen and I gave to my Cousin, wife and child, each of them a gold Ring, and after they had stayed awhile they went away. And this day did my Servant, Mr. Thos. Strickland, and his man, Lancelot Machell, ride from his own house near Kendal called Garnett House towards Appleby whither they came that night to gather my Candlemas Rents, and he lay in the Barron's Chamber there and his man in the Musty Chamber. And to-day I had one or two very ill fitts. Yet I slept well in the night, thank God.

I went not out of my house nor out of my Chamber to-day.

17th day. This morning did I sett my handwriting to four good letters of Hasell's writing, one to my granddaughter of Thanett, one to my Lord Northampton, one to Sir Thomas Wharton, and one to Mr. William Edge, all in answer to letters I received from them by the last post.

The 20th Day. And tho' to-day was Sunday, yet I went not out to Church nor out of my Chamber all this day, but my two Gentlewomen and three of my Laundry Maids and most of my chief men Servants went to this Church called Ninekirks where he preached a good Sermon, vizt., Mr. Grasty, our Parson, so them and the rest conjectured tho' one part thereoff seemed to reflect upon the writer, so that I thought he spoke to none but me.

After dinner Mr. Grasty said Common Prayers, and read a Chapter and sang a Psalm as usual upon Sundays to me and to my Family.

The 21st Day. I remembered how this day was 60 years did my first Lord and I go out of Little Dorsett House in London Town on our Journey Northwards so as that night we lay in the Inn at Dunstable in Bedfordshire as were in our Journey, I towards Brougham Castle to my Blessed Mother and he to sett me on my way as farr as Lichfield in Straffordshire. Eccle., c. 3rd, etc.

The 22nd Day. I remembered how this day was 60 years my first Lord and I went out of the Inn at Dunstable and so through Stony Stratford and hard by Grafton House, in Northamptonshire, into the Inn at Towcestor in that County as we were in our Journey Northwards.

Before I was out of my bed did I pare off the tops of the nails of my fingers and toes, and when I was up I burnt them in the chimney of my chamber, and a little after in this same chamber of mine did George Goodgion clip off all the hair of my head, which I likewise burnt in the fire, and after supper I washed and bathed my feet and legs in warm water, wherein beef had been boiled and brann. And I had done none of this to myself since the 13th of December that George Goodwin cut my hair for me in this chamber of mine. God grant that good may betide me and mine after it.

I went not out of my House nor out of my Chamber to-day.

The 23rd day I remembered how this was 60 years my first Lord and I went out of the Inn at Stony Stratford, into my Cousin Thomas Elmes's House at Lillford, in Northamptonshire, for awhile and so that day into the Inn at Warwich, in Warwichshire, where we lay that night.

And to-day there dined with my folks in the Painted Room Mr. Samuel Grasty, our parson, and afterwards he said Common Prayers and read a Chapter as usual on Wednesdays to me and my Family and there also dined without with my folks Mr. Thomas Ubank of Ormside, the Doctor, so after dinner I had him into my Chamber, and I took him by the hand and I gave him six shillings, and caused him to go up into Arthur Swindon's Chamber to see him and he came up and sayed prayers and then he went away, and afterwards I paid Mr. Samuel Grasty his twenty shillings for saying prayers to me and my family for a month last past, and then they all went away.

I went not out of my House nor out of my Chamber to-day.

The 24th Day. I remembered how this was 60 years my first Lord and I after I had been to see Warwick Castle and Church went out of the Inn and so into Guy's Cliff to see it, and from thence that night we went into the Inn at Litchfield where we lay two nights because the next day was Sunday.

I went not out of my House nor out of my Chamber to-day. Psa. 121.

The 25th Day. I remembered how this was 60 years and then Sunday. My first Lord and I went forenoon and afternoon into the Church at Litchfield to the Sermon and Service there and afterwards into other the most remarkable places in that town and that night we lay again in the Inn there.

And this day did Mr. Thomas Strickland, one of my chief officers, and his man, Lancelot Machell, ride on horseback towards Appleby Castle, to receive there the rest of my Candlemas rents; and the 28th day they returned and came back hither to me and us here.

And this day there dined without with my folks my cousin, Mr. Thomas Burbeck of Hornby Castle, and his wife and their little daughter, and his father-in-law, Mr. Catterick, and his wife and his mother, and there also dined here Mr. Robert Carleton, only son to the widdow, Lady Carleton. So after dinner I had them all into my chamber, and kissed the women and took the men by the hand, and I gave to my cousin, Mr. Burbeck, and his wife each ten shillings, and his mother ten shillings, and his father-in-law Mr. Catterick, and his wife each of them ten shillings, and six shillings to the child, and gave Mr. Carleton a pair of Buckskin gloves, and then all went away.

The 26th Day. I remembered how this day was 60 years I and my first Lord went out to the Inn at Litchfield in Sir George Curzon's House at Croxall in Derbyshire, from whence we went to Burton-upon-Trent in Darbyshire where my first Lord and I then parted, he returning back to Litchfield where he was to stay for four or five days then about a great foot race that was then there, but I proceeded on my Journey towards Brougham Castle and came to Darby and lay in the Inn there.

I went not out of the House nor out of my Chamber to-day.

The 27th Day. I remembered how this day was 60 years did I go out of the Inn at Darby into two Houses at Hardwick now both belonging to the Earl of Devonshire and so from thence into the Inn at Chesterfield in that County where I lay out one night. And tho' to-day was Sunday yet I went not to the Church nor out of my Chamber all this day. Psa. 23rd, but my two gentlewomen went and two of my Laundry Maids and most of my men Servants, rode on Horseback to Ninekirks where Mr. Grasty, the parson, preached a very good sermon to them and to the Congregation.

The 28th Day. I remembered how this was 60 years I went out of the Inn at Chesterfield in Darbyshire into the Earl of Shrewsberries' House called Sheffield in Yorkshire to see it and that Evening I went to the Inn at Rotherham in that County where I lay that one night.

And to-day there dined here in the Painted Room with my folks Mr. Christopher Dalston of Acorn Bank, oldest son to my cousin Mr. John Dalston, and his wife, so after dinner I had them into my Chamber and kissed his wife and took him by the hand and likewise talked with them a good while and I gave to his wife a pair of Buckskin Gloves and then they went away.

I went not out of the House nor out of my Chamber to-day.

The 29th day. I remembered how this day was 60 years I went out of the Inn at Rotherham in Yorkshire into a poor Parson's House at Peniston in that County where I lay that one night. And this afternoon did Mr. Thomas Strickland pay to Mr. Edward Hasell for my use £305 5s. od. of my Westmoreland Rents, due at Candlemass last for which I now gave Strickland an acquittance under my hand and saw the money put up in a trunk in my Chamber.

I went not out of the House nor out of my Chamber to-day.

March The 1st Day. I remembered how this day was 60 years I went out of the poor Parson's House at Peniston in Yorkshire over Peniston Moor, where never coach went before mine, into the Inn at Manchester in Lancashire where I lay that one night.

254

I went not out of the House nor out of my Chamber to-day.

The 2nd Day. I remembered how this day was 60 years I went out of the Inn at Manchester into the poor cottage at Chorley where I lay there in a poor Ale House there that one night, which was within three miles of Latham House but I did not see it by reason of the Mist.

And to-day there dined without in the Painted Room with my folks Mrs. Willison of Penrith, and after dinner I had her into my Chamber and kissed her and took her by the hand but told her I would have no more Wine of her husband because he used me so badly and then she went away.

I went not out of the House nor out of my Chamber to-day.

The 3rd Day. I remembered how this day was 60 years I went out of the poor Cottage at Chorley, though it was Sunday, by reason the lodgings were so bad, into the Inn at Preston in Adersey in Lancashire, where I lay that one night.

I went not out of the House nor out of my Chamber to-day.

The 5th Day. I remembered how this day was 60 years I went out of the Inn at Lancaster town into the Inn at Kendall in Westmoreland where I lay that one night. And to-day there dined without with my folks in the Painted Room Mr. Samuel Grasty and my two Farmers here, so after dinner I had them all into my Chamber, and Mr. Grasty was paid his twenty shillings for saying prayers to me and family for a month last past, and after he said Common Prayers and read a Chapter and sung a Psalm (as was usual upon Sundays) to me and them afforesaid and then when prayers were ended they all went away.

I went not out of the House nor out of my Chamber to-day.

The 6th Day. I remembered how this day 67 years my blessed Mother with many in our company brought me from her house in Austin Fryers to the Court of Little Dorsett house in Salisbury Court in London town to live there with my first Lord, being but married to him the 25th of the month before. Eccl., c. 3, and c. 8, v. 6.

And I remembered how this day was 60 years I went out of the Inn at Kendal to Brogham Castle to my Blessed Mother.

I went not out of the House nor out of my Chamber to-day.

The 7th Day. And this morning died Arthur Swindon, my under Butler, who has served me about fourteen or fifteen years, and the next day about two of the clock in the afternoon was his dead Body burried in Ninekirks Church, where Parson Grasty preached his Funeral Sermon and most of my Servants and others attended the Corps to the Funeral.

I went not out of the House nor out of my Chamber to-day.

The 9th Day. And to-day there dined with my folks in the Painted Room My Cousin Mr. John Dalston of Acorn Bank, and after dinner I had him into my Chamber and took him by the hand and talked with him and then he went away.

And there also dined with my folks Mr. John Gilmoor, the Keeper of Whinfell Park, and his man, Wm. Labourn, dined below in the Hall, and after dinner after my Cousin was gone from me, I had them both into my Chamber and took them by the hand and talked with them and then they went away.

I went not out of the house nor out of my Chamber to-day.

10th Day. And this morning I saw George Goodgion paid for two hundred and forty-nine yards of linnen cloth that he bought for me at Penrith, designed for twenty pair of sheets and some pillow-veres for the use of my house; and after dinner I gave away several old sheets which were divided amongst my servants, and this afternoon did Margaret Montgomery, from Penrith, the sempstress, come hither, so I had her into my chamber and kiss'd her and talked with her, and she came to make up the twenty pair of sheets and pillow-veres.

The 13th Day. I remembered how this day was 60 years I went from my blessed Mother to Naworth Castle, in Cumberland, to the Lord William Howard, my first Lord's Uncle, and his Wife, and the Lady Elizabeth Dacres (my Father's cousin German) and many of their sons and their Wives and their Daughters and their children and their Grandchildren and I lay there in it for two nights.

I went not out of the House nor out of my Chamber to-day.

The 15th Day. I remembered how this day was 60 years in the morning I went out of Naworth Castle, from Lord William Howard and his Wife into the City of Carlisle where I went into the Castle there, wherein was born into the world the Lady Anne Dacres, she that was afterwards Countess Dowager of Arundale and I went into the Cathedral Church there, wherein was burried my great Grandfather William, Lord Dacres, and from thence I went the same day into Brougham Castle where I continued with my Blessed Mother till the second of the Month following that I went from her and never saw her after.

I went not out of the House nor out of my Chamber this day.

The 17th Day. And to-day nobody dined here by my folks so there is nothing to be superadded.

The 19th Day. Being Sunday, Palm Sunday, and this morning I had a violent fitt of the wind, so that it caused me to fall into a swoning fitt for above half an hour together so as I thought I should have died, but it pleased God, I recovered, and was better afterwards. And to-day there dined without with my folks in the Painted Room Mr. Grasty, our Parson, and my two Farmers, so after dinner they came into my Chamber and Mr. Grasty said Common Prayers and read a Chapter and sang a Psalm as usual on Sundays to me and my Family, and after Prayers they all went away.

I went not out of the House nor out of my Chamber this day.

20th Day. I remembered how this day was 60 years did I and my blessed mother in Brougham Castle give in our answer in writing that we would not stand to the award the four Lord Chief Judges meant to make concerning the lands of mine inheritance, which did spin out a great deal of trouble to us, yet God turned it to the best.

Deut., c. 23, v. 5. "Nevertheless the Lord thy God would not hearken unto Balaam, but the Lord thy God turned the Curse into a Blessing unto thee, because the Lord thy God loved thee."

The 21st Day. I went not out all this day.

The 22nd Day the Countess of Pembroke died [in another handwriting].

NOTES

Source information for the diaries appears in the Select List of Women's Diaries under the diarists' names. Should there be two sources for a diarist, the first pertains unless otherwise specified.

INTRODUCTION

1. Bernard, *Female World*, 1.
2. M. Shelley viii, xv; Clairmont vii, viii.
3. Nor are there any extensive up-to-date bibliographies. Matthews's lengthy 1950 *British Diaries: An Annotated Bibliography* was compiled only until the 1940s and is not sorted by gender. Begos's 1977 *Annotated Bibliography of Published Women's Diaries* is selective, international, and not limited to actual diaries. Barrow's 1981 *Women 1870–1928: A Select Guide to Printed and Archival Sources in the United Kingdom* includes only a minimal list of diaries. Huff's 1985 *British Women's Diaries: A Descriptive Bibliography of Selected Nineteenth-Century Women's Manuscript Diaries* has the restrictions indicated by its title, but does cover fifty-eight non-working-class diaries and supersedes Batts's 1976 *British Manuscript Diaries of the Nineteenth Century*.
4. For specifically English female diarists collectively, recent critical attention has been sparse and limited. Huff's bibliography (see my note 3) contains a useful twenty-five-page critical introduction limited to nineteenth-century diarists. Mendelson's 1985 "Stuart Women's Diaries and Occasional Memoirs," covering twenty-three women's serial writing, also is a period study. In book-length criticism, Dyson's 1978 *Various Range: A*

Study of the Journals and Memoirs of British Men and Women in the Indian Sub-continent, 1765–1836 is concerned with lives, not the diary form, besides having the restrictions indicated by its title. Likewise, although Dobbs allots chapter ten of his English-focused 1974 *Dear Diary . . . : Some Studies in Self-Interest* to eleven women's diaries because "there is still something to be said for considering the woman's diary as a specific subject" (178), he leaves that something yet to be said and addresses only the particular lives of the diarists. However, Fothergill incidentally reaches tentative conclusions about a few characteristics of female English diary keeping in his 1974 *Private Chronicles: A Study of English Diaries*. (He also discusses Anaïs Nin's non-English diary as a culminating work.) Some earlier critical books inclusive of or limited to female English diarists are Willy's 1964 pamphlet for the British Book Council, *Three Women Diarists: Celia Fiennes, Dorothy Wordsworth, Katherine Mansfield*; Spalding's 1949 *Self-Harvest: A Study of Diaries and the Diarist*; and O'Brien's 1943 *English Diaries and Journals*. Ponsonby's 1923 *English Diaries: A Review* and 1927 *More English Diaries: Further Reviews* are descriptive anthologies. The first includes random generalizations about women's diaries in its lengthy introduction, though based, as Ponsonby sometimes admits, on a very limited sample; his book describes only twenty-one female diaries (but ninety-eight male ones).

5. The foreword to the 1974 anthology *Revelations: Diaries of Women*, ed. Moffatt and Painter, for example, theorizes on the female diary. The 1982 *Ariadne's Thread: A Collection of Contemporary Women's Journals*, ed. Lifshin, offers a summary analysis of its contributor-diarists' attitudes and approaches, with suggestive generalizations. The 1985 *A Day at A Time: The Diary Literature of American Women from 1764 to the Present*, ed. Culley, includes a valuable introductory essay characterizing women's diaries as literary texts. Diary anthologies aside, the 1980 *Women's Autobiography: Essays in Criticism*, ed. Jelinek, includes some comments on the female diary as a form. Hampsten's 1982 *Read This Only to Yourself: The Private Writings of Midwestern Women: 1880–1910*, which analyzes stylistic characteristics of American diaries and letters, transcends the particular historical period under study, though not class distinctions; and Motz's 1983 *True Sisterhood: Michigan Women and Their Kin 1820–1920* offers a very brief discussion of diaristic language codes per se.

Short theoretical essays include Godwin's 1976 "Diarist," Juhasz's 1978 "Some Deep Old Desk," Sloman's 1978 "Fragmentary Genres," Dehler's 1978 "Need to Tell All," Metzger and Meyerhoff's 1979 "Dear Diary," and Lensink's 1987 "Expanding the Boundaries of Criticism." *Women's Diaries: A Quarterly Newsletter* (1983–1986) contains reviews and brief articles that sometimes include theoretical comments.

6. Metzger and Meyerhoff, "Dear Diary," 45. See Abbott's *Diary Fiction* on contemporary proponents of the therapeutic diary such as Anaïs Nin, Tristine Rainer, and Ira Progoff. Lessing's *Golden Notebook* was published in 1962; Nin's *Diary*, between 1966 and 1976.

7. Moffatt and Painter, *Revelations*, 4–5, 4.

8. No hard data prove (or disprove) the popular assumption that females are more avid diary keepers than males. However, Ponsonby surveyed one hundred educated adults, randomly chosen to include fifty-six males and forty-four females, and discovered that female diarists slightly preponderated among them (*English Diaries*, 41). Allport speaks of a Russian study that claims two-thirds of adolescent girls, but only one-third of boys, keep diaries (*Use of Personal Documents*, 96).

9. *Self* is a prickly term. Theorists of autobiography, as Eakin points out in *Fictions in Autobiography*, debate whether the self is autonomous and transcendent or contingent and provisional, dependent for its existence on language and on others. Does the "I" validate its own uniqueness? Or is the self but an illusion produced by language? (181–182). When I speak of the female sense of self, I assume that the self is an enduring illusion derived from experience. Although I believe that language is enormously significant in the formation and perpetuation of a female self, like Eakin (191ff.) and like Cameron in *Feminism and Linguistic Theory*, I "cannot accept . . . the privileged status accorded language" as sole cause in the construction of a female subjective reality (169). Like Chodorow (*Reproduction of Mothering*), I assume that female gender identity initially develops pre-Oedipally in relation to the mother rather than upon entry into the symbolic, phallocentric order of language in the Oedipal phase. But even if language is not the only or even the earliest mode of effecting gender identity, it accelerates the emergence of a female self and thereafter sustains self-consciousness, in the process obliging females to internalize male cultural values as reality. In keeping a diary and personally speaking of her self, however, a female has some opportunity to distinguish her sense of self from the male constructs culturally imposed on her.

10. Spacks, *Imagining a Self*, 310, 311; Culley, *Day at a Time*, 12.

11. Wolf, "Diary," 69. When I insist on the diary as a form of literature, and therefore of art, I have in mind attacks on it like Stauffer's in *English Biography* (1930):

The diary makes no attempt to see life steadily and see it whole. It is focussed on the immediate present, and finds that the happenings of twenty-four hours are sufficient unto the day. It becomes, therefore, not the record of a life but the journal of an existence, made up of a monotonous series of short and similar entries. . . . in a study of biography as a literary form, the diary has scant claim to consideration, for it makes no pretence to artistic structure. The diary should . . . be considered as . . . raw material. (255)

Such prejudices still flourish, for despite a growing acceptance of diaries as literature, they are not customarily part of literature courses when other forms of writing are available. Moreover, autobiographies constructed on the diary model are suspect, for, as Juhasz observes in "Towards a Theory of Form," while "no one would question the autobiographical nature" of the personal diary, "its status as 'autobiography,' which is a formal and public literary genre, has traditionally been denied" (222).

12. Matthews, *British Diaries*, xv. I prefer the term *diary* to *journal*, although for all practical purposes the terms are interchangeable. The *Oxford English Dictionary* distinguishes the diary as the more personal of the two types of records. However, as Ponsonby says in *English Diaries*, "The word *Journal* should be reserved for the purely objective historical or scientific records, and the word *Diary* for the personal memoranda, notes and expressions of opinion," but "as it is, the words are used quite indiscriminately" (5). How indiscriminately, diarist Fanny Anne Burney (Wood) illustrates: "I am now able to 'write up' my *Journal* so sadly interrupted, for how could I have leisure of mind enough to make entries in my *Diary* when darling Baby was in danger?" (January 1841, 319; my emphasis).

13. Woolf 1:266.

14. Sloman, "Fragmentary Genres," 26.

15. Woolf 1:233–234.

16. Hampsten, discussing an American woman's diary that is forceful though mundane in events and laconic in expression, makes the valuable observation that the writer's "focus on the moment and on herself within it" renders her diary successful as art. Having no requirements of formal content to meet—no obligation to include exposition or background—free to record entirely at close range, the diarist projects her personality all the more intensely (*Read This*, 24–25).

17. Woolf 1:19; Thrale 1:448–449.

18. Grove 7; Miner, "Literary Diaries," 48.

19. C. Fox 2:105; Eleanor Butler 259; Northumberland 158; Sitwell 305; Hoby 195.

20. I follow the precedent set by diary scholar Ponsonby (*English Diaries* and *More English Diaries*) in including Wales.

21. One diary in the main study spans the sixteenth and seventeenth centuries, and three were written in the latter century. One spans the seventeenth and eighteenth centuries, and ten were written in the latter century. Eleven span the eighteenth and nineteenth centuries, and thirty-two were written in the latter century. Five span the nineteenth and twentieth centuries, and six were written in the latter century. Thus five diaries speak of the seventeenth century; twenty-two of the eighteenth; forty-eight of the nineteenth; and eleven of the twentieth (to which the Afterword adds nineteen more).

22. Extant servants' diaries from the past being almost nonexistent, it is worth pointing out the 1854–1873 *Diaries of Hannah Cullwick: Victorian Maidservant* (see under Cullwick). They are not part of this study because they were written for Arthur J. Munby, the admirer who became her husband.

23. Guest translated the *Mabinogion* from medieval Welsh (1838–1846) and was a collector, large portions of whose collections of china, fans, and playing cards are now in the Victoria and Albert Museum and the British Museum under her second marital surname, Schreiber.

24. Eisenstein and Jardine, *Future of Difference*, xix.

25. Bouchier, *Feminist Challenge*, 31, 35.

26. Thrale 1:375, and letter of 19 April 1813 to John Salusbury Piozzi, quoted in the introduction to her diary, 1:xvii; Webb 1:153.

27. Woolf, "John Evelyn," 689 (See List of Other Sources Cited).

28. Wordsworth, *Grasmere Journals*, 15–16.

29. Bond, "Reconsidering Dorothy Wordsworth," 203.

30. Fanny Burney, *Early Diary of Frances Burney*, ed. Ellis, 1:4 (27 March 1768), 1:18 (July 1768).

31. Fanny Burney, *Journals and Letters of Fanny Burney*, ed. Hemlow, 1:xxxii.

32. Fanny Burney, *Early Diary*, 1:253 (1773).

33. Fanny Burney, *Journals*, 1:xxxi–xxxii; Hemlow, *History of Fanny Burney*, 43.

34. Fanny Burney, *Journals*, 1:xxxiv, xxxvi, xxxvii, xli.

35. Weeton 1:174; C. Fox 2:236.

36. Ponsonby, *English Diaries*, 5.

CHAPTER 1

1. Woolf 1:266.

2. Fothergill, *Private Chronicles*, 35. He notes, by the start of the nine-

teenth century, "the growing consciousness in the mind of the diarist of diary-writing as literary composition, a process in which the writer has an eye on himself [or herself] writing, and in which increasingly he [she] invests a deliberate 'literariness'" (32).

3. Cowper 1; Powys 59; George 311; Cavendish 1:94–95. So too Virginia Woolf pens, "trying to tell whichever self it is that reads this thereafter that I can write very much better; & take no time over this; & forbid her to let the eye of man behold it" (20 April 1919, 1:266).

4. Fothergill, *Private Chronicles*, 35. In this paragraph the observations about women's performance are mine, but otherwise I have drawn on Fothergill's second chapter and on the list of early diarists in Matthews's *British Diaries*.

5. *My Daughter's Manual*, 256.

6. For the 1793 diary see Ann Woodforde 35; for the other diary see Grove v, vi. Grove is quoted from pages 86–87. Further descriptions of bound nineteenth-century diaries can be found in Huff's *British Women's Diaries*. During the course of the century the printed extras changed, most notably from entertainments like puzzles and songs to advertisements for purchasable goods (Huff xiv–xv).

7. Gray 230, 237; Powys 277.

8. Diarist Mary Frampton's *Journal* for 1779–1846 consists of annual summaries, except for 1800, 1830, and 1831, which have a few brief, single-day entries, so cursory as to suggest that she kept no daily memo books, but relied rather on memory or notes, another possible arrangement.

9. The same process is probably true for the "diary" of Abigail Gawthern (not a principal diarist), whose retrospective chronicle (1751–1810) was composed between 1808 and 1813 from entries in her pocket books, which were then presumably destroyed. The 1570–1617 "diary" of Mildmay has not been published in full, but extracts are included in Wiegall, "An Elizabethan Gentlewoman" (see under Mildmay).

10. Matthews, *British Diaries*, 1–7.

11. Ponsonby, *More English Diaries*, 8. He credits the soldier's diary of Thomas Coningsby with the same leap. Despite Ponsonby's claims, O'Brien's historical sketch in *English Diaries* ignores Hoby entirely and honors Sir William Dugdale as first English diarist. Fothergill notices Hoby only by way of remarking on her rudimentary style as a Puritan diarist (*Private Chronicles*, 19).

12. As an heiress-widow, Hoby needed to remarry, but married Thomas only reluctantly. She may have begun her diary some time before 1599. Because much of the page bearing the first entry is torn away and the manu-

script has been rebound, editor Meads cannot confirm that the first page is actually the start (62, 243 n. 175).

13. The early history of Thomas Hoby's manuscript appears in the introduction to his *Travels and Life of Sir Thomas Hoby*, v, vi. That Margaret was on friendly terms with her in-laws is indicated by her often visiting them during trips to London. See Margaret Hoby's diary for 19 and 26 October, 150, 151; 16 and 17 November, 153, 154; 11, 19, and 21 December 1600, 157, 159, 159. See also 18 and 24 January 1600; 21 November 1604; 162, 163, on Lady Russell. See 16 and 19 November, 18 December 1600; 153, 154, 158, on Edward Hoby, with whom Margaret stayed. For her interest in Foxe, see, e.g., 24 October 1599, 80, on her reading Foxe and 28 September, 1 and 4 October 1599, 74–75, on having others read Foxe to her.

14. T. Hoby, *Travels and Life*, 128, 130.

15. M. Hoby 71, 94, 184, 206.

16. How much Hoby's diary strayed from Puritan practice will be evident from Watkins's description of the self-examination for which sixteenth- and seventeenth-century Puritan diaries were intended. After the Reformation abolition of oral confession to a priest, it was replaced by confessional diaries wherein one "would write of his [or her] progress and setbacks in the lifelong struggle with the enemy. In such a book the practice of mortification could be systematized," and "by remembering mercies received day by day at the hand of God he [she] might prevent lapses into ingratitude and unfaithfulness" (*Puritan Experience*, 18).

17. M. Hoby 171.

18. Pomerleau, "Emergence of Women's Autobiography," 28. Worth remarking also is that the first full autobiography in English, composed ca. 1432, was by a woman: *The Book of Margery Kempe*.

19. Clifford 70.

20. Northumberland 95.

21. *Note-Books of a Spinster Lady* (listed under Anonymous in Select List of Women Diarists). Likewise, Frances Wynn's ten-volume "diaries" (1797–1844), not included in this study, are really only anecdotes, gossip, and extracts from other people's letters. See *Diaries of a Lady of Quality* under Wynn.

22. Jelinek, "Women's Autobiography," 10.

23. Ibid., 8.

24. Byrom 401–405.

25. Gawthern 2.

26. Hardy 78.

27. Howard 47, 50, 66, 86.

28. M. Shelley, from October 1826 review, quoted in the diary of Claire

Clairmont, 454. Brownell Jameson, *Diary of an Ennuyée*, 1. Brownell Jameson's fictionalized travel diary is prefaced by an unpaged testimonial to its veracity: "Published exactly as it was found after the death of the Author. . . . a real picture of natural and feminine feeling." It does partly derive from her own experiences, for a wealthy family that she served as governess had taken her along on its Italian tour, but unlike her fatally afflicted lovelorn persona, she survived to return to England, where she became active in the feminist movement of the 1850s.

29. Holland 1 : 53–54.

30. Burney (Wood) 337.

31. Trant 238; Brownell (Jameson), *Diary of an Ennuyée*, 45.

32. Trant 237.

33. A later, possibly fictional diary without acknowledgment is Roberts's 1910 *Pages from the Diary of a Militant Suffragette*. Because David Doughan of the research staff at the Fawcett Library of London (letter to me of 6 June 1985) believes that "whether it began as a genuine diary is open to doubt," I include it only in my List of Other Sources Cited.

34. Spurious diaries continue to deceive. A notable instance is the 1964 edition of *Diary of a Farmer's Wife*, ostensibly by Anne Hughes, which Schnorrenberg and Hunter propose as one of the few sources of authentic information about the lower-class woman in "Eighteenth-Century Englishwoman," 184. The diary is actually self-revealing as an imposture because Hughes speaks of her husband by his given name in violation of eighteenth-century practice. Nonetheless, the imposture went undetected until 1979, when Michael Croucher wrote the foreword included in the Penguin edition (1981) that identified the actual author as twentieth-century Jeanne Preston. Yet in 1982, Nikolai Tolstoy was still objecting to the widespread acceptance of the book as a genuine diary ("*Diary* as Forgery," 35–39).

35. Knightley xv.

36. Mansfield 3, 21; Gladstone 410; Asquith 249.

37. *My Daughter's Manual*, 257, 259. The author is anonymous, but, as her constant "we" and "our" indicate, also female.

38. Frampton extracts from the journals of an Anne Agnes Porter and a Lady Susan O'Brien in her entries for 30 October–7 November 1796, 9 and 11 February 1805; 86, 127.

39. Coke 1 : 166.

40. Duncannon 43 n. 1; Sitwell 177; Barrett (Browning) 202; Woolf 2 : 62, 2 : 234; Asquith 474.

41. Huff, *British Women's Diaries*, xviii.

42. Matthews, *British Diaries*, ix. I do not mean to imply that only

women read others' diaries, though I do believe they are more inclined to do so than men. Kagle has already taken Matthews to task on the issue of solitary diarists, though Kagle draws on American and European men of letters to assert: "Many diarists have shared their work, inspiring others not only to take up the habit of diary keeping but also to respect the intrinsic value of the genre" ("Diary as Art," 417).

43. Shore 261.

44. Metzger and Meyerhoff, "Dear Diary," 42.

45. Ibid., 48.

46. Bain 39; Twysden 121; Gray 82.

47. Hamilton 137; Burney (Wood) 65; Frampton 203.

48. Rosenblatt, *Bitter, Bitter Tears,* 169. Rosenblatt closely studied fifty-six diaries, forty-six of which were archival; two others he collated with the originals to detect any edited-out material. Thus his findings are based essentially on diaries not intended for publication. He found significant censoring of sexuality. Aside from gossip about others' sex lives, "no diarist wrote about sex" except one man who spoke of his premarital sexual adventures. One male physician mentioned birth control. No widowed diarists spoke of sex as a need (56, 136). Ponsonby, *English Diaries,* 29. Ponsonby asserts: "Reticence and reserve are national characteristics outwardly and probably inwardly too. . . . Most Englishmen think it bad form to be too expansive. . . . conceive it improper to write down their innermost feelings" (10). Matthews believes of diaries in general that "passages of extended reflection are not so common . . . as one might imagine; . . . usually only puritan diarists . . . indulge in extensive self-analysis" ("The Diary," 292).

49. Amberley 1:403, 2:47; Thrale 2:847, 2:801; Woolf 1:66, 3:254. On menstruation in Woolf, see also 25 January 1918, when Woolf writes, "Another event kept me recumbent," and 26 April 1918: "I was recumbent [yesterday]" (1:113, 1:144). Although Woolf's editor, Anne Bell, indexes 11 January 1918 as a menstrual day, on that day Woolf says only "Another sedentary day" (1:104).

50. More specifically, "some diarists occasionally used a code or wrote parts of some entries in a foreign language. (Many of these instances seem to have been records of menstrual periods)" (*Bitter, Bitter Tears,* 173). Of course the reason for keeping track of one's menses would be as a clue to pregnancy. Crawford has shown how the 1687–1688 manuscript diary of Sarah Savage, who desperately wanted to become pregnant, is also a record of her periods. Though they are not named as such, the references are very clear because they chart her disappointed expectations ("Attitudes to Pregnancy," 43–45).

51. Asquith 212; Clifford 62, 65, 65, 75.

52. Raper 15, 20; Thrale 1:583; Webb 1:17, 1:275, 1:357. On Webb's marriage, see also 23 March 1890, 1:332.

53. Brittain, entry for 4 March 1913, 30–31.

54. The first quote, from Mansfield 12–13, dated simply "Sunday Night" ([1 June] 1907), continues its theme as the entry for 1 June, 13–14, after several illegible lines. The second quote is from an undated entry that belongs between the entries for 29 June and 11 August 1907 and is quoted in Waldron's "Katherine Mansfield's *Journal*," 13. Alpers gives a slightly different version of the entry in *Life of Katherine Mansfield*, 49–50, dated as 29 June. Chiefly, he reads *unclear* as *unclean*, *cast* as *past*, and the illegible words as *Heigh Ho* plus numerous exclamation points. Possibly Murry's suppression of the Maata passage (after granting Mansfield her homoeroticism) was an attempt to diminish the impression of promiscuity.

55. Woolf 2:320.

56. Fox 1:xxx; Asquith xi, 485 (See her index entry for Asquith, John).

57. Waldron, "Katherine Mansfield's *Journal*," 12. For the 1954 edition of Mansfield's journal, Murry added much previously unpublished material to the version he had originally published in 1927, and he incorporated passages from her 1939 *Scrapbook*. But Waldron finds that besides suppressions, Murry also indulged in arbitrary dating and arrangement of passages, unwarranted changes in punctuation, and carelessness (11–18). Murry's editing is also censured in Gordon's edition of Mansfield's travel journal, *Urewara Notebook*, 13–19, to which Gordon restores material Murry suppressed.

58. Cowper's editor, C. S. Cowper, reports (xii–xiii) such motivation for her. The conjectures about Clairmont's motivation are also her editor's (Marion Kingston Stocking) 60 n. 24, based on entries in Mary Shelley's diary. Grove vi.

59. Bagot vii.

60. Wolf, "Diary," 75.

61. Barrett (Browning) xxxiii.

62. Barrett (Browning) 17, 118, 1. Berridge's abridged edition of Barrett Browning's diary explains her state as a schoolgirl's "crush" on a beloved teacher, with Boyd bridging "the perilous gap between father and lover" (*Barretts at Hope End*, 27, 26), but the evidence of the diary says otherwise. Schoolgirls accept and luxuriate in their crushes; Barrett Browning's response is otherwise.

63. Barrett (Browning) 79, 111–112, 180, 12, xxiii.

64. Schlüter 22, 56, 147; Eleanor Butler 259, 216, 226, 66, 55, 340.

65. M. Shelley 40, 84, 126, 208, 180, 122, 190.

66. M. Shelley 170, 203, 180, 182, 199.

67. However, her editor, Anne Olivier Bell, omits overlapping entries from the separate diary Woolf kept at Aseham when "neither in style nor content do they supplement the much fuller diary she was now keeping" in London and elsewhere (1:179 n. 5; see also 1:68). In volume 5, omissions have been made to protect reputations (other than Woolf's), as follows: "[Hugh] saw Ld C [*name omitted*] naked; saw Ld B [*name omitted*] in the act with a boy"; also "I forgot my shudder at Helen's son [*omission*]" (30 March and 28 July 1939; 211, 227).

68. Woolf 1:266, 1:79. According to Morrell, as quoted by Woolf's editor, Anne Bell, Woolf 'opened her eyes wide in astonishment" at Morrell's claim that her own diary 'was filled with thoughts and struggles of my inner life' (1:79 n. 28).

69. Woolf 1:315; 2:26, 2:234, 2:304; 3:241; 4:89; 2:235; 5:251.

70. Woolf 1:141; Hardy 14, 35; Northumberland 148; Thrale 2:868 side note 3. On Sapphism, see also Thrale, 1 April 1789, 2:740, 17 June 1790, 2:770, and 9 December 1795, 2:949.

71. Thrale 1:459 n. 1. Mansfield is the only other diarist to speak of her bodily functions. Ill with tuberculosis, she reports "a queer bit of psychology: I had to disappear behind the bushes to-day in a hollow. That act made me feel nearer to normal health than I have felt for years. Nobody was there; nobody wondered if I was all right, *i.e.* there was nothing to distinguish me, at that moment, from an ordinary human being" (June 1922, 320).

72. Thrale 1:xv.

73. Pinkney (*Tacita Tacit*, 2:276) is quoted in Brightfield, *Victorian England*, 4:276; Miller, *Toward a New Psychology*, 39.

74. S. Ardener, *Defining Females*, 21; Spender, *Man Made Language*, chapter 3; Kristeva, "Women's Time," 24–25; Cixous, "Laugh of the Medusa," 87.

75. Powys 75.

76. Hamilton 203; Elizabeth Wynne 2:161; Gladstone 376; Monkswell 1:1; Woolf 4:18.

77. Trant 306.

78. Schlüter 60; Monkswell 1:147 (see also Woolf 15 March 1919, 1:253).

79. Gray 72; Hardy 61; Carlyle [1] 2:29, 30. Carlyle left two notebooks, labeled [1] and [2], together covering 1855–1856. The Froude edition of her diary takes almost all its extracts from [1]; therefore, I always designate it [1]. The Carlyle edition, which draws entirely on [2], I designate as [2].

80. Mansfield 255; Waldron, "Katherine Mansfield's *Journal*," 12; Mansfield 294; Thrale 1:464. Concerning Thrale's intermittent contrary desire for posthumous reading, because of the mixed nature of *Thraliana*, see the comments of her editor, Balderston (Thrale 1:xvi).
81. Huff, *British Women's Diaries*, xvii; Asquith 43, 81, xi.
82. Shore 189.
83. Mendelson, "Stuart Women's Diaries," 183–185.
84. Elizabeth Wynne 1:242.
85. Asquith 3; Woolf 5:107; Guest 2:28. For Guest, volume 1 always refers to Guest's 1833–1852 diary, and 2 to her 1853–1891 diary, which declares itself a "continuation." The latter diary bears the diarist's second marital surname, Schreiber, but for consistency and because her name is still Guest for part of that volume, I continue to refer to it always as Guest's diary.
86. F. Shelley 1:314; Clifford 42. For Clifford's comments on needlework, see 15 June, 28 August, 4 and 9 November 1616, 34, 40, 41; also 11, 14 and 22 March 1617, 57, 58, 60. On gambling, see 15 February, 20 November, 28 December 1616, 18, 42, 45; also 5 and 19 March, 12 and 13 August 1617, 57, 59, 76; also 2 November, 30 and 31 December 1619, 109–110, 112. Meads, M. Hoby's editor, reports Clifford's claim in her manuscript autobiography that, during two unhappy marriages, "I gave myself wholly to retiredness as much as I could . . . and made good books and virtuous thoughts my companions" (Hoby 59).
87. Shore 262–263, 263.
88. Woolf 2:317; Shore 263; Fox 1:234; Webb 1:63.
89. Barrett (Browning) 1; Woolf 2:72.
90. Rosenblatt, *Bitter, Bitter Tears*, 169.

CHAPTER 2

1. Elizabeth Wynne 1, 3.
2. Huff, *British Women's Diaries*, xxv.
3. Powys x; Asquith 3.
4. A. de Rothschild 88, 96–97.
5. Fothergill, *Private Chronicles*, 66, 72.
6. Dobbs, *Dear Diary*, 8.
7. Fox 2:297; Potter 319.
8. Powys 2:52; Hamilton 135; Holland 1:148; Eleanor Butler 251; F. Shelley 2:224–225; Woolf 5:65.

9. Powys 212; Amberley 2:269; N. Woodforde 51; Eleanor Butler 173, 78; Astry 164, 160; Clairmont (as reported by her editors) 8.

10. Brownmiller comments, "Women are instructed from childhood to be keepers of the heart, keepers of the sentimental memory. In diaries, packets of old love letters and family albums, . . . a woman's emotional history is preserved. . . . Men are busy; they move forward. A woman looks back" (*Femininity*, 215–216). This stereotype accounts poorly for the heterogeneous contents of women's diaries.

11. Freke 110, 111, 127–128, 128–129, 65.

12. Barrett (Browning) 164; Asquith 310; Woolf 1:255; Stevenson 137.

13. Hamilton 187; Gladstone 151; Cavendish 2:166; Monkswell 2:114.

14. Cowper 1, 84–85; George 311.

15. Schlüter 177.

16. Rosenblatt, *Bitter, Bitter Tears*, 14. Compare Ponsonby: "Is egotism the mainspring of diary writing? The answer to this is yes" (*English Diaries*, 6).

17. Webb 1:20; Woolf 4:167; Thrale 1:468.

18. Miller, *Toward a New Psychology*, 60–61, 63. Miller's emphasis on relationships is shared by Gilligan, whose theory of female moral development posits an "ethic of responsibility as the center of women's moral concern, anchoring the self in a world of relationships" (*In a Different Voice*, 132). Insofar as Miller envisions the world's redemption in the spread of female behaviors, her psychology draws on the nineteenth-century ideology of the family. But as it foregrounds the enforced self-abnegation of women, it accounts for the consequences of an ideology of female subordination as old as the Bible and Aristotle in Western culture, to cite only two influential texts.

Winston notes a comparable pattern in female autobiography. Uneasy about nontraditional lives and desirous of projecting womanliness, professional writers who published autobiographies before 1920, she finds, deprecate themselves and claim that they write their life stories only to satisfy others: to entertain readers, publicly defend past actions, or leave a record for their children. Only as they become more confident about the legitimacy of their lives do some women use their autobiographies for explicitly personal and self-validating reasons ("Autobiographer," 93–111).

19. Berry 3:445; L. de Rothschild 26; Shore 260; Weeton 2:362.

20. F. Shelley 2:3; Webb 1:25; Woolf 1:234, 3:58, 5:162, 3:125, 4:193.

21. Shore 139; Potter 60; Trant 118–119; Elizabeth Wynne 2:65; Webb 3:327, 3:356; Guest 2:196.

22. M. Shelley 189; Woolf 5:205. See also, e.g., Thrale, 24 November 1779, 1:410; A. Woodforde, 13 November 1819, 238; Russell [n.d.] 31; and Woolf additionally on 19 December 1920, 2:80.

23. Waite, ed., *English Diaries*, 17. Lifshin reports how the women who furnished entries for her contemporary anthology "talked of the difficulty in going back and rereading diaries" and even "found the experience . . . at times overwhelming" (*Ariadne's Thread*, 11).

24. Nonetheless, interestingly Byron proclaims of his diary, "But I can't read it over; and God knows what contradictions it may contain" (diary entry for 6 December 1813, *Letters and Journals*, 3:233). Also Pepys gives no evidence of having reread more than recent entries, to revise them. According to editor Matthews, Pepys "may occasionally have read [his diary] for pleasure" but "he never records having done so during the diary period" (*Diary of Samuel Pepys*, 1:68).

25. Woolf 3:230.

26. Woolf 5:227; Webb 1:120; Mansfield 205.

27. Hoby 70, 216.

28. Cavendish 1:45; C. de Rothschild 78; Webb 1:270; Eastlake 1:34; Barrett (Browning) 1; Berry 2:318.

29. Berry also labored without due recognition. Although, according to her own editor, Theresa Lewis, it was Berry who edited for publication the various manuscripts Horace Walpole, Lord Orford, had left jointly to her father and his two daughters, her father took credit for the five-volume work, praising her only as his assistant in the preface he wrote (xix).

30. Berry 2:319; Mansfield 271, 63, 327.

31. Weeton 2:158–159; Thrale 1:1.

32. Thrale 2:799. For the history of Thrale's massive diary, see the introduction to *Thraliana*, 1:x ff. Concerning cessation of her children's diary, see *Thrales of Streatham*, 217–219 (both under Thrale).

33. Mansfield 255.

34. Woolf, "Terribly Sensitive Mind," 73.

35. Mansfield 85–86, 94, 96, 97.

36. Curator Lola Szladits of the Berg Collection, New York Public Library, which holds the manuscripts, in a letter to me (30 March 1987) reports plans to publish the early diaries, with Mitchell Leaska as editor.

37. Siganto, "Emergence of Literary Form," 70.

38. Woolf 1:55, 5:162, 2:208, 2:319. See also 20 April 1919, 1:266.

39. Woolf 3:239, 5:251, 2:276, 2:120, 2:106, 5:8. See also 21 April 1937, 5:80, 28 July 1939, 5:227.

40. Eliot 3:121, 3:324; Webb 1:220; Carlyle [1] 2:35.

41. Rose in *Parallel Lives* suggests that Jane's diary constitutes her deliberate and "spectacularly successful" revenge on her husband for marital wounds (250). Thomas was impervious to the nonverbal tactics women usually use to create spousal guilt; therefore, Jane cleverly used written statement, and he "swallowed the story hook, line, and sinker" (254). The tenor of Rose's remarks is less flattering to Jane than it might be, for Jane's marital distress is not her fabrication and the impulse to confide it to her diary is a legitimate one. Since Jane, moreover, as Rose herself points out, died "suddenly" of a stroke or heart attack (255), she may have intended to destroy her incriminating diary without having opportunity to do so. She did at some time destroy her other diaries, according to editor Froude (Carlyle [1] 1:172 n. 1). However, embittered wives may use their diaries as weapons. Lady Louisa Hardy (not included in this study) twice transcribed her 1807–1847 diary for her children, taking care always to retain vengeful attacks on her husband for being wed to his naval career.

42. Webb xvii, 1:28, 1:16, 1:63, 1:19.

43. Freke 101–102.

44. Trant 215; Guest 1:14; Schlüter 23, 31, 64, 83; Webb 1:17; Mansfield 270; Berry 3:445.

45. M. Shelley 180–181, 196.

46. Guest 1:14.

47. Dobbs, *Dear Diary*, 8, 229. As Dobbs perhaps has in mind, Marie Bashkirtseff's declared motive for her diary is to write (and publish) it lest death obliterate her name (*Journal of a Young Artist*, ix, xiv).

48. Clairmont 305; Woolf 1:304 (see also 22 January 1922, 2:158); Shore 280, 350.

49. From *Beatrice Webb's Diaries*, ed. Cole, 1:16. The Cole edition, which includes some passages not incorporated into the larger edition, ed. Mackenzie and Mackenzie, will be designated (Cole) henceforth and is included in the Select List of Women's Diaries under Webb.

50. Willy, *Three Women Diarists*, 7.

51. Fox 1:126, 1:105, 1:127, 2:22; Webb 1:273–274.

52. Fothergill, *Private Chronicles*, 87–88, 87.

53. I am adapting the latter idea from Eakin's statement in *Fictions of Autobiography*: "It is nonetheless the case (as Derrida himself suggests when he posits the system of *s'entendre parler* as the basis of self-presence) that, psychologically speaking, reflexive consciousness—the self's sense of itself as a self—is liveliest and most immediate in the moment of speech" (225).

54. Miller, "Women's Autobiography," 266; Stanton, "Autogynography," 15.

55. Beauvoir, *Second Sex*, xix.

56. Juhasz, "Some Deep Old Desk," 664; Moffatt, *Revelations*, 5; Jelinek, "Women's Autobiography," 19; Juhasz, "Towards a Theory," 223–224. More recently, Lensink also assumes that the diary is "a female text" ("Expanding the Boundaries," 40). But Culley strongly objects to this "type of life/art fallacy for which feminist critics must invent a pithy name in order to stop its easy use" (*Day at a Time*, 3).

57. Shumaker claims memory as autobiographers' "chief source" of subject matter, not documents; "It is not even certain that autobiographies characteristically rely heavily on materials drawn from diaries" (*English Autobiography*, 36, 103). Yet the autobiographer-diarists not only draw on their diaries, but sometimes write their diaries with autobiographies in mind. Asquith, for example, who quotes her diary in her autobiography, in her diary fears she may "strain after sensation to make copy for my autobiography" (15 April 1915, 3). Webb, who rereads her diary to compose her autobiography, has long since decided "These books are more or less an autobiography" (28 November 1880, 1:39). So too Belloc Lowndes claims her diary "has been a great help" in composing her autobiography (letter of 6 May 1945 to Susan L. Marques, bound with the diary, 256). See also my note 67 concerning Clifford's use of her diaries.

58. C. de Rothschild 333.

59. Spender, *Man Made Language*, 192; Weeton 1:173.

60. Cott, who studied the personal writing (diaries, memoirs, letters) of one hundred New England women, 1780–1835, also remarks the discrepancy between contemporary assumptions and past realities. The women of her study, unlike modern feminists, rarely perceived an antithesis between their domestic obligations and their general progress in life (*Bonds of Womanhood*, 197, 199).

61. Hoby 109.

62. Shore 356.

63. Juhasz, "Some Deep Old Desk," 668. She takes her metaphor from Woolf, 20 April 1919, 1:266.

64. Westwater, "Surrender to Subservience," 520, 527, 523, 524, 525.

65. Pomerleau, "Emergence of Women's Autobiography," 22.

66. Women's use of such strategies in imaginative literature has become a critical commonplace. Showalter, for example, discusses it in *Literature of Their Own*, and asserts in "Feminist Criticism" that women's fiction is a "double-voiced discourse . . . we must keep two alternative oscillating texts simultaneously in view" (34). Likewise, for Gilbert and Gubar in *Mad-*

woman in the Attic, women's writing is "palimpsestic": the "surface designs conceal or obscure deeper, less accessible (and less socially acceptable) levels of meaning" (73). So too Nancy Miller's "Emphasis Added" identifies a variably muted protest against limited gender roles, "an emphasis . . . always there to be read . . . it points to another text" (47).

67. Reported by diarist Hoby's editor, Meads, 61. Besides personal daily diaries, Clifford also inaugurated a Great Diary of family records and, later, of estate affairs, compiled by secretaries and annotated by herself. Begun with her mother's help, to use in the fight for Clifford's inheritance, it also contains an autobiography, much of whose information has apparently been summarized from a day-by-day book no longer extant. The Great Diary and Anne's probable daily diaries are described in Williamson's *Lady Anne Clifford*, 357–367 (see under Clifford).

68. Weeton xiii; Shore 138.

69. Metzger and Meyerhoff, "Dear Diary," 46.

CHAPTER 3

1. Freke 52. On Astell, see Smith, *Reason's Disciples*, 117–139.

2. Wollstonecraft, *A Vindication*, 9.

3. Mansfield 36–37.

4. Bouchier, *Feminist Challenge*, 13.

5. West, *Letters*, 3:219–220, Letter 13.

6. Branca, *Silent Sisterhood*, 10–11.

7. Freke 54. On seventeenth-century conditions, see Smith, *Reason's Disciples*, 28–29, and Thompson, *Women in Stuart England*, 162–163. Thompson (182 n. 20) also notes the oddity of Clifford's circumstances.

8. Rendall, *Origins of Modern Feminism*, 7–32. Rendall questions the common assumption that Enlightenment thinkers fostered concern about women's natural rights. Their preoccupation with psychology and epistemology, she points out, led rather to detailed exploration of the assumed differences between the sexes, and their concern with social institutions to justification of women's position within the family.

9. See Hall, "Early Formation," 15–32, for the Evangelical influence; Banks, *Faces of Feminism*, 86.

10. Houlbrooke, *English Family*, 119; Rowbotham, *Hidden from History*, 20.

11. Cott, *Bonds of Womanhood*, 200.

12. See Banks, *Faces of Feminism*.

13. Freke 21; Holland 2:137, 1:157.
14. Holland 1:53.
15. Thompson, *Women in Stuart England,* 170. Earlier in the seventeenth century, only annulment and separation, granted by ecclesiastical courts, were possible, without right of remarriage, though Puritans also practiced private divorce and separation (Thompson, 169–172). Significant improvements in divorce laws came only in the latter half of the nineteenth century, beginning with the Divorce and Matrimonial Cause Act of 1857, which at least made divorce more accessible to women by allowing them to bring suit and by creating a new, less-expensive procedure through a divorce court. But the injustice that the 1857 act allowed a wife to divorce only for adultery plus additional cause (desertion, cruelty, incest, and so on) whereas a husband could divorce for adultery alone was not rectified until 1923. See Stetson, *Woman's Issue,* for divorce legislation.
16. Brophy and Smart, "Position of Women," 209. The act gave morally fit mothers custody of children under seven, with right of access to older children.
17. Thrale 2:692.
18. Monkswell 1:14.
19. Monkswell 2:82; Trant 264.
20. Schnorrenberg and Hunter, "Eighteenth-Century Englishwoman," 198. Rogers also finds "some evidence of feminist feeling in practically all the . . . women writers of the period, even the most timid and conventional": namely, "a particular sensitivity" to women's situation and needs. But that this is very minimal feminism Rogers acknowledges in discussing writers like Austen, Edgeworth, and More, who "were far from feminists in the modern image. Some of them explicitly defended the patriarchal status quo, allowing feminist protests to slip out only in unguarded moments" (*Feminism in Eighteenth-Century England,* 4, 231).
21. Powys 65; Berry 3:332, and see also memorandum of 7 May 1797, 2:22.
22. Gray 76.
23. Thrale 1:369; Berry 2:268, 2:375.
24. West, *Letters,* 3:98, Letter 12; Guest 1:55.
25. Stone, *Family, Sex and Marriage,* 329–330. I do not say that Stone should also have looked at female letters, because he does—and ignores them. Thus, for example, of a couple named Banks he says, "The pursuit of personal happiness through domestic intimacy was clearly uppermost in the mind of her husband, despite the continued use of [on] his wife's part of the old formal mode of address" (330). Stone claims that formality was revived

by the 1830s, when "wives were once more addressing their husbands in public and apparently in private" as "Mr." (668): a pattern directly contrary to the diaries. Judith Lewis has sensibly suggested that formal usage after 1830 does not show resurgence of an old custom but rather delay in catching up with a new one; change occurred far more slowly than Stone assumes (*In the Family Way*, 11).

26. Asquith 5.

27. Holland 1:93; Webb 1:223; Stevenson 165.

28. Powys 82; Hamilton 212; Berry 3:22; Jeune 14; Gladstone 120 side note; Monkswell 2:131.

29. Belloc Lowndes 89; Asquith 231; Monkswell 2:131.

30. Rich, "Compulsory Heterosexuality," 646. She quotes from Kathleen Barry's *Female Sexual Slavery* (1979).

31. Hamilton 167–168; Guest 2:50, 2:13; Webb 1:38; Thrale 2:978.

32. F. Shelley 2:10.

33. West, *Letters*, 3:120, Letter 12.

34. Fox 2:142, 143.

35. M. Shelley 205; Opie 306; Webb 1:355; Asquith 129; Monkswell 1:58.

36. Jane Lewis, *Women in England*, 83, 87–88.

37. Webb 1:63, 3:318.

38. Gray 201; Bagot 241; Fox 2:142; Cavendish 2:201; Bain 65; Hamilton 178.

39. More academically oriented day schools for secondary education were founded during the last quarter of the century (see Gorham, *Victorian Girl*, 20–27, on reforms in secondary education). Moreover, Girton (1873) and Newnham (1880) colleges at Cambridge, and Lady Margaret Hall (1879), Somerville (1879), and St. Hugh's (1887) at Oxford were founded. The much older Queens (1848) and Bedford (1849), reports Banks, actually offered secondary rather than university education (*Faces of Feminism*, 40).

40. Hamilton 217; Jeune 127; Frampton 395; Gladstone 64.

41. Guest 1:253; Eastlake 1:39; Eliot 2:14.

42. Webb 1:157; Potter 313; L. de Rothschild 70; Cavendish 2:290; Cowper 14; Trant 267.

43. Elizabeth Wynne 3:247; Trant 174; Eastlake 1:164; Jeune 81; Asquith 206; Woolf 1:188.

44. Lower middle-class diarists Nancy Woodforde (late eighteenth century) and Elizabeth George (mid-nineteenth century) do not complain of their single states, possibly because each was fortunate enough to have a good niche, George as her uncle's and Woodforde as her father's house-

keeper. But very little of their diaries is extant. Neither may lament spinsterhood simply because she has already accepted it as irrevocable. George, as earlier noted, speaks resignedly of not having descendants.

45. Berry 2:320; Gladstone 166, 237, 277; Eastlake 1:173.

46. Jeffreys, *Spinster and her Enemies,* 86. Jeffreys observes that in the late Victorian period almost one in three of all adult women was single and one in four would never marry. The proportion of women relative to men in the population increased from 1,036 women to 1,000 men in 1821 to 1,068 in 1901 (88).

47. Webb 1:261.

48. Freeman and Klaus, "Blessed or Not?" 394–414; and Jeffreys: "Numbers of spinsters, at least until after the First World War, made a positive choice not to marry," either "because they regarded marriage as a form of humiliating slavery and dependence upon men, or because they wanted to pursue a career and fulfill their potential." On statistical evidence, she designates 1911 the year when marriage was least popular between 1801 and 1931 (*Spinster*, 88, 89).

49. Webb 1:169, 1:226.

50. Eastlake 219.

51. Elizabeth Wynne 3:312; Cavendish 2:272, 2:31; Woolf 1:225.

52. Beauvoir, *Second Sex,* 589–590.

53. Spacks, *Adolescent Idea,* 22–23.

54. Clairmont 37; Fox 1:313; Jeune 57, 98–99; Sitwell 217, 232; H. Wynne 3:191; Woolf 1:136.

55. Powys 356; Berry 2:431; Grove 84; Bain 80; Shore 149; Northumberland 310.

56. F. Shelley 1:33, 2:41; Eastlake 1:188; Webb 1:261; Asquith 71; Northumberland 174; Asquith 233.

57. Cavendish 1:87; Northumberland 112; Lytton 89; Monkswell 2:131; Trant 303; Monkswell 2:175.

58. Asquith 53; Cavendish 1:74; Shore 144; Monkswell 1:159.

59. Jeune 21; Beauvoir, *Second Sex,* 593.

60. Frampton 34; Shore 38; Potter 141, 324; Thrale 1:393; Powys 357.

61. Monkswell 2:12; Davidoff, *Best Circles,* 93.

62. Clifford 71; Powys 152; Hamilton 185; Thrale 2:868; Eleanor Butler 118; Powys 243.

63. Beauvoir, *Second Sex,* 589.

64. N. Woodforde 52, 62, 62, 67. See also 29 June, 63.

65. Northumberland 158; Beauvoir, *Second Sex,* 600; Woolf 3:183, 3:81, 1:226.

66. Carlyle [2] 2:95; Clifford 42; N. Woodforde 79; Lumb 28.

67. Potter 425; Monkswell 1:69.
68. Banks, *Faces of Feminism,* 247.
69. Pomerleau, "Emergence of Women's Autobiography," 36; M. Shelley 204.
70. Eastlake 175.
71. Rendall, *Origins of Modern Feminism,* 276. My summary history of the women's movement follows Rendall 311, 313, 315, 319, and Kamm, *Rapiers and Battleaxes,* 144–145, except as otherwise noted.
72. The Married Women's Property acts of the 1870s and 1880s gave a wife control over her property for her own use and entitled her to her wages, but she did not gain the same capacity as an unmarried woman to acquire, hold, and dispose of property until 1935 (Jane Lewis, *Women in England,* 78). See Stetson, *Woman's Issue,* for detailed discussion.
73. Webb, 1:303.
74. Monkswell 1:163. Phillipa Fawcett's achievement is reported in Kamm, *Rapiers,* 133.
75. Cavendish 2:22; Monkswell 2:208.
76. Webb 1:288, 1 (Cole): 122; Woolf 1:104, 1:125, and see also 24 October 1918, 1:207.
77. Webb 3:325, 1 (Cole): 148 n. 3; Woolf 2:167; Gladstone 308, 316; Stevenson 8, 190.
78. Amberley 1:63, 1:464.
79. Amberley 2:291, 2:391, and see also 25 May 1870, 2:330, 2:298–300.
80. Monkswell 2:208.
81. Northumberland 159–160; Trant 127.
82. Carlyle [2] 2:102; Asquith 452; F. Shelley 2:3; Holland 1:119.
83. Hamilton 217; Woolf 4:201.
84. The Select List of Women Diarists includes three anonymous diarists. The reference here is to the 1919 *Notebooks of a Spinster Lady,* 166, 264.
85. Jeune 11; Carlyle [1] 2:32; Monkswell 2:11; Holland 1:132.
86. Weeton 2:386; F. Shelley 2:312; West, *Letters,* 3:221–222; Letter 13.
87. Monkswell 1:67; Webb 1:14; Woolf 4:75.
88. Mansfield, 37; Webb 1:346; Clairmont 407, 408.
89. Thrale 1:421; M. Shelley 207; Weeton 2:377, 2:386–387.
90. Huff remarks of nineteenth-century British manuscript diaries of girls that a frequent topic is "the desire to be male. . . . Some fantasized about being missionaries in India to convert unbelievers, but many . . . wished to become soldiers, and virtually all desired the escape from confinement which they felt males enjoyed" (*British Women's Diaries,* xxvi–xxvii). I find express

desire to be male only in a very few eighteenth-century diaries, but the discrepancy is understandable because her sources include a much greater number of youthful diaries; they also include devotional and colonial diaries.

91. Shore 324; Cavendish 1:98, 1:128; Sitwell 263; Cavendish 1:279; Sitwell 269–270.

92. Fitzgerald 43; Berry 2:454, and see, e.g., 21 September 1807, 2:330; Shore 181; Barrett (Browning) 197; C. de Rothschild 114; Webb 1:77.

93. Thrale 1:465, 1:590–591.

94. Holland 1:159; Amberley 2:268, 2:275; Woolf 3:200; Gladstone 193, 239. The degree circumstances under which Brittain attended Oxford were frustrating, for the university did not award women the B.A. before 1920, though by 1914 they were allowed to write the examinations and have the results published officially (Brittain, 352 n. 63).

95. Gladstone 239; Brittain 287. Berry, in a letter to Cholmeley on March 1805 (bound with her diary) complains, "My time is now frittered away by myself, because I have no sufficiently strong motive to oppose any intrusion on my attention by others, because everyone seems to think that *they* have an equal right to what I don't appear to make any decided use of myself" (2:296–297). Extracts from her manuscripts, also bound with her diary, inveigh against the typically shallow female education of her day.

96. Clifford 48, 27.

97. Raper 30; Trant 111, 233. Trant's 1823 entry appears in a portion of her diary that Trant rewrote for her daughter.

98. Webb 1:111–112; Potter 150. Webb apparently married Sidney with the understanding that their marriage would be sexless, because "personal passion has burnt itself out" (1 December 1890, 1:345). "If I marry," she declares, ". . . it will be an act of renunciation of self and not of indulgence of self as it would have been in the other case" (22 May 1891, 1:355–356).

CHAPTER 4

1. Trant 308; Guest 1:22 (and see also 29 July 1833, 1:14); C. de Rothschild 82; Jeune 119; Monkswell 1:174.

2. My observations on the changing bases for marriage reflect Thompson, *Women in Stuart England*, 115–117; Stone, *Family, Sex and Marriage*, 543–544; and Judith Lewis, *In the Family Way*, chapter 1.

3. Stetson, *Woman's Issue*, 3. Such, she explains, is the spirit underlying English common law.

4. Jane Lewis, *Women in England*, 3. Lewis reports that between 1871

and 1951 the proportion of married (or formerly married) female adults never fell below 60 percent and that the popularity of marriage increased between the late nineteenth century and the interwar period (3–4)—for all that the "New Woman" spinster was a late Victorian-Edwardian phenomenon. In the decade immediately after the Great War of course expectations of marriage were sharply curtailed.

5. Thompson, *Women in Stuart England*, 115.

6. Eugenia Wynne 3:153; Trant 276; Jeune 64; Sitwell 277; F. Shelley 2:230.

7. Trant 307; Gladstone 376; Cavendish 1:212, 1:258; Monkswell 1:14, 1:40. See also Amberley 8 March 1867, 2:20.

8. Eugenia Wynne 2:206, 3:76; C. de Rothschild 165; Gladstone 226; Trant 276, 126.

9. Holland 1:278, 1:276, 1:273; Asquith 118, 310, 373.

10. H. Wynne 3:271; Fitzgerald 44; A. Woodforde 238.

11. Raper 23, 30; Trant 306; Webb 1:266, 1:267.

12. Gray 26; Amberley 1:411; Cavendish 1:248, 1:192–193, 1:195, 1:210.

13. Elizabeth Wynne 2:103, 2:106; Eugenia Wynne 3:263.

14. Elizabeth Wynne 2:162; Thrale 2:1060; Russell 59; Webb 1:371; Cavendish 1:219; Elizabeth Wynne 2:161; Eugenia Wynne 3:291; Burney (Wood) 61.

15. Powys 93–94; Gray 29; Elizabeth Wynne 2:162; Trant 310; Cavendish 1:221; Eugenia Wynne 3:291; Burney (Wood) 60; Guest 1:15.

16. For remarriage entries, see Eliot, 6 May 1880, 3:393; Holland, July 1797, 1:147; and Guest, 10 April 1855, 2:45. On the changing status and form of the wedding-day ritual, see Judith Lewis, *In the Family Way*, 32–33.

17. Monkswell 1:2–3; Gladstone 381.

18. Burney (Wood) 63; Trant 310–311; Russell 62, 201; Cavendish 1:228; Amberley 1:347, 2:388, and see also 29 September 1867, 2:53, and 8 November 1871, 2:419.

19. Hamilton 287; Powys 353; Guest 2:48; Eliot 2:75, 2:394; Stevenson 23; Webb 1:224, 2 (Cole): 272.

20. Woolf 1:318, 5:115, 3:30, 1:70. On Woolf's good marriage, see also 8 April 1925, 3:8–9, 28 May 1931, 4:27, 10 November 1932, 4:130.

21. Mendelson, "Stuart Women's Diaries," 193. There is some overlap with this book. Her study includes diarists Clifford, Freke, Hoby, Twysden, and M. Woodforde.

22. Holland 1:43; Monkswell 1:144, 1:46; Stevenson 96; Amberley 1:359; Guest 1:42.

23. Trant 304; F. Shelley 2:319; Burney (Wood) 63.

24. Webb 1:95; Miller, *Toward a New Psychology,* 60–61.
25. Woolf 2:290; Webb 1:359, 1:328.
26. Holland 1:40; Jeune 4.
27. Jeune 4, 49.
28. Jeune 2, 41, 22, 9, 5.
29. Jeune 53.
30. Stevenson 140, 147, 160.
31. Stevenson 189, 67, 161, 149, 186.
32. Woolf 2:241, 1:190; Monkswell 2:159.
33. Cowper 75; Thrale 1:436; Holland 1:257.
34. Guest 2:181; L. de Rothschild 167; Gladstone 465, 466; Cavendish 2:318.
35. M. Shelley 181, 195; Stevenson 153; Carrington 491. Woolf too "should not wish to live if L[eonard] died" (12 November 1938, 5:190). She and Leonard argue "which would mind the other's death most," Virginia "happy to think I was so much needed" (28 April 1939, 5:216). In 1940 they were to plan a joint suicide in the event of a German invasion.
36. Thrale 2:1010, 1:487 n. 2, 2:1099. For Thrale's resentment, see, e.g., 21[?] January, 1:424, and 21 March 1780, 1:432.
37. Northumberland 177; F. Shelley 2:310, 1:39. For Asquith's marital relationship, see, e.g., 12 August, 203, and 24 September 1916, 219, and 28 August 1918, 468.
38. Trant 272; Eugenia Wynne 3:251; Amberley 1:477.
39. Hoby 133, 267 n. 357.
40. Clifford 106, 110, 67, 103 side note. Williamson's *Lady Anne Clifford* (126, 132, 141; see under Clifford) first alerted me to Dorset's affair, so well hidden by Anne's discreet reporting that I had overlooked it. Anne's second marriage in 1628 to Philip Herbert, earl of Pembroke, a man "with hardly a grace to recommend him," as Williamson puts it, was no joy to her either; indeed, contemporary scandal linked him to an affair with his niece. He and Anne separated before five years of marriage (160, 175, 177). Her extant diary does not cover her second marriage. Hoby 36, 38, 45.
41. Guest 2:105.
42. Weeton 2:159.
43. Carlyle [2] 2:101, [1] 2:29, 31; Clairmont 409, 410.
44. Stone, *Family, Sex and Marriage,* 416.
45. Brookes reports that an average family size of six children in the 1860s declined to 2.19 children born to those married from 1925 to 1929 ("Women and Reproduction," 152). See also my note 64.
46. Amberley 1:412; Monkswell 2:189.

47. As Branca points out, only in the 1880s did women learn to watch for bluish discoloration of the vaginal passage; before then, they had to wait almost five months to be certain of pregnancy (*Silent Sisterhood*, 83, 82).

48. Clifford 107 side note; Amberley 2:65; Burney (Wood) 100.

49. Elizabeth Wynne 3:75; Thrale 1:308.

50. Judith Lewis, *In the Family Way*, 216; Rosenblatt, *Bitter, Bitter Tears*, 63.

51. H. Wynne 3:201; Elizabeth Wynne 3:312; Guest 1:31; Amberley 1:400; Gray 49; Burney (Wood) 101.

52. Hoby 63; M. Hardy 36; Asquith 67; Powys 113; Eleanor Butler 179.

53. Thrale 2:974–975. For eighteenth-century obstetric practices, see Rich, *Of Woman Born*, chapter 7.

54. Rich, *Of Woman Born*, 143; Branca, *Silent Sisterhood*, 64, 82; Brookes, "Woman and Reproduction," 153. Brookes reports that maternal mortality came second to tuberculosis as a major cause of death for married women, 1911–1930; moreover, between 1923 and 1936 the maternal death rate even rose.

55. Thrale 1:322; Amberley 1:401. It was during this period of first childbirth that Kate's husband kept up her diary for her, reporting that Kate suffered pressure from her inability to nurse, which he attempted to relieve by sucking her breasts, "but I could not get much. . . . It is no wonder the infant found it too hard for him" (14 August 1865, 1:403).

56. Schlissel, *Women's Diaries*, 111. See also 57, 108, 120, 129, 199–201.

57. M. Shelley 208; F. Shelley 2:2; Guest 1:197.

58. Freke 27; Thrale 1:401, 1:401 n. 2, 1:400. Thrale dates the stillbirth, in a note added later, as occurring on 3 August (1:400 n. 1), but dates her description of the coach trip as 10 August (1:401 n. 1) even though the trip necessarily preceded the birth.

59. Freke 24.

60. Judith Lewis, *In the Family Way*, 77; Branca, *Silent Sisterhood*, 84–86. Printed with Russell's diary (99–100) is a letter from Simpson in Edinburgh, March 1848, offering to deliver her next child and presenting as inducement that "with almost all my medical brethren here I use chloroform in all cases. None of us, I believe, could now feel justified in *not* relieving pain, when God has bestowed upon us the means of relieving it."

61. Asquith 195. Feminist Cicely Hamilton's *Marriage as a Trade*, with just such a message, was published in 1909. See Bland, "Marriage Laid Bare," 135–141, for Edwardian feminist attitudes to sexuality.

62. Russell 100, 65; Thrale 1:446; Monkswell 2:20.

63. Hoby 206; Cavendish 1:299, 2:76.

64. Brookes reports that childless marriages doubled from slightly over 8 percent in the 1870s to 16 percent after 1919 ("Woman and Reproduction," 152).

65. Woolf 3:107, 2:221, 2:159, 3:298, 5:148, 2:221, 5:189. On wanting Nessa's children, see also 13 September 1919, 1:298; 4 January, 3:214, 15 August, 3:241, and 21 September 1929, 3:254.

66. Mansfield 142, 142–143, 3; Alpers, *Life of Katherine Mansfield*, 98, 122. Despite Mansfield's medical history, her editor-husband Murry comments in his edition of her diary—and indeed her diary shows as much— "Katherine spent much of her secret life in hoping against hope for the child which never came" (44).

67. Mansfield 58, 136–137, 168, 187, 193. Mansfield uses a child metaphor for her love in the 15 December 1919 entry, in which the Mansfield-Murry intimacy is a "love child" destroyed by Murry's self-referring attitudes (187). But her fantasy-child is no metaphor; it is a wish-fulfillment child.

68. Mansfield 51.

69. It is her title for the second chapter of her *Of Woman Born*.

70. Thrale 2:628, 1:389; Asquith 236, 412.

71. Guest 1:88, 1:154, 1:196. For other of Guest's deliveries, see, e.g., 28 March 1839, 1:88, and 1 July 1843, 1:154. Elizabeth Wynne 3:325; H. Wynne 3:201; Elizabeth Wynne 3:155.

72. Brookes, "Woman and Reproduction," 162–164; Branca, "Silent Sisterhood," 130–133, 138, quotation from 74; Webb 1:240; Amberley 2:71.

73. Eugenia Wynne 3:251; Cowper 46; Weeton 1:60 (letter to Miss Chorley).

74. A noteworthy child's diary was also kept by Elizabeth Gaskell (not one of the principal diarists): *My Diary: The Early Years of My Daughter Marianne*, spanning March 1835–October 1838. She commences her precise observations when Marianne is six months old, as a token of "her Mother's love and extreme anxiety in the formation of her little daughter's character" (5). Gaskell assumes that "all a woman's life . . . ought to have a reference to the period when she will be fulfilling one of her greatest and highest duties, those of a mother" (4 August 1835, 10). A summary of the Gaskell diary is available in Robertson, "Home as Nest," 413–414.

75. Thrale 2:709. The cover of Thrale's book reads "The Children's Book or rather Family Book." Begun on her first daughter's second birthday in 1766 and kept until 31 December 1778, the book includes material about Thrale, her husband, her mother, and family friend Samuel Johnson. Nonetheless, Thrale brandished it as evidence of maternal devotion during her struggles over her remarriage with her "ungrateful Girls!—let 'em look at

this Book & blush for Shame—I cared for nothing else [than them], twenty long Years together" (19 February 1788, 2:709). The Children's Book has not yet been published in full, but is extensively excerpted in Hyde's *Thrales of Streatham* (see under Thrale). Diary quotations from the Children's Book will henceforth be labeled (Hyde).

76. Elizabeth Wynne 3:104, 2:204; Guest 1:35; Monkswell 1:35.

77. Clifford 66; Thrale (Hyde) 21; Twysden 126.

78. Burney (Wood) 322; Jeune 62; Guest 2:79 (for etiquette, see David-off, *Best Circles*, 50); M. Woodforde 15; Bain 66; L. de Rothschild 70, 67; Weeton 2:384, 2:385.

79. Clifford 67, 105, 67. On 3 August 1617 Clifford's child also gets to sleep with both her parents (75). M. Woodforde 15; M. Hardy 19; Thrale (Hyde) 86; Gray 80; Twysden 117. On nursing practices, see McLaren, "Marital Fertility," 22–53.

80. Thrale (Hyde) 35; Freke 25, 26; Holland 1:136; Amberley 1:413, and letter to Georgy Russell of 24 October 1865, 1:414–415.

81. Davidoff, *Best Circles*, 53; Janet Lewis, *In the Family Way*, 225.

82. Lady Mary Wortley Montagu introduced the process of inoculation with material from another human case; Daniel Sutton, a physician, devised an improved method supplemented with drugs and given official medical approval in 1745; Edward Jenner devised the better-known and more dependable cowpox inoculation in 1796 (Thrale [Hyde] 25–26). A Sutton injection gave one Thrale infant, Ralph, a virulent case of smallpox from which he never quite recovered. See Thrale, 28 November and 19 December 1774 in Hyde, 110.

83. Gray 80.

84. Jeune 48, 47; Thrale 1:580; Holland 2:125; L. de Rothschild 50. See Powys, 25 October 1793, 277, and Holland, 18 May 1799, 1:249, for typical reports on smallpox sufferers.

85. Ross, "Labor and Love," 94 n. 29; Stone, *Family, Sex and Marriage*, 679; Jane Lewis, "Reconstructing Women's Experience," 3.

86. M. Shelley 122; Eliot 3:102; Clairmont 365; Elizabeth Wynne 3:326; Powys 113.

87. Ilick, "Child-Rearing," 315; Stone, *Family, Sex and Marriage*, 70.

88. Thrale (Hyde) 37, 55; F. Shelley 2:379.

89. Asquith 19, 20, 18, 155, 166, 357.

90. Chodorow, *Reproduction of Mothering*, 109, 166.

91. Powys 248; Thrale 1:55; Powys 276, 330, 331.

92. Holland 1:263, 1:266, 2:103–104.

93. Clairmont 78, 222.

94. Weeton 2:258, 2:356, 2:401–403.
95. Guest 2:52, 2:58; Thrale 1:504, 2:839, 2:708, 2:947, 2:984.

CHAPTER 5

1. Woolf, 2:309. Franklin likewise observes of American women's diaries, "Self-deprecating remarks are often found. . . . even the most accomplished women join in the refrain" ("Diaries of Forgotten Women," 472).

2. Morgan, *Descent of Woman,* 240. Spender puts it even more forcefully: Women "must first unlearn what a patriarchal society has taught them about themselves. Having been initiated into a male-dominated society they have been well instructed in the art of woman-devaluation, and if they have learnt their lesson well women will have emerged with their confidence undermined, their assurance dissolved, and their sense of self debased" (*Feminist Theorists,* 4).

3. Russell 24, 27; Trant 132; Asquith 219; Monkswell 1:174; M. Shelley 189; Eliot 1:481.

4. Byrom 386; Russell 59, 215; Woolf 2:69; Eliot 2:401.

5. Trant 265; Barrett (Browning) 224; Weeton 1:134; 2:387; Eastlake 1:156.

6. Rogers, *Feminism in Eighteenth-Century England,* 39.

7. Cavendish 2:19.

8. All references to Horney in this and the next paragraph will be to her 1934 paper *Overvaluation of Love,* 182–213; quotation from 209.

9. Mansfield 320–321.

10. Eastlake 1:40; Monkswell 2:113, 2:150.

11. Monkswell 1:163.

12. All references to Bardwick in this paragraph will be to chapter 9, "The Ego and Self-Esteem," in *Psychology of Women;* quotations from 158, 155.

13. Webb 1:64, 1:82, 1:44, 1:121.

14. All reference to Miller in this and subsequent paragraphs will be to *Toward a New Psychology,* quotations from 58, 110, 57, 57.

15. Jeune 102; Eliot 3:192.

16. Stevenson 195.

17. Monkswell 2:8.

18. Trant 270–271, 266.

19. Guest 1:112, Russell 163.

20. Guest 1:89, 2:72, 2:111.

21. Guest 1:67, 1:68, 1:146–147.

22. Daly, *Church and the Second Sex*, 37, 38; Beauvoir, *Second Sex*, 193; Rogers, *Troublesome Helpmate*, 188, 190. Diarist Woolf recognizes the bias in religion when reading that "first of the masculinists" John Milton, who tells "what men thought of our place in the universe, of our duty to God, our religion" (10 September 1918; 1:193), but other diarists do not comment on it.

23. Rogers, *Troublesome Helpmate*, 190. She illustrates with a sermon preached by the Reverend J. F. Stearns in 1837 telling women that the restrictions Saint Paul imposed on female conduct were "'designed, not to *degrade*, but to *elevate*,'" the female character, "'not to cramp, but to afford a *salutary* freedom. . . . Let woman throw off her feminine character, and her power to benefit society is lost.'"

24. Jeffreys, *Spinster and Her Enemies*, 141.

25. Webb 1:334.

26. C. de Rothschild 109; L. de Rothschild 7; Amberley 1:49.

27. Hoby 64; Schlüter 58; Shore 175; Russell 69, 25.

28. Thrale 1:454; Berry 3:446; Trant 149; Opie 261, 202, 207. See also Barrett (Browning), 19 June 1831, 22, and Weeton, 19 June 1825, 2:395, on being a slack believer.

29. Hoby 217; Jeune 50; A. de Rothschild 83.

30. Berry 3:361; Woolf 2:176; Opie 211; Sitwell 230; Woolf 2:184, 2:190, 5:95; Mansfield 113.

31. Woolf 2:94, 3:6.

32. Mansfield 280, 36, 240, 67, 95, 221, 255.

33. Eliot 3:129, 1:411; Webb 1:16, 3:220.

34. Northumberland 58; Elizabeth Wynne 2:105; Trant 129; Opie 259.

35. A. de Rothschild 79; Shore 336–337; Barrett (Browning) 79, 75.

36. Woolf 2:263, 2:77, 1:214. See also 16 January 1915, 1:20, 5 December 1919, 1:316, 12 December 1920, 2:79, and also 20 February 1937, 5:58, 24 September 1939, 5:240.

37. Mansfield 294, 269; Webb 1:158.

38. Cavendish 2:319; Thrale 1:459; Shore 237.

39. Holland 2:135; Webb 1:64; Barrett (Browning) 5, 149, 169; Woolf 5:227.

40. Potter 256; Barrett (Browning) 197; Trant 120, 123; Gray 25; Mansfield 240; Potter 390; Asquith 232. On reading, see, e.g., Hamilton, 25 June 1784, 212; Holland, 20 November 1798, 1:206; Weeton, [July?] 1810, 1:275.

41. Russell 25; Gladstone 159; Mansfield 73; Woolf 3:132, and see also 11 March 1939, 5:208, on being old and ugly.

42. Hamilton 231; Opie 255; L. de Rothschild 33; Elizabeth Wynne 2:78; Stevenson 193; Potter 78.

43. Weeton 1:174 (essay-review incorporated into diary); Woolf 2:135, 5:75; Berry 2:534.

44. Eliot 2:324, 3:251, 2:306, 2:307. On Eliot's doubts as a writer, see also 18 September 1859, 2:133, 30 July 1861, 2:311, 17 July 1864, 2:386, 23 July 1865, 2:406, 11 September 1869, 3:99, 31 December 1877; 3:324.

45. Chesler, *Women and Madness*, 64; Potter 118.

46. Seligman, *Helplessness*, 99; Arieti and Bemporad, *Severe and Mild Depression*, 372. Rohrbaugh, reviewing present research, reports that "no evidence establishes a biological cause for depression, much less a cause that is sex-linked. On the other hand, there is plenty of evidence that depression is always accompanied or caused by psychological factors. . . . This does not mean that biological factors do not accompany or even contribute to depression, but it does suggest that the social and emotional aspects of depression are crucial" (403).

47. Weissman and Klerman, who reviewed rates of depression in industrialized Western countries for the past forty years, almost consistently found a 2:1 female-to-male ratio. "The female preponderance," they say, "is real" ("Sex Differences and Epidemiology of Depression," 103). While their findings cannot speak for the past four centuries, they are suggestive.

48. Woolf 3:235, 3:290; Berry 3:34; Webb 1:259; Carlyle [2] 2:89; Holland, e.g., 5 August 1793, 1:82; Clifford 72, 103; Weeton 2:87. For Clairmont, see, e.g., 13, 14, and 16 January, 269; 7, 10, and 16 March, 278, 279; 8 and 9 April, 1822, 283; also 9 July, 337, 13 September, 358, and 15 November 1825, 379.

49. L. de Rothschild 29; Trant 192.

50. Gladstone 52; Pomerleau, "Emergence of Women's Autobiography," 37; Bernard, *Female World*, 176 n. 6; C. de Rothschild 340.

51. Berry 3:493; Powys 318.

52. Thrale 1:383; Woolf 3:230; Asquith 261, 217, 220, 348.

53. Holland 1:232, 1:122; Eugenia Wynne 2:146–147; Fox 2:101, 2:157; Thrale 1:447; Woolf 1:112, 1:234; 2:167.

54. Berry 2:60, 2:336; F. Shelley 2:108–109; Mansfield 65; M. Shelley 196.

55. Belloc Lowndes 30; Trant 305; Holland 1:147.

56. Mansfield 204; Monkswell 1:14, 1:162; Thrale 2:733–734; Woolf 1:65.

57. Eastlake 1:204; Jeune 6; Holland 1:211; Cavendish 2:257; Guest 2:29.

58. Other women's menopause apparently is also a taboo subject, though Stevenson breaches it to attribute another woman's softer, sadder manner partly to religious conversion and "partly I imagine to a 'change of life!'" (20 January 1935, 299).

59. Thrale 2:801.

60. Woolf 3:254, 3:219. For her positive attitude to aging, see also 31 March, 11 April, 2 and 7 August 1939; 5:212, 5:214, 5:229, 5:230.

61. Gladstone 201; Monkswell 2:23; Eastlake 1:60; Cavendish 1:138; F. Shelley 1:313; Thrale 1:553–554.

62. Hamilton 52–53; Fox 1:41, 1:126; Mansfield 33; Asquith 254, and see also 8 May 1917, 302.

63. Cavendish 1:181; George 285–289; Opie 311; Northumberland 194; Carlyle [1] 1:173–176; C. de Rothschild 113, and see also 1885, 204; Sitwell 173.

64. Potter 54; Schlüter 147; Stevenson 268; Weeton 2:393; Monkswell 1:196.

65. Cavendish 1:164; C. de Rothschild 278; Shore 236; Belloc Lowndes 96.

66. Webb 1:354; Woolf 4:79; Stevenson 110; Potter 205.

67. Rich, Of Woman Born, 226.

68. Thrale 2:768, 1:355, (Hyde) 70.

69. Chodorow, Reproduction of Mothering, 167, 198. Chodorow contends that both mother and daughter "maintain elements of their primary relationship" (110) after the daughter's oedipal phase. Signe Hammer, to whom Chodorow refers, also believes that "at some level mothers and daughters tend to remain emotionally bound up with each other in what might be called a semisymbiotic relationship, in which neither ever quite sees herself or the other as a separate person" (Daughters and Mothers, 165).

70. C. de Rothschild 201, 75, 241.

71. Shore 33, 272; Asquith 466, 300, and see also 13 August 1915, 68, 26 February 1916, 136; Schlüter 103; Elizabeth Wynne 2:165; Powys 214.

72. Eastlake 1:225; Mansfield 154; Carlyle [1] 2:31; Trant 127; Cavendish 2:34, 1:101. On mother as a reference point for appropriate behavior, see, e.g., for Trant, 24 October 1824, 130, 3 June 1831, 296; for Cavendish, 11 November, 1:76, and 30 December 1858 1:79.

73. Belloc Lowndes 171, 185; Weeton 2:384, 2:385; Thrale 1:355; Carlyle [2] 2:107.

74. George 311; Webb 1:273; Thrale (Hyde) 198.

75. Trant 130; Barrett (Browning) 88; Russell 128; Gray 74–77.

76. In 1814, she notes, "I in a fit of fury write a letter to Mama but do

not send it" (20 October, 52–53); in 1821, "In the Evening [I] write to Mrs. G" (28 June, 238). But thereafter it is "write to my mother" (13 February and 2 March 1822; 275, 277; see also 23 August 1825, 355).

77. Potter 338.
78. N. Woodforde 75.
79. Fitzgerald 32; Amberley 2:90.
80. Guest 2:92; Stevenson 33.
81. Webb 1:18, 1:188, 1:56.
82. Webb 2 (Cole): 306.
83. Weeton 2:254, 1:175, 1:174, 2:173.
84. Smith-Rosenberg, "Female World of Love," 15, 17.

AFTERWORD

1. Houghton 106.
2. The three who did not publish their diaries are Vera Brittain, Kathleen Isherwood, and Sarah Macnaughtan (on the last, however, see also my note 3). The six diarists reappearing from the main study are Asquith, Mansfield, C. de Rothschild, Stevenson, Webb, and Woolf.
3. Macnaughtan, *Woman's Diary of the War*, 13; henceforth, Macnaughtan [1]. She published this version of her diary herself. A relative published a second, more inclusive version: *My War Experiences*; henceforth, Macnaughtan [2].
4. Jephson 35; Thurstan 3 (note that this diary, limited to 1914; gives no interior dates); Brittain 281–282.
5. Brittain 89; Isherwood 431; Houghton 159, 187, 191–192, v.
6. Macnaughtan [2] 5, [2] 19, [2] 184; see 22 December 1915, [2] 213 for her age. Stevenson's diary provides another interesting glimpse into attitudes to women early in the war years. She reports a suggestion for new taxation Lloyd George received from "a man who thinks that the women of the country are not paying enough towards the War": "a tax on corsets!" (30 November 1914, 15). By 1915, however, when they became subject to compulsory national registration, women began to be sought for the munitions factories and as land-army and male-replacement workers; and after the universal male conscription of May 1916, large numbers of women were brought into war work (Marwick, *Women at War*, 73).
7. VAD (like FANY) designated both the organization and an individual member. Although VADs were also employed as drivers, the main VAD work was nursing, to assist professional hospital staffs in military hospitals

both abroad and in England. Because VAD service could assimilate untrained women, it was enormously popular.

8. See, e.g., Stevenson, 12 October 1915, 68, for her daring even to anger him by doing so.

9. Asquith 31. Her choice of metaphor is noteworthy. Fussell designates the metaphor of theater as characteristic of male self-protective psychic reactions to war, permitting a man to perform his soldiering without implicating his "real" self or his deep sense of a still-rational universe (*Great War and Modern Memory*, 192). But as Asquith's diary, which speaks elsewhere of melodrama (22 April 1915, 9) and here of tragedy, indicates, the theater figure in fact is gender free (see also Stevenson, 4 August 1916, 112). The ironic pastoralism and ruralism Fussell finds typical of male war writing (*Great War*, chapter 7) are likewise common in women's diaries. Both genders had the same cultural training in literature and myth; hence, their wartime visualizations could match.

10. Marwick, *Women at War*, 162.

11. Asquith 97; Brittain 208; Webb 3:324; Asquith 91, 190; Boyle 65.

12. Isherwood 471, 481; Brittain 300.

13. Stevenson 83; Finzi 109; Macnaughtan [1] 113.

14. Bagnold 133 (note that her diary gives no dates); Farmborough 101, 102, and see also 21 April 1915, 42. Service abroad cost some diarists more than peace of mind. Thurstan suffered a shrapnel wound in her leg, and Finzi was so "broken in body" by 1916 (10 February, 258) that she had to return home. Macnaughtan was already elderly and ill when she undertook her strenuous hospital and canteen work in Belgium and France, besides returning home in 1915 to give thirty-five lectures to reluctant munitions workers. Fatally weakened by hardships endured while attempting to serve also in Russia, she died in 1916.

15. Morrell 83; Houghton 222; McDougall 20; Finzi 85; Brittain 339.

16. Lloyd 121; Houghton 248; Macnaughtan [2] 31, [1] 159–160; Webb 3:289; Macnaughtan [1] 162; Courtney 34. Courtney, who afterwards became a member of the Executive Committee of the International Women's League for Peace (3 October 1915, 62), should not be confused with Dame Kathleen Courtney (1878–1974), a league founder and a participant in the Hague Congress.

17. Woolf 1:229; Pless 275; Macnaughtan [1] 27.

18. Finzi 53; McDougall 132; Sinclair 13; Thurstan 142; Sinclair 224. Sinclair is more perceptive (or candid) on 5 October 1914: "But now . . . I realize what the insatiable and implacable self is after, how it worked in me

291

against all decency . . . ; how it actually made me feel as if I wanted to see Antwerp under siege" (135).

19. Finzi 57; Kennard 49.

20. Farmborough 352; Morrell 235; Sinclair 247; Adam 223; Bagnold 25. See also Asquith, 6 September 1915, 76, and 29 May 1918, 442.

21. Anonymous 52–53 WWI: the label WWI will always signify the anonymous Great War nurse. Asquith 34, 248, 437; Farmborough 390; Kennard 72. See also Brittain, 27 June 1915, 213; Anonymous, 1915, 112–114 WWI; Kennard, September 1916, 55; Thurstan, [1914], 27.

22. The new pride was partly constructed out of a sense of successful rivalry with men (see, e.g., Macnaughtan, 16 October 1914, 21 May 1915; [2] 29, [2] 41. But more significantly, it issued from a dawning respect simply for women's capabilities. As critic Gilbert says, "The liberating sisterhood experienced by women was mostly untainted by hostility to men . . . in fact frequently associated with admiration for male soldiers" ("Soldier's Heart," 443). "Union among women," Auerbach points out too, "is one of the unacknowledged fruits of war" (*Communities of Women*, 161).

23. Thurstan 174–175; Macnaughtan [1] 53–54; McDougall 78; Finzi 83; McDougall 180.

24. See, e.g., Finzi, 8 April 1915, 125–127; Sinclair, 10 October 1914, 213–214; Macnaughtan, 18 February 1915 [2] 89.

25. Macnaughtan [2] 112–113; Thurstan 28; Sinclair 128–129; Anonymous WWI 57; Finzi 118; Farmborough 299, 303. On all-women endeavors, see also Finzi, 1 November 1914, 41; Sinclair, 4 October 1914, 127, 130.

26. Brittain 178; Bagnold 78, 35, 128; Asquith 451; McDougall 92.

27. Finzi 85; Pless 340; Bagnold 76.

28. Macnaughtan [2] 135; McDougall 74; Brittain 172; Kennard 129; Farmborough 322; Anonymous 89 WWI. See also Thurstan 66.

29. Sinclair 196, 204; Anonymous 37 WWI; Farmborough 30; Macnaughtan [2] 103; Houghton 92–93.

30. Pless 384; Kennard 164; Farmborough 247; Thurstan 12; Finzi 4.

31. Bagnold 47.

32. Gilbert, "Soldier's Heart," 449.

33. Adam 234.

34. Jane Lewis makes a similar claim: "The two world wars probably increased the confidence and sense of independence (and thus the expectations and aspirations) of individual women of all classes, and, despite the frustrations women experienced in the years following both wars, may have

been comparable to the feminist movement of the 1970s in terms of their consciousness-raising effect" (*Women in England*, 223).

35. Mitchell, *Monstrous Regiment*, xvi.

36. Principally, the Sex Disqualification Removal Act of 1919 opened jury service, the magistracy, and the practice of law to women, and it permitted some entry into the upper reaches of the Civil Service. Under the National Insurance Acts (1918, 1920, 1921), they became eligible for national insurance benefits as wage-earners (Marwick, *Women at War*, 162).

37. Jane Lewis, *Women in England*, 4; Davidoff, *Best Circles*, 99.

38. Lewis, *Women in England*, 135, 5–6, 70. Lewis reports that the marital fertility rate, declining since the 1870s—at that time, over 295 legitimate live births per 1000 married women aged 15–44—fell to 222 by the first decade of the twentieth century and 111 by the 1930s, with approximately 50 percent more childlessness among non-manual-worker families (5–6).

39. Banks, *Faces of Feminism*, 166–177.

40. Bridenthal, "Something Old," 425. Bridenthal decides that despite "glimmers of progress and future promise" in female attitudes interwar, most women resolved the increased tension between work and family by acceding to a reactionary impulse (442).

41. By the 1950s, middle-class women "in significant numbers" had begun to continue with careers after marriage (Banks, *Faces of Feminism*, 252). By the early 1960s, large numbers of women were pursuing higher education, enabled by the 1944 Education Act grants and expansion of the university system. Beauvoir's *Second Sex*, with its extensive analysis of women's cultural relegation to inferiority, already translated in 1953, was available in a cheap paperback edition in 1961 (Bouchier, *Feminist Challenge*, 33, 35).

SELECT LIST
OF WOMEN'S DIARIES

Diaries are listed under the diarist's name. Principal Diarists, upon whose diaries this study is based, are listed without a symbol; the World War I Diarists of the Afterword are indicated by an asterisk (*); and diarists not included in the study, though in a few instances cited as supplementary, are denoted by a dagger (†). Restrictions such as privacy, immediacy, and pre-1940 composition have not been imposed on these additional eclectic diaries. The time span for each diary appears either in its title or following the title in brackets.

*Adam, Mrs. Helen Pearl (Humphrey 1882–?).
   Paris Sees It Through: A Diary, 1914–19, London: Hodder and Stoughton, 1919.
Amberley, Kate (Katharine Louisa) Russell (née Stanley); Viscountess Amberley (1842–1874).
   The Amberley Papers: The Letters and Diaries of Lord and Lady Amberley [1859–1872]. Edited by Bertrand and Patricia Russell. 2 vols. London: Hogarth, 1937.
Anonymous (d. 1908).
   The Note-Books of a Spinster Lady [1878–1903]. [Editor not identified]. London: Cassell, 1919.
Anonymous (no dates available).
   Recollections of a Spinster Aunt [1849–ca. 1859]. Edited by S. Sophia Beale. London: William Heinemann, 1908.

*Anonymous (no dates available).
A War Nurse's Diary: Sketches from a Belgian Field Hospital [1914–1915].
New York: Macmillan, 1918.
Asquith, Lady Cynthia Mary Evelyn Charteris (Mrs.) (1887–1960).
Lady Cynthia Asquith: Diaries, 1915–1918. Edited by E. M. Horsley. London: Hutchinson, 1968.
Astry, Diana (Mrs. Orlebar) (1671–1716).
Frederica St. John Orlebar. Orlebar Chronicles in Bedfordshire and Northamptonshire: 1553–1733 [1701–1708], 160–168. London, 1930.
*Bagnold, Miss Enid Algerine (1889–1981).
A Diary Without Dates. London: William Heinemann, 1918.
Bagot, Miss Mary (no dates available).
Mrs. Charles [Sophy Louisa] Bagot. Links with the Past [1820–1855], 157–284. London: Edward Arnold, 1901.
Bain, Mrs. Louisa (1803–1883).
James S. Bain. A Bookseller Looks Back: The Story of the Bains [1857–1883], 39–89. London: Macmillan, 1940.
Barrett, Miss Elizabeth Barrett (later Mrs. Browning) (1806–1861).
Diary by E. B. B.: The Unpublished Diary of Elizabeth Barrett Barrett 1831–1832. Edited by Philip Kelley and Ronald Hudson. Athens, Ohio: Ohio University Press, 1969.
†Bedingfield, Lady Charlotte (d. 1854).
The Jerningham Letters (1740–1843): Being Excerpts from the Correspondence and Diaries of the Honourable Lady Jerningham and Her Daughter Lady Bedingfield [1809–1833]. Edited by Egerton Castle. 2 vols. London: R. Bentley and Son, 1896.
Belloc Lowndes, Mrs. Marie Adelaide (1868–1947).
Diaries and Letters of Marie Belloc Lowndes: 1911–47. Edited by Susan Lowndes. London: Chatto and Windus, 1971.
Berry, Miss Mary (1763–1852).
Extracts of the Journals and Correspondence of Miss Berry from the Year 1783 to 1852 [retrospection 1762–1783, 1848–1849; diary 1783–1848]. Edited by Lady Theresa Lewis. 3 vols. London: Longmans, Green, 1865.
Bessborough, Countess of. See Duncannon, Harriet Spencer
†Boscawen, the Honorable Frances Evelyn (1719–1805).
Cecil Aspinall-Oglander. Admiral's Wife: The Life and Letters of the Hon. Mrs. Edward Boscawen from 1719 to 1761 [January–December 1748], 67–134. London: Longmans, Green, 1940.
*Boyle, Mrs. Laura (no dates available).
Diary of a Colonial Officer's Wife [1916–1917]. Oxford: Alden Press, 1968.
*Brittain, Miss Vera (1893–1970).

War Diary, 1913–1917: Chronicle of Youth. Edited by Alan Bishop with Terry Smart. London: Victor Gollancz, 1981.

Browning, Elizabeth Barrett. See Barrett, Miss Elizabeth Barrett

Burney, Fanny Anne (Mrs. Wood) (1812–1860).
A Great-Niece's Journals: Being Extracts from the Journals of Fanny Anne Burney (Mrs. Wood), from 1830 to 1842. Edited by Margaret S. Rolt. Boston: Houghton-Mifflin, 1926.

†Burney, Fanny (Frances) (Mme. D'Arblay) (1752–1840).
The Early Diary of Frances Burney, 1768–1778. Edited by Annie Raine Ellis. 2 vols. London: George Bell, 1889. Reprint. Freeport, N.Y.: Books for Libraries, 1971.
The Diary and Letters of Madame D'Arblay [1778–1840]. Edited by C. Barrett. 6 vols. London: Macmillan, 1904.
The Journals and Letters of Fanny Burney (Madame D'Arblay) [1791–1840]. Edited by Joyce Hemlow with Althea Douglas and Patricia Boutilier. 12 vols. Oxford: Clarendon, 1972–1984.

†Bury, Lady Charlotte Susan Maria (1775–1861).
The Diary of a Lady-in-Waiting [1810–1820]. Edited by A. Frances Steuart. 2 vols. London: John Lane, 1908.

Butler, Lady Eleanor (Miss) (1739?–1829).
The Hamwood Papers of the Ladies of Llangollen and Caroline Hamilton [September–December 1785; 1788–1821 with large gaps]. Edited by Mrs. G. H. Bell. London: Macmillan, 1930.

†Butler, Lady Elizabeth Southerden (1846–1933).
An Autobiography [1862–1918]. London: Constable, 1922.

Byrom, Miss Elizabeth (1722–1801).
"The Journal of Elizabeth Byrom" [1745–1746]. In *The Private Journal and Literary Remains of John Byrom,* edited by R. Parkinson. Chetham Society Publication 44 (1847): 385–410.

Carlyle, Mrs. Jane Baillie Welsh (1801–1866).
[1] *Letters and Memorials of Jane Welsh Carlyle* [13–27 April 1845; 1855–1856]. Edited by J. A. Froude. 2 vols. in one, 1:172–177, 2:29–39. New York: Harper and Bros., 1883.
[2] *New Letters and Memorials of Jane Welsh Carlyle* [15 October 1855–5 July 1856]. Edited by Alexander Carlyle, 2:87–109. London: John Lane, 1903.

Carrington, Dora de Houghton (Mrs. Partridge) (1893–1932).
Carrington: Letters and Extracts from Her Diaries [1915–1932]. Edited by David Garnett. London: Jonathan Cape, 1970.

†Castle, Barbara (b. 1911).
The Castle Diaries, 1974–76. London: Weidenfield and Nicolson, 1980.

Cavendish, Lady Lucy Caroline (née Lyttleton) (1841–1925).
The Diary of Lady Frederick Cavendish [retrospection to 1854, diary 1854–1882]. Edited by John Bailey. 2 vols. London: John Murray, 1927.

Clairmont, Miss Claire (Clara Mary Jane) (1798–1879).
The Journals of Claire Clairmont [1814–1827]. Edited by Marion Kingston Stocking assisted by David Mackenzie Stocking. Cambridge, Mass.: Harvard University Press, 1968.

Clifford, Anne (Mrs.); Countess of Dorset, then also of Pembroke and Montgomery, and Baroness Clifford (1590–1676).
The Diary of the Lady Anne Clifford [retrospection 1603, diary 1616–1619]. Edited by Vita (Victoria Mary) Sackville-West. London: William Heinemann, 1924.

George C. Williamson. *Lady Anne Clifford: Her Life, Letters and Work* [1 January–21 March 1676], 265–280. 2d ed. Wakefield, England: S. R. Publishers, 1967.

†Clive, Caroline Meysey-Wigley (1801–1873).
Caroline Clive: From the Diary and Family Papers of Mrs. Archer Clive [1835–1865]. Edited by Mary Clive. London: The Bodley Head, 1949.

†Coke, Lady Mary (1726–1811).
The Letters and Journals of Lady Mary Coke [1756–1791]. Edited by J. A. Home. 4 vols. Edinburgh, 1889–1896. Reprint. Bath: Kingsmead Reprints, 1970.

Collier, Mary. *See* Monkswell, Mary Josephine

*Courtney, Lady Kate (Catherine) Potter (Mrs.) (1847–1929).
Extracts from a Diary During the War [1914–1919], n.p.: privately printed, 1927.

Cowper, Mary Clavering (Mrs.); Countess Cowper (1685–1724).
Diary of Mary, Countess Cowper, Lady of the Bedchamber to the Princess of Wales [1714–1716, 1720]. Edited by C. S. Cowper. London: John Murray, 1864.

†Cullwick, Hannah (1833–1909).
The Diaries of Hannah Cullwick, Victorian Maidservant [1854–1873]. Edited by Liz Stanley. New Brunswick, N.J.: Rutgers University Press, 1984.

†D'Abernon, Helen Venetia Duncombe Vincent; Viscountess D'Abernon (b. 1866).
Red Cross and Berlin Embassy 1915–1926: Extracts from the Diaries of Viscountess D'Abernon. London: John Murray, 1946.

†Devonshire, Georgiana Spencer; Duchess of Devonshire (1757–1806).
Walter Sichel, *Sheridan, From New and Original Material* [1788–1789], 2:399–426. New York: Houghton Mifflin, 1909.

†Dixon, Agnes Margaret Powell (no dates available).
The Canteeners [1915?–1916]. London: John Murray, 1917.
†Duberly, Frances Isabella (1829–1903).
Journal Kept during the Russian War [1854–1855]. London: Longman, Brown, Green and Longman, 1855.
Campaigning Experiences in Central India and Rajputana during the Suppression of the Mutiny [1857–1859]. London: Smith, Elder, 1859.
Duncannon, Harriet Spencer (Mrs.); Countess of Bessborough (1761–1821).
"Lady Duncannon's Diary." In *Lady Bessborough and Her Family Circle* [March–April 1789]. Edited by the Earl of Bessborough, 43–53. London: John Murray, 1940.
Eastlake, Lady Elizabeth Rigby (Mrs.) (1809–1893).
Journals and Correspondence of Lady Eastlake. [1842–1848]. Vol. 1. Edited by Charles Eastlake Smith. London: John Murray, 1895. Reprint. New York: AMS Press, 1975.
Eliot, George [Mary Ann Evans] (Mrs. Cross) (1819–1880).
J. W. Cross. *George Eliot's Life* [1854–1880]. 3 vols. London, 1885.
†Evans, Jane (1826–1906).
Major Gambier-Parry. *Annals of an Eton House: With Some Notes on the Evans Family* [1878–1900], 308–326, 358–380. London: John Murray, 1907.
*Farmborough, Miss Florence (1887–1978).
Nurse at the Russian Front: A Diary 1914–18. London: Constable, 1974. (Also published as *With the Armies of the Tsar: A Nurse. . . .* New York: Stein and Day, 1974.)
†Field, Joanna [Marion Blackett Milner] (b. 1900).
A Life of One's Own [1926 and undated later entries]. London: Chatto and Windus, 1934. Reprint. Los Angeles: J. P. Tarcher, 1981.
†Field, Michael. [joint pseud. for Katherine Bradley (1848–1914) and Edith Cooper (1862–1913).]
Works and Days: From the Journal of Michael Field. Edited by T. and D. C. Sturge Moore. London: John Murray, 1933.
*Finzi, Miss Kate John (no dates available).
Eighteen Months in the War Zone: The Record of a Woman's Work on the Western Front [1914–1916]. London: Cassell, 1916.
Fitzgerald, Lady Lucy (Miss) (later Lady Foley) (1771–1851).
Gerald Campbell. *Edward and Pamela Fitzgerald* [ca. 1796–1798 and undated entries]. London: Edward Arnold, 1904.
Fox, Miss Caroline (1819–1871).

Memories of Old Friends: Being Extracts from the Journals and Letters of Caroline Fox from 1835–1871 [1835–1867]. Edited by Horace N. Pym. 2d ed. 2 vols. London: Smith, Elder, 1882.

Fox, Elizabeth. *See* Holland, Elizabeth

Frampton, Miss Mary (1773–1846).
Journal of Mary Frampton, From the Year 1779, Until the Year 1846 [retrospection 1779–1788, diary 1789–1831]. Edited by Harriot Georgiana Mundy. London: Sampson Low, Marston, Searle, and Rivington, 1885.

Freke, Mrs. Elizabeth (1641–1714).
Mrs. Elizabeth Freke, Her Diary: 1671 to 1714. Edited by Mary Carbery. Cork: Guy, 1913.

†Gaskell, Elizabeth Cleghorn (1810–1865).
My Diary: The Early Years of My Daughter Marianne [1835–1838]. London: privately printed, 1923.

†Gawthern, Abigail (1757–1822).
The Diary of Abigail Gawthern of Nottingham, 1751 [sic]*–1810.* Edited by Adrian Henstock, Vol. 33 of Thoroton Society of Nottinghamshire Record Series, 1980.

George, Miss Elizabeth (no dates available).
"The Journal of Elizabeth George, 1840–47. Kept at the farmhouse of the Duke of Buckingham's 'good old Tenant' at Stowe." *Cornhill*, no. 180 (1974): 283–311.

Gladstone, Mary (Mrs. Drew) (1847–1927).
Mary Gladstone (Mrs. Drew): Her Diaries and Letters [1864–1920]. Edited by Lucy Masterman. 2d ed. London: Methuen, 1930.

Gray, Faith (née Hopwood) (1751–1826).
Papers and Diaries of a York Family: 1764–1839 [1764–1826]. Edited by Mrs. Edwin Gray. London: Sheldon Press, 1927.

Grove, Miss Harriet (later Mrs. Helyer) (1791–1867).
The Journal of Harriet Grove for the Years 1809–1810. Edited by Roger Ingpen. London, 1932.

Guest, Lady Charlotte Elizabeth (née Bertie) (then Mrs. Schreiber) (1812–1895).
[1] *Lady Charlotte Guest: Extracts from her Journal 1833–1852.* Edited by the Earl of Bessborough. London: John Murray, 1950.
[2] *Lady Charlotte Schreiber: Extracts from her Journal 1853–1891.* Edited by the Earl of Bessborough. London: John Murray, 1952.

Hamilton, Mary (Mrs. Dickenson) (1756–1816).
Mary Hamilton: Afterwards Mrs. John Dickenson: At Court and at Home

[1777–1788]. Edited by Elizabeth and Florence Anson. London: John Murray, 1925.

†Hanbury, Charlotte (1830–1900).
Charlotte Hanbury: An Autobiography (1848–1869). Edited by Mrs. Arthur Head, 21–87. London: Marshall Bros., 1901.

†Harcourt, Mary (no dates available).
"Mrs. Harcourt's Diary of the Court of King George III" [1789–1791]. *Miscellanies of the Philobiblon Society* 13 (1871–1872): 13–57.

†Hardy, Lady Louisa Berkeley (1788–1877).
John Gore. *Nelson's Hardy and His Wife* [1807–1847], 40–235 passim. London: John Murray, 1935.

Hardy, Mrs. Mary (1733–1809).
Mary Hardy's Diary [1773–1809]. Edited by B. Gozens-Hardy. Norfolk Record Society Publications, 37. Norfolk: Norfolk Record Society, 1968.

Hoby, Lady Margaret Dakins (Mrs.) (1571–1633).
Diary of Lady Margaret Hoby [1599–1605]. Edited by Dorothy M. Meads. London: Routledge and Sons, 1930.

Holland, Elizabeth (née Vassall) (Mrs. Webster, then Mrs. Fox); became Baroness of Holland House (1770–1845).
The Journal of Elizabeth, Lady Holland [1791–1811]. Edited by the Earl of Ilchester. 2 vols. London: Longmans, 1909.

*Houghton, Mrs. Mary (no dates available).
In the Enemy's Country: Being the Diary of a Little Tour in Germany and Elsewhere During the Early Days of the War [July–September 1914]. London: Chatto and Windus, 1915.

Howard, Mrs. Katherine (1672–1765).
The Diary of George Booth of Chester, and Katherine Howard, His Daughter, of Boughton, Near Chester, 1701–1764 [1721–1764]. Edited by the Reverend Gibbs Payne Crawfurd, 27–86. Reprint from *Journal of the Chester and North Wales Architectural, Archaeological and Society,* n.s. 28. Chester, Eng.: G. R. Griffeth, 1928.

†Hurnscot, Loran [Gay Stuart Taylor] (no dates available).
A Prison, A Paradise [1922–1958 and undated entries]. New York: Viking, 1959.

*Isherwood, Mrs. Kathleen Machell Smith (1868–1960).
Christopher Isherwood. *Kathleen and Frank* [1881–1940]. New York: Simon and Schuster, 1971.

†Jacquier, Ivy (b. 1890).
The Diary of Ivy Jacquier: 1907–1926. London: Victor Gollancz, 1960.

*Jephson, Lady Harriet Julia (Miss) (d. 1930).
A War-Time Journal: Germany 1914 and German Travel Notes. London: Elkin Mathews, 1915.
Jeune, Mrs. Margaret (1818–1891)
Pages from the Diary of an Oxford Lady [1843–1862]. Edited by Margaret Jeune Gifford. Oxford: Shakespeare Head Press, 1932.
†Jones, Agnes Elizabeth (1832–1868).
[J. Jones.] *Memorials of Agnes Elizabeth Jones: By Her Sister* [10–11 November 1846, 1853–1867], 12–13, 27–230 passim. London: Daldy, Isbester, 1877.
†Kemble, Fanny (Frances Anne) Butler (1809–1893).
Records of a Girlhood [1831–1832]. 2d. ed. New York: Henry Holt, 1879.
Journal by Frances Anne Butler [1832–1833]. 2 vols. London: John Murray, 1835. Reprint. New York: Benjamin Bloom, 1970.
Fanny, the American Kemble: Her Journals and Unpublished Letters [1831–1832, 1835, annotated excerpts]. Edited by Fanny Kemble Wister, Tallahassee, Fla.: South Pass Press, 1972.
Journal of a Residence on a Georgian Plantation in 1838–39. Edited by John A. Scott. New York: Alfred A. Knopf, 1961.
*Kennard, Lady Dorothy Katherine Barclay (Mrs.) (no dates available).
A Roumanian Diary: 1915, 1916, 1917. New York, Dodd Mead, 1918.
†King, Mrs. Robert Moss (Emily Augusta) (no dates available).
The Diary of a Civilian's Wife in India, 1877–1882. 2 vols. London: Richard Bentley and Son, 1884.
†Knight, Cornelia (1756–1837).
The Autobiography of Miss Knight: Lady Companion to Princess Charlotte [1805–1812, 1815–1816]. Edited by Roger Fulford, 88–101, 199–211. London: William Kimber, 1960.
†Knightley, Lady Louisa (1842–1913).
The Journals of Louisa, Lady Knightley, 1856–84. Edited by Julia Cartwright. London: John Murray, 1915.
†Knox, Elizabeth Jane (1824–1855).
Memoirs of a Vanished Generation, 1813–1855 [20–23 October 1848]. Edited by Mrs. Warrenne Blake, 250–251. London: John Lane, 1909.
†Knox, Jane Hope Vere (1790–1875).
Memoirs of a Vanished Generation, 1813–1855 [January–July 1813, May–July 1841], 5–10, 135–144.
*Lloyd, Miss Gladys (1889–?).
An Englishwoman's Adventures in the German Lines [1914]. London: C. Arthur Pearson, 1914.

Lumb, Mrs. Anne (later Mrs. Milnes) (no dates available).
Diaries of Mrs Anne Lumb of Silcoates, near Wakefield, in 1755 and 1757.
Edited by Charles M. Gaskell. London: privately printed, 1884.

Lytton, Edith Villiers (Mrs.): Countess Bulwer-Lytton (1841–1936).
Lady Lytton's Court Diary: 1895–1899. Edited by Mary Lutyens. London:
Rupert Hart-Davis, 1961.

*McDougall, Miss Grace (d. 1963).
A Nurse at the War [1914–1916]. New York: Robert M. McBride, 1917.
(Also published as *Nursing Adventures: A F.A.N.Y. in France.* London:
Heinemann, 1917.)

*Macnaughtan, Miss Sarah Broom (d. 1916).
[1] *A Woman's Diary of the War* [1914–1915]. London: Thomas Nelson
and Sons, 1915.
[2] *My War Experiences in Two Continents* [1914–1916]. Edited by Mrs.
Lionel Salmon. London: John Murray, 1919.

Mansfield, Katherine [Kathleen Mansfield Beauchamp] (Mrs. Bowden, then
Mrs. Murray) (1888–1923).
Journal of Katherine Mansfield [1904–1922]. Edited by J. Middleton Murry.
London: Constable, 1954.

†Mildmay, Lady Grace Sherrington (1551–1620).
Rachel Wiegall. "An Elizabethan Gentlewoman" [1570–1617]. *Quarterly
Review* 215 (1911): 119–135.

Monkswell, Mary Josephine (née Hardcastle) Collier; Baroness of Monkswell (1849–1930).
*A Victorian Diarist: Extracts from the Journals of Mary, Lady Monkswell:
1873–95.* Also, *A Victorian Diarist: Later Extracts from the Journals.* . . .
[1895–1909]. Edited by E. C. F. Collier. 2 vols. London: John Murray,
1944–1946.

*Morrell, Lady Ottoline Violet Anne Cavendish-Bentinck (Mrs.) (1873–
1938).
Ottoline at Garsington: Memoirs of Lady Ottoline Morrell, 1915–1918.
Edited by Robert Gathorne-Hardy. New York: Alfred A. Knopf, 1974.

†Murray, Mary (b. 1759).
William Henry Bagshawe. *The Bagshawes of Ford* [August–October 1776],
532–538. London: Mitchell and Hughes, 1886.

Northumberland, Elizabeth Seymour Percy (Mrs.); Duchess of Northum-
berland (1716–1776).
The Diaries of a Duchess [1752–1774]. Edited by James Greig. New York:
Doran, 1927.

Opie, Mrs. Amelia (1769–1853).

Cecilia Brightwell. *Memorials of the Life of Amelia Opie* [1827–1853], 199–394. Norwich: Fletcher and Alexander, 1854.
†Partridge, Frances Marshall (b. 1900).
  Julia: A Portrait by Herself and Frances Partridge. [1933, 1940–1967], 122–123, 173–289 passim. London: Victor Gollancz, 1983.
†Pepys, Emily (1833–1877).
  The Journal of Emily Pepys [July 1844–January 1845]. Edited by Gillian Avery, Charlottesville, Va.,: University of Virginia Press, 1984.
Percy, Elizabeth. *See* Northumberland, Elizabeth Seymour Percy
*Pless, Daisy (Mary Theresa Olivia) Cornwallis-West, (Mrs.) Fürstin von (1873–1943).
  Daisy, Princess of Pless: By Herself [1902–1918]. Edited by Major Desmond Chapman-Huston. New York: E. P. Dutton, 1929.
  From My Private Diary [1896–1914]. Edited by Major Desmond Chapman-Huston, 35–281. London: John Murray, 1931.
Potter, Miss Beatrix (later Mrs. Heelis) (1866–1943).
  The Journal of Beatrix Potter from 1881 to 1897. Edited by Leslie Linder. London: Frederick Warne, 1966.
Powys, Caroline (née Girle) (1739–1817).
  Passages from the Diary of Mrs. Powys [1756–1808]. Edited by Emily J. Clemson. London: Longmans, Green, 1899.
†Pym, Barbara (1913–1980).
  A Very Private Eye: An Autobiography in Diaries and Letters [1932–1980]. Edited by Hazel Holt and Hilary Pym. New York: E. P. Dutton, 1984.
Raper, Miss Elizabeth (later Mrs. Grant) (d. 1778).
  The Receipt Book of Elizabeth Raper [1756–1761]. Edited by Bartle Grant, 5–31. London: Nonesuch Press, 1924.
†Ritchie, Lady Anne Isabella Thackeray (1837–1919).
  Letters of Anne Thackeray Ritchie [1854–1879]. Edited by Hester Ritchie. London: John Murray, 1924.
Rothschild, Lady Annie de (Miss) (later the Hon. Mrs. Yorke) (1844–1926).
  Lucy Cohen. *Lady de Rothschild and Her Daughters, 1821–1931* [1858–1859]. London: John Murray, 1935.
Rothschild, Lady Constance de (then Lady Battersea) (1843–1931).
  Lucy Cohen. *Lady de Rothschild and Her Daughters, 1821–1931* [1858–1931]. London: John Murray, 1935.
Rothschild, Lady Louisa de (née Montefiore) (1821–1910).
  Lucy Cohen. *Lady de Rothschild and Her Daughters, 1821–1931* [1837–1878]. London: John Murray, 1935.

Russell, Frances Anna Maria (née Elliott); Countess Russell (1815–1898).
Lady John Russell: A Memoir, with Selections from Her Diaries and Correspondence [1830–1878, 1892–1898]. Edited by Desmond MacCarthy and Agatha Russell. London: Methuen, 1910.

Russell, Kate. *See* Amberley, Kate

†Sackville-West, the Hon. Vita (Victoria Mary) (1892–1962).
Nigel Nicolson. *Portrait of a Marriage* [1907, 1911–1923]. New York: Atheneum, 1973.

Schlüter, Miss Auguste (1850–1917).
A Lady's Maid in Downing Street: 1877–1890. Edited by Mabel Duncan. Boston: Small Maynard, 1922.

†Scott, Lady Kathleen (later Lady Kennet) (1878–1947).
Self-Portrait of an Artist: From the Diaries and Memoirs of Lady Kennet, Kathleen, Lady Scott [1911–1946], 91–361. London: John Murray, 1949.

†Sewell, Elizabeth Missing (1815–1906).
The Autobiography of Elizabeth Missing Sewell [1845–1885]. Edited by Eleanor L. Sewell. New York: Longmans, Green, 1907.

Shelley, Lady Frances (née Winckley) (1787–1873).
The Diary of Frances Lady Shelley [retrospection 1787–1812, diary 1813–1817, 1818–1873]. Edited by Richard Edgcumbe. 2 vols. London: John Muray, 1913.

Shelley, Mary Wollstonecraft (née Godwin) (1797–1851).
Mary Shelley's Journal [1814–1840]. Edited by Fredrick L. Jones. Norman, Okla.: University of Oklahoma Press, 1963.

Shore, Miss Emily (1819–1839).
Journal of Emily Shore [1831–1839]. [Editor not identified]. London: Kegan Paul, Trench, Trübner, 1898.

*Sinclair, Miss May (1865–1946).
A Journal of Impressions in Belgium [1914–1915]. London: Hutchinson, 1915.

Sitwell, Miss Florence Alice (1858–1930).
Two Generations [1873–1877]. Edited by Osbert Sitwell, 147–308. London: Macmillan, 1940.

†Stanley, Catherine (1792–1862).
Arthur Penrhyn Stanley. *Memoirs of Edward and Catherine Stanley* [1809–1862], 129–333. London: John Murray, 1880.

Stevenson, Frances Louise (then Countess Lloyd-George) (1888–1972).
Lloyd George: A Diary by Frances Stevenson [1914–1937, 1944?]. Edited by A. J. P. Taylor. London: Hutchinson, 1971.

†Strachey, Julia (1901–1979).

Julia: A Portrait by Herself and Frances Partridge [1928–1966 and later, undated entries]. London: Victor Gollancz, 1983.

Thrale, Mrs. Hester Lynch Salusbury (then Mrs. Piozzi) (1741–1821).
Thraliana: The Diary of Mrs. Hester Lynch Thrale, 1776–1809. Edited by Katharine C. Balderston. 2d ed. 2 vols. Oxford: Clarendon, 1951.
Mary Hyde. *The Thrales of Streatham Park* [1766–1778]. Cambridge, Mass.: Harvard University Press, 1977.

*Thurstan, Miss Violetta (d. 1978).
Field Hospital and Flying Column, Being the Journal of an English Nursing Sister in Belgium and Russia [1914]. London: G. P. Putnam's Sons, 1915.

Trant, Clarissa Sandford (Mrs. Bramston) (1800–1844).
The Journal of Clarissa Trant: 1800–1832 [retrospection and rewritten diary 1800–1823, 1828, 1830; unretouched diary 1824–1827, 1829, 1831–1832]. Edited by C. G. Luard. London: John Lane, 1925.

†Trench, Maria Melesina Chevenix (1768–1827).
The Remains of the Late Mrs. Richard Trench, Being Selections from Her Journals, Letters, and Other papers [1798–1827]. Edited by the Dean of Westminster, 25–520 passim. 2d. ed., rev. London: Parker, Son, and Bourn, 1862.

Twysden, Lady Isabella Saunder (Mrs.) (1605–1657).
"The Diary of Isabella, Wife of Sir Roger Twysden, Baronet of Royden Hall, East Peckham, 1645–1651." Edited by F. W. Bennitt. In *Archaeologia Cantiana* 51 (1939): 113–136.

†Victoria, Queen of England (1819–1901).
The Girlhood of Queen Victoria: A Selection from Her Majesty's Diaries Between the Years 1832 and 1840. Edited by Viscount Esher. 2 vols. London: John Murray, 1912.
Leaves from The Journal of Our Life in the Highlands from 1848 to 1861. Edited by Arthur Helps. New York: Harper and Bros., 1868. Reprint. New York: Kraus Reprint Company, 1969.
Queen Victoria: Leaves From a Journal: A Record of The Visit of the Emperor and Empress of the French to the Queen and of the Visit of the Queen and H. R. H. The Prince Consort to the Emperor of the French, 1855 [April–May and 18–28 August 1855]. Edited by Raymond Mortimer. New York: Farrar, Straus and Cudahy, 1961.
More Leaves from the Journal of a Life in the Highlands, from 1862 to 1882. London: Smith, Elder, 1884.

Webb, Beatrice (née Potter) (1858–1943).
The Diary of Beatrice Webb [1873–1943]. Edited by Norman and Jeanne Mackenzie. 4 vols. Cambridge, Mass.: Harvard University Press, 1982–1985.

Beatrice Webb's Diaries [1912–1932]. Edited by Margaret I. Cole. 2 vols. London: Longmans, Green, 1952–1956.

Weeton, Ellen (Mrs. Stock) (1776–1844).
Miss Weeton: Journal of a Governess 1807–1825 [including also retrospection 1748–1809]. Edited by Edward Hall. 2 vols. London: Oxford University Press/Humphrey Milford, 1936–1939. Reprinted as *Miss Weeton's Journal of a Governess*. Newton Abbot, Eng.: David and Charles, 1969.

†White, Dorothy Vernon (b. 1877).
The Groombridge Diary [1907–1913]. Oxford: Oxford University Press, 1924.

Woodforde, Miss Ann (d. 1861).
Woodforde Papers and Diaries [5–17 November 1819]. Edited by Dorothy Heighes Woodforde, 237–238. London: Peter Davies, 1932.

Woodforde, Miss Julia (1789–1873).
Woodforde Papers and Diaries [February–December 1818]. Edited by Dorothy Heighes Woodforde, 181–183, 201, 217. London: Peter Davies, 1932.

Woodforde, Mrs. Mary Norton (d. 1730).
Woodforde Papers and Diaries [1684–1690]. Edited by Dorothy Heighes Woodforde, 3–34. London: Peter Davies, 1932.

Woodforde, Miss Nancy (Anna Maria) (1757–1830).
Woodforde Papers and Diaries [January–December 1792]. Edited by Dorothy Heighes Woodforde, 35–85. London: Peter Davies, 1932.

Woolf, Mrs. Virginia Stephen (1882–1941).
The Diary of Virginia Woolf [1915–1941]. Edited by Anne Olivier Bell, assisted by Andrew McNeillie for vols. 2–5. 5 vols. New York: Harcourt Brace Jovanovich, 1977–1984.

†Wordsworth, Dorothy (1771–1855).
The Journals of Dorothy Wordsworth: The Alfoxden Journal, 1798; The Grasmere Journals, 1800–1803. Edited by Mary Moorman. 2d. ed. Oxford: Oxford University Press, 1976.
The Journals of Dorothy Wordsworth [1798–1828]. Edited by E. De Selincourt. 2 vols. New York: Macmillan, 1941.

†Wright, Myrtle (no dates available).
Norwegian Diary, 1940–45. London: Friends Peace and International Relations Committee, 1974.

†Wynn, Frances Williams (1773–1857).
The Diaries of a Lady of Quality [1797–1844]. Edited by Abraham Hayward. London: Longman, Green, Longman, Roberts, and Green, 1864.

Wynne, Elizabeth (Mrs. Fremantle) (1779–1857).

The Wynne Diaries [1789–1820]. Edited by Anne Fremantle. 3 vols. London: Oxford University Press, 1935–1940.
Wynne, Eugenia (Mrs. Campbell) (b. 1780).
The Wynne Diaries [1789–1811]. Edited by Anne Fremantle. 3 vols. London: Oxford University Press, 1935–1940.
Wynne, Miss Harriet (b. 1786).
The Wynne Diaries [1803–1806]. Edited by Anne Fremantle. 3 vols. London: Oxford University Press, 1935–1940.

LIST OF
OTHER SOURCES CITED

Abbott, H. Porter. *Diary Fiction*. Ithaca, N.Y.: Cornell University Press, 1984.

Allport, Gordon W. *The Use of Personal Documents in Psychological Science*. New York: Social Science Research Council, 1951.

Alpers, Antony. *The Life of Katherine Mansfield*. New York: Viking Press, 1980.

Ardener, Shirley, ed. *Defining Females: The Nature of Women in Society*. London: Croom Helm in association with the Oxford University Women's Committee, 1978.

Arieti, Silvano, and Jules Bemporad. *Severe and Mild Depression: The Psychotherapeutic Approach*. New York: Basic Books, 1978.

Auerbach, Nina. *Communities of Women: An Idea in Fiction*. Cambridge, Mass.: Harvard University Press, 1978.

Banks, Olive. *Faces of Feminism: A Study of Feminism as a Social Movement*. Oxford: Martin Robertson, 1981.

Bardwick, Judith M. *Psychology of Women: A Study of Bio-Cultural Conflicts*. New York: Harper and Row, 1971.

Barrow, Margaret. *Women 1870–1928: A Select Guide to Printed and Archival Sources in the United Kingdom*. New York: Garland, 1981.

Bashkirtseff, Marie. *The Journal of a Young Artist*. 1887. Translated by Mary J. Serrano. New York: E. P. Dutton, 1919.

Batts, John Stuart. *British Manuscript Diaries of the Nineteenth Century*. Totowa, N.J.: Rowman and Littlefield, 1976.

Beauvoir, Simone de. *The Second Sex*. Translated by H. M. Parshley. New York: Random House, Vintage Books, 1974.

Begos, Jane Du Prée. *Annotated Bibliography of Published Women's Diaries.* Pound Ridge, N.Y.: Begos, 1977. Supplement I, 1984.

Bernard, Jessie. *The Female World.* New York: Free Press, 1981.

Berridge, Elizabeth, ed. *The Barretts at Hope End: The Early Diary of Elizabeth Barrett Browning.* London: John Murray, 1974.

Bland, Lucy. "Marriage Laid Bare: Middle-Class Women and Marital Sex, 1880s–1914." In *Labour and Love: Women's Experience of Home and Family, 1850–1940,* edited by Jane Lewis. Oxford: Basil Blackwell, 1986.

Bond, Alec. "Reconsidering Dorothy Wordsworth." *Charles Lamb Bulletin,* n.s. 47–48 (1984): 194–207.

Bouchier, David. *The Feminist Challenge: The Movement for Women's Liberation in Britain and the USA.* London: Macmillan, 1983.

Branca, Patricia. *Silent Sisterhood: Middle Class Women in the Victorian Home.* London: Crom Helm, 1975.

Bridenthal, Renate. "Something Old, Something New: Women Between the Two World Wars." In *Becoming Visible: Women in European History,* edited by Renate Bridenthal and Claudia Koonz. Boston: Houghton Mifflin, 1977.

Brightfield, Myron F. *Victorian England in Its Novels.* Vol. 4. Los Angeles: University of California Library, 1968.

Brookes, Barbara. "Women and Reproduction, 1860–1939." In *Labour and Love: Women's Experience of Home and Family, 1850–1940,* edited by Jane Lewis. Oxford: Basil Blackwell, 1986.

Brophy, Julia, and Carol Smart. "From Disregard to Disrepute." In *The Changing Experience of Women,* edited by Elizabeth Whitelegg, Madeline Arnot, Else Bartels, Veronica Beechey, Lynda Birke, Susan Himmelweit, Diana Leonard, Sonja Ruehl, and Mary Anne Speakman. Oxford: Martin Robertson in association with the Open University, 1982.

Brownmiller, Susan. *Femininity.* New York: Simon and Schuster, 1984.

Byron, George Gordon. *Byron's Letters and Journals.* Vol. 3. Edited by Leslie A. Marchand. London: John Murray, 1973.

Cameron, Deborah. *Feminism and Linguistic Theory.* New York: St. Martin's Press, 1985.

Chesler, Phyllis. *Women and Madness.* New York: Avon Books, 1973.

Chodorow, Nancy. *The Reproduction of Mothering: Psychology and the Sociology of Gender.* Berkeley and Los Angeles: University of California Press, 1978.

Cixous, Hélène. "The Laugh of the Medusa." Translated by Keith and Paula Cohen. *Signs* 1 (1976): 875–893.

Cott, Nancy F. *The Bonds of Womanhood: "Woman's Sphere" in New England, 1780–1835*. New Haven: Yale University Press, 1977.

Crawford, Patricia. "Attitudes to Pregnancy from a Woman's Spiritual Diary. *Local Population Studies*, no. 21 (1978): 43–45.

Culley, Margo, ed. *A Day at a Time: The Diary Literature of American Women from 1764 to the Present*. New York: Feminist Press at City University of New York, 1985.

Daly, Mary. *The Church and the Second Sex*. New York: Harper and Row, 1975.

Davidoff, Leonore. *The Best Circles: Society Etiquette and the Season*. London: Croom Helm, 1973.

Dehler, Kathleen. "The Need to Tell All: A Comparison of Historic and Modern 'Confessional' Writing." In *Feminist Criticism: Essays on Theory, Poetry and Prose*, edited by Cheryl L. Brown and Karen Olson. Metuchen, N.J.: Scarecrow Press, 1978.

Dobbs, Brian. *Dear Diary . . . : Some Studies in Self-Interest*. London: Hamish Hamilton, 1974.

Dyson, Ketaki. *A Various Range: A Study of the Journals and Memoirs of British Men and Women in the Indian Subcontinent, 1765–1836*. Delhi: Oxford Univeristy Press, 1978.

Eakin, Paul John. *Fictions in Autobiography: Studies in the Art of Self-Invention*. Princeton: Princeton University Press, 1985.

Eisenstein, Hester, and Alice Jardine, eds. *The Future of Difference*. Boston: G. K. Hall and Barnard College Women's Center, 1980.

Faderman, Lillian. *Surpassing the Love of Men: Romantic Friendship and Love Between Women from the Renaissance to the Present*. New York: William Morrow, 1981.

Fothergill, Robert A. *Private Chronicles: A Study of English Diaries*. London: Oxford University Press, 1974.

Franklin, Penelope. "The Diaries of Forgotten Women." *Book Forum* 4, no. 3 (1979): 467–474, 557–559.

Freeman, Ruth, and Patricia Klaus. "Blessed or Not? The New Spinster in England and the United States in the Late Nineteenth and Early Twentieth Centuries." *Journal of Family History* 8 (1984): 394–414.

Fussell, Paul. *The Great War and Modern Memory*. London: Oxford University Press, 1975.

Gilbert, Sandra. "Soldier's Heart: Literary Men, Literary Women and the Great War." *Signs* 8 (1983): 422–450.

Gilbert, Sandra, and Susan Gubar. *The Madwoman in the Attic: The Woman*

311

Writer and the Nineteenth-Century Literary Imagination. New Haven: Yale University Press, 1979.

Gilligan, Carol. *In a Different Voice: Psychological Theory and Women's Development.* Cambridge, Mass.: Harvard University Press, 1982.

Godwin, Gail. "A Diarist on Diarists." *Antaeus* 21/21 (1976): 50–56.

[Gore, Catherine.] *The Diary of a Désennuyée.* Paris: Baudry's European Library, 1836.

Gorham, Deborah. *The Victorian Girl and the Feminine Ideal.* London: Croom Helm, 1982.

Hall, Catherine. "The Early Formation of Victorian Domestic Ideology." In *Fit Work for Women,* edited by Sandra Burman. London: Croom Helm, 1979.

Hammer, Signe. *Daughters and Mothers: Mothers and Daughters.* New York: Quadrangle/New York Times Book Co., 1975.

Hampsten, Elizabeth. *Read This Only to Yourself: The Private Writings of Midwestern Women: 1880–1910.* Bloomington, Ind.: Indiana University Press, 1982.

Hemlow, Joyce. *The History of Fanny Burney.* Oxford: Clarendon Press, 1958.

Hoby, Sir Thomas. *The Travels and Life of Sir Thomas Hoby, Kt. of Bisham Abbey, Written by Himself: 1547–1564.* Edited by Edgar Powell. *Camden Miscellany* 10 (or 3d ser., vol. 4). London: Royal Historical Society Publications, 1902.

Horney, Karen. *The Overvaluation of Love.* Reprinted in Horney, *Feminine Psychology.* Edited by Harold Kilman. New York: W. W. Norton, 1973.

Houlbrooke, Ralph A. *The English Family 1450–1700.* London: Longman, 1984.

Huff, Cynthia. *British Women's Diaries: A Descriptive Bibliography of Selected Nineteenth-Century Women's Manuscript Diaries.* New York: AMS Press, 1985.

Hughes, Anne [Jeanne Preston]. *The Diary of a Farmer's Wife 1796–97.* Edited by Suzanne Beedell. [England]: Countrywise Books, 1964. Reprint. Harmondsworth, Middlesex: Penguin, 1981.

Ilick, Joseph E. "Child-rearing in Seventeenth-Century England and America." In *The History of Childhood,* edited by Lloyd de Mause. New York: Psychohistory Press, 1974.

[Jameson, Anna Brownell Murphy.] *Diary of an Ennuyée.* 2d ed. London: Henry Colburn, 1826. (Originally *A Lady's Diary,* 1826.)

Jeffreys, Sheila. *The Spinster and Her Enemies: Feminism and Sexuality 1880–1930.* London: Pandora, 1985.

Jelinek, Estelle C. "Women's Autobiography and the Male Tradition." Introduction to *Women's Autobiography: Essays in Criticism*, edited by Estelle C. Jelinek. Bloomington, Ind.: Indiana University Press, 1980.

Juhasz, Suzanne. "Some Deep Old Desk or Capacious Hold-All": Form and Women's Autobiography." *College English* 39 (1978): 663–668.

———. "Towards a Theory of Form in Feminist Autobiography: Kate Millett's *Flying* and *Sita*; Maxine Hong Kingston's *The Woman Warrior*." In *Women's Autobiography: Essays in Criticism*, edited by Estelle C. Jelinek. Bloomington, Ind.: Indiana University Press, 1980.

Kagle, Steven Earl. "The Diary as Art: A New Assessment." *Genre* 6 (1973): 416–427.

Kamm, Josephine. *Rapiers and Battleaxes: The Women's Movement and Its Aftermath*. London: George Allen and Unwin, 1966.

Kempe, Margery. *The Book of Margery Kempe: A Modern Version*. Edited by W. Butler-Boudon. London: Oxford University Press, 1954.

Kristeva, Julia. "Women's Time." *Signs* 7 (1981): 12–35.

Lensink, Judy Nolte. "Expanding the Boundaries of Criticism: The Diary as Female Autobiography." *Women's Studies* 14 (1987): 39–53.

Lewis, Jane. "Reconstructing Women's Experience of Home and Family." Introduction to *Labour and Love: Women's Experience of Home and Family, 1850–1940*, edited by Jane Lewis. Oxford: Basil Blackwell, 1986.

———. *Women in England 1870–1950: Sexual Divisions and Social Change*. Sussex, Eng.: Wheatsheaf Books, 1984.

Lewis, Judith Schneid. *In the Family Way: Childbearing in the British Aristocracy, 1760–1860*. New Brunswick, N.J.: Rutgers University Press, 1986.

Lifshin, Lyn, ed. *Ariadne's Thread: A Collection of Contemporary Women's Journals*. New York: Harper and Row, 1982.

McLaren, Dorothy. "Marital Fertility and Lactation 1570–1720." In *Women in English Society, 1500–1800*, edited by Mary Prior. London: Methuen, 1985.

Mansfield, Katherine. *The Urewara Notebook*. Edited by Ian Gordon. Oxford: Oxford University Press, 1978.

Marwick, Arthur. *Women at War, 1914–1918*. London: Fontana Paperbacks in association with the Imperial War Museum, 1977.

Matthews, William. *British Diaries: An Annotated Bibliography of British Diaries Written between 1442 and 1942*. Berkeley and Los Angeles: University of California Press, 1950.

———. "The Diary: A Neglected Genre." *Sewanee Review* 85 (1977): 286–300.

———. "The Diary as Literature." In *Diary of Samuel Pepys*. Vol. 1. Edited by William Matthews and Robert Latham. Berkeley and Los Angeles: University of California Press, 1970.

Mendelson, Sara Heller. "Stuart Women's Diaries and Occasional Memoirs." In *Women in English Society, 1500–1800*, edited by Mary Prior. London: Methuen, 1985.

Metzger, Deena, and Barbara Meyerhoff. "Dear Diary (or, Listening to the Silent Laughter of Mozart while the beds are unmade and the remains of breakfast congeal on the table)." *Chrysalis*, no. 7 (1979): 39–49.

Miller, Jean Baker. *Toward a New Psychology of Women*. Boston: Beacon Press, 1977.

Miller, Nancy K. "Emphasis Added: Plots and Plausibilities in Women's Fiction." *PMLA* 96 (1981): 36–48.

———. "Women's Autobiography in France." In *Women and Language in Literature and Society*, edited by Sally McConnell-Ginet, Ruth Borker, and Nelly Furman. New York: Praeger, 1980.

Miner, Earl. "Literary Diaries and the Boundaries of Literature." *Yearbook of Comparative and General Literature*, no. 21 (1972): 46–51.

Mitchell, David. *Monstrous Regiment: The Story of the Women of the First World War*. New York: Macmillan, 1965.

Moffat, Mary Jane, and Charlotte Painter, eds. *Revelations: Diaries of Women*. New York: Random House, 1974.

Morgan, Elaine. *The Descent of Woman*. New York: Stein and Day, 1972.

Motz, Marilyn Ferris. *True Sisterhood: Michigan Women and Their Kin 1820–1920*. Albany: State University of New York Press, 1983.

My Daughter's Manual: Comprising a Summary View of Female Studies, Accomplishments, and Principles of Conduct. New York: D. Appleton, 1837.

O'Brien, Kate. *English Diaries and Journals*. Britain in Pictures Series. London: William Collins, 1943.

Pepys, Lady Charlotte Maria. *The Diary and Houres of the Ladye Adolie, A Faythfulle Childe, 1552*. London: Addey, 1853.

Pomerleau, Cynthia S. "The Emergence of Women's Autobiography in England." In *Women's Autobiography: Essays in Criticism*, edited by Estelle C. Jelinek. Bloomington, Ind.: Indiana University Press, 1980.

Ponsonby, Sir Arthur. *English Diaries: A Review of English Diaries from the Sixteenth to the Twentieth Centuries*. London: Methuen, 1923.

———. *More English Diaries: Further Reviews of English Diaries from the Sixteenth to the Twentieth Centuries*. London: Methuen, 1927.

[Rathbone, Hannah.] *Lady Willoughby; or Passages from the Diary of A Wife and Mother in the Seventeenth Century*. 2 vols. 1844–1848. Reprint. New York: A. S. Barnes and Burr, 1860.

Rendall, Jane. *The Origins of Modern Feminism: Women in Britain, France, and the United States, 1780–1860.* London: Macmillan, 1985.

Rich, Adrienne. "Compulsory Heterosexuality and Lesbian Existence." *Signs* 5 (1980): 631–660.

―――. *Of Woman Born: Motherhood as Experience and Institution.* New York: Bantam, 1977.

Roberts, Katherine. *Pages from the Diary of a Militant Suffragette.* Letchworth and London: Garden City Press, 1910.

Robertson, Priscilla. "Home as a Nest: Middle Class Childhood in Nineteenth-Century Europe." In *The History of Childhood,* edited by Lloyd de Mause. New York: Psychohistory Press, 1974.

Rogers, Katharine M. *Feminism in Eighteenth-Century England.* Urbana, Ill.: University of Illinois Press, 1982.

―――. *The Troublesome Helpmate: A History of Misogyny in Literature.* Seattle: University of Washington Press, 1966.

Rohrbaugh, Joanna Bunker. *Women: Psychology's Puzzle.* New York: Basic Books, 1979.

Rose, Phyllis. *Parallel Lives: Five Victorian Marriages.* New York: Random House, Vintage Books, 1984.

Rosenblatt, Paul C. *Bitter, Bitter Tears: Nineteenth-Century Diarists and Twentieth-Century Grief Theories.* Minneapolis: University of Minnesota Press, 1983.

Ross, Ellen. "Labour and Love: Rediscovering London's Working-Class Mothers, 1870–1918." In *Labour and Love: Women's Experience of Home and Family, 1850–1940,* edited by Jane Lewis. Oxford: Basil Blackwell, 1986.

Rowbotham, Sheila. *Hidden from History: Rediscovering Women in History from the Seventeenth Century to the Present.* New York: Random House, 1975.

Schlissel, Lillian. *Women's Diaries of the Westward Journey.* New York: Schocken Books, 1982.

Schnorrenberg, Barbara B., and Jean E. Hunter. "The Eighteenth-Century Englishwoman." In *The Women of England: From Anglo-Saxon Times to the Present,* edited by Barbara Kanner. Hamden, Conn.: Archon Books, 1979.

Seligman, Martin E. P. *Helplessness: On Depression, Development, and Death.* San Francisco: W. H. Freeman, 1975.

Showalter, Elaine. "Feminist Criticism in the Wilderness." In *Writing and Sexual Difference,* edited by Elizabeth Abel. Chicago: University of Chicago Press, 1982.

———. A Literature of Their Own: British Women Novelists from Brontë to Lessing. Princeton: Princeton University Press, 1977.

Shumaker, Wayne. English Autobiography. Berkeley and Los Angeles: University of California Press, 1954.

Siganto, Marie Gabrielle. "The Emergence of Literary Form in the Diaries of Virginia Woolf." Master's thesis, University of Queensland, 1980.

[Skene, Harriet.] The Diary of Martha Bethune Baliol, from 1753 to 1754. London: Chapman and Hall, 1853.

Sloman, Judith. "The Fragmentary Genres: Women Writers and Non-Canonical forms." Canadian Newsletter of Research on Women 7 (1978): 26–29.

Smith, Hilda L. Reason's Disciples: Seventeenth-Century English Feminists. Urbana, Ill.: University of Illinois Press, 1982.

Smith-Rosenberg, Carroll. "The Female World of Love and Ritual: Relations between Women in Nineteenth-Century America." Signs 1 (1975): 1–30.

Spacks, Patricia Meyer. The Adolescent Idea: Myths of Youth and the Adult Imagination. New York: Basic Books, 1981.

———. The Female Imagination. New York: Knopf, 1975.

———. Imagining a Self: Autobiograpy and Novel in Eighteenth-Century England. Cambridge: Mass.: Harvard University Press, 1976.

Spalding, Philip A. Self-Harvest: A Study of Diaries and the Diarist. London: Independent Press, 1949.

Spender, Dale. Man Made Language. London: Routledge and Kegan Paul, 1980.

———, ed. Feminist Theorists: Three Centuries of Women's Intellectual Traditions. London: Women's Press, 1983.

Stanton, Domna C. "Autogynography: Is the Subject Different?" In The Female Autograph, edited by Domna C. Stanton and Jeanine Parisier Plottel. New York: New York Literary Forum, 1984.

Stauffer, Donald. English Biography Before 1700. Cambridge, Mass.: Harvard University Press, 1930.

Stetson, Dorothy M. A Woman's Issue: The Politics of Family Law Reform in England. London: Greenwood Press, 1982.

Stone, Lawrence. The Family, Sex and Marriage in England 1500–1800. London: Weidenfield and Nicolson, 1977.

Thompson, Roger. Women in Stuart England and America: A Comparative Study. London: Routledge and Kegan Paul, 1974.

Tolstoy, Nikolai. "The Diary of a Farmer's Wife as Forgery." Encounter 58 (1982): 35–39.

Waite, Vincent, ed. *English Diaries and Journals.* Exeter, Devonshire: A. Wheaton, 1952.

Waldron, Philip. "Katherine Mansfield's *Journal.*" *Twentieth-Century Literature* 20 (1974): 11–18.

Watkins, Owen C. *The Puritan Experience: Studies in Spiritual Autobiography.* New York: Schocken Books, 1972.

Weissman, M. M., and L. Klerman. "Sex Differences and the Epidemiology of Depression." *Archives of General Psychiatry* 34 (1977): 98–111.

West, Mrs. *Letters to a Young Lady in Which the Duties and Character of Women Are Considered.* Vol. 3. London: Longman, Hurst, Rees, and Orme, 1806.

Westwater, Sister A. Martha. "Surrender to Subservience: An Introduction to the Diaries and Journal of Eliza Wilson Bagehot." *International Journal of Women's Studies* 1 (1978): 517–529.

Willy, Margaret. *Three Women Diarists: Celia Fiennes, Dorothy Wordsworth, Katherine Mansfield.* Writers and Their Work, no. 173. London: Longmans Green, 1964.

Winston, Elizabeth. "The Autobiographer and Her Readers: From Apology to Affirmation." In *Women's Autobiography: Essays in Criticism,* edited by Estelle C. Jelinek. Bloomington, Ind.: Indiana University Press, 1980.

Wolf, Christa. "Diary—Aid to Work and Memory." In *The Reader and the Writer: Essays, Sketches, Memories,* translated by Joan Becker. New York: International Publishers, 1977.

Wollstonecraft, Mary. *A Vindication of the Rights of Women.* Edited by Carol H. Poston. New York: W. W. Norton, 1975.

Women's Diaries: A Quarterly Newsletter. Pound Ridge, N.Y., 1983–1986.

Woolf, Virginia. "John Evelyn." Review of *The Early Life and Education of John Evelyn, 1620–1674, Times Literary Supplement,* 28 October 1920: 689–690.

———. "A Terribly Sensitive Mind." Review of *The Journal of Katherine Mansfield,* ed. J. Middleton Murry. New York *Herald Tribune* 18 September 1927. Reprinted in Woolf, *Granite and Rainbow.* New York: Harcourt, Brace, and Co. 1958.

INDEX

319